All of Baba's Children

All of Baba's Children

Myrna Kostash

NeWest Press
Edmonton

First edition 1977. Published by Hurtig Publishers Ltd. Edmonton

Canadian Cataloguing in Publication Data

Kostash, Myrna.
      All of baba's children
      Includes index.
      ISBN 0-920897-11-8
      1. Ukrainian Canadians – Canada, Western – History.
I. Title.
FC106.U5K68 1992 971.2'00491791 C92-091147-1
F1035.U5K68 1992

Credits:

Cover design: Diane Jensen
Interior design: Bob Young/BOOKENDS DESIGNWORKS
Editor for the Press: Eva Radford

Financial Assistance: NeWest Press gratefully acknowledges the financial assistance of Alberta Culture and Multiculturalism, The Alberta Foundation for the Arts, The Canada Council, and The NeWest Institute for Western Canadian Studies.

Cover photo by permission of Mary Babiuk

Printed and Bound in Canada by Best Gagné Book Manufacturers

NeWest Publishers Limited
#310, 10359-82 Avenue
Edmonton, Alberta
T6E 1Z9

Contents

Preface

No writer consciously sets forth to write a "classic," of course. Indeed, had I known, in the summer of 1975, what I know now – of Ukrainian and Ukrainian-Canadian history, of literature and language – I would never have written *All of Baba's Children*: I would have been too inhibited by my own naiveté. But I was blissfully unaware that my notions were largely impressionistic and so I was able to barge through the project without second-guessing myself.

It turned out to be the right strategy, for I hit a nerve – several nerves – in writing the book as passionately and stridently and self-confidently as I did. All across Canada I heard from Ukrainian-Canadians, among others, that I had finally told *their* history, the history of ethnic loss and pain and regret as well as the trumpeted story of ethnic pride and achievement. I was thanked by labour organizers and women activists for not having relegated them to the margins of official ethnic history. Young people asked for my autograph, thanking me for voicing their own ambivalence as third and fourth generation Ukrainian-Canadians.

On the other hand, there were those who attacked me for having aired the community's dirty laundry in public, for being "pinko" in my political sensibilities and a betrayer of my interviewees (I had actually quoted them and put them in print), not to mention for being a mere scribbler bereft of scholarship.

But people went on reading it nevertheless, several thousands of people over the years, including readers in the United States, Australia, England, Ukraine. On the basis of *All of Baba's Children*, I have been invited to speak from Prince Rupert to Halifax, in Dallas,

Texas, and Melbourne, Australia. And there is talk now of a Ukrainian-language translation in Kiev.

The publication of the book changed my life, in fact. Not only did it put me into direct and intimate contact with my ethnic community from whom I had been estranged for many years, it provided me some of the most exciting intellectual work of my career as I struggled with certain imponderables: "Is assimilation a good or bad thing?" "What future has multiculturalism in a society torn by racism and mistrust?" "What identity do we want to pass on to the next generation?" "How does ethnicity shape literature?"

And it finally propelled me on a trip I never thought I would care to make: travels to Ukraine and reunions with my Baba's relatives in the village she left as a young woman and never saw again.

I am very pleased, then, to see a new edition of my book in the anniversary year of the Ukrainians' first arrival to Canada: let it be my grateful memorial plaque to their great adventure. Let it also be a kind of honouring of those who stayed behind, in the villages and cities of Ukraine, who struggled for their lives as an independent people against ferocious odds and who, in 1991, won it.

Mnohaya lita!

M.K.
Edmonton
February 1992

Preface to the First Edition

At the beginning of 1975, I was living in Toronto, working as a free-lance writer, and comfortable in the assumption that my identity proceeded in its totality from the white, English-speaking middle class of this country. If one put it in terms of "us" and "them," I was a member of the former, the privileged daughter of a nuclear family in a single-family dwelling, beneficiary of higher education, travel in Europe, and an interesting career. I understood my inheritance to be the BNA Act and the history of the CPR; my personal sources the Anglo-Saxon novelists and poets, Yankee bohemians and New Leftists, and women – as far back as the Amazons. To the fact that I was incontrovertibly of Ukrainian origin I gave a passing, friendly nod; I was vaguely pleased to be able to number a *baba* and *dido*, a familiarity with Slavic inflections, a taste for sauerkraut and Greek Orthodox church music among my blessings. But in no way did I consider these blessings facets of my self-definition. They were just there, like the weather.

It was with some surprise, then, that in mid-1975 I packed my boxes and returned to Alberta to write a book about Ukrainian-Canadians. Up to the moment of filling out an application for a Canada Council grant, I did not know I was going to do this. Of all the things to write about, why would I choose the Ukrainian-Canadians? I did not feel particularly attached to their community; I did not speak Ukrainian; lessons in Ukrainian history and literature had made no impression and, besides, compared to the stories of, say, Louis Riel or Gabriel Dumont, of American blacks and chicanos, of the expelled Acadians, Ukrainian-Canadians were uncompelling as the subject of a book.

Or so I had imagined, until it was time to decide what my book would be about. I have only retrospective explanations for the choice. As one of a handful of Ukrainian-Canadians working in the media, I was in an advantageous position to publicize ethnic history. As an Albertan, I sought a theme remote from the self-centredness of Toronto. Most important, as an outsider – a Canadian outside the American heartland, a woman outside the Boy's Club, a "progressive" outside the bourgeois establishment's world view – I was keen to apply this consciousness of otherness to my own cultural roots: the history of Ukrainian-Canadians in western Canada. By this choice I was admitting, in fact, to membership in the ranks of "them" rather than "us."

And so I went to Two Hills, Alberta, an almost exclusively Ukrainian-Canadian community ninety miles east of Edmonton. I chose it because no Kostash had ever lived there and also – I confess to a certain sentimentalism – because it was only twelve miles from the village of Hairy Hill, a place about which I had heard much: my parents had met there and so it marks my true beginnings. I set up shop in the Two Hills motel and spent four months interviewing local residents. (All unattributed quotes in the text are from these interviews.) The book starts from them. The book is not about the immigrants; it is about their children – my parents' generation – the ones who had to find their identity, their purpose, their community and their pride somewhere between Galicia and downtown Canada. In the choices they made, in their self-definition and explanations, in their experiences between 1920 and 1950, I believe lie not a few clues to my otherness. And to the otherness of all those Canadians who know, despite Coca-Cola and Bob Dylan, despite university degrees and a consumer society, despite the Protestant work ethic and democratic ideals, that we are not Anglos. Not mainstream Canadians, not the "us" at the summit of the vertical mosaic.

In a way, I have stayed on in Two Hills. I have bought a small farm there and call it Tulova, the Galician village the Kostashchuks left behind. I know that, urbanized and Americanized, I am not one of these people, but I am of them and it gives me a certain pleasure to live awhile each year in the midst of a community that nurtured us all.

As to the "bias" of this book, it begins and ends with my desire to demystify the prevalent mythologies, indulged in by both Ukrainian-Canadians and non-Ukrainian-Canadians, about ethnic history in the prairies. There is a very good reason why I had for so long felt no common ground with the Ukrainian-Canadian community: I simply failed to identify with the ethnic establishment's view of who we are and what has happened to us. If the only way to be a "real" Ukrainian-Canadian was to accept romanticization of our history, trivialization of our culture and piece-meal demands for restitution, then I refused it. Instead, the attempt I have made in this book to go beyond conventional wisdom has been among the most exhilarating work of my life. And so, at the end of it, I feel at home in Two Hills.

M.K.
Tulova
Two Hills, Alberta
July 1977

Foreword

GEORGE MELNYK

This reprinting of *All of Baba's Children* in a mass-market paperback format a decade after it first appeared is a sign of the book's vitality and importance. In an age when most books are short-lived, it continues to attract attention because it has the stuff that classics are made of – an authentic voice, an original vision and literary merit.

For a work of non-fiction to become a classic means that it has made a significant contribution to a particular culture by creating a breakthrough in its consciousness and by heralding a new stage in its evolution. *All of Baba's Children* achieved this by its vibrant, radical, and revisionist perspective on multiculturalism. It turns its back on the old clichés; it dares to question and to criticize. For the contemporary generation of Canadians, it, more than any other book, has revealed the true nature of ethnicity, which has often been hidden under a veneer of assimilation. *All of Baba's Children* has become a manifesto that is yet to be surpassed.

Stylistically, the book combines an energetic, free-flowing journalism with a vocabulary blended from a variety of sources: ethnic, regional and popular. Culturally, the book is influenced by the ongoing struggle for equality and pride of the women's movement and oppressed minorities, who in the sixties and seventies were rediscovering their lost past in strong, confident tones. This book is part of that social literature and its author is a product of that protesting generation.

I first met Myrna Kostash in 1975, which was the year she returned to Alberta from Toronto to research and write this book.

She had decided to exchange a successful career in national journalism for a modest Canada Council Explorations Grant and the opportunity to search for her roots.

Our paths crossed because we were both living in Edmonton; we were both of Ukrainian descent, and we had both come back from the East. I had returned to the West from Toronto in 1972 and so shared with her the identity of returnee. This return to the region, which some might characterize as a return to the "homeland," was an attempt by rootless intellectuals to overcome the alienation of life in Toronto, where we had to identify with a history and peoples other than our own.

Her response to this alienation was the writing *All of Baba's Children*, while my response was the launching of a regional magazine called the *NeWest Review*. Both projects were an affirmation of our having found meaning in the West. That the two projects were related became clear when Kostash began writing for the magazine. In May 1976 the *NeWest Review* published, "Out There is the Prairie: The Two Hills Diary of Myrna Kostash." In the article she explained her personal mission.

This morning a CBC announcer kept exclaiming about how disillusioned he was to find out I really did mean what I'd said about wanting to live and work here. He thought I'd be a super-sophisticated media starlet merely passing through like a tourist to a health spa, restoring myself on my way back to the Big Time. I don't know how to convince such people that I do in fact feel at home here; that, when it comes down to it, all other identities and roles fall away and I find myself to be a Ukrainian-Albertan who wants to settle down near the same places her grandparents chose as immigrants.

And this is precisely what she did. She bought some property near the town of Two Hills, a Ukrainian settlement not far from Edmonton. There was a one-room cabin on the land and she refurbished it as a writer's retreat and named it "Tulova" after her ancestral village in the Ukraine. This is where she wrote *All of Baba's Children*. She then matched this rural retreat with a small house in Edmonton's inner-city core. From its front yard one could see the Ukrainian Credit Union and one of the city's landmark Ukrainian cathedrals. These physical links with her history played an important role in her process of self-discovery and they expressed to others the depth of her commitment.

From this it is clear that her choice of the West, her conscious rediscovery of her ethnic past and her decision to continue living in Edmonton was a major personal revolution. Edmonton, the city of her childhood and youth, has now become the base for her literary career. Her 1975 rejection of a mere "tourist" relationship to Alberta has become permanent.

All of Baba's Children, which was published by Hurtig in 1977, established her credentials as a senior Western Canadian writer. As a powerful existential statement about the impact of a hinterland and its people on a returning native daughter it is unsurpassed. The narrative combines empathy with scrutiny, criticism with understanding, social history with autobiography. The themes of racism, nationalism and social conflict are revealed through the lives and words of those she interviewed. They constitute one Canadian ethnic group's sense of "otherness." In the seventies, the issue of separatism was very much in the air and what Kostash was attempting to do was show that English Canada was not a monolithic Anglo culture but a diverse reality made up of numerous contradictions and tensions, some of which were very deep.

Even though on the surface the book seemed to deal with a limited topic – Ukrainian-Canadians in the West – it received immediate national attention. This happened because the author was well-known and her views were provocative and out of the ordinary. It become evident very quickly that here was an investigation of the darker corners of the Canadian identity the like of which had not been seen for some time. The book made it to the *Maclean's* bestseller list.

Reviews appeared across the country. Novelist Adele Wiseman, writing in the Toronto *Star*, praised Kostash for "taking the bull by the horns." A reviewer for the Calgary *Herald* stated bluntly, "It's not often that a book raises one's blood pressure level to boiling point." The book became a *cause célèbre* among Ukrainian-Canadians, who quickly divided into those who stood behind it and welcomed its insights and those who condemned it as divisive, unflattering, and counter-productive for the ethnic cause. But the author's goal was summed up by a letter to the *Financial Post,* written by W.R. Petryshyn, in which he stated firmly, "We French, Indians, Jews, and Ukrainian-Canadians expect our ethnicity to be fully recognized, as is the Anglo-Canadian, in the definition of Canadian society." It is a goal the book achieved.

Kostash had honed her provocative writing style in the early seventies, when she was writing a feminist column in *Maclean's. All of Baba's Children* simply confirmed this special ability. Yet it would be unfair to conclude that the author's purpose was to aim a gun at the myth of the happy ethnic and blast it. She did much more. The book portrays a restless and questioning spirit that honestly seeks new understanding. The essential Kostash is a highly-charged, emotional seeker of polarities and contradictions that cry out for resolution. The end result of her probing is a new level of self-knowledge that is meant to touch her readers.

Just because the book contains more questions than answers does not mean that it is somehow cheating the reader. It simply means that it is true to its journalistic objective, which is to investigate, reveal, and pass judgement. The solutions are left to theorists and visionaries. What Kostash has done is to open up the dusty closets of a forgotten topic and with her strong language and cleansing imagery let in fresh air.

The book's impact on Western Canadian non-fiction writing is similar to that made by Maria Campbell's autobiographical *Halfbreed.* Both were stories waiting to be told and both were free of conventional stereotypes. In poetry a comparable example is Andrew Suknaski's *Wood Mountain Poems* and in fiction John Marlyn's *Under the Ribs of Death.* But it would be wrong to label Kostash as a purely ethnic or regionally-oriented writer simply because of this one book. Her second book, *Long Way From Home*

(1981), dealt with the sixties in Canada and her third book, *No Kidding* (1987), deals with the problems faced by teenage women. Without turning her back on region or ethnic identity, she has remained open to the world. She has proven she is not a single issue writer.

All of Baba's Children developed out of a cultural milieu that was more strident, confrontational and iconoclastic than today's, yet it remains accessible to contemporary readers. V.S. Naipaul, writing in a recent issue of *The New York Review of Books*, explained the task of a major writer in the following terms:

Every senior writer has to be original; he cannot be content to do or to offer a version of what has been done before.

The critics agree that Kostash's treatment of the ethnic question is original. They have remarked on its forthrightness and intensity. Her language is stripped of false optimism and genteel tones. It is bold, rich and savoury. It engages its audience and pulls them into the debate. It is difficult to be detached when reading *All of Baba's Children*.

That sensibility is captured in this unrevised reprinting. The frank discussion of Ukrainian social history in the West is left unaltered, with each episode filled with the spirit of an immigrant people coming to grips with a new land. A decade later the author could have clarified some points and refined others, but the tone of revelation would have been muted. The book you are about to read is filled with the enthusiasm of first discovery and with the thrill of fresh insights. It is this quality which has made *All of Baba's Children* a part of the literary heritage of the West and its author, Myrna Kostash, an example of how fruitful a reciprocity can exist between place and the self.

George Melnyk
May 1987
Calgary, Alberta

ONE
EMIGRATION

There were hardships. No chance of earning a living at the time and no hope of earning enough to acquire more land. They would work for the landlord – the *pan* – and they would have to cut twelve bundles or sheaves for this lord to get one for themselves. So you can imagine how many bundles you have to tie in a day to get enough grain to feed your family.

– Jack Malenka

* * *

What did your father have in the old country?
He had 2 1/2 *morgs* [about four acres].
What kind of set-up was it?
We worked for the landlord at twelve cents a day.
What kind of work?
Hoed potatoes, beets, picked them in the fall, took them to market.
Did you work for the pan *because you had to?*
Yes, we had no money. Everyone worked.
When did you work on your own land?
Those who had none of their own worked for the *pan* full-time.
Those who had a bit of land worked on it in the spring and fall, when they could get away.

– Peter Teresio

* * *

Even though my mother's side was wealthy, the Ukraine was not beautiful. Oh, beautiful for weather, beautiful for countryside, but the living wasn't anything you could boast about. There was too much suffering. In that social system, you'd have to be happy with very little.

— Alice Melnyk

The first generation of Ukrainian-Canadians are the great-grandchildren of serfs and the grandchildren of peasants, more or less miserably poor. Serfdom was abolished in Western Ukraine in 1848 by the Austrian Ferdinand I and certain odious and violent practices of feudalism were thereby eliminated: peasants could no longer be dragooned into military service at the landlord's pleasure, they no longer required his permission to buy or trade or marry, and they were released from the obligation to provide wage-free service on his lands.

But the new regime had a desperate character of its own. Because the act which abolished serfdom also provided for compensation to the landlord, the burden on the peasant landholder, taxed to pay the compensation, was enormous. Forty years after the act, the debt had yet to be paid off: with interest, the original assessment of 97 million Austrian marks had compounded to 121 million, with 9 million in principal still outstanding.[1]

There was more. Although the serfs were now freemen, the act required that they pay the landlord for any use they made of his forests and pastures. This legislation was particularly oppressive because, until 1848, large portions of the forests and pastures had been used as communal property. When, after 1848, the landlords laid claim to these as well, the peasants sought relief from the courts. In 1860 alone, of 32,000 suits, the peasants won exactly 2,000.[2] Loss of these free lands reduced many to absolute impoverishment. By 1908, 80 per cent of individual peasant holdings consisted of fewer than twelve and a half acres and almost 50 per cent were less then five acres. It was estimated that to survive as full-time farmers, a family would need to own a minimum of fourteen and a half acres. Clearly, it was no longer possible to divide and subdivide such small holdings among heirs. Even if a young man were to inherit a parcel, years of compulsory military service in the Austrian army would keep him away from his work

> Alexander Bochanesky was born on January 16, 1866, in the village of Kisyliw, province of Bukovyna, Ukraine. At the age of twenty-seven, Alexander married Magdalena, born on July 27, 1869. Alexander and Magdalena were married in 1893 in the Ukrainian Greek Orthodox church in Kisyliw.
>
> Alexander's parents were poor, even by the low standards of his times. To set Alexander and Magdalena up on their own when they were married, Alexander's father reportioned his small holding and gave them half a morg of land (about two acres). Obviously, this small parcel of land could not even begin to provide a livelihood for the young couple. Therefore, like so many of his countrymen, Alexander hired himself out to the local landlord (pan), under conditions of employment which gave Alexander little time to take care of his own bit of land. So the responsibility fell on Magdalena.[3]

The Austrian government, as exacting as it was, did not create half the hardships for the Ukrainians as did the Polish landlords. Themselves former sovereigns of Western Ukraine until the division of Poland among Austria, Prussia, and Russia, the Polish aristocracy remained in Galicia, a province of Western Ukraine, as landlords and administrators, and judges, and it was against them that all the bitterness and fury of the Ukrainian peasants were directed. The feeling was mutual. The Poles rejected the notion of a distinct Ukrainian nationality, prohibited the establishment of Ukrainian language schools, and suppressed Ukrainian nationalist organizations. In Bukovyna, another province of Western Ukraine under Austria, the same situation prevailed with Rumanian landlords.

Squeezed between the Polish landlords and the Austrian army, reduced to a strip of land that could support fewer and fewer people, denied literacy and cultural self-expression, consigned to high taxes and low wages, suspicious of the priests' compromised position within a state-financed church and harassed by personal debts piling up at the tavern, the Ukrainian peasant was at his wit's end precisely when the Canadian government opened the Northwest Territories for settlement.

To keep the record straight: millions stayed behind. Those who had substantial landholdings, secure jobs in the cities or who had become Polonized, Roman Catholic civil servants, didn't leave. Nor did those who were so poor they could not put enough money together to pay the passage overseas and the ten dollars required to lay claim to a homestead. But, between these two classes, there were large numbers who were not only in an economic position to emigrate but psychologically prepared to do so. Those who had ambitions as farmers, who resisted the fatalistic doctrine *yakos to bude* (whatever will be, will be) and insisted on their right to material and intellectual security, who were draft-resisters and political agitators, who had had a taste of status and mobility and wanted more than they were going to be able to get at home – these left.

A foreman on a Polish landlord's estate, himself the owner of three acres of land – a small fortune! – and educated to the third grade packed up and left so that his children might go even farther. A young man, working as a messenger boy in the town of Chernovetz, yearning for independence and adventure, borrowed money for the trip from his parents who had grain and corn, sheep, and cows. A village councilman and magistrate whose son might be a lawyer, over there in Canada; the blacksmith who, literate, wanted to be a teacher; the student who sought escape from the excesses of the aristocracy and the hypocrisy of the priests – these left too.

As for the women, rarely would an unmarried girl voluntarily pull up roots and emigrate. She could not get her hands on the money. She had even less education than the male villagers. She would not be allowed by Canadian law to claim a homestead of her own. She had no skills other than housekeeping to trade for wages in a Canadian city. Momentarily inspired to throw in her lot with the emigrés, she would finally succumb to the social pressures of family and village organized against such self-assertion. The women who did travel to Canada were the daughters or wives or mothers of men who had made the decision to go. Or the fiancées. A girl's father is visited by a local boy who says he wants to marry her. First he would go to Canada, get a job and build a house. Two years pass. Money is sent from Canada for her voyage. She is not asked if she wants to go and she never says one way or the other.

Men, women, and children collected at the nearest railway station on the first leg of the journey that would take them by train to Lviv and Hamburg and Antwerp, by ship to Quebec City, by train to Winnipeg and Strathcona, by wagon or foot to the homestead. The rejoicing would be saved for the arrival, for the first crop in the new earth. Here at the railway station, leaving home, the people were forlorn and already weary. To quote the Ukrainian poet Ivan Franko:

> If in some railway station you should spy
> Like herrings in a keg, tightly packed, a crowd,
> Women so gaunt and pale you want to cry –
> Like wheat stalks hit by hail, broken, wilted, bowed –
> The children huddled close, without a smile,
> The men morose, of stern, fanatic glance,
> With care and thwarted dreams each forehead lined,
> Their ragged, dusty bundles round them piled –
> Those are the emigrants.[4]

They carried with them what was most precious – millstones, flail, sickle, axe, linens, spoons and forks, or just the clothes on their backs – and the understanding that they would never return. In some cases, whole families of two or three generations moved together, but the majority of emigrants were leaving their relatives behind, spreading a branch of the family tree halfway round the world.

They should have been advised to have at least one hundred dollars capital with them – they would be months in Canada before they could achieve an income off their farms – but unscrupulous steamship agents, eager for bonuses and commissions, often misled even the poorest emigrants about what their needs would be. Leaving with nothing but their "ten fingers," the ten-dollar fee to file on a homestead, they trusted the account of "Shipping Agent Mr. Michael Morawec of Hamburg, who distinctly promised them not only free land but that the Canadian government would further assist them by grants for subsistence and by gifts of cattle and tools."[5] It was a lie.

A story. The head of the household is already in Canada. He sends some money, the rest is gathered from the sale of tools and domestic articles – the family must pay for the immigration papers provided by the agent. There is enough for the passage and food and the twenty-five dollars to show the immigration officer in Quebec City. The mother is illiterate. In Lviv, where she goes to the agent's office to buy her ship-card, she discovers its price is coincidentally the same as the amount of money she has in her pocket. In Antwerp, she discovers there is a five-day wait for the ship and four nights' accommodation to pay. In Quebec City she has thirty-five cents to show, and no food for the train trip to Pincher Creek, Alberta. Typical of such cooperative gestures, fellow immigrants donate their bread, apples, and sausage.

As it was, the immigrants' journey was a pilgrim's progress. They ran a gauntlet of Prussian border police, fraudulent moneychangers, greedy steamship agents and careless dock workers – more than one emigrant lost cash and baggage before embarking at Hamburg; they endured seasickness, the discomforts of steerage accommodation and stale food; they were herded through customs halls, immigration halls and land offices. Upon entry to Canada (or at any point after that until they were naturalized) they could be deported, sent back where they came from. Just cause for deportation in 1906-07 might be: "tuberculosis, insanity, varicose veins, old age, pregnancy, vicious tendencies, likely to become a public charge, frostbite, failing eyesight, bad character, or criminal," to name a few.

If, by the time they arrived at Edmonton, they had any money left, they bought some sacks of flour and a plough, loaded up a wagon and walked fifty, sixty, ninety miles to their homestead, following Indian trails. What they had chosen, of course, was uncleared, virgin brush – all that wood! free! – and here they deposited themselves and dug a hole in the ground for shelter. The emotional accounting they made at this point must have been immeasurable. The isolation and confusion, the weariness and doubt, the inclination to submit without complaint. "It is primarily important," wrote Dr. Joseph Oleskow in a book about emigration, "to get rid of the stigma of slavery in the course of the trip, to lift one's head and look squarely into the people's eyes instead of looking from under the brow like an animal chased by dogs."[6]

Oleskow upbraided his compatriots for their "psychology of servility," the reflex passivity and docility that had "permeated the blood and bones"[7] of a people socialized for centuries within the heavy-handed institutions of imperialists, warmongers, tyrants, and thugs. This wasn't the whole story, of course; there had been those heroes romantic enough to throw themselves against the knives of the overlords and there would be those who would organize revolutionary cadres. But the majority had cleaved themselves to the earth, eyes to the ground, minding their straitened business while the boss minded his expansive one. Coming to Canada to till the soil at the behest of yet another government did not, at first, seem to be such a different proposition. If anything, it seemed worse: no home, no village, no ancestors, no music. Sitting under the stars of a foreign sky in the middle of their nowhere, they must have thought perhaps they had made a terrible mistake.

The Canadians, however, were satisfied by their arrival, or rather, Sir Clifford Sifton, Minister of the Interior under Prime Minister Laurier, was satisfied. "I think a stalwart peasant in a sheepskin coat, born on the soil, whose forefathers have been farmers for ten generations, with a stout wife and a half-dozen children is good quality. . . . These men are workers. They have been bred for generations to work from daylight to dark. They have never done anything else and they never expect to do anything else."[8] One man's servitude is another's enterprise. It is ironic that the conditions from which the Galicians were escaping, as from a penal colony, had bred in them the very characteristics that Canadian social planners hoped to turn to their own use. There are more sentimental views of this event, but those who lived it know better. Without the men and women in sheepskin coats there would have been no prairie economy outside the Hudson's Bay Company, native hunters and trappers, and the NWMP in their forts. In exchange, the peasants believed they would be given the chance to spare the generations after them the penury of the land.

> I found no path, no trail
> But only bush and water
> Wherever I looked I saw
> Not a native (land) – but foreign.

> I found no path, no trail
> only green bush
> Wherever I looked I saw
> A foreign country.[9]

Two

Arrival and Settlement

At first, my parents didn't realize what they were up against. If they had, they would have walked back to the Ukraine. Back in the old country, emigration agents had come to the village and talked to the men in the *korshma* [pub] about Canada. Father brought pictures home for us to see, pictures of horses and machinery and big houses. People thought they could get money off trees.

– Maria Teresio

* * *

My father came over in the spring of 1899. He came over for the forests. You understand, he came from a regime where you had to pick up every twig and ask the lord for everything. He went out to the Mundare area and picked out the bushiest land he could find.

– Peter Shevchook

* * *

When my mother's family came to Canada they stayed with here uncle. One day everything burned down and they lost what they had brought. To make some money she worked for different families looking after children and doing housework. They used to say there was nothing but mosquitoes.

– Mary Spak

* * *

My mother lived on the homestead, Father went out working, and this was in winter. Her baby was born in 1904, her baby wasn't a year old yet. She lived alone out there, her father died and the closest neighbour was two and a half miles away. There was no road, she had to walk through the bush, carry this baby in winter through the snow, to let someone know that her father had died.

– Bill Hnydyk

* * *

There were no oxen. There were no roads. So they would walk to Edmonton. One hundred miles. It would take them a week. Walking for half a bag of flour.

– Walter Kitt

* * *

Of course they worked hard, harder than in the old country. Our homestead had only seven acres of open land. My parents cleared the other ninety acres by hand with oxen, then ploughed it with a hand plow. It took fifteen years to clear it. But we got used to it, and we had neighbours within two miles. But they knew that in the old country they would have been poorer and their children would never have been anything else than peasants. They believed they could become rich in no time here. Even if they didn't, they saw a future for their children.

– Stephen Mulka

* * *

These voices, of fifty, sixty, and seventy-year-old men and women, belong to the children of the immigrants, those who are old enough to remember themselves as young children growing up on a settlement only recently cleared of the bush. The younger ones, born late in a large family, grew up on operating farms. For these Ukrainian-Canadians, the early, bitter years of pioneering were already "the old days," transcribed in the storytelling of older brothers and sisters and less frequently by their parents. Almost as though there were no pleasure in the story, the pioneer parent was reticent about these beginnings. When the child grew up to want to hear the tale, the parent was dead, or alive and well on a half-section or in the town, luxuriating in a decent price for wheat, and willing only to tell a story of pride and success. The litany: "we worked hard, we suffered hard, and we overcame." They are too modest.

If they had arrived in Edmonton in the fall, they had then to wait through the winter, using up precious capital before they could get to the homestead. Impatient and anxious, sharing accommodation with earlier arrivals – two families in two rooms – and dependent on their largesse, such as it was, they were dumbfounded by the prairie winter, scarcely believing how it went on and on until they thought they would go crazy. This was the first nostalgia, the longing for early spring and blossoming pear and plum and cherry trees while all about them were poplar saplings, willow bush, and native grass under the snow.

The wood they were glad enough for, and come spring they picked homesteads that had a lot of bush; with this they had all the firewood and building materials they needed, for free. No matter that it took a decade to clear: to them the wood, as spindly and crooked as it grew, was as valuable as any crop that could have been seeded in its place.

It was land on which English settlers had tried to establish ranches. It was land that distribution agencies in Strathcona had sent them out to, saying "pick your quarter here" where the CPR was or would be running. And it was land on which the American or English or French refused to settle, fertile enough but covered in bush so that only those prepared for the tedious labour of the grub hoe would accept it. The CPR and the Hudson's Bay Company and school lands picked off twenty out of thirty-six sections in every township. "The area became a checkerboard of settlement where four immigrants could file on the black spaces but the adjoining white sections remained empty. This handicap had the effect of dispersing the Ukrainians far more widely than they had anticipated."[10] So much for the picture postcards of the immigration agent back in the old country, so much for Arcadia.

According to agreement the settler was obligated, during the three-year term of the contract, and for the sum of $10.00, to build a house on the land alloted to him, buildings for cattle, and to clear and plough at least thirty acres of land. Only after carrying out these terms of the contract could the land be considered as belonging to him. If these terms were not carried out he lost his rights to the land and the three years of work and effort that was put into it was lost and wasted. To make sure that this wouldn't happen and that he would have the right to settle permanently on his contracted land, the settler and his family worked from sunrise to sunset to clear the forest and cultivate the thirty acres demanded in the contract. Without horses and oxen – the people themselves donned the harness, ploughing the earth and harrowing it with their own strength. And just as in the old days of serfdom, in the time of Shevchenko, "people were harnessed to the yoke," so here in Canada, in the "new land," they were also forced into harness to keep from dying of hunger. It was the same serfdom – only in a different form. [11]

The work that had to be done was formidable, considering that they arrived without tools and without livestock. Of course, those who had had disposable property in the old country and who had arrived with plenty of cash were able to buy equipment, horses, seed, and supplies right away and thresh a crop within a year. J.G. MacGregor records such a success story:

> During the summer of 1896, Kost Nemirsky had worked hard, and as well as putting up a house had cleared and broken four acres. With the $600 that remained on his arrival at Edmonton he had purchased a wagon, which he shared with Halkow, a pair of large oxen, two cows which cost him $56, a $26 plough, a $516 stove, a tent for summer use costing $10, kitchen utensils to the value of $60, some small implements on which he expended $35, and two small rifles for which he paid $20.

A bonanza! For the rest, it would take almost a generation to catch up and meant the absence of the father, gone to town or to the railroad or the sawmill for a paycheque.

Women and children together would begin the work of transforming the prairie into farmland. To undertake this monumental project they had odds and ends of clothing, some dishes and pans, grindstones (to grind for flour the still unrealized wheat), some tea, sugar and flour, a pick, axe and grub hoe. Their first shelter was a dugout *(burdei* or *zemlyanka)* measuring about 4' x 10' x 15' without walls and with a roof of poplar saplings covered with sod. It was a dark and smoky cavern, damp and cramped. Within it women cooked, mended, washed, spun, sang, prayed, and gave birth. They fed themselves and their children from the natural harvest of the land – mushrooms, berries, rabbits, prairie chicken, bush partridge, rosehips for tea – until a garden could be planted in one of the clear spots. With the tools at hand they began the struggle against the bush.

From time to time, the man would return from his job with what was left of his wages after he had bought a plow, seeds, and a team of oxen. Sometimes he was able to stay and help with the clearing and seeding; sometimes he was not there at all but only sent money. From Clover Bar in the coal mines to Fort Macleod on the railroad, from Red Deer on a ranch to Golden in the iron mines, Ukrainian men earned one wage for two jobs: their own, and their families'. "With the two oxen, Magdalena plowed and cultivated a bit more land; the seeding she did by hand. That summer Alexander sent her some money and she bought a cow. . . . Her experience with harvesting done entirely by hand, and the help from the boys, enabled her to cut, thresh, bag the wheat, stack the straw and cut some hay that was plentiful in the low meadow and excellent fodder for the cow and oxen."[12] Or even, more succinctly, one man's mother "ploughed a little clearing, harrowed it by hand, threw on the seed and got a bumper crop."

In retrospect, the story is sanguinely told, even by those who, as children at the time, worked alongside their parents. Unrealized, between the lines, lies the feeling of the experience. One has to recreate forcibly the pathetically lightweight plough jabbing away at the root-infested sod, the oxen heaving on ropes to pull out a thousand tree trunks, the women and children banging at the furrows with hand-made hoes, the arms swinging eighteen hours a day at poplar saplings and willow bush, the buzzing cloud of mosquitoes settling on their sweat, and the blisters rising up on their hands, for the rememberings will only give you the outlines:

Dad came here with just his "ten fingers." He took a homestead, he was using the pick and axe and tore up a little at a time. That was a lot of hard work. We never had no cash, and very little when there was some.

My mother's father passed away quite early after he arrived here and Mother was the oldest of the children and she had to help Grandmother. There was only Mother and then a brother and two girls. My grandmother never did remarry. Just kept up the farm with the kids to help. Mother cut brush and burned it and always had to dig out the roots. They cleared it acre by acre.

And every now and then a story slips out, of a fire which destroyed the little bit the family had accumulated, of feet frozen black from the intense cold, of husbands who went to look for jobs and were never heard of again, of starving women and children shuffling along a trail towards Fort Saskatchewan to get food from the police,[13] of graves being dug in blizzards.

In 1897, Corporal G.D. Butler of the NWMP stationed at Edna, in the middle of the new Ukrainian settlement east of Edmonton, reported to his commanding officer at Fort Saskatchewan on the living conditions of the homesteaders in the area, most of whom had been settled only a few months. Some had already managed to put in a small garden but it was obvious that by winter their meagre resources would be exhausted. The commissioner of the NWMP in Regina wrote his superior in Ottawa that, "there is certain to be great destitution among the Galicians and other foreigners, who have grown nothing of any account this year, and are now living in a most miserable manner and many of them are sick, caused, it is said, by want of nourishment." Butler's report confirmed the commissioner's impression in a series of notes made as he visited each homestead.

> Dmytro Balan: Has nothing. This man has also built a house and is working out when he can get any work. Has four small children. George Klapatiuk: Has nothing. Three children. He owed Ivan Scraba $200 for passage money to this country. Wasyl Hunka: Has two cows, but nothing else of any account. Has six children. Giorgi Melnyk: Has one horse, one cow and four children. His wife had twins about a month ago and caught cold from laying on the ground. He started to take her to Edmonton once but had not gone any more than a quarter of a mile before she started to groan and say she could not stand being taken that distance. She has not been any better since. Wasyl Stecko: Has nothing. Sends wife amongst the neighbours to work.[14]

In 1898, another NWMP officer, Inspector P.C.H. Primrose, visited the settlements and reported that the children he saw had hardly any clothes or shoes and had to stay indoors all the time as a result. Because there was no money for blankets, the people were forced to sleep with their clothes on. "The houses I found with few exceptions very hot, there not being much ventilation. All these houses with the exception I think of two had mud floors, and I would not consider any clean and in a great many they keep their hens in with them, and in some the hens were nesting on the beds. The insides of some of these houses struck me as filthy with mildewed walls as soft as putty. . . . The most flour I saw in any house was three bags. . . . About twenty have no stock." The suggestion from an agent of the Dominion Lands Office in Edmonton that the poor should get work he thought "an excellent one, but some are prevented from doing so having no wives, and children to look after; through having to get out the logs for their houses; through sickness; through not having the proper clothing in which to go and look for work, etc. Whilst on this subject of work I may say some are reluctant to go to work as they say they do not get their pay. . . . Fifteen families have no land broken at all. Only one has ten acres, and the others six and under. You will also notice that but one family had meat of any sort of description (piece of pork) in the house. Several had nothing but a few potatoes and many are deriving their sustenance from bread made from shorts, which diet is hardly suitable for human beings in mid-winter, and, as the visit was made when the preparations were in progress for the celebration of their New Year's Festival, it is to be presumed that they were as well provisioned as they could be."[15]

The Ukrainian homesteaders were examined a third time, also in 1898, by Thomas Bennett, an immigration officer in Edmonton, authorized to provide relief to the most destitute. Over and over again in his report occur the phrases: "very poor," "wretched poor house," "wretchedly poor," "no provisions," "destitute," "clean but poor." And again the data from the house-calls: "Paulo Gudzan: Wife and three children, arrived in May, 1987. Has one cow and calf, good house and cook stove but was short of provisions sufficient to carry him through until he could get a crop in. I explained that any assistance the government might give must be secured by a lien on his homestead, to which he willingly assented. I therefore gave him relief to the amount of $10. Panko Onuczko: Wife and one child. Two children having died since his arrival in Dec., 1897. No land broken but timber cut and hauled to build a house. At present living with a neighbour. John Sliwka: This man owes $7 for baggage but has given order on CPR for that amount as he has been working for that company and has not yet been paid. Rosalia Sawkowa: Widow and four children. Good house and cook stove, eight acres broken, two horses, two cows and two calves. Raised fourteen bu. of wheat but such poor quality that they would not grind it for her at the mill."[16]

How, from this assembly of poor and desperate people, hungry enough to accept government help in exchange for dispossession of their land, one is to construct the intrepid, freedom-fighting and muscle-bound figure popularized by the conventional histories such as MacGregor's is a puzzle. The contemporary accounts do not have it so. Father Nestor Dmytriw, Greek-Catholic priest, visiting the Edna colony the same year of Butler's, Primrose's, and Bennett's reports, gave this sobering counsel to the poor still in the Ukraine:

> Let none dare come to Canada without a cent. Let such stay in Galicia, for it is easier to be a beggar there than here. There, a beggar is handed a piece of black bread, but here none will give away anything gratuitously. They may pay for work done, but work is not to be found on the farms, except on your own farm. And how can you work your own farm if you do not have oxen and a plough, even if you are dying of hunger, and die you surely will. To start farming and to last out until you can enjoy the fruits of your toil, you must have not less than three hundred dollars in your pocket on arrival at the site. Without that modest capital, a person will either perish or forever be a pauper. A grave error was committed by those of our people who arrived in Canada towards winter. It is certainly obvious that, in winter time, you will not get bread from under the snow. Your money will all be spent for food in the course of a long and hard winter, and in the spring, you will be left without a cent – and then try beating your head against a wall.[17]

The shocked observations of police and priest notwithstanding, there were those among the authorities who were not convinced that the "Galicians" were having a hard time of it. Their conviction rested, perhaps, on the assumption that poverty among Galicians was all that they deserved or expected, that a Galician was happy with little and required even less. It was commonplace, at the turn of the century, to describe the East European immigrant as a person of only the rudest needs: "the Slav came single-handed, alone. Wife and children had he none, nor wished for them . . . he was satisfied to live in almost any kind of place, to wear almost anything that would clothe his nakedness, and to eat any kind of food that would keep body and soul together."[18] From that generalization to the satisfied appraisal of an agent of the Dominion Lands Office in Edmonton, in 1897, is not far:

> Several of them [the settlers] said that they would like it if the government would advance them some seed grain and flour in the spring and they would pay it back in the fall with interest. I gave them to understand that they must not expect any help from the government and that they must go out and work among the farmers and earn their grain and flour and that there was plenty of work all over the country this year. . . . On my way back to Edmonton I met Mr. Porte, president of the Fort Saskatchewan Agricultural Society. He had been to every house to ascertain how much crop per acre each farmer would have and he informed me that he had never seen a more contented and happy lot of farmers. . . .[19]

There were, of course, reasons why so many of the homesteaders were impoverished, reasons having nothing to do with pseudo-scientific explanations of a "national character," with primitive needs, or with supposed laziness or lack of imagination. As has already been pointed out, the amount of capital on arrival was crucial in determining how quickly land could be cleared and cultivated, how quickly an income could be realized from it. The less money the immigrant had to begin with, the longer he had to spend working away from the farm and the longer he had to postpone transforming the homestead into an economic unit. As late as the end of the 1920s Charles Young, a sociologist who travelled through the Ukrainian settlement in northeastern Alberta, was still obliged to explain to his Anglo-Saxon readers that the time between arrival in Canada and the establishment of a working farm could be long indeed, and did not necessarily reflect poorly on the Galician.

> And in a much greater degree is this true of the unaccompanied males who have come with the intention of settling on the land they loved but have been compelled to do day labour on

construction gangs or work in the mines or in the bush, in order to pay off old debts or to bring the family or sweetheart from the homeland. Three years compulsory service in the militia at home, or five years – or perhaps a lifetime – with railroad gangs in Canada! That was the choice for many who came to this country.[20]

There were acts of God which could wipe out even the most enterprising: death of a spouse, fire, early frost, drought or grasshoppers, a disabling accident. There was the possibility of being cheated out of wages or of failing to receive relief to tide one over until harvest. There was, as Oleskow warned in his book on emigration, the temptation to buy a great number of expensive items on credit only to be ruined through exorbitant interest charges.[21]

And there was the element of the land – its quality, its accessibility, its topography. It was Charles Young who observed that the "economic and social progress of the Ukrainians is closely dependent . . . on the nature of the land which they have settled."[22] The connection is simple enough. By 1896, during the first major wave of Ukrainian immigration to the prairies, the best homesteads – those in the open, flat country and those close to the large towns and cities – had already been colonized by immigrants from eastern Canada, the United States, Great Britain, and Western Europe. The Ukrainians were offered the leftovers and thirty-five years later, when Young wrote his book, had still not caught up. "The standard of living of the people on the whole in the rural settlements is lower than the standards of other nationalities."[23] But he noted, to his satisfaction, that Ukrainian families who had sent daughters out to work as housekeepers and maids in Anglo-Saxon homes had the cleanest homes and an almost "Canadian" standard of living.

At what point do an observer's biases make him incredible? Evaluations of "cleanliness" and "standard of living" are notoriously subjective and proceed largely from the eye of the beholder. Young, for instance, bases his remarks about the standard of living among Ukrainians not on what Ukrainians themselves reported to him but on questionnaires filled out by non-Ukrainian neighbours![24] Subject to prejudice and ignorance, can such observations be believed? Similarly, in the case of the Edna colony in its first years, one runs a strange and narrow course between the inevitable and real suffering of pioneers and the culture shock experienced by Anglo-Saxon authorities encountering their first sheepskin coats and *pyrohy*. Fifty years and two generations later, it is a question of succumbing neither to the liberal notion that the pioneers lived invariably in dignity and health, nor to the racist notion that in the difference between the Ukrainian and the Anglo-Saxon lay the difference between the barbarian and the sophisticate. When faced with the fact that some Ukrainians had flour but no shoes, does one call it a lie, or a racial characteristic? Between the two is the truth of the matter: when you're poor and have only fifty cents to spend, you'll feed yourself before you clothe yourself. When you have a dollar, you'll do both.

Not only were Ukrainians settling on marginal or bushland, they were also, in Alberta, homesteading miles and miles from the nearest transportation system. Those who chose their quarter sections in the Ukrainian bloc settlement east of Edmonton made their way home along wagon trails which branched off from three major "roads"; one on the south side of the North Saskatchewan River made its way around lakes and through gulleys and eventually emerged at the Vermilion River near present-day Two Hills. The nearest train station was at Edmonton, which was anywhere from thirty to one hundred miles from the farms, a journey of two to five days with oxen and much longer by foot. Like it or not, this was home.

By 1914, 30,000 Ukrainians had arrived in Alberta, most of them settling in the parklands northeast and southwest of Edmonton and in the coal mining districts near Lethbridge. Their greatest concentration lay in the 1,000-square-mile territory from Bruderheim to Derwent (west to east) and from the north bank of the North Saskatchewan to Holden (north to south).[25] The new communities of Willingdon, Andrew and Wostok, Smoky Lake,

Vilna, and Spedden were to be organized by people from villages called Kysyliw, Boriwtsi, Shypyntsi, and Stawchan in the Ukrainian province of Bukovyna. The Canadian towns of Lamont, Mundare, Vegreville, Myrnam, and Two Hills grew up among emigrants from Galicia, from villages called Nebyliw, Ispas, Zawale, and Tulova. Some of these names were transplanted and applied to schools and post offices and villages in Canada but most were left behind as Ukrainians moved into areas already named by the Anglo-Saxon and the French.

Their children, the first Ukrainian-Canadians, are the problematic ones, the citizens balanced on the contradiction between a desire to pay respect to the roots of their ancestors, and the need to endorse their own Canadian experience. More precisely, it is the Ukrainian-Canadian who, as an historian, must make sense of the immigrants' tribulations and complaints within the context of the next generation's adjustment to the dominant culture's values, who must, in retrospect, make "good Canadians" of tens of thousands of Ukrainian peasants who never asked for more than a respite, at last, from poverty and exhaustion. Such an historian, Paul Yuzyk, in summarizing the Canadian experience of his parents' generation, describes the "opportunities" for freedom and material wealth of which the pioneers supposedly took advantage.

> The immigrants found in Canada homesteads, land on easy payments, remunerative even though hard work, prospects of advancement, business opportunities, the freedom to change their type of work, and a higher standard of living. . . . Individuals had the protection of the law, before which all were equal. . . . In Canada, where individual work is recognized, a person may improve his financial situation and social standing through work, thrift, or business ability . . . mutual respect for others, cooperation and harmony meant peace and welfare for all in the Canadian polyglot population.[26]

This is a familiar, not to say hackneyed, version of the Canadian myth of the pursuit of happiness. The extent to which one subscribes to it is a measure of the degree to which one has accepted the middle-class, Anglo-Canadian view of our history, no less true for ethnics than for anybody else. Of course, the success stories of Ukrainians in Canada are legion – all those doctors and lawyers, politicians and entrepreneurs – and Ukrainians in Canada did progress beyond semi-feudal life in the old country (for that matter, so did the Ukrainians who stayed behind). But Yuzyk's vision is simplistic and misleading, even though it does correspond to the prevailing mythology among most Ukrainian-Canadians today. It belies the fact that financial security was tenuous in the extreme, that their labour was far from remunerative, that their "freedom" to an education was to an anglicized one; the law was discriminatory, their non-Ukrainian neighbours were racists, their leftist political activists were persecuted; and the admonitions to "work" and "thrift" applied precisely and only to the working people – the resident elite had neither to work nor be thrifty.

There is a tendency, then, among the historians and storytellers of these events, to ascribe to an often miserable and thankless way of life a dimension of glory and to the people enduring it a prophetic vision, or at least a nobility of character, as though the unedited reality of their experiences is somehow vulgar or banal or even shameful. "Only her sturdy constitution and a determination born of a life of toil, self-reliance and resourcefulness enabled her to overcome. . . ."[27] As if it were awkward and embarrassing just to let be the pain and loss and even failure of so many of these lives, the "official" histories demand that we see their lives as heroic or nothing at all.

The Ukrainian-Canadian has had to make a choice, when describing his or her parents' lives, between a romantic cover-up and a rude protest, between homilies about "freedom" and "success" and this voice:

In search of fortune I rushed over here,
To such a far and distant land.
I've suffered much
And I still endure all kinds of hardships.

But good fortune is a rare thing here,
And few will ever find it;
More people perish in the mines than anywhere else,
And no one will ever hear them again.

Others have their hands cut off –
Victims of machines,
While still others die of hunger
Because they can't speak the language.

O save us, Mother of God,
And all you heavenly powers above!
So that we can earn another
Hundred dollars for our pockets;

So that we can sail back to our families
Over that frightful ocean;
It is there that our hearts will be lighter
And the black days will be forgotten.[28]

Between those choices lies something like the true story of the immigrant. And one may have to leap a generation to find it.

THREE

Racism

I recall my dad telling me that way back when he was just starting out he went to buy a lantern in Duvernay from the French storekeeper and he was a couple of cents short. He asked her to wait a couple of weeks for him to bring her the other ten cents. And she said: "No! Russian credit no good!" So Dad walked back the eight miles without a lantern.

– Nick Olinyk

* * *

At Hinton I had several services, performed marriages. There our people, who were only a bit religious, sent their children to the United Church or Church of England. But after some of them got together they realized that they were given very high positions – like a broom and a pail. But to. be elected to the board – oh, no! Nor would the older people be allowed to take the collection. The younger ones were good for shovelling snow.

– Father Peter Zubrytsky

* * *

People just became subservient to the English nationality. If you wanted a better job, if you wanted some consideration, you learned to tow the rope because people who got into better positions, well, they just couldn't talk. And you knew – even today – that when you made an application, there was going to be a prejudice against Ukrainians. When Mr. H — was on the school board, he said, "As long as I'm here, there will not be a Ukrainian teacher in Vegreville."

– Dick Geleta

* * *

As a Ukrainian, there are some things I don't like that the English people do to Ukrainians. They call them bohunks and whatnots. I was in Vegreville at the hockey game two or three years ago. There was John K — sitting by me, another young guy sitting next to him. And Two Hills and Vegreville, when they played hockey, there was quite a rivalry between these two teams. I said something in Ukrainian, and this fellow says to me, "Talk English, you bohunk." I told him, "I am a Canadian, just like you." People are funny. If they want to hurt your feelings, they either call you a bohunk, or a farmer.

– Metro Shepansky

* * *

By 1940, we were all working together for a common cause. I don't think that we were called names, you didn't hear that kind of thing anymore. But maybe you cannot blame the English. Maybe you cannot blame the English for saying things. I wonder what the Ukrainians would do, most of them nationalists, if the English were a minority and they were immigrants like this to a Ukrainian country? I wonder what the Ukrainians would do? Whether they would call some fancy names. Hard to tell.

– Mike Tomyn

While immigration to western Canada may have satisfied the long-range economic plans of the CPR and Ontario capitalists for the prairie provinces, it infuriated, disgusted, appalled, and plagued just about everybody else. The sense of proprietorship which the Anglo-Saxon establishment held for the western provinces and the wounded dignity they felt in the face of the "hordes" unloading on the platform at Strathcona's CPR station were near the surface of the protests they registered as soon as the first statistics were available. In 1897 the editor of the Edmonton *Bulletin* speculated that, if only Clifford Sifton (author of this iniquitous immigration policy) could see a photograph of a newly-arrived Ukrainian "in all the glory of its ultra negligee attire as it parades through our streets, he would have a violent and nauseating feeling in the region of his watch pocket."[29] In 1899 a writer for the Calgary *Herald* took a look at the figures supplied him by the immigration agent in Edmonton and noted that, of 1,792 immigrants to northern Alberta that year, 1,075 were "dirty, frowsy Galicians" and only 38 came from the "mother country." He feared that the Ruthenian "mass of human ignorance, filth and immorality" would give the rest of Canada a bad name: "Like a hotel, or other public place, a country is gauged and sized up according to the class of people who frequent it. [30]

Repeatedly, in this era, the equation is made between defense of self-interest and defense of the interests of "British civilization." Unless this civilization prevailed against the "alien invasion" and the mass of "human dregs" from Eastern Europe, one's family life, one's career, one's self-esteem would be dragged about in the muck of the foreigners' culture. These were, remember, "people emerging from serfdom, accustomed to despotism, untrained in the principles of representative government, without patriotism."[31] Stephen Leacock, pontificating from Ontario, deplored the fact that the continental European immigrant did not exhibit the characteristics of the "strenuous, adventurous and enterprising" pioneers who had first settled British North America and had envisioned a Republic and a Confederation. Would the "mere herds of the proletariat of Europe," he wondered, be capable of carrying on the work of the Anglo-Saxon heroes or would they, conversely, drag the federation down to the depths of their own ignorance? He asked the question of the Americans:

> It is beyond the scope of the present inquiry to ask whether the United States is proving itself able in reality to assimilate this enormous influx of alien elements; whether in elevating the

mass of the illiterate and the untrained, it will not of necessity depress the level of its own general standard; whether after all the spacious environment of a fertile and prosperous country will of itself create a unified people of as high an intellectual and moral standard as that of the pioneer settlers and their descendants, by whom, under vastly different circumstances, the republic was founded.[32]

He was in part answered by the Toronto *Globe* who reassured its readers (and those of the Vegreville *Observer* where the editorial was reprinted) that Anglo-Saxon civilization was holding its own in the West; there was nothing to fear in the "Slavic inundation" so long as the elite and its institutions remained WASP – white, Anglo-Saxon, and Protestant. What influence could a pack of mere farmers bring to bear against the genius of the WASP bourgeoisie?

The immigrants from the United States and Great Britain and the migrants from eastern Canada so outnumber the settlers from continental Europe that the West is today definitely Anglo-Saxon. . . . The legislators, the teachers, lawyers, ministers and newspapermen are almost invariably from the East and at this formative period the West is to them as clay in the hands of a potter.[33]

By 1929, however, there were those – the Ku Klux Klan, the anti-immigration National Association of Canada, and the Anglican bishop of Saskatchewan, George Exton Lloyd – who could not share in such self-assured complacency, who feared in fact that the opposite was the case:

If this theory [the "melting pot"] is persisted in, it will produce in Canada what it has produced in the States, a series of hyphenated Canadians who will demoralize our British institutions. As the president of the Jesuit College of Regina voiced it, "It is too late to talk British institutions and British language in the West." In other words, that Jesuit father thinks that in our Western "melting pot" the British element is already at the bottom. And he is very nearly right![34]

These men were very much disturbed by the fact that the majority of immigrants were Slavs. What could have been further from the Anglo-Saxon ideal of blond-haired manhood than these swarthy, squat, high-cheeked, long-haired, buxom people in skins (except perhaps for Asians, who were beneath contempt)? In the diatribes printed against them, in the choice of adjectives and verbs, in the reliance on mystical references to "morality" and "national character" and "manhood," one can feel the real malaise of the writers, their discomfort at having to consider and deal with such people at all.

The general attitude was that the "Russians" or "Galicians" were undoubtedly good workers, but that they were not "white" and were certainly very inferior to English-speaking people. One might condescendingly speak to "John" or "Mike" in bastard English which the Canadian fancied was "Russian." But any other form of social intercourse was unthinkable. The Galician was presumably dirty; he smelled powerfully of garlic and treated his women in a way which did not meet the approval of our people. Stories were circulated about his under-ventilated house, which, quite often, sheltered pigs and chickens as well as human beings. The prevailing opinion, right or wrong, was that the Galician was an untrustworthy and vindictive person.[35]

Reverend J.S. Woodsworth observed that the Ukrainians worked "with a physical endurance bred of centuries of peasant life and an indifference to hardships that seems characteristic of the Slav. . . . Drunk, he is quarrelsome and dangerous. The flowers of courtesy and refinement are not abundant in the first generation of immigrants. But he is a patient and industrious workman. . . . The girls as a rule make good domestics."[36] The saving grace.

On the face of it, Woodsworth was a sympathetic and

compassionate commentator surrounded as he was by the more virulent racism of yahoos. He searched his soul and found the sympathy that human decency demanded when confronted, in 1908, by the mass of humanity arriving daily in the West; it was the sympathy of the elitist. An honest democrat would not resort to the occult categories of "clean blood" and degrees of "whiteness," as Woodsworth did, in forming judgements, nor imagine that any human being could ever become "indifferent" to hardship and oppression. A writer close to the subject would not describe Ukrainians as, in Woodsworth's words, "unenterprising farmers," nor award them the condescending compliment of being "patient" workers and good housemaids.

The fact that Ukrainians had a lower standard of living than the Canadian-born population seems to have been generally accepted. But it was rarely appreciated that this was a temporary state of affairs – who wouldn't have a low standard of living on an uncleared quarter section with minimal tools, meagre crops, and exorbitant transportation costs? In 1898, Commissioner of Immigration W.F. McCreary, in reply to NWMP Inspector Primrose's account of hardship among the settlers, thought he knew better. He chastised the Inspector for expecting too much of "European immigrants" and excused their poverty by explaining they found it acceptable.

> The report of Inspector Primrose in many points is true but his ideas of the requirements of these people are not in accordance with their habits even when they are well off – as for instance he speaks of the women and children having no clothing except a linen shirt. I may say that in the whole colony it would be impossible to find a woolen undergarment and I have never seen any of them yet wear stockings. . . . The bed consists of straw or hay with a coarse linen cover, but no blankets or eiderdown quilts were visible in the colony, so that while Inspector Primrose's kind heart was touched by their apparent discomfort it is evident they are quite content to sleep in their sheepskin coats as their fathers have done before them and

would consider our requirements an extravagant luxury.[37]

In the Ukraine, of course, they had not had to live like this. There they lived in orderly whitewashed homes with sufficient linens and clothing – a superfluity of clothing if one is to judge from the photographs of families in full regalia – furniture, dishes and tools. But most of this they had had to leave behind. Once they had money in Canada, they bought themselves clothing and made themselves blankets and quilts and wore stockings. To say they were "content" to be poor is to repeat the bogus logic of the smug.

The sympathy of the liberal was very often only a facade. Charles Young, who presented himself as a friend of the Ukrainians, did not deny their distress but believed that "it is not so much the harm to them resulting from their low standard [of living] that is important, for they have been accustomed to it, as the effect of this standard of living on the country at large. There is no reason to doubt that they will contribute materially to the retarding or lowering of the Canadian standard of living."[38] Listing his reasons for such retardation, Young mentions social disorganization among the immigrants, their high crime rate, inter-group trouble, and slow assimilation rate. Eventually he presents statistical evidence to support his claims but, even so, to conclude that Ukrainians should not be admitted to Canada because of what amounts to the effects on them of Canadian capitalism is illogical: the Ukrainian was an object, not an instigator, of distress. To talk in 1931 of "social disorganization" among the intensely community-oriented and socially organized Ukrainian-Canadians, and of "retarded assimilation" when a whole generation was becoming bilingual, self-consciously patriotic and committed to the Canadian mythologies of hard work, progress, and fair play, is to parade one's ignorance.

Better, in a way, to deal with the undisguised and unapologetic prejudice of a die-hard bigot like "H.D.," a regular columnist for the Vegreville *Observer* in the 1910s and 1920s.

The average present-day Ruthenian is still a pretty slippery proposition; his word isn't good for much, meester; he will break his promise and go back on his agreement if he feels the least bit like it; and the eighth commandment has a very slender hold on him. With exceptions of course, a good many, particularly among the ladies, have a strong touch of kleptomania; they will commandeer the linen off your wash-line, annex the clothes from your wardrobe and adopt the spoons out of your drawer. . . . They have the instincts of a primitive people and I have known them to take very mean vengeance for fancied wrongs.[39]

Earlier he had been offended by the appointment of Peter Svarich as a weed inspector in the district:

It is quite possible that English-speaking generations yet unborn will come to look upon the descendants of Galician emigrants as their equals and friends; at the present time we do not so consider them. In view of their education, ideas, moral standards and mode of life, we justly regard them as inferiors. We are prepared to treat them with fairness and civility; we are not prepared to be bossed by them. . . . When it comes to investing a Russian yokel with authority to dictate, in the Government's name, to English-speaking British subjects, we think that this is going too far, and anticipating too boldly on the future. We resent it as a humiliation; and it is unlikely that white men in this Province will stand for it. [40]

The Ukrainian as nigger? In retrospect, these tirades are almost amusing; they are the tragicomic crowings of a ruffled rooster, shocked and amazed that his little barnyard kingdom can no longer be considered his private fief.

Some Anglo-Canadians were never to be placated. As late as 1931, the *Observer* suspected that a great deal about the Depression could be explained by the foolhardiness of immigration policies – what a waste of good land to put it into the hands of undifferentiated foreigners: "Fairly bribing them to come, bonussing transportation companies to bring them in, turning excellent land over to them for the $10 entry fee, naturalizing them in wholesale lots practically without any investigation, all contributed to the difficulties under which this country is now labouring." [41]

It is true that the Ukrainians were never without their admirers and supporters, and these "friends" I call the "positive" racists. They believed themselves to be good-willed and open-minded about the immigrants' habits and aptitudes and professed an admiration for their good qualities, such as they were. In the things they chose to admire lies the nature of their prejudice, for a "good" Ukrainian was a person most closely resembling an untroublesome rustic who knows his or her place.

> All goodness does not centre in the native born or the English stock. For his lights the Galician is a worthy citizen. He is eager and quick to learn, pays his school rates willingly, is anxious for his children to have a good education. He is thrifty and a good farmer, and his scale and style of living show improvement every year. There are a few sheepskin coats now in the first generation and none at all in the second. He is pious, builds churches, pays for them and goes to them regularly. Also he glimpses the truth that cleanliness is next to godliness, and that washing ought to be a daily habit. . . . The Galician may have his faults, but he is not nearly so hard to digest as the Doukhobor. [42]

Speaking at a conference of Ukrainian-Canadian farmers in Edmonton in 1920, Dr. Henry Marshall Tory, president of the University of Alberta, "marvelled at the rapidity with which all Ukrainians grasped the elements of the English language." [43] Peter Bryce, on a tour of inspection for the federal government in 1928, remarked on the "pretty gardens," "some old picturesque cottage," and the "women stooking the grain alongside the others, as in the old Scotch days of 'Comin' Through the Rye.'" [44] Their attachment to the land – had they a choice? – was to be viewed not as a sign of their low station in life, but as their peculiar virtue:

For centuries they have lived their simple lives in the villages of
the Carpathian Mountains, and gone out to their small plots to
cultivate them in an intensive fashion and so learned the value
of every foot of ground. . . . As a Calgary banker, who had lived
in Alberta all his life, said to me: They love the land, since, as
one of his clients in real estate told him, he had refused to sell a
piece of land to an American, who simply wanted to speculate
with it, but sold it on easy terms to the Ukrainian, who loves
the soil. [45]

In the same vein, an Edmonton *Journal* reporter, travelling through
the Ukrainian districts in 1923, was enchanted by the "pretty
blouses," the beads – "Ukrainians love pretty things and bright
colours" – and the "glowing head covering" of the peasant woman's
"ensemble."

Is it really necessary to see picturesqueness and artfulness in the
perfectly mundane in order to accord the Ukrainians dignity and
personality? It is only necessary if you had imagined them otherwise.

As we shall see, the Ukrainian-Canadians' response to racist
attitudes was either to develop a romantic and consoling mythology
around their European culture and character or to become
politicized, together with Finns and Germans and Poles, around
their class position; in both cases, it was a question of self-defense.
The Anglo-Canadian establishment was, after all, in a position to
institutionalize its biases, as many Ukrainian-Canadians learned
when they left home to find jobs. They had also heard tales from
their parents, reluctantly related, of ill-treatment and humiliation:
the shopkeeper who refused credit to a "Russian"; the man who was
trailed in the streets of Vegreville by children bleating "ba-a-a" at
the back of his sheepskin coat; the woman who was forced to wait
outside the post office, in sub-zero weather, because the interior was
for the "English" only; the teacher who, "herself a first-generation
Ukrainian-Canadian, used to tell us that when we had dirty
fingernails and ate with our mouths open and gawked and farted we
were being just like a 'bunch of stupid Ukrainians.'"

One has the impression, when talking to their sons and daughters, that the immigrant Ukrainians seldom spoke of these incidents, either in fear of the consequences of being heard to complain while still without citizenship or out of the resignation of the victim – "It was ever thus" – or the personal pain of recollection. Instead, they instilled an ethic which they hoped would serve as protection enough: "Father used to tell us, whatever you do, do right, and it won't matter what people say about you." But it was not always enough; it was not just a question of what people would say about you but of what they could do to you. "When I went out practice teaching I had a hard time in one school because the demonstrating teacher seemed to favour the fellow I was teamed with. He had a pronounced English accent and the teacher was Anglo-Saxon." "As a kid my brother changed his name to Chapman. He wanted to work for B.C. Telephones and they said, 'Well, you know, we'll never promote Germans or Ukrainians.'" "I was told I would not be hired by the Edmonton Public School Board with a name like Winarsky. A year later I tried again. Same face but new name. Wynn. I was hired." "In my teen years, if you were an Anglo-Saxon, a government job was already half yours, automatically. But if you were a Ukrainian – forget it. Even the post office." "The Ukrainians have been tillers of the soil and there have been those who felt they should be tillers forever."

It was the Ukrainian-Canadians' quintessential dilemma. They were raised by parents very often intimidated by the authority of the Anglo-Saxon majority, parents who urged them not to complain or protest but to "prove" themselves as good as the Englishman. But the Englishman they were asked to emulate and please was the one who called them bohunks and sneered at their names and faces. They were called upon to be an example for their race, to be the first Ukrainian in law school or in the Chamber of Commerce or the House of Commons, but the obstacles were considerable, the accent was too strong, their names were unpronounceable, their parents too poor, their racial quota already filled, their non-Ukrainian neighbours scandalized by their pretensions. They were expected to exhibit only the best characteristics of a Canadian if they would be rewarded, but the reward was often withheld because they could not be Canadian enough. They took for granted their parents' and the establishment's message that if they worked hard and kept their noses clean they could leave the farm forever, only to learn that their parents had been allowed into Canada precisely to engender a farming class on the prairies. They weren't supposed to be a middle-class success story.

> We educate our Ukrainians living in Canada to live up to the highest ideals of intelligent and active citizenship; we ask them not only to enjoy their rights but to fulfill their duties, not only to expect privileges but to assume responsibilities. Unfortunately, in their noble efforts as Canadian citizens, the Ukrainians are being unduly hindered by prejudices . . . as if we were a less desirable and a less valuable element in the population of Canada. . . . Although they possess all the required qualifications, despite the moral stability of their characters and their intelligent concept of their civic status, our young Ukrainian-Canadians are experiencing grave difficulties in their attempts to gain for themselves their rightful place in Canada's social and economic life. [46]

Retrospectively, in Two Hills it is said: "You have to have continuous striving. That's when you accomplish things. You have to have opposition. It's good for you." So he says, comfortable enough these days. Only the secure and the beguiled can be so sanguine.

FOUR

World War I

One of my brothers joined the army in the First World War. He stayed the full four years or so. Well, that was the best promise of living at that time, and adventure as well. Better than trying to farm. There was so much allotted for your clothes and you could see the country and so much pay on top of it. I suppose it was a lot of glamour for those young boys, and the uniform, and three decent meals a day.

– Jack Malenka

* * *

I know that Germans were put in concentration camps during the First World War but Ukrainians were never bothered. No, I never heard of that. Unless it was somebody who was speaking out too roughly.

– Walter Kitt

The period of the First World War and immediately after (1914-1919) gave Ukrainian-Canadians their first taste of the repressive and hostile capacities of the Canadian state and their first awareness of how vulnerable they were when anti-foreign sentiment was exercised on a mass scale. Most of the first generation were too young at the time to recall now any personal experiences; but with or without knowing what happened in detail during those years, they were to encounter over the next two decades the consequences and reverberations of that period. The fact that, for apparently so little reason, Ukrainians could be persecuted in a country they had been invited to and a country which advertised itself as a haven of democracy undermined their sense of security for decades. Whether they retreated into caution and fearfulness or expressed their outrage through political organizations or jumped onto the Anglo-Canadians' patriotic bandwagons, the varying responses of the Ukrainian-Canadian community to persecution at this time marked the beginnings of an internal struggle that would divide it right up to the present.

The problem began with Canada's declaration of war against Austria in 1914. Ukrainians who had been born in Canada or whose fathers had acquired Canadian citizenship before 1905 were regarded as safe enough but everybody else, the vast majority, were considered to be Austrian subjects still, especially those who were not yet naturalized. It was absurd: the Ukrainians were no more "Austrian" in nationality than were Canadians, yet they were considered "enemy aliens" by the Canadian government for the unavoidable coincidence of having emigrated to Canada on Austro-Hungarian passports.

The concern of the government about the loyalty of the Ukrainians had been intensified by a pastoral letter issued in July 1914, by Bishop Budka (a Greek Catholic bishop who had been in Canada less than three years) who came to the support of Austria (where he had been trained as a seminarian) when it declared war on Serbia after the assassination at Sarajevo. Budka's mistake was to assume that the Ukrainians in Canada were as sympathetic to the Austrian cause as he was initially, or at any rate as sympathetic to the beleaguered monarchy and the notion that Austria and the Ukraine were one and the same homeland:

> The Canadian Ruthenian Ukrainians, sympathizing in the grief of our ancient Fatherland, made evident their sentiments in church services for the assassinated ones, and in their prayers for the fate of their native land. . . . To Canada there came an official appeal that the Austrian subjects who are duty-bound to serve in the army should return to Austria in order to be prepared to defend the state. . . . All Austrian subjects must be

at home in positions ready to defend our native land, our dear brothers and sisters, our Nation. [47]

A week later, upon Canada's declaration of war, the bishop, mindful perhaps of who now buttered his bread, retracted his statements and urged Ukrainians to join the Canadian army. But the damage had been done. The government and the Anglo-Saxon majority assumed that the Ukrainians' loyalty to the Canadian state was equivocal at best and they moved to protect themselves from the menace of the enemy alien within. "The Canadian government chose to ignore the fact that Ukrainians were in this country because the yoke of Austrian imperial oppression was unbearable and they desperately wanted another chance to build a new life in what they believed was a new land of promise and opportunity. Instead, the dream became a nightmare as they fell victim to the terrible provocation of the ambivalent bishop and the hysteria of the Anglo-Saxon chauvinist."[48]

In September 1914, a federal order-in-council required all Germans and "Austrians" to hand in their firearms. In October another order-in-council permitted the establishment of internment camps. As the Edmonton *Bulletin* explained it:

> Those [Germans and Austrians] who are destitute and those who it is considered should be kept under surveillance will be held in places of detention as prisoners of war. They will be in the charge of the military authorities and work will be provided for them. These latter plans have not been definitely worked out as yet. An effort will be made to find work which will not be unduly in competition with Canadian labour. The Austrians and Germans detained in the West, for instance may be put at the cleaning up of the national parks of dead or fallen leaves.[49]

By June 1915, 5088 persons were interned and 48,500 paroled.[50] All "aliens" of German and Austrian nationality were ordered to present themselves at NWMP registration offices; those under or over military service age or those unfit for the army were allowed to leave the country, the rest were to report once a month to the police.

Edmonton had 4,000 unemployed at the time, most of them European immigrants;[51] these were the men categorized as "destitute" and sent off to the labour camps. Hundreds of Ukrainians were dismissed from their jobs – "Because of his ethnic origin [Nick] Gavinchuk could not remain in teaching during the war"[52] – their property looted, their church services disturbed, their persons assaulted.[53] It became risky for an "alien" to walk about without papers, to voice dissatisfaction about such treatment, or to belong to an organization designated subversive. "Timofey Koreychuk, before the First World War, went to Canada and was an organizer of the Ukrainian Social Democratic Party, for which at the time of the first imperialist war, he was sent to a concentration camp in British Columbia where he died." [54]

By September 1918, at least fourteen such organizations were banned from meeting and carrying out their activities, including the International Workers of the World, the Ukrainian Revolutionary Group, the Ukrainian Social Democratic Party and the Workers' International Industrial Union, and their more obstreperous members were interned in the camps. Newspapers in fourteen different languages, including Ukrainian, were suppressed and meetings held in these languages prohibited. Naturalization for Ukrainians, among others, was suspended and, by the War Times Election Act of 1917, they were disenfranchised. (There was speculation that Prime Minister Borden feared they would vote for the opposition Liberals who were against conscription.[55]) "'It comes as a great surprise to Austrians to learn that they are enemies of the British Empire,' said one of the officials who is dealing with them. 'The Germans know all right, they are against us, but the Austrians seem to think that they are still our friends and are greatly shocked at being arrested as prisoners of war.'"[56]

The "Austrians" are the Ukrainians and although it is impossible to know exactly how many were interned, one can estimate that of the 2,087 interned and 79,057 on parole by June

1918, half were Ukrainians. It was a staggering number of people under coercion and the experience was an enduring lesson to the Ukrainians. How arbitrarily their lives could be circumscribed and their rights abrogated.

Those many Ukrainians not interned also felt the resentment and insensate chauvinism of the Anglo-Saxon communities. In January 1917, an official for the Canadian Patriotic Fund reported to a meeting of Whitford, Alberta, farmers that he had been encountering "cases of indifference and one instance of violent opposition" to the work of the Fund as he went canvassing among the Ukrainian farmers. The meeting told him that "those unfriendly to the Patriotic Fund are unfriendly to the country and by being so give comfort to the enemy – which is treason."[57] In January 1918, the Great War Veterans' Association held a provincial convention in Edmonton and called upon the government to take drastic action again "enemy aliens": "All such enemies should be set to work on works of national importance, that those not so engaged should be interned, that all such as are disenfranchised under the Election act report at thirty-day intervals and be required to reside within certain defined limits and that a supertax be placed on the incomes of such aliens, that they should not be allowed to acquire additional land under any circumstances."[58] In March 1919, months after the war's end, members of the Ukrainian Literary Society in Vegreville were prevented from staging a play (half the proceeds were to have gone to the Memorial Hall fund) by a Constable Nicholson who "forbade the play to proceed unless presented in English and translated into Ukrainian,"[59] which is to say translated back into Ukrainian. Of such stuff are the defenses of the realm.

While thousands of Ukrainians were being harassed and threatened, interned and kept under surveillance, others publicized their personal loyalty and steadfastness to government and Empire. An organization of Ukrainian Presbyterians sent a telegram to the governor general in June 1916:

[We extend] our expression of loyalty and devotion toward our adopted fatherland, Canada, and the British Empire, with the assurance that we stand firmly in this grave hour of national trial by the British flag; stimulated and united with other citizens of our common empire by the deepest faith in the certain and glorious victory of the highest ideals of true liberty and democracy of Great Britain and her allies; believing that these make for the progress and civilization of the world . . . including the thirty-five million Ukrainians. God Save The King![60]

In July 1916, the editors of six Ukrainian-language newspapers wrote an "Address to the Canadian People" which was printed in English-language papers and which attempted to correct the misapprehensions of Anglo-Canadians about Ukrainian political sentiments. The coincidence of their complaint and their loyalty is almost palpably uneasy. "We proclaim that after Canada and the British Empire to which as Canadian citizens we owe allegiance, we have love only to Ukraine in Europe, and we want to see there such another democratic government as we enjoy in Canada. . . . We realize that all the injury done Canadian Ukrainians in the name of the government of Canada was due in part to the ignorance of the Canadian people concerning the Ukrainian question. . . . It was also due to the unfortunate pastoral letter of Bishop Budka on the eve of the war. . . . But a whole nation should not be answerable for the mistake of one man, and during the two years of the war that has been over and over again wiped out by the loyal conduct of Canadian Ukrainians to the land of their adoption and the great empire that guarantees liberty and justice."[61] While it was undeniably true that they no longer lived under the semi-feudal and outrageously exploitive regime of Austro-Hungary (and for this they were naturally grateful), it was also patently obvious that under the exigencies of the War Measures Act many Ukrainians in Canada were deprived of "liberty and material prosperity." To pretend it was otherwise was unconscionably naive.

When the Ukrainians (with the exception of the socialists and Communists) did protest, it was with the characteristically defensive apology of those who "know their place." In January 1918, a public meeting of disenfranchised farmers and merchants discussed the anti-Ukrainian resolutions of the Great War Veterans' Association; aggravating the situation was the fact that they had been endorsed by the press and various "prominent public men." A newspaper report of the meeting commented: "The Ruthenians in Canada are well-known as being peaceful and loyal citizens who pursue their respective callings to the best of their ability. They have liberally contributed to the Patriotic Fund and the Red Cross and subscribed for Victory Bonds; and more than that they have sent thousands of their young men and boys to the front."[62] It is to the point that they, no more than the other patriots, argued not that their treatment was unjust on principle but simply that they should have been exempted.

By 1918 it should have been obvious to every Ukrainian-Canadian that no amount of patriotic genuflection would effect the slightest modification of the government's wartime policies. If anything, the assertions of loyalty and gratitude, the hosannas about civilization and the empire, and the categorical silence on the subject of interned, deported, and otherwise persecuted compatriots helped perpetuate an atmosphere in which the government could continue to act with impunity: who was to gainsay them? In March 1919, anticipating the return of Canadian veterans from the front, the Ukrainian shareholders of the National Co-operative Company Ltd. in Vegreville appealed for the swift restoration of their own Canadian naturalization and then went on, as though in retreat from their audacity, to assure the Canadian public that "we will greatly appreciate the presence of the returned men in our communities who would be able, willing and anxious to teach us the great British ideals, to promote our loyalty and to help us to attain the standard of British citizenship."[63]

For all this, no less than ten thousand Ukrainian-Canadians fought in the Canadian armed forces.[64] One has to ask why. Perhaps some were sincerely motivated by anti-Austrian and pro-British sentiments, some simply fulfilled an obligation without a fuss and some, especially if they were unemployed or wanted to get away from the farm, saw the army as a source of food, wages, and travel.

But there were others who were apathetic or even hostile to the war effort. Some were intellectuals who, in the old country, had been mollified by the Austrian emperor's relative liberalism and were genuinely afraid that the war, and an Austrian defeat, would jeopardize the liberal experiment in Europe. For others, opposition to the war was a function of their disillusionment or cynicism about their own situation in Canada. In the first place, many of them were prevented from serving, even if they had wanted to, by their Austrian citizenship. Secondly, they were becoming disaffected by the treatment of Ukrainians in Canada – the bigotry, the harsh working conditions of manual labour, the economic instability of the homestead, the violence done to "enemy aliens," the unemployment. Thirdly, they were becoming radicalized – by Anglo-Saxon radicals and by their own Ukrainian Social Democratic Party, which had been formed in Winnipeg in 1911.

Even before the war, in their workplaces, in political campaigns, in national halls, and in the ethnic socialist press, they had heard arguments that the war was an inevitable spasm of a decadent capitalism, that wealth, not men, should be conscripted and they heard about the Bolshevik Revolution. The more sensational the news from Russia, the more outspoken the Ukrainian socialist leaders in Canada became. Matthew Popowich, later a founding member of the Communist Party of Canada, attempted a prophecy for the future in front of an audience in Winnipeg in 1917, gathered to honour the birthdate of poet Taras Shevchenko: "I am confident that the workers and peasants, our class brothers, will not stop. Now that tsarist autocracy is cracked and Nicholas has abdicated, the people will go on from this provisional government forward to government by the working people and thus forward to socialism."[65]

These experiences, and their own hardships, "provided ammunition for men [and women] who felt and argued that the various layers of government in Canada were treating them just as the Hapsburgs and Romanovs had in Europe. Anglo-Saxon support of the authorities' dealings with the recent immigrants confirmed radical suspicions that Canadian society was hostile and oppressive."[66]

The Bolshevik Revolution, then, was good news to many. Lenin's platform of a forcible seizure of power by workers, peasants and soldiers' soviets, his renunciation of the Russian war effort and his theory of the self-determination of nations excited many Ukrainians in Canada, socialists and otherwise, who were themselves rendered powerless as workers and farmers, who were disgusted by the carnage of the war and still hoped for an independent Ukrainian state in Europe. As a Communist put it:

> The Canadian government, like those of other imperialist countries, was shaken by the events in Russia. A workers' state, for the first time in history, was established by the Russian Revolution in 1917. It had a tremendous impact on the workers of this country, as it did throughout the world. And it stimulated the growth of revolutionary ideas as well as the ranks of the socialists in the country.[67]

It also stimulated the authoritarian reflexes of the government. The close attention paid by East European immigrants to Bolshevik successes and the continued anti-conscription activities of Canadian socialists inspired an order-in-council banning left-wing organizations and ethnic newspapers and putting a seal on the property of ethnic organizations with pro-Bolshevik sympathies. A socialist Ukrainian was a double-headed menace. In 1918, a Montreal lawyer, C.H. Cahan, was appointed director of the Public Safety Branch in the Department of Justice; in his interim report on radical activity in Canada he noted that "there is considerable mental unrest among the people of Slavic origin in Canada, Russian, Ukrainian, and Austrian, which is directly attributable to the dissemination in Canada of the Socialist doctrines, espoused by the Russian Revolutionary element, and more recently by the Bolshevik Party in Russia. . . ."[68] At the same time, however, he admitted that he could find no evidence that "aliens" had committed "any acts in contravention of the orders and regulations made under the provisions of the War Measures Act"[69] and went so far as to suggest that their "mental unrest" may have been the expression of the "growing belief that the . . . government is failing to deal effectively with the financial, industrial and economic problems growing out of the war which are, perhaps, incapable of any early satisfactory solution."[70]

The apparent contradiction between his observation of unrest caused by Bolshevik propaganda on the one hand and by government (non)policies on the other was resolved in his full report a few months later:

> The Russians, Ukrainians and Finns who are employed in the mines, factories and other industries in Canada, are now being thoroughly saturated with the Socialistic doctrines which have been proclaimed by the Bolshevikii faction of Russia. . . . Since the outbreak of the present war, revolutionary groups of Russians, Ukrainians and Finns have been organized throughout Canada. . . . They are known to hold public or private meetings and to direct revolutionary propaganda. . . . Considerable quantities of literature in the Russian and Ukrainian languages . . . have recently been sent into Canada direct from Petrograd. . . .[71]

It had become clear to Cahan at least that left-wing radicals were at the root of all the unrest – the IWW had disseminated piles of literature "advocating destruction of all state authority, the subversion of religion and obliteration of all property rights"[72] in mining areas where many Slavs worked. Two weeks later the order-in-council banning seditious organizations was passed.

The anxiety about Bolshevism and subversion had its effects on the Ukrainian-Canadian community in Alberta and the situation was enough to provoke a cautionary editorial in the Vegreville *Observer* in 1917:

Silence is a Golden Policy

It becomes citizens of this country to walk warily and not let themselves into any situation which is precarious even in the slightest degree. The *Observer* is pointing straight at anti-conscription or Socialistic meetings which are being held among the Ukrainians. . . . There are agitators extant who are imposing their opinions on the half-educated classes of Ruthenian farmers and apparently bent on making trouble. It seems a pity that these unoffending Ruthenian farmers whose course hitherto has been irreproachable should be misled by half-truths. . . into a position of apparent hostility to the sentiment of the loyal citizens of Canada.[73]

The editor's word of caution was prophetic. In 1919, after the upheaval of the Winnipeg General Strike, the government added amendments to the Immigration Act and the Criminal Code which threatened even further the status of Ukrainian-born "troublemakers" and others caught in the federal net of reaction. Article 98 of the Criminal Code – an infamous article in the history of left-wing movements in Canada – outlawed "any association, organization, society or corporation whose professed purpose or one of whose purposes is to bring about any governmental, industrial or economic change within Canada by use of force, violence or physical injury to person or property . . . or which teaches, advocates, advises or defends the use of force, violence, terrorism or physical injury to person or property. . . ."[74] As for the Immigration Act amendments, they now prohibited from entry to Canada such classes of immigrants as "persons . . . *likely* [italics mine] to become a public charge . . . persons who believe in or advocate the overthrow by force of violence of the Government of Canada . . . enemy aliens or persons who have been alien enemies and who were or *may be* [italics mine] interned." In other words, the act refused people on the basis of their political beliefs, the accident of having been born within the superannuated Austro-Hungarian Empire and the misfortune of looking like they may someday lose their jobs.

In an attempt to protect itself from ambitious foreign revolutionaries, the Canadian government also threatened thousands who were simply frustrated or unlucky. It was not the most propitious atmosphere in which to grow up Ukrainian-Canadian. The bitterness of their parents' experience would be the ghost at the next generation's feast.

FIVE

The Homestead

They already had quite a nice set-up on the farm where I was born. A three-roomed home with an upstairs. The nicest home in the district. My dad bought it off a man who was in trouble with debts. My dad was quite well off. He already had some cattle. He had a store there, too, and people had a bit more money. And he'd be trapping muskrats and coyotes, and everything under the sun. Because Mom and Dad worked together so closely they were able to make a go of it. Dad did not linger at work. In the spring they got up at 4 o'clock to make sure they got the seeding done just when he wanted it done. Other farmers were maybe slower and lazier. Dad had the post office and the telephone. It was a centre, a stopping-point for the ranchers who grazed their cattle along the river. My mother fed those cowboys, eggs, potatoes, whatever she had. Sometimes it was just tea or bread but she would give it.

– Helen Marianych

* * *

By the time I was born he had a good farm. He had a gang plough, harrows, seed drills, discs, binder. A lot of farmers didn't have these things. It was just a two-room house, though, with a thatched roof. In 1916 they started a new house and hauled the logs from Musidora because there was no more heavy bush near Royal Park. But in 1918 Dad was killed and everything got set back. No money to finish the house. They stored grain in it.

– Paul Spak

* * *

When I was thirteen years old it was the first year that I worked with a threshing machine. We were still using horses then. We were short of help, and at that time I had to miss school to do threshing. And I worked as long as twenty-eight days with the threshing machine. I had blisters from the fork – in the morning I couldn't take the board in my hand. That's how sore my hands were.

– Metro Rewega

* * *

My mother died in 1917; not quite two years after Dad passed away. She was only forty-six, but in those days, you know, there were no hospitals. There were doctors – Dr. Archer was establishing his residence at Lamont – but there was no phone. She died, I understand, contracting cold and pneumonia, and the same thing when Dad passed away. He had quite a bit of cattle and there wasn't that much land under cultivation. He used to make hay with the scythe, but this summer was so wet and he was cutting with the scythe this hay for about a week, and pushing, pulling it to the side. He was constantly wet and he contracted rheumatic fever. He did go to Lamont to see the doctor, and they had already a little hospital, but they couldn't save him. About two, three months later he was gone. And so we were left, my oldest brother was about fourteen, left without the parents, and sister about sixteen.

– Jack Malenka

* * *

Mrs. Dodinsky was a kind of *vorozhka* [healer] and whenever anything troubled Mother, she would go to her. She could, as they say, *strakh zlovyty* [cure fears]; when a kid was scared of something she'd melt some wax and pour it in the water and tell you what the kid was scared of. And you wouldn't be scared anymore. And it's true! We took our own little girl to her because she was waking up every night screaming. Mrs. Dodinsky said she was scared of a black dog – and there was one wandering around the neighbourhood – and Eileen never screamed again.

– Anton Shchurek

There were farms and farms. By 1929, in the Shandro district of Alberta, the average farm was 400 acres of which 248 had been cleared.[75] The people who lived on them were no longer peasant pioneers; they were farmers. But there were those who fell below the average, lacking, even in 1923 when an Edmonton *Journal* reporter visited the Ukrainian settlements, the "necessary money with which to buy good cattle and proper seed." There were those, too, who had, in a burst of ill-founded optimism, bought a great deal of high-priced land during the period of the First World War, only to have it revert back to the mortgage companies when the price of wheat slumped a few years later. And there were those who exceeded the average, the celebrated master farmers with their clean fields, fat barns and houses with verandas, the sturdy backbone of the prairie rewarded at last. "They are a hardy class," wrote the *Journal,* "and live in the manner of all peasants: they are economical, hard-working and religious. . . . Patience must be exerted with them and then one can work wonders."

The wonders were entirely of the farmers' own doing. Gambling without the cushions of subsidies and debt adjustments, without even agricultural literature in the Ukrainian language, they nevertheless enjoyed a modicum of security. Seeking an explanation, Charles Young made a note of the "exceptionally large families" among the Ukrainians, a population increase which was "about one-half again as large as that for the British stock."[76] He made a note also of the fact that, while the Anglo-Saxon farmer hired help, "on the Ukrainian farm everybody shares in the work, from the man of the house to the children just out of the cradle!"[77] Note the exclamation mark. The statement is, in any case, exaggerated: infants were not expected to work. But everyone else was. And it is almost a cliche among Ukrainians to observe with disdain the fact that "Angliki" contracted out the dirty work – "an English woman near here used to hire Ukrainians to weed her radishes." A number of the Anglo-Saxon farms had been deprived of manpower as a result of casualties in the First World War; the

Ukrainians had not been so affected; they had been classified as "enemy aliens" and were prohibited from serving in the Canadian army. Young neglects to mention the numbers of Ukrainians forcibly interned in prison camps during the same period.

Besides, hired help cost money, a point that does not seem to have occurred to Young. Mystified by the Ukrainians' ability to live on very little, to persevere in an enterprise others abandoned, he concludes: "Frugal living! That is their secret! With comparatively few wants and inured to hardship through a traditional background of poverty, they survive . . . where Anglo-Saxons and others accustomed to more of the comforts of life cannot do this and so get out."[78] Superficially, it is an accurate enough observation: people practised in the arts of survival within feudal and penurious conditions can, of course, survive as homesteaders as well; in the case of Ukrainian immigrants, they would even put up with a temporary setback in their standard of living, having to recreate in ten years in Canada what five hundred years of peasant culture had built in the Ukraine. But to assume that they had "comparatively few wants" is to assume quite erroneously that what they had was somehow good enough; that their enforced frugality was a form of acceptance of their class position; that, unlike more ambitious and proud breeds, the Ukrainians measured their satisfaction in niggardly rewards.

The fact was that the Ukrainian families worked together so devilishly hard and made do with minimal returns for two reasons: one, they had no choice, there being no alternate forms of work or support available to them. Not a good living but the best there was: the choice between the homestead and the CPR extra gang was a choice between the devil and the deep blue sea. Secondly, they were driven by the conviction that, unlike feudalism, the Canadian economy would allow them to make progress to establish bigger and more productive farms that would ultimately allow the next generation to leave altogether. They worked for a future pay-off. In the thirties, as we shall see, when this future was jeopardized and even sabotaged in some cases, there were numbers of Ukrainians who fought furiously to snatch it back.

There were farms and there were farms and somewhere between impoverishment and modest comfort, the majority of Ukrainian-Canadians grew up. Already the farms had switched from oxen to horsepower and nine or ten head of horses would be feeding in the barn. Already they would be pulling on a binder and seed drill as well as the plough. There were cows and heifers, and milk and cheese to sell in the towns and cities. A man would consider his operation prosperous enough if he could butcher four hogs a year and a calf, so the children weren't hungry. For those who could not measure success in terms of heads of horses or a multi-roomed house, feeding the children became a standard in itself. "It was rough. The crops were so poor. Hailed out. Frozen out. But we always had food." Poverty snapped at their heels: a family of ten children who took turns going to church because there were not enough boots or pants to go around; a child sent to school with no lunch; and families who had to pay their bills at the local store in chickens because they had no cash.

It was the land that made the difference. The families who settled near Royal Park, near Andrew and Vegreville, had a fighting chance with good soil lying flat; but east and south from there, at Plain Lake or Yspas, the land was often dismal with swamp and rocky hills. Too wet, too dry. Pastures failed, bush fires took the rest and mother would have to take the wagon all the way to Royal Park to buy feed. Father had to work out. Draying, hauling, cutting wood, he'd do anything that needed to be done in the towns, working for seed money and still having to borrow $800 in the spring to see the cattle through the summer and then off to the railroad in the winter to pay back the loan. "You see how it was. He was paying off little by little every year, until it was all paid off ten years later."

On good land, a family could be the first in the district to deliver a wagonload of wheat, to buy a tractor or car, to acquire a second quarter and then a third, to order a radio from Eaton's catalogue, to raise registered Herefords or grow fruit trees. And to hire help. This surely was a turning point: the farm had grown too large, become too diversified and too productive for one family's labour to manage. The Ukrainian farm had come full circle when the hired hand had become in turn an employer of hired men.

Besides good soil, it helped to have inherited a cleared farm with buildings; it helped to have cash to buy, for $300, an extra quarter; it helped to have cooperative neighbours – "One family's home was destroyed by fire. Well, all us neighbours pitched in and rebuilt it" – and it helped to have an imagination:

> The land around Bellis is piss-poor land, it's all sand. Around Bellis, a lot of them reverted to home brewing, so home brewing was a big trade. During the war, a lot of real tough, sharp brewers who had agents in Edmonton made fortunes. They'd sell it to people in town here, who would sell it to the Yanks during the war, and the troops loved it. The Bluebird Hall in Edmonton was a drunk every night on Ukrainian brew from Smoky Lake.

Progress was measured by the abandonment first of the *burdei*, that sod-roofed hole in a hill, then of the hut or shack, constantly replastered to get rid of the tormenting bedbugs in the woven-willow walls, and then even the handsome thatched-roof, whitewashed, two-room, poplar log and plaster house. A real house, this was. In one room were the beds and in the other an oven for baking bread and behind that a high, plastered ledge where the children slept in winter (hence the Ukrainian prepositional phrase, "to sleep on the stove"). The clay plaster was made by mixing water and clay by foot and adding chopped straw and manure. The earthen floor was packed down hard, smoothed over with clay and "waxed" with a solution of cow dung and water. Until bricks were available, the chimney was made of woven willow branches plastered over with mud. Glass was expensive and windows tiny.

In such homes the kids were raised in their early years. Cozy in the winter, wonderfully cool in the summer, rainproof, these shelters utterly charmed an Edmonton *Journal* reporter in 1923 who was, perhaps, expecting something a good deal less cheerful from the "races of dark-skinned people." In his rhapsodies about these "quaint picturesque dwellings" and "pretty little spotless white-walled cottages with dainty straw thatched roofs" lies the surprise of the Anglo-Saxon that the Ukrainian should be so aesthetic. The Ukrainian houses were not, however, "dainty." Sturdy and squat, they are still to be seen, gently sliding into the soil, decades after the original occupants have let them go.

For the families had moved into two-storied frame farmhouses just like the "Angliki" had built for themselves. It was progress Canadian-style: shingled with a wood floor and siding, a stairway, a veranda, a cast iron stove, a living-room with furniture from the catalogue, windows all around! And the old thatched cottage was turned over to the hay bales or the pigs. In 1929, a *Journal* reporter was back again. "The women are good cooks and good housekeepers. . . . Farmyards are well arranged, showing taste, industry and an appreciation of sanitary practice." Well done.

Clothed, fed and housed: the bottom line of security. But they were vulnerable nonetheless. In 1918, the farming districts were ravaged by influenza and neither the efforts of a few, scattered doctors nor the home remedies of face masks and garlic could save the sick. Between October 4 and November 11, 3,259 Albertans died as a result.[79] And today the cemeteries under the weeds, the broken stone tablets and withered wood crosses, the pathetic rows of babies' graves, one after the other in the family plots, are the document. If it wasn't the flu, it was scarlet fever, whooping cough, tuberculosis, or diphtheria and with the nearest doctor still thirty miles away it was literally a race against death for the feverish victim bouncing in the back of the wagon or sleigh as the horses staggered over ruts or snowdrifts.

We were pretty strong kids but you know how it is. There's chicken pox, measles, tonsillitis, appendix. The closest doctor was in Vegreville. When I was eleven I got sick just before Christmas. Mother tried all kinds of things but nothing helped. I figured I was going to die because I couldn't breathe anymore. [It was decided to take her to Vegreville; they hitched up the team and drove in.] They had to put their horses in a stable there behind somebody's house. The doctor came over and looked at me and threw up his hands. "Oh, oh, we're going to have to quarantine this house." I had diphtheria and that was considered very dangerous then. The people who had the stable were screaming. They had people coming and going from the stable. It was their living. And they said, "No, no, take this child away! We don't want this house quarantined." Where was I going to go? Out into the frost? Mom and Dad grabbed the doctor and tried to make him understand how sick I was, that I needed to go to the hospital. They couldn't explain too well and the doctor was English. They took me to the hospital and left me. There was only one patient, the laundry lady, the cook. I started crying and said I wouldn't stay alone. . . . They let the nurse sleep in the next bed to mine and I held her hand.

There were the special hazards of poverty, children constitutionally weak from malnourishment, (too few vegetables and protein, too much white flour dough) and vulnerable because of inadequate clothing. Too poor for glasses, a girl quit school because she could no longer read the writing on the blackboard – glasses cost the price of a cow – and a boy had three teeth pulled by the time he was fourteen since there was no money for annual checkups. There were lice, the shame of the fastidious. "Mother combed and combed the children's hair every day after school. You could catch them so fast."

High birth rates, high infant mortality rates: historically, they are associated and the Ukrainian-Canadians were no exception. Charles Young, writing in 1931, said that at the same time that Ukrainians led "the list of groups in the Dominion as having the highest percentage of racial population under ten years of age," they also had an infant mortality rate, 11.24 per thousand, that was higher than for Czechs, Bulgarians, Serbo-Croatians, and British-Canadians.[80] They were also disproportionately represented in the tuberculosis sanitoriums in Alberta. According to one doctor's cryptic explanation they suffered "economic conditions trying to the lungs."[81] Substandard housing, inadequate clothing, unbalanced diet.? In that case, it was the poor who were so sick. "Diseases of the gastro-intestinal tract due to little variety of diet." "Little or no attention is paid to the teeth." "Skin diseases are general, especially the itch, due, as one doctor remarked, 'to unclean beds and no sheets.'"[82] Venereal diseases, however, were rare.

Accidents. The terrifying list of casualties illustrates the hazardous and even sinister nature of the farmyards and the heartache of family members maimed and killed, lost because they could not get treatment. "In 1924, my mother had an accident with the binder and lost her foot. There was a phone about two miles away and somebody called for the doctor. He didn't know too much and gangrene set in and the whole leg had to be amputated."

A father dies at forty-nine of blood poisoning, from a scratch on his nose when gathering piles of bush to burn. The neighbours lose their little boy when he bleeds to death from a cut from a scythe. Children are disfigured by the kick of a horse to the face. Others are lost in snowstorms on their way back from school, their bodies recovered months later in the thawed stubble of a wheat field.

My parents had another girl, but that girl died, small. I don't know what she died of. My father was killed by a train crossing a track in Vegreville. He was in a hayrack and wagon. It was sometime in November when the ground was frozen already and there was a blizzard, and he had a big fur coat collar over his head, and a team of horses and he didn't hear the train. So the horses went across the track and the train caught the wagon. Brother Bill died before Father died. Bill was sick with something, some infection in his foot. Whatever he had, we don't know, but he died. I think it was at seventeen. There were no doctors. There was only Dr. Archer in Vegreville and that was about fourteen miles.

They were not, however, without their own medical resources. Women in particular had skills to which the community resorted: midwives aided women in childbirth, a masseuse could fix ruptures, farm women knew about the cathartic properties of wild plants and herbs, and the *vorozhka* cured children of nightmares. Greek Catholic nuns ministered to the sick as best they could.

To call Ukrainian-Canadians "heroic sufferers" and "fatalists,"
then, as Charles Young does,[83] is nonsensical – when they were sick
or wounded they tried to save themselves – and to attribute the
Ukrainians' apparent reluctance to use doctors and hospitals to this
"characteristic" is insensitive. What doctors? What hospitals? As
late as the 1930s a doctor would still have to travel forty miles on a
round trip to a patient near Two Hills suffering from pneumonia. It
wasn't until 1929 that a public health lecturer visited Two Hills,
Myrnam, and Plain Lake to talk about sanitation, sewage disposal,
and water purification (a translator was provided), and, although
there was a Methodist missionary hospital operating in Pakan as
early as 1907, Dr. Lawford's fees were too high for many of the
farmers:

> It is impossible to show the people the justice of when they call
> the Doctor to their home and do not ask him to return and he
> sees fit to make several visits more and charges them for each of
> these visits. . . . They consider they have been robbed and
> especially so in cases where they cannot see the benefit of the
> additional visit. . . . To them it is stealing and the worse because
> it is done by the Church.[84]

In spite of it all – sod houses and poor soil, plagues and fatal
accidents, cabbage soup, and well-meaning Methodists – the
Ukrainian-Canadians were growing up healthy and robust enough.
For every child who died weak and helpless, there were three or four
who flourished; for every husband killed, there was a woman with
children who carried on, taking up the slack; for every house burned
down, another was erected; for every acre lost to mortgage
companies or the implacable bush (sometimes a family could take
no more and they would pack it in, loading up a wagon with the
odds and ends and head out for somewhere, anywhere), there were
ten or twenty that were added on, like patches on a quilt.
Ukrainian-Canadians were past settling, and the kids, at least, felt
at home.

Six

School

My parents had a very, very high opinion of education. I had an older brother who dropped out of school – and how my dad begged him to stay in! He told me, "Son, don't give up. And don't worry about the finances. We'll scrounge if we have to to get you to university." I wanted to quit school in grade ten, to go to work in a store or whatever. So, my dad said, "You want to quit school, do you?" He took me out to the farm on the hottest day of the summer and told me to pick the weeds. In those days there weren't weed sprays; the kids walked up and down the rows and picked the blossoms off the sow thistle. It was ninety above and all day I picked thistle. The first day of school in September one of the first guys in school was me!

– Nick Olinyk

* * *

My parents always promoted my older brother. I had an older sister too but Mother would say, if anything, he should go to school. But he didn't want to go past grade eight. I was dropping out half-way from grade ten and the teacher came and pleaded with mother, "Send her to school, she's doing well." When he left she said to me, "What do you need that for? You already know how to keep house and milk the cows." I was disappointed.

– Lena Geleta

* * *

I liked school. I would run away to school too. I wish I had not had so much to do on the farm so I could have continued going to school. After grade nine, if I went on, I would have loved to be a Home Ec teacher, very much so. For grade ten, I would have gone to Edmonton. There was nothing in Vegreville for a college. Maybe if I had some relatives there that I could've stayed with. . . . See, my father let my brothers all go to grade twelve. Why? You need school and you have to go to school and they went. My brother was finished grade twelve and he went and he took diesel, like garage work, repair cars. Mechanic, that's right. And my other brother he was farming, he didn't go anywhere. And my brother Sam, he finished grade twelve and he joined the Air Force. . . . I had a hard time getting to grade nine anyway. . . . I just understood that I was expected to stay home, and work and help. I got married after that.

– Anne Svekla

* * *

I wanted to be a teacher. But father's crops froze in '33, there was no money whatsoever and he couldn't afford to keep me at school. He had to send the young ones to public school, we had to buy all our books and scribblers and pencils. When the prices were good he was doing all right. He could pay the mortgage, clear more land, dig a deeper well. That's what he invested his money in. Necessities. Improved the fence. It broke my heart not being able to become a teacher but . . . I went ahead and decided to go to the Vermilion Agricultural College. I had the $10 for the uniform, I sewed the apron and bib and two blue dresses, but then my girlfriend who was going to go with me couldn't go because her father didn't have the money so I didn't go either.

– Kay Palamaruk

* * *

Dad got a job as principal in Bellis which was an extremely good place for him. Bellis was rough and tough but people liked him. They really liked my dad there, they understood him. He was extremely bad-tempered. He was eight years in the armed forces. He was four years in the Austrian Army, and four years Ukrainian national army. And he had kind of a military thing, his stance, his manner. And he grew up with this European discipline which was extremely autocratic and harsh. He was very hard on the kids, but the parents were pretty hard on the kids too, so it worked quite well. He always got along in Ukrainian communities, but whenever he taught kids who were non-Ukrainian, anytime he had trouble in a community it was with non-Ukrainian kids, the WASP kids. They'd petition the school board to fire him. He would forgive anybody if they tried and he would do anything for the brilliant. You could do anything in his classes if you were smart. Even if you were lazy and smart, he'd forgive you, he admired you. But he couldn't stand those who were rude and lazy, especially if they were dumb, rude, and lazy.

– Oleh Kupchenko

* * *

I was very proud to be at university – I was the third person from Two Hills to go. And when I came home for visits people would point me out on the street, "There goes the university student." They would gawk at me like at some animal in the zoo. So I tried my damnedest not to flunk anything. I was afraid of letting myself down, my parents down, the town down – and there was a little bit of Ukrainianism there too. Letting the Ukrainians down.

– Nick Olinyk

The vicious circle: in the old country, only minimal schooling was available to peasants and because the peasants had no schooling, there were always peasants, generation after generation. In Canada there was the chance to break the curse of illiteracy – "inconceivable illiteracy," said Charles Young, who estimated that 50 percent of Ukrainian immigrants were illiterate on arrival: according to the 1921 census, 40 percent still were, twenty years later.[85] "Dad felt that the Ukrainians had been tillers of the soil too long." The protest was unmistakable. No sentimentality here about the harsh nature of farm work and its attendant status; the children, as many of them as possible, were bred for destinies more rewarding than picking rocks, pulling roots, stooking, baling hay, and shovelling grain. A threat, in fact. As if they were saying, if you can't read and write, you are doomed to slog out a life like all the generations before you; bending your back until you can't straighten up again. If the immigrants were willing to do it one more time, it was only because they would be the last. When they died, their land would be sold, not inherited.

A sister from the Basilian monastery at Mundare tells this story:

> One evening, recalls Sister L., two children came to us a brother and sister. They came from Saskatchewan. They heard that the Sisters had a school and they came walking. Their clothing showed signs of poverty. They were grasping a small bundle. They were tired. The Sisters fed them and noted blisters on their young hands. "What were you doing that your hands are covered with wounds?" "We trapped muskrats all summer to earn enough to buy clothes for the journey. Here are $3.00 for books. We will work for the tuition. We know how and are not afraid to work. . . . !"[86]

A fable, perhaps, but a document for all that. Whatever was necessary to provide an education would be done, so long as there were in fact the means to do it, to hire a threshing crew at harvest time, for instance, so that the children could stay in school instead of helping out, to board out a son in a town that had a high school so he would eventually study medicine at the university, to cash in a life insurance policy to pay for tuition. The refrain: "I do this for you so you won't have to work so hard. I do this so you can get out in the world, talk to people, get a good job, learn something about the world a hundred miles away. I do this so you can learn English, because wherever you turn, there is an English person speaking." "To School!" then, as Peter Svarich, pedagogue and sloganeer, announced.[87]

Since school districts could only be organized where there was a minimum enrollment to support them, schools were not always available to growing children. Plain Lake School, for instance, wasn't organized until 1910 – and even when organized, operated only intermittently between seeding and harvest times or was deserted after a few months by desperate teachers gone "bush crazy" or even when working smoothly, did not provide all that the parents expected in basic education. For all these reasons those parents who could read and write gave instruction at home. Little Moose School was opened in 1921 and in 1922 a ten-year-old boy went for a month. At home, his father, schooled to grade four in the old country, taught him to read and write Ukrainian. His mother, who had been a housemaid in a Polish household, sang him Polish lullabies.

There is a William Kurelek painting of a Ukrainian mother teaching her son to read. They are bent over a book laid on the table under a kerosene lamp which throws a bulky shadow behind them on the wall. The mother is wearing a white head-scarf and points out letters on the page. There is something wrong with this picture. In most Ukrainian farm homes, it would have been the father giving the lesson, for if half the Ukrainians as a group were illiterate, the women were much more often so than the men.

> We'd come home and Dad would help us read, under the coal oil lamp. How to write. My mother didn't know how to read or write because her father said that it was important for the boys to learn because they'd be going into the army, in the old country. "What do you, a girl, need to go to school for? You have to cut the *sichka*, the feed for the cattle, you have to take the cattle to pasture, go work in the field. Learn to work."

As we shall see, the same assumptions about education for girls applied to the next generation. Even in homes where the father had a modicum of education and the sons a great deal, female illiteracy was not considered unusual. This was one vicious circle notoriously difficult to break out of, for the so-called natural role of the female members of the family to service the needs of the males meant generations of women tied to the peasant economy while brothers and sons, thanks largely to women's labour, made their escape.

There were exceptions. There were women who were roughly literate in Ukrainian but not English, some self-taught, some with two or three years of old country schooling, and there were those who could understand some English and speak it in broken sentences. A woman who could read and write was depended on by the others to read the letters from the old country and write the replies. A woman who could speak three languages, Ukrainian, German, and Polish, was the postmistress at Plain Lake.

As for the fathers, they passed on what they had. After supper, with mama in the kitchen washing dishes, father and son sat down at a table, backs bent against the need to go to sleep, and read together a Ukrainian story book. Besides Ukrainian, many could speak Polish, German or Rumanian (the language of the ruling classes in the old country) and if they had gone to school could read and write to a certain extent in these languages as well. There were homes, then, with Polish and English newspapers as well as Ukrainian and the children read the comics in the *Free Press* and *Prairie Farmer*. Reading in the English language was rare, for the vast majority of homes were unilingually Ukrainian in language spoken and read. This was the universal standard of literacy: competence in the "mother tongue."

> Our parents were such, you learn ten languages if you want but you must learn your own. It was a must in our home. There was never an English word spoken at meals. It was a rule. After supper, whether it was winter or summer, but not in harvest, we were all put behind the table like chickens and each one had to read and write. At that time I thought it was silly but now I thank them for it.

English would come later for the men, and many times not at all for the women. When the men went out working on jobs beyond the farm, they came in contact with English-speaking co-workers and bosses, on the railroad, on ranches, in the mines. The man who failed to pick up some English was the man who would be hoodwinked and overruled, who had to depend on the sometimes sketchy knowledge of a fellow countryman to get him through the vicissitudes of application for naturalization, application for patent rights to the homestead, appeals to the foreman for unpaid wages. The women, however, confined to the homestead, almost never heard English spoken and became old ladies still speaking only Ukrainian, for they had never communicated with anyone but family, relatives, and neighbours. There is some irony, then, in the sentimentalization of the Ukrainian mother as the essential conduit of Ukrainian culture: she could not be otherwise.

At the table, under the lamp, this is what the children learned: the Ukrainian alphabet and elementary reading and writing skills; folk tales and songs; occasionally something about the Cossack *sich*, Taras Shevchenko and the Ukrainian armies of liberation; without exception, the Bible. A rudimentary education but psychologically as well as intellectually formative. As it turned out, the lessons were a kind of vaccination against assimilation, a dose of an ethic that upheld the sovereign right of the parent to pass on to the children the characteristics that would stamp them as members of the tribe, "one of us," in spite of the contradictory pull of Anglo-Saxon institutions. "Outside of knowing how to read and write and to sing there was nothing given me at home about being Ukrainian. But the tradition was given me. Faithfully observed. And I miss it today."

The will to educate, to be educated, was fierce, the means to achieve it uncertain. The problem was money. Money to clothe and equip the children for school; money to pay for "advanced" education beyond the eight grades provided in the rural school – money for tuition, room, and board in a town or city high school; money for the school tax levied on organized school districts. The conditions under which a family had settled ten years back upon immigration caught up with them at this point for poor and uncleared land would not yield the tax.

And for many families the choice had still to be made: to send a child to school or to keep him or her on the farm as a working hand. It was the communal good versus individual advancement; where a farm was already prosperous, with more land under cultivation and a larger herd of cattle than neighbouring ones, then a decision could be made to invest some profit in high school or even university education for one or two children – usually the middle ones, the young ones still too young for consideration, the older ones already working full-time on the farm or already too old when the school was finally built and functioning. Those who were given the opportunity, who were not necessarily the brightest or most ambitious of the children, might realize their potential and hence justify the labour of the rest.

Obviously, if a family already lived in town, where the father ran a store or the post office, the question of having to pay room and board while the child attended high school was not a consideration. A man whose father could afford to send him to town – "My parents had a little bit more money. They raised wheat, a few head of cattle, some hogs, and my mother milked sixteen to eighteen cows everyday, twice a day" – recalls that most of the students in the high school with him were from the town, perhaps only six of thirty-two were from the farms. One boy rode nine miles back and forth by horseback. Another "brilliant boy" took his grade twelve by correspondence and won all the honours. But the family didn't have the money to send him further so he went to work for the post office.

In a good year, when the prices were up, the child in grade eight would be sent on; when the prices were bad, the child in grade eight would drop out. "Nobody had more than grade eight. There was no such luck." There was luck, however, in having relations in town with whom the child could live. Or the luck of being born late enough that by the time you were fifteen, the district had a two-room school that included grades nine and ten. Or, perhaps most telling of all, the luck of being a boy instead of a girl.

A case in point is my own father's family. The Kostashes have a reputation of almost mythical proportions for having sent all six sons to university from their Royal Park homestead. (A composite photograph of them in their graduation caps and gowns is endlessly reproduced in ethnic histories.) The lone daughter, Helen, however, had a different destiny. She left the Ukraine, at four years of age, before she could get any schooling there. In Canada, she looked after her brothers and married at age sixteen a Ukrainian labourer from Edmonton. They homesteaded in the Athabasca area on two acres of cleared land, while her brothers were at university earning two or three degrees each. She had been able, however, to squeeze some education in at the summer school at Kolomea School and through private lessons from a teacher who boarded with the Kostashes one winter. Enough fragments of learning to enable her to teach her children the alphabet on a gunny sack. When Ukrainian girls were educated, it was often accidental.

One can understand the thinking, if not approve it: spend a couple of thousand on a girl and she gets married and raises a kid! But a boy who becomes an engineer will always be an engineer. The man whose father scraped from the bottom of his shallow barrel to send his son to medical school thought grade eight was achievement enough for his daughters, and by that simple decision defined the class lines of the future, for the son would grow up to be a high school principal, the daughter a store cashier. So, when the parents' expectation was that a farmer did not need a fancy education and the farmer's wife needed it even less, when male teachers derided a girl's ambition to be a teacher and told her to marry instead, when parents refused to send a daughter to art school, fearing for her virtue, then the fact that Ukrainian-Canadian women were schooled to the extent they were is a minor miracle.

* * *

What did the Lanuke community build first?
A church. And a school. Both in 1906.

The community was precocious. As for the rest of the Ukrainian "colony," by 1912, 90 school districts had been organized; by 1915, 130 schools. This was not, however, free-lance organizing. While there is considerable evidence to support the prevailing belief that ethnics in general and Ukrainians in particular have an intense and principled commitment to education, this is not to say that they had complete freedom, as a community, to determine the nature and style of that education. As if anticipating nationalistic or racial zeal among the settlers to educate their children as Ukrainians, the government of Alberta moved quickly to ensure the opposite. In 1907, Robert Fletcher was appointed as supervisor of schools for non-English-speaking districts and was headquartered in the midst of the Ukrainians at the village of Wostok. His mandate was to give "every possible assistance to the non-English settlers in the establishment of school districts, the erection of schools, the employment of teachers, etc."[88] This sounds more benign than it was in practice: Fletcher had in effect the power to suspend the powers of local boards of trustees of school districts and to impose upon the districts a government-appointed official trustee in order to carry out his work. In the Prosvita School District, for example, which balked at hiring a teacher they couldn't afford, Fletcher had an official trustee appointed and the teacher was duly assigned.[89] Fletcher was also providentially the secretary of eight schools over which he thus maintained control of finances and correspondence.

The majority of schools, however, were organized and administered directly on the initiative of the Ukrainians themselves, and usually by the resident *intellihent* if the area happened to have a representative of the intelligentsia of the Western Ukraine among them. Peter Svarich was such a person – seven years of high school (*gymnasium*) in Kolomea – and with considerable gusto and ambition, he established a string of schools bearing Ukrainian names: Kolomea, Pobeda, Oleskow, Kiew, Brody, Myroslaw, Krasne, Sich, Stanislaw, Volodomyr, Wolia, Zaporoze, and Franko. He won the contract to build several of the schools and was hired as secretary-treasurer and auditor at others. It was a lucrative business personally, and ultimately resulted in a network of schools four miles apart, available to settlers and over which, through their elected trustees, they could maintain substantial local control as long as they observed the regulations of the School Acts. School attendance was compulsory, state bilingual schools were prohibited and, in 1914, the year-round operation of the school was legislated.

Take, for example, the work of the Krasne School District #2245 board of trustees. Their first meeting was in August 1910; present were Karl Adamowski, Michael Samoil, and Hrynko Malowanyj. Their first two decisions were to hire Peter Svarich as secretary-treasurer for the salary of $30 a year and to levy a school tax of 6 1/4¢ per acre. In September they moved that "the school house be built immediately and plans for it be specified as follows: 22' x 30' x 12', porch 8' x 12' x 9', 4 windows on each side, foundation of boulders, walls of matched lumber ceiled [sic] inside. J. Janishewski contractor made an offer to build such school as specified for the sum of $800 providing the ratepayers will haul all necessary material." In March of 1911 they got around to the matter of the teacherage, referred to in the minutes as a "shack." In 1912, the "shack" had still not been built, and it was obvious that a new secretary-treasurer had been appointed, for the minutes become ungrammatical (Svarich's English had been substantially correct):

Feb. 13/1912

Mooved by H. Cymbaluk second by K. Adamowski that shack have to be build wright away and have the school open for second term. Caried.

All trustee was agree to get a teatcher for second term. Moved by Adamowski second by Cymbaluk to have the carpenter wredy soon is they Material gets ther. Caried.

By 1914, the grammar and spelling had improved but the finances were in trouble.

By-law No.1:

Whereas the money required for the purposes of Krasne SD #2245 for the year 1914 have not been paid by the ratepayers and whereas in the meantime it is necessary to have money to meet current expenses therefore be it enacted that the Board of School Trustees of this district do borrow from the Merchants Bank of Canada in Vegreville upon the credit of the Board the sum of One Hundred and fifty dollars. . . .

By-law No. 2:
Whereas the money required for the purpose of Krasne SD No. 2245 for the year 1915 have not been paid by the rate-payers and whereas in the meantime it is necessary to have money to pay teacher salary therefore be it enacted that the Board of this district do borrow from the Merchants Bank the sum of $125.00. . . .

Lanuke School District #1610 was in better shape. In 1907 they had receipts of $1254.55 (from taxes and the school debentures, a mortgage purchased by the Department of Education) and expenditures of $933.90, leaving them a balance of $320.65. The money was spent every which way. In June, they purchased a rubber stamp and postage (90¢) and cashbooks and ledgers ($8.80), in October, school seats ($91.00) and a stove ($18.00); in November, schoolhouse construction ($700.00), lumber for a well ($8.10); in December, wages to Dmytro Soldan for digging the well ($28.80), the secretary-treasurer's salary ($20.00) and fire insurance ($16.00). By 1908, they were paying for the teacher's salary ($525.75 to Mr. G.E. Heber Smith), notices of school meetings, freight on maps and blackboards, a caretaker's services and a pump. In 1910, expenditures included basin and towels, school clock, ground improvements and a new teacher's salary. In every case they were solvent, receiving money not only from taxes (from the Teresios, Monkmans, Dadynskis, Hmilyars, Kaminskis, Snychuks, etc.) but in government grants and in receipts from "books and slates sold to scholars," meaning pupils.

For eight months a year the school was open, closing down only for the deepest winter, but attendance was often irregular, Truancy Act or no. During the peak labour seasons of spring and fall, education was temporarily suspended for the more urgent needs of the farm. "When I was eleven, my parents took me out of school for two weeks to help with the harvest and to do the milking, fill the mangers and take the lunches out to the men in the fields – they had promised me a bicycle in exchange."

They walked to school, never more than four miles, along buffalo and old Indian trails and their own pathways, tramped out through thickets and around sloughs. The summer walk was a bucolic affair, raiding strawberry patches, examining wild flowers, hunting birds' nests, snaring gophers, skinny-dipping in the roadside ditch, but in winter the journey became a horror. They sank to their waists in the snow, huddled together through blizzards and arrived at school with their extremities deep-frozen. If they were lucky, father would drive them by sleigh; otherwise they bundled up and prayed that the teacher or janitor would get to school before them and start the fire in the stove.

The schoolhouse cost about $800 to build (between 1920 and 1930 it would cost $3,000) and displayed the standard design: one room with a porch, a cloakroom with hooks for coats and shelves for lunchpails, a woodburning stove or forty-five gallon steel drum in the middle or in the rear, and at the front, the Union Jack, portraits of the King and Queen, and a map courtesy of Neilson Company with pictures of chocolate bars in each corner. Outside was a lean-to cum stable, a well or pump, outhouses, and often a teacherage.

The school was a log building, with siding; in other words no grander than the homes the students lived in, and in some cases even less comfortable. It was a log building chinked with moss and mud and had no lights or lamps; if it was dark outside, it was dark inside. It was a one-room school with a stove in the back that was useless unless you were sitting on it; a breeze blew under the door, and ink and lunches froze. To keep warm, teachers and students ran around the room in a snake dance, sat on top of their desks to keep their sodden feet out of the draughts, and hung wet clothing in the heat of a stove, enduring then a stench as well. In the summer, they sat alongside a smudge pot lit to keep the everlasting mosquitoes at arm's length.

One room held up to fifty students, aged seven to seventeen, in double-seated maplewood desks which bore little relation to the height or breadth of the student within. Scribblers were a luxury item, most classwork was done on a piece of slate with a slate pencil or up on the blackboards behind the teacher's desk. Depending on the financial position of the school district, there might have been a globe, chalk, window netting, storybooks, and writing paper. For the rural, one-room school, this was as good as it was ever going to be.

In April 1919, an inspector of schools, Mr. J.A. Butchart, filed a report on Wolia School to the Minister of Education and sent a copy to the secretary-treasurer of S.D. #2591, M. Tomyn, Esq. Among his observations were the following:

> Fence: Page wire, in very bad repair
> Closets: two; fair condition
> Teacher's residence: small one
> Water supply: well; water good, pump broken
> Interest taken in tree planting: none apparently
> General appearance of grounds: poor
> Schoolhouse: good but needs to be painted
> Equipment: fairly sufficient
> Attendance: irregular
> Punctuality: good
> General standing of the classes: fairly satisfactory; retarded by irregularity of attendance
> General remarks: The school-house is in good repair but it is badly in need of being painted. This should be done as soon as possible. The fence is in very bad repair and should be attended to at once to keep cattle out of the grounds. The grounds are in bad shape but it would not take much to render them quite attractive.

Seven years later, in an inspector's report on Sherentz S.D.

#2614, it is apparent that the Department of Education was less interested in the physical layout of the school than in the intellectual content of the classes. Inspector Owen Williams stayed at the school from one o'clock to half-past three in the afternoon, watching forty students (from fifteen in grade one to three in grade eight) go through their paces in science, writing, art, music, composition, history, and arithmetic. He found the students "attentive and industrious," their work neat, their teacher with only three months' experience "energetic and resourceful." The year-round school was having its effect. "With continuous operation of school, grading is becoming properly stabilized and the pupils have attained the grades proper for their ages." There is in his report a general tone of satisfaction and approval, except for one condition. "Due to overcrowding, school environment is not very satisfactory. This has also affected the appearance of the school. . . . Owing to poor seating accommodation, discipline is a hard problem. . . . The overcrowding of the school hampers efficient presentation [of lessons]." From irregular attendance to overcrowding.

There were other kinds of education. A night school in Edmonton was operated by the Sisters Faithful Companions for Ukrainian girls living and working in the city and here they were taught English reading and writing (as well as Ukrainian handicrafts and religion).[90] The Basilian fathers in their mission at Beaver Lake, near Mundare, concurrently operated a chapel and a schoolroom, even though regular school districts were already organized nearby at Limestone Lake and Creekford. The Protestant churches were likewise committed. On the north bank of the North Saskatchewan River, south of Smoky Lake, Reverend George McDougall of the Methodist Church had been celebrated for his missionary work among the natives and Métis; in 1905 his mission at Victoria-Pakan redirected its efforts from heathens to superstitious and papist (as they saw them) Ukrainians but lost out to the Greek Orthodox mission in 1908. The Methodists were rather more successful in the operation of their day schools at Kolokreeka, Chipman, and Radway where the rudiments of counting and reading were more easily digested than the world view of John Wesley. The education of young "new Canadians" was fertile ground for the Presbyterians as well. They opened a Boys' and Girls' Home in Vegreville, a residential school, principally for Ukrainians with an aim to "supervise their schoolwork and teach them Canadian ways, thereby training them to become good Canadian citizens," as Superintendent Mrs. Jean Robertson put it as late as 1932. For twenty-eight years the institution taught the English language, the principles of Presbyterianism and, in the evenings, Ukrainian reading and writing and history under the direction of converted Ukrainian ministers or teachers. Presbyterianism and good Canadian citizenship were apparently synonymous. The town was "out of bounds" during the week and only on Saturdays and with permission could the students visit the provocative territory of downtown Vegreville. Use of the Ukrainian language during the day was actively discouraged, not to say prohibited. Boys and girls were made responsible for the chores appropriate to their sex: boys weeded the garden, cut wood, carried water, and tended the cows and chickens; girls cooked, sewed, baked, and cleaned house.

I was sent to the Nesbit School Home which was a Presbyterian school for boys. They only charged $15 a month including laundry. A lot of Ukrainians ended up there. This is where we were taught the Bible and had to go to the Presbyterian church every Sunday. Some of the boys were even converted. I won an Eversharp Silver Pencil for being able to recite long passages from the Bible.

The end result was several hundred Ukrainian-Canadians reared in the Protestant ethic: "They were brought up in a sound moral environment, self-disciplined and self-reliant, prepared and inspired to reach for higher and better things."[91] Conversion to the Presbyterian faith itself would have been almost redundant.

The variety of educational institutions available to Ukrainian-

Canadian schoolchildren did not disguise the fact that, except for the schools run by religious orders belonging to the Greek Catholic Church, each institution was committed to the same objective: the Anglicization of the Ukrainian child. "This is an English-speaking province . . . and every Alberta boy and girl should receive a sound English education in the public schools of the province."[92] The Minister of Education understood himself to be only reasonable. English was the language and WASPism the culture of the establishment and it was the responsibility of liberal and free-thinking establishments to make available at least the rudiments of middle-class, Anglo-Saxon culture to the benighted classes. "And, as we view their uncouth ways, their laxity of morals, their alien ideals, the ignorance and superstition of many of them, we sometimes have reason to fear that to us is coming a tremendous contribution of the worse – a contribution against which we will have cause to measure our highest ideals of manhood, our noblest conceptions of womanhood sanctified by faith in the God of the nations and a knowledge of the Gospel of His Son."[93] It was in response to this sort of declaration (from the *North-West Baptist*) that J.S. Woodsworth, who could be as parochial as the rest of them, gently counselled: "We must divest ourselves of a certain arrogant superiority and exclusiveness, perhaps characteristic of the English race."[94] But the fact was that even the most well-meaning of middle-class Anglo-Saxons were convinced that assimilation into the culture of the Empire was a necessary, even ennobling, procedure and that the principal agency of this assimilation would be the English-speaking public school system. An editorial in the Vegreville *Observer*, September 10, 1913, spoke for all such reasonable people: "The province owes it to the coming citizens, that everyone of them shall possess a working knowledge of English. This cannot be obtained by the employment of Ruthenian teachers on permits, and the Dept. of Education in taking a firm and unmistakable stand on the matter is doing the right thing both for the present and the future."

The "matter" referred to here was the question of who was to be entrusted with this mandate to assimilate the young. Who, in other words, was to be allowed to teach? Up to this point, in 1913, the schools had been serviced, intermittently and undependably in many cases, by a grab bag of Anglo-Saxon men and women wandering in the West from eastern Canada or Great Britain, who were more or less qualified to teach. Since many of these people were students looking for summer work, they were often contracted for only a month at a time and so a school would be staffed by two or three different teachers during the year. At the same time there were also a few Ukrainian teachers, graduates of the Ruthenian Training School (a normal school) in Winnipeg, who had been hired by the school trustees in Alberta's Ukrainian settlements to teach in their schools (on "permits" until they could be certified in Alberta). By 1913, a similar school, the English School for Foreigners, was operating in Vegreville. The crucial difference to the trustees between the two categories of teachers – the English and Ukrainian – was that it was impossible to understand the former. Not only their language, but their habits, attitudes, deportment. How was such a stranger to be trusted with the children? How were they to communicate, neither speaking the other's language, and the one in a position of authority to impose, out of ignorance or arrogance, his or her Protestant and urban values? "Ever present too was the vestigial anxiety carried over from the Ukraine where the officials – usually Poles – used the schools as an instrument to impose a new language on the children and thus to wipe out their Ukrainian mother tongue and culture. In Alberta, might not the sole use of English in the schools also be a plot aimed against their Ukrainianism?"[95]

The concern about one's "Ukrainianism" was usually an intellectual luxury of the intelligentsia – Peter Svarich, for example, wanted a Ukrainian seminary, a Ukrainian school organizer, the use of Ukrainian textbooks in the school. To ascribe the Ukrainians' initial resistance to exclusively English-language schools and teachers to the "continued perseverance in the struggle for their national identity which they had struggled for in the old country"[96] is to offer an overly sophisticated explanation. To be sure, this local intelligentsia in Alberta, publicizing its criticism in the press, gave broad currency to the point of view of Ukrainian nationalists who did have a consciousness of imperialistic patterns in Europe and an ideological commitment to the restitution of the Ukrainian "nation." They were not, however, always supported in these views by their compatriots:

> These Ruthenian teachers have only one idea and that is to instruct the children and parents that as they were persecuted in Galicia by Polaks, in Russia by Russians, so they are persecuted in Canada by English fanatics; at election time their idea is to work against the government. We all saw teachers on the platform in Vegreville and Mundare talking to the people and telling them that "the rule of English cowboys is finished; we are now in charge; we are a nation able to govern our own matters, etc." Signed, A. Ruthenian.[97]

And some communities were indifferent. Impatient for the school at Lanuke to open, the parents and students didn't care one way or the other if the teacher was Ukrainian. In fact, says an ex-student, they were just as glad for the English ones. "They taught us good pronunciation."

The intelligentsia were supported, when they were supported, by communities less concerned with issues of European politics than with the simpler questions of inter-generational communication, solidarity, and community control of education.

In any event, the bureaucrats in the Department of Education were unhappy with the fact that great numbers of newly-organized schools were under the direction of uncertified Ukrainian-speaking "permit" teachers from Manitoba (and Alberta) and thus were determined to counteract the tendency by enforcing a regulation that only qualified teachers could teach. Enter Robert Fletcher again, the supervisor of Foreign Schools in Wostok. He was now appointed as official trustee with authority to dismiss unqualified teachers and replace them with the qualified. In his report to the

Minister of Education in 1913, Fletcher argued the case against the
so-called Ruthenian teachers; referring to the appointment of such
teachers by Ukrainian school boards as "raiding," he gave this
description of their qualifications and motivations:

> The majority of these young men had a very indifferent
> education. Their written English was faulty in idiomatic
> expression, while their speech was characterized by indistinct
> articulation. Some of them could scarcely make themselves
> understood in either written or spoken English. For instance,
> one of them who happened to be a witness on a case in court
> asked for an interpreter, but when the presiding magistrate
> learned that he was a teacher, teaching English in one of our
> rural schools, he refused his request with the result that his
> conduct as a witness was deplorable.
>
> It soon became apparent that an organization was formed to
> place these young men in Ruthenian schools. It encouraged
> them to come from Manitoba and Saskatchewan to this
> province and distributed them among the various schools when
> they arrived here. The organization was composed of certain
> well-known agitators, who had ulterior motives to serve, but
> who, to conceal their personal desires, took advantage of the
> natural and praiseworthy love the Ruthenian people have for
> their mother tongue.[98]

Fletcher's modus operandi against recalcitrant school boards was
invariable:

> The next school I visited was Kolomea which is also close to
> Mundare. I made the same request [that the teacher be
> removed] and gave the same warning [that he, Fletcher, would
> be appointed official trustee of the school] to the board but they
> refused to make a change of teachers. I reported their refusal to
> the department and was promptly appointed official trustee of
> the district. I placed a qualified teacher in charge of the school
> immediately. The board of trustees visited the department to

protest my conduct, but my action was sustained.[99]

Owing to the "good services of Mr. Fletcher," as Charles Young put it, by 1916 there were not more than a half-dozen Ukrainian-speaking teachers in the province. A whole generation would have to grow up, finish high school, and go to normal school, before the Ukrainian districts would see a Ukrainian teacher again. As far as the authorities were concerned, it was a job well done. It was the opinion of the editor of the Vegreville *Observer* that "in place of developing into Canadian citizens the Ruthenians were clinging more strongly to racial characteristics and the continued employment of these unqualified teachers was simply retarding the progress of the people towards full-fledged citizenship."[100] To most non-Ukrainians, the situation seemed clear cut: since the immigrants had voluntarily availed themselves of the economic opportunities in Alberta, they should likewise adopt its language and make use of a school system developed out of the tradition of Anglo-Saxon literacy and operated by the best examples of it. To avoid such opportunity, to insist on a markedly inferior compromise, to huddle together in ghettos of like-minded rustics and patriotic die-hards was unfriendly, not to say hostile. "The sheepskin-wearing immigrants were not only undesirable in the first instance, but they were stiff-necked, intractable, and nationalistic; they wanted to establish a Ukraine in Canada and were unwilling to learn the English language."[101] This kind of sentiment was particularly pronounced during the First World War when Anglo-Canadians began to equate cultural uniformity with national unity -- a precondition of a successful war effort.

One persons' "intractability" is another's "resistance." And the Ukrainians didn't need the grandiose version of a "Ukraine in Canada" to drive them to it. All they needed was a righteous anger against Fletcher and the department, an anger at being pushed around and preached at, and a disappointment that in a country whose propaganda was pro-democratic and anti-authoritarian they manifestly did not have the right to determine the nature of their children's schooling, in spite of the fact that they were paying for it – for the building, for the teacher's salary, for the books. So they struck back. It was not a question of being hostile to the idea of schooling per se; if there was "jealous aversion, dogged silence, watchful inactivity and at times open opposition"[102] among them, it was to the notion of enforced unilinguality and general high-handedness.

At Bukovyna School, Fletcher fired William Chumer and replaced him with a Mr. Armstrong. Uncowed, the trustees in short order built another school adjacent to the first and promptly re-hired Chumer. Armstrong twiddled his thumbs in an empty school while Chumer continued to hold classes until December 1, when the ratepayers voted to accept the dictum of the official trustee. They let Chumer go and agreed to let their children return to the care of Armstrong. Unfortunately, the matter did not end there.

In the interim, there was much agitation in the district over the action of the official trustee in seizing chattels of the trustees of the school for illegally paying wages to Chumer who had been dismissed by him.

"The last move of the agitation," reports the Edmonton *Bulletin* of early January 1914, "was against the English teacher, and women seem to have been employed as the instruments in this case. On January 4, when Mr. Armstrong returned to his shack alongside of the school after the vacation, two women came into his shack, and when his back was turned struck him on the head with a pot, and proceeded to beat him up generally, using teeth upon him fiercely. He succeeded in ejecting them from the house. He was then set upon by a couple of men with clubs who beat him up unmercifully. Of course, the offenders will be prosecuted."[103]

The Ukrainian press printed inflammatory headlines – "Punitive Action Against the Ukrainian People"; "Ugly Lies of the Minister of Education"[104] – and the Basilian monastery in Mundare defiantly opened a school-orphanage in 1914 (in 1909 their parishioners had had charges against them dropped for sending their children to the Sisters' school instead of to the recently built public school) to counteract the "denationalization" of the Greek-Catholics by the government's attempt to "gain control not only of the teaching programme, but over the very souls of our settlers, not so much to make Canadians because they were such, but to assimilate them into the Anglo-Saxon element of the Canadian population."[105]

It is an interesting distinction – between Canadians and Anglo-Saxons – which became lost in the public urgency to assimilate the immigrants with all their strangeness and inscrutability into what was then perceived to be the mainstream of Canadian culture. It would not be revived again until, during the debates surrounding multiculturalism, it was argued that loyalty to and identification with Canada wasn't necessarily the same thing as allegiance to the British way of life.

Before the children could be thoroughly assimilated into the majority culture, they had first of all to learn the English language, without which even the most strenuous propaganda could not be absorbed. Some pupils had picked up a modicum of English from older siblings already at school but for the majority the first day of school was the first exposure to the new language. Imagine the scenario: forty-five Ukrainian speakers, one English speaker, and a curriculum to fulfill whose alphabet, let alone content and intent, was utterly foreign to the students. One would begin with the letter "A," draw an apple on the blackboard, pronounce the word, have it repeated back, progress to "B" with a picture of a bird, and so on. "Once we got to school, we were in a totally Anglo-Saxon environment. We learned everything by rote, often without understanding a word of what we were saying." The wonder is that within a couple of years the students were speaking, reading, and writing English with considerable flourish, if not with absolute correctness.

Our Church

The church that we go to belongs to the Greek Catholic Denomination.

I am going from north to the church, There are ten acres of land, and south from the church there is cemetry, The church is on the hill. On Sunday I came to church I see many people there while we stand near there and talk. Upon going inside I see the priest who is standing by the altar. The people kneel down and then pray. The people go nearer to the priest and there is a small table and on the table there is picture which the people kiss and go outside and then depart.[106]

Catching Horses on the Prairie

Last summer I lefted the horses on the prairie at night. In the morning I was going to catch them and I came on the prairie and the horses were grazing there than I called them and one horses came and I caught him. The others were running away.

Then my father went for them and I went too. The horses were about three miles. And there we found them. I caught one horses and my father caught two horses. And we were riding on the horses to home. We were riding very fast and the horses were jumping. I like it.[107]

Yesterday

Yesterday as Mr Butchart [school inspector] came to our school we did not behave all good somebody behave good but not all. As Mr Butchart came to school we all did not stand up at the right time. Somebody stood up a half an hour before and somebody at the right time and somebody did not stand up at all. Few of the children look saw at Mr Butchart as they have had never seen him before. As they were going to ask something walked like if there were about a hundred them they to much noice.[108]

In several ways, the English language would never be totally comfortable to them. For this generation and even the two following, a Ukrainian accent would be distinguishable in the speech (by now, the accent is so characteristic of some small-town and rural speakers it is almost a dialect of English). The vocabulary would be sufficient but limited in nuance. The temptation to insert Ukrainian words and phrases that seemed more expressive or were simply there on the tip of the tongue would never vanish. And the complex transition from language study to reading the literature would befuddle many, even the university graduates. "We gobbled up math and science but the only course I ever flunked in school was grade 12 English. Physics – 81. Social Studies – 71. English – 37! I was heartbroken. I'll admit I really didn't know how to write an essay until I went to university; none of us could write English very well."

In a classroom in which the teacher was the single English-speaking individual, it was imperative, from her point of view, to enforce a rule that no Ukrainian be spoken in school or even on the school grounds. For one thing, it was the only means she had to ensure she'd understand what was being said around her; for another, it was a way of providing at least one English-language environment for the students who otherwise would hear only Ukrainian spoken, at home, in town, in church, at meetings and dances; for yet another (and this applied as well to Ukrainian-speaking teachers who took their socializing roles seriously), it provided an object lesson in the inevitability of the de-nationalization of the "alien" by means of imposing the language of the ruling class. It was a political lesson. If you were punished and humiliated for speaking your native language, it was apparent that there was something "bad" about it, something undesirable and unworthy. If you were never rewarded for speaking it, you would stop using it to get what you wanted and would depend more and more on English to make your way through the school system and any other Anglo-Saxon environment that represented achievement. Eventually, you would not even find this strange, that

Ukrainian-Canadian teachers themselves would refuse to acknowledge their Ukrainian sources, but would accept that they were in the class, not as representatives of the community but as agents of the Department of Education. "In those days, we got spanked if we spoke Ukrainian in school. I got seven straps for saying *moya horbata zymna*. That's the only straps I got from grade one till grade eleven, for saying 'my tea is cold' in Ukrainian." Of course, not speaking English fluently, it was always easier to speak to each other in Ukrainian even when playing at recess. And if the teacher caught anybody speaking Ukrainian, they had then to write 500 times, "I will speak English."

Once the elements of the English language were mastered, the teaching of the curriculum began in earnest. By the time the student wrote the grade eight public school leaving examination,[109] he or she had studied arithmetic, literature, composition, grammar, spelling, geography, hygiene, art, agriculture, history, and civics. Language mastery was crucial: one was judged for reading speed, "voice inflection to express feeling involved in what is read," a general knowledge of *Ben Hur* or *The Merchant of Venice* or *Heroes of Land and Sea* and the memorization of poetry, among other things. Clearly, a failure to conquer the language would jeopardize chances to go on to high school. No wonder the teachers, even the Ukrainians, insisted on the priority of the English language: to do otherwise would be to prejudice a non-Anglo-Saxon student.

The table of contents of a reader reveal the intent of the curriculum; one was not merely learning how to read, one was also absorbing information and attitudes about Canadian society. More specifically, a student was learning that to be really Canadian was to be Anglo-Saxon (if not British), Protestant and male. Witness the *Introduction to Literature*, edited by G. Fred McNally and published in Toronto in 1934. The selections include: "The United Empire Loyalists," "King Arthur and His Knights," "Kew in Lilac-Time," "The Heavens Declare the Glory of God," "The Mounted Police," "Gentlemen, The King!," "Brutus and Anthony," "The Battle of Agincourt," "Ivanhoe and Isaac of York," and "O God, Our Help in

Ages Past." Witness the writers: Duncan Campbell Scott, Alfred John Church, Alfred Noyes, the Evangelists, Robert Service, Harold Begbie, Shakespeare, Sir Walter Scott, and Isaac Watts. There is, in the whole table of seventy-four items, one non-Anglo-Saxon (Victor Hugo) and one woman (Eugenie Foa). There is demonstrably no reference in the titles to Eastern European, Canadian immigrant, non-Protestant, or feminine experience.

Witness Book IV of the *Canadian Readers* series published by Gage and Company in Toronto in the first decade of this century, a book for more advanced readers. Here we have one Frenchman (Louis H. Frechette) and two women (George Eliot and "Mrs. Moodie") and, where there is reference to Canadian content, it is to Upper Canadian scenarios ("A St. Lawrence Rapid," "Canadian Boat Song," "Niagara Falls") except for an essay on Manitoba, which includes a reference to Edmonton and an essay on "Northwestern Canada," described as a region devoid of population. Inevitably, there are the poems about extraordinary Englishmen ("Death of Wellington"), the psalms ("The Lord is My Shepherd"), the homiletic essays from abroad ("Love of Country" by Sir Walter Scott and "The Greatness of England" by William Gladstone), and from Toronto ("Canadian Loyalty" by Rev. Dr. Ryerson) and the masculine enthusiasms ("The Taking of Roxborough Castle," "Recollections of My Boyhood," "Advice to Young Men," "The Soldier's Dream").

Addressing himself to the subject of Canadian loyalty, Rev. Ryerson defines it thus:

> Loyalty in its true essence and meaning is the principle of respect to our Sovereign, the freedom of our institutions, and the excellences of our civilization, and it is therefore a feeling worthy to be perpetuated by the people. . . .
> Canadian loyalty is the perpetuation of that British national life which has constituted the strength and glory of Great Britain, and placed her at the head of the freedom and civilization of mankind. . . . Canadian loyalty, therefore, is not a mere sentiment, or mere affection for the representative or

person of the Sovereign; it is a reverence for, and attachment to, the laws, order, institutions, and freedom of the country. . . . Canadian loyalty is a firm attachment to that British Constitution and those British laws, adopted or enacted by ourselves, which best secure life, liberty, and prosperity, and which prompt us to Christian and patriotic deeds by linking us with all that is grand and noble in the traditions of our national history.

The editor writes a "Counsel for the Young Men and Women of Canada":

Happily you live in a land whose inhabitants are as free as the air they breathe, and there is not a single prize which the ambition of man can desire, to which you may not aspire. . . .

Perhaps in no country in the world, under no possible conditions which can be imagined, do a body of young men, such as those I see around me, start in life under more favourable auspices, or enter upon their several careers with a more assured certainty that, by industry, by the due cultivation of their intelligence, by sobriety of manners and of conduct, they may attain the greatest prizes of life. I would remind you that you are citizens of a country in which all the most cherished prizes of ambition are open to all, – that, however humble the origin of any of you may have been, there is no position in the service of the country to which you may not hope to attain.

A geography text, The British Isles, lists "Our Island Home," "Amongst Our Ancient Mountains," and "London, the Mother of Cities" among its chapters.

This then was schooling. A child in handmade cotton clothes arrives at school after a three-mile barefoot walk from a two-room log house (chattering in Ukrainian along the way); enters the classroom, salutes the Union Jack and sings God Save the King; gazes out the window at uninterrupted miles of oat fields and poplar groves, at the fluorescent dome of a Greek-Catholic church, at the figure of an old *baba*, kerchief on her head, embroidered felt jacket around her body, walking down the road with her cow; opens the textbook and reads. The world within the book is unrecognizable but unmistakably admirable and exemplary. In fact, everything which is therein described as "heroic" and "lovely" and "virtuous" and "ours" is, by definition, "not like me." Not Ukrainian, not western Canadian, not rural, not poor, not Greek-Orthodox or Cyrillic, not female. No honour or dignity or piety attaches to these characteristics and there is no model of "good citizenship" or "loyalty" or "manhood" for such a queer kind of person. If the only actions worth performing take place in western Europe or eastern North America, where can I make a mark? If only blond and blue-eyed aristocratic boys are sung about, who will find me worthy? If "Canadian loyalty" is measured only by one's commitment to the "perpetuation of British national life," does that mean I'm disloyal for living as a Ukrainian farmer? If "Christian" means "Anglican," does that make me a heathen? If the "cherished prizes of ambition" really are "open to all" then why are all the powerful people around me only the English? If we really do live in a land "whose citizens are as free as the air we breathe" then why was Uncle Panko arrested in 1916 and Mr. Fedorchuk fired from the school and my sister crying because somebody said she stank like a sheep and why did my aunt and uncle have to leave their farm after working so hard on it?

The generation responded in various ways. There were those who became Anglophiles, identifying personally and passionately with the glories of Empire and Westminster, who assumed, by emotional and intellectual osmosis, the accomplishments of Anglo-Saxon culture as their own and who found the exploits and rhetoric of the Anglo-Saxon many times more exciting and attractive than the hardship and banality of their immediate environment. Some accepted the propaganda of the textbooks and instruction as the only available model of "Canadianism"; wishing heart and soul to be thought of as good Canadians, they voluntarily validated the contemporary definition. Some related positively to the pro-British bias out of contempt for their own Ukrainian origins (the psychology of the minority). Some were apparently unaffected. "Before my time the teachers would call us Russians. We learned all about how Britons never will be slaves and how Britannia rules the waves. It didn't bother me, it was beyond my comprehension." Some simply related to the literature as to adventure stories about exotic lands – a fantasy – keeping their consciousness as Ukrainian-Canadians intact. And, later in life, some were to cultivate a zealous Ukrainian nationalism as if to redress the imbalance of an earlier, chauvinistic, and untenable education.

In addition to instruction in the "three R's," the school concert played an important role in the indoctrination of the young into Anglo-Saxon values. Pageants, after all, are a theatrical and declamatory exercise in commemorating publicly the epiphanic events of a society (as selected by the establishment: church, army, merchants) and all citizens are expected to identify with these self-congratulatory celebrations as moments in their own history. Less abstractly, the school concert in the rural areas was one of the more important communal activities – everybody went – and an equally important educational tool, as it generally included poetry, music, and drama. More to the point, the concert was directed and produced by the teacher and so reflected, as did the curriculum, the intent of the school system: Anglicization. In 1928 the Deputy Minister of Education circulated a letter to teachers suggesting how Empire Day might best be observed:

The Flag Ceremony (used last June)
     The School Flag should be raised to the masthead by a committee of older boys especially selected for this duty. The rest of the school will stand at attention until the Flag is in position. Then the entire school will stand at salute and repeat this pledge:

"I salute the Flag and pledge my loyalty to my King and Country."

O Canada!

Recitation from Lord Dufferin:

"Love your country, believe in her, honour her, work for her, live for her, die for her. Never has any people been endowed with a nobler birthright or blessed with prospects of a fairer future."

Speech by one of the pupils – "Canada's Future."

Recitation.

Song "The Maple Leaf."

"God Save the King."

I trust that you will cooperate with the Board in making this program a memorable one for the children.[110]

The tone is patriotic, monarchist, militaristic, and virile, in the manner popularized throughout the British Empire. Even *The Maple Leaf Forever* is only superficially local. The verses were written exclusively from the point of view of an Englishman witnessing the extension to a foreign shore of the British army, flag, and constitution; for a Ukrainian-Canadian school child on the prairies to celebrate the entwining of the "shamrock, thistle, and rose" is at the least nonsensical and alienating. But they did, for a whole generation.

Less perversely, the Shandro school had a Hallowe'en concert in 1932, the details of which simply illustrate how the Ukrainian-Canadians were being introduced to Anglo-Saxon popular culture. "The room was decorated with jack-o-lanterns, with pumpkins and apples," according to a writer for the Vegreville *Observer*. The concert opened with the obligatory O *Canada,* followed by a recitation, "The Old Maid" by Rosie Moisey, a duet, "The Willows," by Kate and Mary Huculak, a game, "Ducking for Apples," a chorus singing "Song of the Brook" and chocolate-apple-on-a-string game won by Paul Hawreliak. It was simple, fun, good-natured and unrelievedly Anglo-Saxon (except, one can imagine, for the accents of the children).

The Christmas concert was the crucial one: the climactic expression of both secular and religious sentiments and the celebration most closely identified with the spirituality of children. This was the concert the community expected to be the most ambitious, sophisticated, and meaningful, and the Shandro district, in 1934, witnessed "the best ever held." It was, by the account in the *Observer*, an extravaganza, featuring two- and three-part harmonies in the choruses, an organ lent by the Community Club, an enlarged platform, and "brilliant performances by little Reta Ulchek, Netty Shandro, Nick Ewanchuk," et al. "The Nine Jolly Negroes and Two Little Maids pleased greatly the overcrowded audience, and are still the talk of the district."

Now Christmas is a very serious holiday among the Ukrainians as well, and a host of preparations and rituals surround it. It is intensely devotional and intimate and was practised, as much as finances and circumstances would permit, in Canada as in the Ukraine. But the Christmas that the Ukrainian community witnessed in the schoolhouse was something else again. "Jack Frost," junior room chorus; "Merry Christmas Drill"; "Jolly Old St. Nicholas," song by grade one; "While Shepherds Watched Their Flocks By Night," by senior room; "Drink To Me Only With Thine Eyes," senior chorus; "A Christmas Dinner," a play by grades three and four; "Nine Jolly Negroes," by senior girls; "Jingle Bells," a two-room chorus. And, penultimately, Arrival of Santa Claus (just before *God Save the King*).

From the parents' point of view, it must have been simply an "entertainment," a revue of pleasantries without emotional or religious significance, a sociable means of being shown the progress their children were making in the English language. They must either have adopted this attitude or been deeply and visibly offended and estranged by the secularization of the celebration and the categorical absence of any references to the Ukrainian tradition. Perhaps they went to the Christmas concert as to the Ringling Brothers Circus and the All Star Baseball tournament.

From the students' point of view, it was a question not only of doing what the teacher required, doing it well and achieving honour, it was an exercise in "becoming good Canadians." It was the beginning of a compromise. The Ukrainian-Canadians would publicly observe the formalities of Anglo-Saxon behaviour, would formally adopt the "Canadian" way of doing things, as much out of pragmatic self-interest as out of admiration or intimidation or nonchalance. Meanwhile, in the privacy of their own homes and churches and halls, they would carry on as they had always done, for another couple of decades anyway.

Although the school boards had lost the right to have their children educated in the Ukrainian language within the public schools, they were not prevented from establishing Ukrainian language lessons after hours. In fact, once Ukrainian-Canadians became available for teaching positions, it was understood that they would be available to conduct such classes and if they could also teach something of Ukrainian history and literature, music and dance, so much the better. Such persons had no trouble finding a job in these districts for their role was crucial, not only in countering the effects of Anglicization (or de-Ukrainianization, as the Basilians put it), but in providing a service the illiterate or semi-literate parents could not. Sometimes hating it, the kids stayed after hours in the schoolroom – it would be dark and scary by the time they set out for home in winter – to be taught not just the Ukrainian alphabet and grammar but folk songs, history, and literature, musical instruments, liturgical music – one class learned the entire mass and would sing it, walking to church, two by two – by teachers who sometimes had no more than a grade six Canadian education. No matter. Their Ukrainian one was impeccable.

Although there were some non-Ukrainians who objected to

this practice, seeing in it a vestigial subversiveness and a reminder of old disputes, Charles Young was more reasonable. He found no reason to be anxious about after-hours instruction to "pupils already fluent in English. The objections to the bilingual system were due to the fact that it put Ukrainian on a par with English in the curriculum."[111] By the thirties, however, there was no such menace. English was the language of the public and institutionalized instruction and Ukrainian was assuming the status of a covert form of communication. No harm then in letting the Ukrainians carry on teaching it wherever and however they could. Within twenty years, it would be a phony issue: English would be the mother tongue of the second generation.

In the broad view, the teacher was the instrument of the assimilationists. At a more personal level, he or she was an unforgettable character, an exotic creature from another world or an unspeakable brute, an impressive scholar or a lazy vagabond of dubious repute. Fifty, sixty years later, the students of these teachers recall them with vivid images, some more affectionately than others.

And he was this type of fellow, he loved beer, but he had a wife. He was a short little fellow and he had a tall wife like this. And now and then she'd come and haul him out of the beer parlour and he would come. But he was terrific in his work. Oh, he was A-1 in his work.

———

Mr. Bray was a very nice teacher. He always had girls in front. And he used to smoke a pipe and he'd want to smoke that pipe and he'd go outside to smoke. Once he came in, his shoes were all slippery and he fell; the whole school shook, because he's a big man. And he pretended that the girls use some perfume, that that's what made him fall down. . . . He made us all dress up and go out and play at recess. Football in winter, we kicked a football, or running around like what they call, the hound or the fox and the geese, and we'd run around. We'd come in and our cheeks would be all red and fresh. He believed in a lot of fresh air. And then we'd have our lunch and he'd have his lunch. In summertime he'd go and sit under the trees and I'd be always sitting there beside him, and the way he was talking about the old country I can still remember.

I was in first year at school. Every morning the teacher would call us up one by one and hit us three or four times on the head and then we went back to our desks. We hadn't done anything! It was just our "medicine" for the day. And he figured that since he had beaten us he had done his job. Then he'd write some numbers on the board, arithmetic or I don't know what, and then he'd go out to his shack for an hour and sneak back. By that time, of course, the kids were all over the place but one of us would be watching at the window and by the time he came back in we'd all be sitting at our desks. After recess we'd be lined up for a strapping. After lunch hour same lousy thing: line up for a beating. Then again after five. Giving everybody their medicine. He was a Ukrainian. I missed a lot of school because of those beatings. I was scared and didn't want to go. My father was dead and what could my mother do? I never did learn to like school after that. I was scared of teachers.

We had a teacher who beat a girl so hard with a big dictionary and a stick that she went out of her mind. Her brothers would lead her to school and leave her outside the schoolhouse and at recess we would come out and see her sitting there not even bothering to chase away the flies on her face. She wouldn't speak or eat her lunch. Then she was sent to Oliver Mental Hospital.

It stretches the imagination sometimes to account for the enormous esteem with which the teacher was usually regarded in the Ukrainian community. Interviewees testify to the "respect and seriousness," the "admiration," felt by them as students towards their teachers (one went so far as to imitate, out of sympathy, the limp of a teacher with a peg-leg) and yet they also relate hair-raising incidents of a teacher's brutality, insensitivity, and plain stupidity. Perhaps it was understood that, while the person holding the office may be contemptible, the office itself was distinguished. For several years after settlement, the teacher was the best educated person in the community – there were no doctors, dentists, or lawyers – and even the merchants, in spite of their relative wealth, had only primary school education and a corresponding status. But the teacher was an *intellihent*, a reader, writer, and mathematician, a person who knew how to write letters to authorities and to make himself or herself understood to the bureaucrats, who could dispense advice on how best to undertake one's business among the "Englishmen." No matter that the teacher might be a drunk or a pederast, an intellectual mediocrity or a bully, no matter that he might be a Ukrainian who referred, out of old-country conceit, to his fellows as *banyaky* ("pots") and *kozhukhy* ("sheepskins"), no matter that she might be an Anglo-Saxon who pointedly favoured the children of the Anglo-Saxon station agent and Anglo-Saxon bank manager, the teacher was the object of collective estimation and deference, a "superior" human being.

There were many teachers who fulfilled this expectation, who conducted themselves with dignity and humility and are remembered with warmth. There were even some Anglo-Saxon teachers who "assimilated very well" into the Ukrainian community, as one man remembers them, who "learned to sing some of the Ukrainian carols and were offended if they weren't invited to a wedding." And a great many Ukrainian-speaking teachers who provided the first "role-model" to young Ukrainian-Canadians wondering if there was something else to life besides tilling the soil.

He taught the girls to be ladies as well. He made sure that when everybody came in their fingernails were clean and hands clean and he'd tell us to go outside and take off our shoes and see if our feet were clean. He gave prizes away to those that were.

And as far as the girls were concerned, menses and all that, you know, some were ignorant. He even had to teach them about that. That was overlooked by the mothers, so he had to.

Many communities were lucky to get a teacher at all. City-bred Anglo-Saxons were extremely reluctant to teach among the "foreigners," alienated as they were from the language and customs, and unhappy at the prospect of being boarded with a farm family in a two-room house. In such cases, teacher turnover was dramatic and "English" teachers earned a reputation as unreliable and money-wasting "adventurers" and "lumberjacks."[112] Living in a teacherage was little consolation: it was usually a mean dwelling, asphyxiating in the summer and bone-chilling in the winter, miles from the nearest neighbour. The loneliness of such a situation was staggering. Eventually, the majority of rural teachers were young women, barely twenty years old, and the public scrutiny of their behaviour and the unstated expectation that their emotional and spiritual life be beyond reproach only increased the loneliness. They were expected not only to teach but to act as school janitors, to stoke fires, diagnose illnesses, and apply first aid. "They counselled, scolded, played games, umpired, cut the children's hair, settled disputes, taught Sunday School, played the organ for church services, trained the choir, helped at school functions and organized cultural activities."[113] (My father recalls witnessing "from the safety of the top of [my] desk, the teacher and an eighteen-year-old boy wrestling for supremacy on the floor between two rows of desks."[114]) Later, when Ukrainian-speaking normal school graduates were hired, they were, in addition to all that, expected to give Ukrainian language lessons after hours.

The questions answered by a school board when making application for the appointment of a teacher reflect what the Department of Education regarded as the salient features of the job: Male or female teacher? When will school open? Length of engagement? Salary offered? (Note: Section 199 of the School Act provides that the yearly salary shall be twelve times the monthly rate.) Distance of school from: a) the railway station; b) the post office; c) the boarding house? Cost of board? Is there a residence? To what extent is residence furnished? Number of children on roll? What grades are taught? Nationality of residents? [115]

How, one wonders, were some schools, miles from the nearest town, unserviced, and preponderantly "foreign," ever chosen except by the most desperate or unsuccessful teachers?

The situation of Ukrainian-area schools improved considerably after 1915, once Ukrainian-speaking graduates emerged from the provincial normal schools and discovered that there was an unofficial barrier to their employment in the cities. They were, however, welcomed by the school districts of Plain Lake, Kiew, Sherentz, Wolia, and others who hoped for a recovery of their losses after Robert Fletcher's "purge" of Ukrainian teachers. By employing these men and women, many only two or three years off the farm, they assumed correctly, they would participate without embarrassment in the community's affairs and would contribute what they could to the advancement of Ukrainian culture. They had, after all, the benefit of a raised consciousness from rubbing shoulders with the Ukrainian nationalist movement in the cities where old-country intellectuals congregated around the newspaper offices, the bookstore, the church, and the residential Institutes. They were fluent English speakers who could still speak Ukrainian, thus satisfying both bureaucratic and popular needs. They were *nashy* – ours – free of the bigotry that prevented many Anglo-Saxon teachers from relating to the community in anything but a constrained and supercilious way.

Ukrainian, Anglo-Saxon, or otherwise, the relationship of the teacher to the board of trustees was problematic. There were issues which polarized them and others which united them against a third group. Take, for example, the Two Hills School Board. In May 1933, a high school teacher, J.J. Laughlin, was told he would receive a $100 bonus if he were successful in passing 75 percent of his students. In June he was allowed to collect 90 percent of all students' tuition fees from the grade twelve students. By June of 1934, however, a serious rift had occurred between the teaching staff and the board.

June 6, 1934

A special meeting called for the purpose of discussing the question of teachers' contracts for the coming term. Those present were Chairman Soldan, Trustees Skakin and Olinyk. The following teachers were also present. Laughlin, Powell and Sherstianka.

The Chairman explained to the teachers that insofar as the Board was concerned their contracts would not be renewed. J.J. Laughlin asked for permission to appeal to the Board why they should consider past services and results before giving any definite decision with respect to the teachers' dismissal. Laughlin proceeded to give an outline in detail regarding his own experiences while on the staff, particularly bringing to the attention of the Board the results he has obtained while in charge of the school.

The Chairman was rather reluctant to carry on further, saying that if the teachers were not satisfied with the treatment that they were getting that they could appeal their cases to the Board of References for a ruling. However, he reconsidered his stand and explained to the teachers that the reason the Board took the stand they did was because it was quite apparent there was no harmony among the teachers themselves, the school had become in a bad state of repair, and one of the teachers was unable to carry out her work on account of sickness and was still not well. The teachers also were not teaching French in any of the grades and were giving no attention to athletics.

The teachers denied all the accusations made against them, replying they did the very best under the circumstances in that the School Board had not asked that they teach French nor give any of their time to athletics, although they had personally financed athletics in previous years but received no further encouragement nor assistance.

The outcome of the discussion was that the Board decided to go through with the dismissals as previously given.

It was, perhaps, a case of teachers exhausted by the demands of a school board which required a heavier commitment from the staff than the salaries warranted. A month later it was also a case of burgeoning union consciousness on the part of the teachers.

July 25, 1934

A Special Meeting of the Ratepayers of the Two Hills S.D. #1941 was held in the school house. All trustees were present.

Soldan proceeded to tell the position the Board was in insofar as the teachers were concerned and that the meeting was called to get the approval of the ratepayers to carry their appeal before the Board of Reference. Moved by N. Dowhaniuk and seconded by Harry Molofy that the Board have full authority to settle the matter of teachers' disputes as they see fit and if necessary secure the services of an attorney to present their appeal to the court. Carried.

Just as the meeting adjourned, John J. Laughlin and representatives of the Teachers Alliance entered the meeting and asked that the same be re-opened so that they could talk settlement with the Board and possibly arrange so that it would not be necessary to go to Court. This was approved of and the meeting proceeded in the Town Hall where lighting facilities were available.

J.W. Barnett on behalf of the teachers asked for a settlement, giving his opinion of the position of both parties. Mike Soldan stated that the Board would consider re-engaging the teachers on a term contract only providing that the teachers would accept the following terms.

That J. Laughlin accept $1200 to carry on the same work for a period of one year. That Miss Powell accept $750, Miss Sherstianka $750 and Mrs. McCutcheon $840. That Mrs.

McCutcheon undertake to teach French I and II as well as teaching her previous grades.

Accepted.

In 1938, a series of incidents at the Two Hills school provoked a solidarity not only between the trustees and the teachers but between them and a parent as well. By this time, the school, acting *in loco parentis*, was supported in its disciplinary function by the father (it is difficult to know how mothers felt about this as it seems women did not attend the trustees' meetings); in fact, I was told several times that a child punished at school would not dare tell his or her father for fear of having the punishment repeated at home. Between the patriarch and the pedagogue, there was a perfect consonance of opinion regarding respect for authority.

March 16, 1938

Investigation made by the Board of Trustees under the authority of Section 119 subsection V of the School Act. Stanley C. Clarke, Principal of the school, informed the trustees Nick Dowhaniuk, Steve Yuskow and Mike Soldan that Peter A — , student of grade twelve, refused to obey teacher's order on December 7, 1937, he used profane language and he tried to organize other students for the purpose not to obey teacher's orders. Principal informed Peter that he will be expelled from the school. Questioned by Soldan, Peter declared that he is twenty years of age, is taking grade twelve and that differences started between him and teacher because he always felt that he and other students are behind in their subjects.

Principal declared that Peter tried to interfere with him while he was straping [sic] Peter's younger brother Steve saying that it will be better for me and you if you don't punish my brother. Peter declared that he went to the teacher because he was afraid that the teacher will give his brother too severe punishment. Teacher told him to get out but Peter said he is not afraid of teacher. Principal wanted to have decent atitude [sic] from

Peter and he will teach Peter five subjects on Saturday but he do not want him in the school on all other days of the week. After long discussion between Principal and Peter the Principal changed his mind and agreed to take Peter back to school if Peter will behave himself. But for any small reason Peter will be expelled from school.

Second case: The Principal informed the Board that he expelled George S — from school for using profane language. Miss Helen Soldan teacher testified that she heard George saying to teacher in Ukrainian language *shlyak trufyw* [literally, may lightning strike you down]. George admitted he is guilty. The Principal decided to give George thirty straps but he gave him twelve straps only because George could not stand anymore. George S — Sr. instructed the Principal to administer seventeen more straps tomorrow but the Principal declared that if George will behave no more straps will be given to him but if he do not behave himself he will get thirty straps instead of seventeen.

Third case: The Principal informed the Board that John S was expelled from school for refusing to rise [sic] his hands for straping. John admitted he is guilty and he received his punishment – thirty straps.

By the Second World War, the teacher's role was undergoing considerable modification. With the organization of larger school divisions and the innovation of bussing farm children to the central town schools (roads too had improved), the rural one-room school was deserted and the teacher became a town resident. The move meant that the teacher was no longer on such intimate terms with the pupils' parents, who had been neighbours, and no longer a singular beacon of enlightenment and accomplishment to the students. By the end of the thirties, there were many people in the towns who could assume leadership of cultural activities – "lead a choir, coach a play, lecture on public health, organize a parish or a *narodny dim* (national hall). In the growing towns, others could, and did, take over some of the teacher's role. The local merchant, the parish priest, the local grain buyer, lawyer or doctor – these were available to do the job."[116] Greater numbers of Ukrainian-Canadians were graduating from high school and the increased economic productivity of the farms, reflected by the expansion of the villages into towns, meant more time could be diverted to recreational and cultural activities.

In 1975 a retrospective look at the teaching profession during those years incites, not bitterness or regret, but nostalgia. From a letter from my father dated June 30, 1975:

My first school was Hamburg – as I've no doubt told you before. It was thirty miles straight east of home – among hills and tall poplar groves. Sunday afternoon a neighbour and brother John drove me in an old Chev and more or less unceremoniously dumped me off at the chairman's place – some three miles away from the school.

Almost the first thing the chairman asked me was whether I could read Ukrainian and then thrust a copy of the *Ukrainian Voice* at me and told me to read. I cannot imagine I passed with high marks as he never again asked me to do it, although I visited him quite often.

Late that evening I walked the three miles to the school, carrying my worldly possessions in a cardboard suitcase that was popular in those days. The teacherage, which was to be my home for the next six months, was a flat-roofed shack that leaked at every rainfall. Anyhow, I gulped down that feeling of helplessness and desolation and proceeded to make the ramshackle teacherage habitable. One thing I do remember doing – presumably to give me physical courage in the event of some sort of attack by a wild animal or wild human inhabitant of the district – I hung in a very conspicuous place on the wall a small hand revolver (which in all the years I had it never once fired – simply because I never bought any bullets for it). That particular precaution was totally unnecessary but the gun was a conversation piece when the young bucks of the neighbourhood dropped in to visit the new "professor."

I do not recall how long I had that funny feeling in my tummy; but I do recall that I enjoyed walking along the winding road – either to the nearest neighbour for milk and bread and eggs; or somewhat further to another neighbour who picked up my mail which was being addressed to Ranfurly.

Receiving mail was by far the most exciting event that summer. I got it about once a week, or perhaps two weeks. And usually there would be several letters – mostly from my former normal school mates (male and female). I seldom wrote home – on the whole we were not very much for correspondence, and still are not. But I would avidly read the letters over and over again; lose myself in recalling the friends, the good days at the normal school, etc., etc.

The letters I received were my link with civilization, as I saw it then. I also got a magazine or two and they never ceased to create wonder and curiosity in the young man who frequently delivered it. No one in that district, I'm sure, had ever seen a copy of *Maclean's* or whatever magazine I was getting at the time.

Eventually, I got used to the long evenings alone, the long walks to the next school, the longer horseback ride (eight miles) to pick up my pay check. It was just a matter of a month or so, and I was as much at home among the unsophisticated rural folk as I had been among my schoolmates.

Time seems to take care of everything.

According to the figures from the 1961 census, the percentage of Ukrainians with a university degree is 2 percent compared to 4.3 percent for the "British" and 3.4 percent for the national average; 2.5 percent with "some university" (British: 4.1 percent and national average: 3.3 percent) and 33.7 percent with "some secondary" (British 54.5 percent and national average 44.5 percent). The clear majority of Ukrainians in Canada – 55.3 percent – fall under the category of "some elementary."[117] Considering that, by 1961, these figures include first and second generation Ukrainian-Canadians as well as the better educated, third wave, post-war immigrants, they tell a depressing story. Ukrainian-Canadians haven't yet recovered from the devastating effects of the twenties and thirties when the first generation was not, in fact, educated beyond a few years in public school. Those who did manage more achieved varying degrees of success. Within·one family, for instance, the children became: an engineer with the federal government, a school superintendent, a dentist's receptionist, a mechanic, a telephone operator, a policeman, and three teachers. The whole panorama from working class to lower middle class to middle middle class! In some families, being bright and ambitious meant an opportunity to attend secretarial school in Edmonton, agricultural college (directly from grade ten), or receive nurses' training. Something practical; job-training, in fact, rather than intellectual expansion and development. To make a living, any kind of urban-based, wage income, was an advance from the farm. Even the government supported this advance when, during the Second World War, it set up sewing and cooking classes for girls in the defunct Communist Hall in Myrnam and "shop" classes for boys in the national hall.

The working class of the towns and cities, the petit-bourgeoisie of shopkeepers and service people, became the inevitable repository of those who would not or could not be supported by the farms. Tinsmiths, hospital orderlies, bakers and butchers, elevator agents, road builders, well-diggers, town clerks, hairdressers, and weed inspectors. Here was the advancement available to them, the privilege accorded, if they had anything from a grade four to a vocational institute education.

Others, with money or ingenuity or luck, went to normal school to train as teachers – the one "profession" readily available to Ukrainian-Canadians – for the rural schools.

I had to get an education because I had nothing else to make my living with. My mother had one of the quarters and my sister and my brother-in-law the other. So I had to go out teaching. At all costs I had to get an education; my brother-in-law even borrowed money to send me on to grade eleven.

Going into teaching was the first stepping stone and besides there was nothing else. No money to send me to university. You had to go into teaching. In eight months of normal school you could get a Second-Class teaching certificate and teach the rest of your life on that.

It wasn't exactly university but it was a cut above the trades, it required only one year's instruction, it was a step in the direction of more lucrative and estimable jobs – school superintendent, secretary of the school division, secretary of the county – and, for women, it was the "logical" career for someone interested in the less appropriate pursuits of science or the arts or commerce.

One begged, borrowed, or worked to earn the tuition fees. Sometimes it was literally the parents' last cent, or cents they didn't have in the first place, and it was understood that the student would live as frugally as possible. There were surprisingly few complaints: to be a teacher, a person of substance and security, was worth every indulgence. One woman had the luck to receive some money from a United Church fund for education. Another had a father who earned a salary and sewed a month's wages into her pocket and sent her off. Others made more desperate sacrifices. In 1935, when the crops froze, a son's tuition to normal school was paid for by the cash surrender value – $400 – of a $1000 life insurance policy. When conditions improved during the war, the father made good his loss. "Blood money," they called it, the money earned by those who stayed on in Canada while brothers died in Europe.

The student's life was not easy, but familiar to anyone who had grown up under the economic regime of the farm or small-town business or rural church.

That was the hardest time of all. I stayed at my sister's place and that was way on the north side of the city, normal school was on the other side and where were we going to get the streetcar? We couldn't get the streetcar tickets, so we tried to walk, and you found you wore out your shoes and shoes cost too much money. . . . We wore the same thing, same dress till Christmas time, getting it cleaned two or three times and after Christmas then we got two blouses and a skirt. That finished your year off. And we walked all over town to get a five dollar gown for graduation, because there was no money. In order to go to the show we had to lug all our books and go right after school in order to get in for seventeen cents. We could afford seventeen cents, but we couldn't afford the thirty-five cents after six. After I got out I paid all my debts and I always had two dollars left every month out of the fifty-six dollars I made.

Although "it's always been a cherished thought in the minds of the Ukrainian parents that their children will go on to university," very few managed to finance such an enterprise. One man's four years at the University of Alberta cost his family $2000, and although that included everything from tuition to laundry to room and board at $40 a month with a Ukrainian family, it was still an extravagant amount. And, in the end, he became a teacher like everyone else.

Dad didn't want me to be a farmer or a store operator. He never suggested anything specific, just wanted me to go to university. When I was studying for the B.Sc. I wanted to go into dentistry or engineering. But in those days dentistry was very closed and ex-servicemen had priority. And engineers were a dime a dozen. And you hated to admit you were in Education; it had very low status. But my chemistry professor recommended it.

The transition from Two Hills to Edmonton could have provoked serious culture shock were it not for the Ukrainian population living there and the institutions they created to keep a large part of the Ukrainian-speaking community cohesive and collectively purposeful. The awareness of the parents' financial sacrifices, the inferiority feelings of someone not only a Ukrainian but also a "hick," and the determination to prove oneself worthy of a university education worked on a student's sense of isolation from the Anglo-Saxon majority and sense of place among fellow "ethnics." Thus, the family with whom the student boarded became, in his or her homesickness, a home away from home. They would all go to church together. There were Ukrainian-Canadian Youth Organization dances and concerts at the Ukrainian halls. The priest's wife would cook up a pot of *pyrohy* or *holubtsi* and invite students for dinner after mass.

Students in the Western Ukraine at the end of the nineteenth century had organized "institutes," or residences where they provided not only room and board for out-of-town students but also political and cultural activities for a new group of intellectuals politicized by the struggle for Ukrainian independence. Some graduates from the institutions emigrated to Canada and eventually organized similar politico-cultural clubs, one of the first of which in Alberta, the Adam Kotzko Society, met in Edmonton in the back room of D. Ferbey's Ukrainian bookstore in 1917.[118] Back in 1912, a "Russo-Ukrainian Bursa" had already been built in Edmonton and was operating as a residence for twenty students and young working people and a place where meetings, plays, and concerts were held. When it was taken over by Presbyterians, the Adam Kotzko Society assumed responsibility for an institute and in 1919, the Mykhailo Hrushevsky Institute was opened in what used to be the Edmonton Bible Institute and the Beulah Mission Hall.

> Prompted by the fact that Protestant churches were setting up "homes" for Ukrainian boys and girls in various centres in Alberta (Wahstao, Smoky Lake, Vegreville), it was decided that the M.H. Institute should be a truly "national" institution, independent of any religious or denominational control. It would be based and supported by membership of all enlightened Ukrainians of Alberta. The *Ukrainian Voice*, a weekly newspaper published in Winnipeg, became its spiritual and moral mentor, urging all enlightened Ukrainians in the West to give their financial and moral support to the Institute.[119]

It was here that numbers of future teachers learned the fundamentals of "Ukrainian consciousness" which they were to take with them into the schools. Besides studying the prescribed high school courses, the students met around the piano every evening after supper – this was compulsory – and learned folk songs and church music. Every day for an hour, they studied the Ukrainian language. When an instructor was available, they studied Ukrainian history; they prepared debates and recitations; they mounted a concert every two weeks and presented Ukrainian plays and the inevitable mandolin ensemble. These were precisely the sorts of activities that many Anglo-Saxons feared and mistrusted; the deliberate, not to say insolent, inculcation of "foreign" habits and non-Canadian cultural modes. When, later, Institute graduates began showing up on committees and executives of ethnic organizations demanding equal time for (middle class) Ukrainian-Canadians in the establishment, the worst suspicion had been realized. It was not entirely true that the ethnic population of Canada was being assimilated beyond recall; organizations like the Institutes were retarding the process, and in some cases subverting it, by providing an alternative identity to the one popularized by the public school system, by making it seem more accessible and therefore more attractive. Well, what else was a Ukrainian-Canadian to do? At the Institute, at least, it was "okay" to be Ukrainian.

What the Institute tried to do was build character; respect for the older students, respect for the teachers, responsibility, and it prepared us when we went out as teachers – and most of us did start out as teachers – to be able to take part in the community and teach plays, concerts, give speeches, do cultural work. It would be very difficult to get or keep a school if you couldn't do these things. You had to be able to teach Ukrainian after hours. And the Institute gave us a family life. Even forty years later when we "boys" get together we still feel part of a family.

The school: a way-station between the past and future, between a Ukrainian culture that could not, in the new circumstances, be transmitted *in toto* and a Canadian one that could not be indefinitely resisted. So the generation grew up half-way between the two, fully socialized in neither one nor the other. Ukrainian instruction was haphazard and intermittent, depending on who there was to teach it and how well. It would be appropriate no farther than the neighbourhood boundaries and down the road to the hall. Anglicization prevailed only to the extent the student exploited it, usually only as far as skilled labour in the town or city. Yet both types of education were absolutely necessary. Whenever and wherever Anglicization failed to satisfy or reward the Ukrainian-Canadian, the Ukrainian education was a reminder to the ethnic and exploited that there did exist meaningful ways-of-being outside the world view of the WASP establishment. If *Ivanhoe* made little sense, the tales of the cossack *sich* were always at hand. The school, after all, was meant only to explain so much.

SEVEN

Church

In the old country, if you wanted to get married you had to go and work for a week for the priest. My grandfather got married in the old country, he had to go and work for one week. And some of the ministers, they weren't helping the church. Instead of bringing the people in, they were chasing the people away from the church, with their talks, with their attitudes towards people. They considered themselves so much better. In plain words it was more of a dictatorship. You do as I tell you and that's all. My parents did, but my generation, they rebelled against that. It has to change and the church has to change.

– Bill Hnydyk

* * *

I would say that my parents were religious people. As children, they wanted us to go to catechism. Of course, we lived five miles away from a church, this was the Plain Lake church, and we used to go with horses and a democrat, or wagon at first, before we had a democrat, pile up and go to church. But then, before the Hungry Thirties, they started building a church and they wanted each family to give $100 towards the building fund, and my dad couldn't afford it. Well, he just couldn't. So then he, well, I wouldn't say he broke away from the church, but he didn't attend church very often. It hurt him when some of the wealthier parishioners had said, "Well, if you don't give us a hundred dollars, you can't come to church. "

– Kay Hnydyk

* * *

I had once one of your institute products. He was in the hospital; I don't want to name him. He was a teacher. I visited the hospital. His mother and a younger brother were with him. I started talking to him. Do you know what he said? He said, "Father, I do not believe in God." I looked at him and said, "Son, I know why; because you are a stupid cow. Goodbye." He told me that he has four years of university. That's nothing to me. If you're educated and a gentleman, you would not say that. I was touched to the quick.

– Father Peter Zubrytsky

* * *

Coming to a small community was like being in a prison. Coming here to Two Hills, even now I have plans that I would be transferred to the city sooner or later where I can be more positive. Then I can give more for the community which is more active. But still, you have to be really idealistic. It is missionary work. You still have to cope with lots of difficulties. . . . You come to people with religious indifference, you come to people who lost their national identity, you come to people who take care only about the biological life. What can you add? The church is not only for baptism, for burial, for marriage. It is something that everyday you are involved with. Your conscience has to be educated by the church.

I think that our people here were neglected before. Priest came as guest once a month to make like a show and I think that is not proper for the church. And then when people are living for long period of time in this indifference then still certain currents are against the religion. Like Communism. Here in Two Hills, there were some very active members that dedicated themselves towards Communism. It was thirty years ago and certain traces are left. The majority of people, they do not belong to the church. They may not be Communists, but anyway they are not religious. People are not actually hostile, but still they are so closed in themselves they are against clergymen and against church. They smile and they are polite but I think still here in this district has, or is left the remains, some influence of this period of time.

– Father Peter Lytwyn

———

A popular and reassuring scenario: the Ukrainians, a pious people unshakeably attached to their church and profoundly respectful of the priest's authority, waste no time erecting churches to care for their spiritual needs in Canada. Despite overwhelming pressures to assimilate, the Ukrainian-Canadians retain their loyalty to this most culturally and psychologically characteristic of their institutions and reject skepticism. If it hadn't been for this inbred piety and collective tenacity, the Ukrainians as a people would have vanished long ago into the Anglo-American woodwork.

The reality is more problematic. It's true that Ukrainians, like most rural populations, went to church, deferred to the priest and incorporated religious practices into their daily lives. It was the only ideology readily available, they were automatically disciplined within it by parents and church, and it provided them a community and a shared ethical code. All the more reason, then, to perpetuate this state of affairs in Canada, where geographical isolation, cultural alienation, and economic insecurity reinforced a Christian's sense of vulnerability in the cosmos.

Nobody denies that Ukrainians have been as religious as any other group. What is frequently overlooked and in fact excluded from the popular scenario is the fact that they have also been very often hostile towards their churches and priests, skeptical in their faith and indifferent to the mythologies propagated by the clerical establishment.

Take, for example, the commonplace that the Ukrainians are a simple folk who cannot be understood unless one is aware of their "deep religious background. . . . The priest was the object of their highest respect. When they met him along the way they would bow profoundly and kiss his hand for this was the traditional custom."[120] There is more than one way of looking at this: an oppressed and exploited peasantry has traditionally adopted a servile posture towards ecclesiastical figures, and intellectuals have traditionally patronized them. The move to Canada lifted the lid off many

Ukrainians' resentment towards the church. In fact, this resentment was by far a more common topic of conversation with me in Two Hills than were declarations of how well they had adhered to their faith. In Galicia and Bukovyna they had little choice but to be pious and respectful but in Canada they could speak more openly and make independent decisions about how a church was to be organized and a priesthood administered.

Typically, the first Canadian-born generation was raised in a moderately religious atmosphere in which the traditional forms were observed. Whenever the priest was officiating at the nearest church (sometimes fifteen miles away) and if the weather wasn't unbearably bitter, the family would go to mass and would be careful not to work in the fields that day (barnyard and domestic chores, like milking cows and cooking meals, were done as usual, meaning women and children worked as usual). The children went to catechism lessons in the summer as a matter of course and, as a matter of course, many played hookey. Most homes had icons of a saint or two and the Madonna (*Bohoroditsa*) hung up high on the walls and sometimes draped with embroidered cloths; everybody had a Bible. Mothers taught the prayers and the important events of life were invariably observed as sacraments; weddings, baptisms, and funerals. Fathers, usually more literate, instructed from the Bible. Fathers could also be less fervent believers – usually the mothers were more devout – and undemonstrative in their faith.

Our family went to church very seldom. We lived in the country in places where they didn't have regular services. In Bellis they had only about ten a year. But I still loved the music and colour and ceremony of it all. My father was much more of a Protestant than he was a Greek Orthodox. He would argue and question tenets of the Bible and he would say, "I do not believe in the resurrection of the body!" He was too educated to swallow it holus-bolus. But he still respected the church as a repository of Ukrainian culture in Canada so he supported it. Mother was a strong Catholic.

Some families produced priests and nuns; more didn't.

We had prayers before you go to bed and prayers in the morning. Then I was going to catechism. Walked to the monastery three miles away. I did that for about three years. I wanted to go for a nun but my mother wouldn't let me, but later on when I grew up a bit bigger and started going to dances and meeting boys she wanted me to. Then it was too late. I started going out, I didn't want to be locked up as a nun.

But there were, for everyone, moments in the religious calendar and events in one's life that were passionately observed. They were part of one's identity as a Ukrainian and could be ignored only by quitting the community altogether. There was Christmas with its weeks of fasting and food preparation, eating and carolling, praying and receiving blessing. Easter: six long days of church services, the prohibition of food and drink the night before confession and communion, the pounding in a child's head and the growling in his gut as he smelled the food in the baskets brought to the priest to be blessed – he thought he would faint – and the terrible spectacle of an old, old woman, crippled with arthritis, crawling grotesquely on her knees to the altar. There was Green Sunday, in May, when prayers were said for the crop. In 1923, and Edmonton *Journal* reporter watched the celebration:

> Thanks are given for the green blades springing up through the earth and for green leaves upon the trees. Parties of worshippers led by the priest journey out into the fields and growing crops and there ask blessings upon their lands. Everywhere and on every farm green branches and sprigs of spruce or poplar are hung; around eaves of their straw thatches; on the outer walls of their cottages; along the rafters and beams of their inner rooms; saplings are cut to decorate the posts of their gates and even their dumb animals are decorated with greenstuffs in their mane or tastily [sic] arranged on their harness.

There was *khram* or the celebration of the saint's day after whom the church was named, a curious combination of religious and secular enthusiasms. The Greek Orthodox Church in Shandro, in 1933, staged a major production and someone who was there wrote about it for the Vegreville *Observer*:

> Bishop Arseny [and five priests] were greeted at the parish door by the above-mentioned priests, the Church procession, ten flower girls and the Church choir. This picturesque procession wended its way to the Church, where the sermon began. Between two and three thousand people, some from thirty and forty miles away, were present.
>
> As is the usual custom on this day the vast throng dispersed to their homes in the district. Every home was the scene of a large feast accommodating the guests as they travelled from house to house. As many as six tables were served at some homes during the afternoon and evening.
>
> As the evening drew near the younger set gathered at the dancing pavilion where a large crowd enjoyed itself till well after midnight. George Achtemichuk and his Smoky Lake Boys supplied some peppy music.[121]

And there were the funerals. From one man's memory these fragments of the scene: a room lighted by candles contains the homemade coffin and around it a group of professional wailers, women paid to spend the night grieving over the deceased's body, tear their hair, and weep bitterly, exclaiming, "Oh, my poor, poor Petro, you worked so hard all your life and now, look, you leave a wife and six little ones! Oh, Petro, how you suffered at the end! Ah, how we shall miss you and long for you!"; the harder they could make the family cry, the more they were paid. At the head of the coffin a man sits reading the Psalms hours on end, with slugs from a bottle of whiskey to keep him awake. Finally, the funeral. An evening prayer service and a morning prayer service are followed by a procession to the church, religious banners flapping ahead in the wind, with the coffin bumped in a wagon over the ruts and stones. Mass at the church, another procession to the cemetery and, finally, as the grave is closed over, candles and money are tossed onto the lid of the coffin so that the dead man may more easily find his way to heaven.

The churches themselves were modest wooden buildings (the Shepenitz church was finally built of brick after fires twice destroyed the wood structures) constructed by parishioners themselves with volunteer labour or, if the parish could afford it, by contractors. "Because Dad had some Clydesdale horses, he hauled the bricks for the Shepenitz church all the way from Vegreville, on his own time. Of course he didn't get paid for it!" There was neither time nor money to build the ostentatious structures that would become popular in the cities. Technology was limited to manual labour, and materials to whatever the earth threw up in the vicinity. The design was rudimentary but fulfilled the basic requirements: a small, cross-shaped chapel facing east, a bulb for a dome, a cross indicating the rite and an iconostas – the partition that separates the congregation from the tabernacle – initially a simple slab of board hung willy-nilly with icons, later elaborately carved and hand-painted screens illustrated with seraphic Madonnas, humourless saints and a judgemental God; perhaps floral motifs painted in a strip along the walls and a glowering Christ inside the dome, if there was an artisan in the district. Always the cloths, embroidered by the women, on the altar, the lecturn, the confessionals and around the icons. Beeswax candles and musky incense. A little bit of stained glass. A plate of bread. All that was necessary to worship God.

Our church was a small wooden one. There were no pews. You stood for the two and a half hours of the mass. No choir, just a *dyak* [cantor] and some singers. There were religious pictures with paper flowers all around them. A group of girls would get together some time before Easter and scrub the church floor and make these flowers. It was so cold in there in the winter! There was just a wood-burning heater that they would start up on Saturday but even so your feet froze during the service.

This was the accomplished church, a dignified if chilly building after years of praying in neighbours' houses or in halls or in old schoolhouses.

On March 26, 1900, the future members (all men) of the Temple of the Nativity of the Most Holy Mother of God at Rabbit Hill had a meeting to propose the building of a church, three years after their arrival in Canada. They began by explaining why they were here:

> We, the undersigned Rusyny [Ruthenians] of the Greek Catholic rite from the land of Halych, in the state of Austria in Europe, emigrated from our land in the years 1896, 1897 and 1898, partly because of poverty-stricken conditions to which Ruthenians were subjected by Polish [landlord] and Jewish [moneylender] elements and which drove Ruthenians of Halych across the seas.

They described what they had been doing for the last three years:

> When each one settled on his land, his first concern was to obtain the necessities of life, expecially the cultivation of his land which was covered with thick impenetrable forest. Since many of us settled on this land without any means of livelihood, we had to leave our homes in quest of different types of labour to provide food for ourselves and our children. As a result of this kind of existence, everyone has made progress and, finding ourselves in better circumstances after two or three years, though we are still far from wealthy, we have embarked on the building of a temple of God after having been visited by a priest two or three times during this period.

They had problems even before they started on the church:

> . . . in making our decision about such an important and blessed task, [we know] we shall suffer a good deal of distress before we conclude the envisioned task. Not only do we suffer because of our lack of finances . . . but we suffer still more from another cause. In spite of the fact that there are altogether sixty-five

Ruthenian families to all of whom the church is essential, yet when it came to building, our brothers divided into three groups. One of the groups supports Orthodoxy, and what causes more sorrow is that not only do they not help us but they also seek to thwart us. Another group . . . have withdrawn because of distance.

Finally they got down to the business of the construction plans.

Construction will begin on March 26, by the Latin calendar, on the Monday following Holy Cross Sunday in the year 1900. Construction under the supervision of Wierzba, a builder of German birth, will continue with God's help and ours. He will be paid two dollars a day. Half of the congregation will undertake to help him the first three days of the week and the other half will help the remaining three days until the building is completed.

They were not without a sense of moment:

We find courage and joy in the hope that we shall derive satisfaction from an accomplished task and can praise God in the Trinity that this temple of God will be a reminder to our descendants that their fathers raised this building for them with much hardship in order that they might honour God and lift up their prayers to Him for their forebears, the founding fathers of this temple, as long as it remains on this spot.

Probably, further down the road and in another generation, they would also decide to build additions, add a cupola, buy a bell, fix up the basement, replace the wood-burning stove with a furnace, install pews and a chandelier. By that point, the church would reflect far more their Canadian lifestyles than Ukrainian traditions and by then – by the time the church was spacious, comfortable, even opulent – it would be half empty.

The Canadian-born generation went to church but did not

necessarily approve of what went on there. Stories about priests in the old country still circulated like ragtags of folklore, stories about greed, lust, treachery, and corruption – like the Jewish tavern-keeper, the priest was the butt of jokes. When this attitude was attached to the fact that the parishes in Canada were organized by the people themselves to ensure a degree of local, democratic control, the Ukrainian-Canadians grew up as the religiously ambivalent generation.

A Greek Catholic priest born in Europe may still believe that "in the old country the priest had dominant influence on the folk and he was appreciated. His work was appreciated and his voice had value." But the folklore says otherwise:

On a hill stands a church
With a large dome.
I have a barrel full of wine
And I drink it everyday,
And I drink it everyday.
In church the bells ring and ring
And in the inside "bom, bom"
"Ever lasting memory," I sing
Because I am a priest.
A rich man has died,
To the funeral I go along the side
Ever lasting memory I sing
Because I am a priest.
The poor unfortunate has a house
Covered with sheaves.
But my house is like a palace
Because I am a priest.
The peasant eats sauerkraut
And borsch with peas,
But I have a fat chicken
Because I am a priest.
A girl is coming to confession

More than once,
Come here my girl!
Let me kiss you,
Because here no one sees us.[122]

A man's older brothers, born in the Ukraine, spoke resentfully of the priest as a spy who would disclose to the landlord the contents of damaging confessions. And several times I was told how food, brought to the priest by the peasants as an offering or payment, was tossed to his pigs. These tales may be apocryphal; more to the point is one woman's complaint that the church collaborated in the overt exploitation of peasants.

> My mother was quite critical. She said that the priest had his own home, he had a servant or two, and he lived very well according to the standards of those days. But he never spent any time educating the people, lecturing or starting schools. The priest was not critical of the going to the taverns. She said the women worked hard, long hours while the men went to these taverns, spending money. She felt it was the duty of the people who were educated, like the priests, to do something about these things but she said they never lifted a finger. In fact she felt they cooperated with the landowners against the peasants.

The behaviour of the church in Canada was far less callous but to a lot of people it was still a reactionary institution. At worst, it was exploitative and self-interested, at best, irrelevant. And the anti-clericalism of the old country intelligentsia became focussed in the new on the figure of the priest himself. Disbelieving the sermons of the priest, they stopped going to church altogether. They complained that the language of the church was incomprehensible and that the European-born priests were too histrionic. Young men flaunted their nonchalance by going to the church only to meet girls. They complained that during the Depression, when the community was poor, the church still demanded donations and that, faced with the poverty and frustration and fear of the people, it couldn't answer their question, "what shall we do?" The church found itself replaced not surprisingly by the Communist party. Years later, many rejoined the church but not without a residue of bitterness.

"During the Depression the priest couldn't go through town without some people laughing at him. But after the war they had to belong somewhere – they were being called Communists – so they joined the church." "In the old country the priests were rich, they owned property. And here you're still not supposed to talk back to them. So the members aren't as strong as they used to be because they've been abused. They've lost faith and the churches are becoming museums." "Mundare, that was the centre of all the trouble. As I said, they [mortgage companies] were selling land and there were quite a few priests who bought it and chased the families out. During the Depression that's how it was and how can you believe in priests like that? And I wouldn't say the Greek Orthodox priests were any better. A priest is a priest." "On Sunday we went to church, a Catholic church. Heavens! The priest began to scold the people, call them swine, fools and sheep. I said to myself, 'Do I have to listen to this?' So I stopped going to church." "I was raised as a Greek Catholic and my parents gave a lot of money but Dad became a socialist and when he died the church at first refused to bury him in consecrated ground. Only after some big shots in the church strong-armed the priest did he finally get buried." "I remember once when the priests came to bless our house and they got their sleigh stuck at the gate. Mother had to go dig them out because they just sat there and refused to do it for themselves. On top of all that, she then gave them ten dollars for the blessing! The next year they came and got stuck again. This time I wouldn't let her go out and help them and, sure enough, eventually they dug themselves out. For the blessing I tossed them fifty cents, which they took, after giving me dirty looks. That was thirteen years ago and they haven't been back since."

Such people, with chagrin and cynicism rooted in painful personal experience or in a political critique of the church as instrumental in the abuse and confounding of the people, reject out of hand any sentimentalities about their history. They would not accept, for instance, that "while etching their way slowly into the Canadian soil, [the Ukrainians'] greatest longing was for their own Ukrainian priest"[123] or, "on this religious background lies the whole history of the Ukrainian settlers in Canada."[124] They would point out that the consolations of a priest were sought out because they were so desperately isolated from their community and profoundly alienated from the Anglo-Saxon culture, that the building of churches and the summoning of priests were acts, not so much of a devout people as of a dislocated one, anxiously recreating the forms of social stability familiar to them. The repetition of old world religious practices in the new was as much an exercise in cultural bonding and group solidarity as it was an expression of authentic spirituality.

As for the true believers, they went to church and prayed and fasted and celebrated much as they had always done. And grumbled about priests. The priest was the convenient target for all the complaints they had about the way the church conducted its affairs, the control it had over their lives and the sophisticated, not to say baffling, points of doctrine it preached in answer to their basic questions. It was difficult to attack a doctrine or an office but it was easy to poke fun at the priest down the road and to keep track of his human frailties. In Canada all the more so, since he didn't have the state's authority on which to prop himself. He was demystified.

I was told about a Greek Orthodox priest defrocked for pederasty and bootlegging. Someone got a laugh out of a priest who refused to baptise children not named for their patron saint. A joke was made about a priest's accent and about a group of "die-hard" church-goers in the thirties who, scandalized by a community decision to install pews in the Shepenitz church, hid them in the belfry. I heard lamentations about priests' arrogance and the pretensions of priests' wives. There was the priest who beat his children in public and whose wife was a careless housekeeper. The parish couldn't afford to continue repainting the house and replacing furniture, so he had to go.

But there are also priests respectfully and affectionately

remembered, their good works still enumerated and their humility gratefully acknowledged. "The priests in those days had a hard time. They worked hard for us and were poor, God bless them. The roads were bad, the parishes didn't have much money, they had to get around in a wagon even in bad weather. Our priest would play the violin for us at christenings, drop in for a visit and a drink of whiskey, help out with the stooking or shovelling grain. What can I say? A good man."

And whatever justification critics, cynics, and wags have had in their hostility towards the institution of the church, the priest has always had his own point of view on the communities he served. He was not always charmed.

Mostly the people living in and around Two Hills, they are farmers. In the work of the community they are very, very slow. For example, when it is a question about making a decision about their own farm, they are making the decision in a few minutes. But when it comes to economical support for the church, then they take years to realize that the priest is also a human being, that they should give him a raise, five dollars a month. You see, if I would say to them, "If you do not give me something this month, I'm quitting!" they would rather close down the church than pay to me.

I think the biggest trouble is economic, maintenance of the life of the priest. In the old country, church was not dependent on their support. Absolutely not. It was supported by the government so that its priests lived as intelligent persons who went to university and were not dependent on the community. In Canada we are dependent and it is something humiliating. If people are church members, they should be honest. It costs for the heating, the lights, the minimum wages for me. But absolutely they are indifferent. Ten years ago they paid ten, fifteen dollars a year for membership and still they are paying that amount. It is not easy for me.

My first responsibility when I came to this area was to visit the people. Do missionary work from house to house. I'll give you an example. The parish at Ispas. I went early in the morning with my wife and called on B—. Then we went to the church and waited and waited. Then came B— at 10:30. But still no one else. I asked him where were all the people? He said, "The secretary, well, his son wrecked the truck. As for the women, they have all become Seventh Day Adventists and the men all became hotel owners. When they quarrel with their wives they go to the hotel." So I did not open the church. I said a prayer – there were six of us by then – then we went to B— 's for dinner. This was my first service at Ispas. You can imagine my impression. However, I had a list of twenty-four Orthodox families. Next day I took a map and a Bible and drove off. For three days I drove and told everybody that on October 31 they will have their first service. "I want to see you and your children there." Seventy-six people came.

And an old Greek Orthodox priest, finishing out his vocation in a small, northern town, recalls the halcyon days of serving in an ethnically cohesive, more or less faithful community in the Two Hills area in the thirties. Oddly enough, it had its rewards.

I never had much money. It's nice to have money but it's even nicer to have a purpose in your life. If you can contribute something to life and make it felt, then you are rich person. I think that's what I've done. I shouldn't say that, I don't like that ego, but sometimes I think, so what? I never wanted to quit. I sometimes wanted a holiday, go somewhere and forget my troubles, but I never had intentions of quitting.

In these towns they respected the priesthood and they were proud of me. The young priest. They responded to me in a friendly way, even when they were Communists. I used to have the service and about three o'clock in the afternoon they would meet outside the church and we would have such meetings! I spoke to them. It was a sunny day and I stood up in a truck. They wanted me to talk. So I prepared seven subjects about an hour and a half each. To give you an example, I compared Christianity and Communism. It was well-prepared and there were two or three hundred people. They listened respectfully, they didn't argue. At the end they nicely asked me questions and I answered. . . . They asked questions about religion. They wanted to know about the liturgy. I didn't hide anything from them. I told them that they are all human people and that I had no right to accuse any of them. And I says, do not hate people, hate their sins. I have seen sinners after they repent become very nice people. I said, hate their sins but not their natures.

They had yet enough to eat, but when it comes to money, they didn't have much money. They had just enough to live. So, one Sunday afternoon after service I told them: "I came here and you are taking good care of me as a priest and I have no complaint against you, but financially, yes. I don't accuse you but I don't have enough money to buy shoes for my kids, so please help me, otherwise I am going to leave you." I used to go visiting in the evening. I'd visit people and they'd say, "Oh, oh, here he comes." I'd say, "Don't be scared of me. I need money but not by force. Talk to your wife, your husband and make a decision and next time if I come to you, maybe you will have a cheque. Big, small, but do help us." And people, somehow, they understood me, and they helped. . . . You have to dedicate your time for people. And it's a pleasure to work for a good cause. Everybody has a certain big cause. Sometimes you are discouraged, but you know you are on the right side.

The Protestant churches in Alberta were as anxious as the Catholic and Orthodox ones to minister to the Ukrainian-Canadians; in fact, they had a double mission. To provide religious services to people struggling to organize their communities and to convert them to a more "civilized" faith than the one they brought with them from the dismal backwaters of Eastern Europe.

They are peasants, the majority illiterate and superstitious; some of them bigoted fanatics, some of them poor, dumb, driven cattle, some intensely patriotic, some embittered by centuries of wrong and oppression, some anarchists – the sworn enemies alike of Church and State. The Slav is essentially religious but his religious instincts have never yet found true expression[125]

To be fair, not every Protestant missionary felt this way. In 1937, a Ukrainian United Church minister criticized the work of his church among the Ukrainians. He felt that the United Church had been too eager to assimilate; that their religious program had been more social than spiritual. They had offered more Canadianism than Christ. Such a policy had, in his opinion, turned the Ukrainians against Protestantism as being unpatriotic to their own race. The Ukrainian who became a Protestant lost stature with his own countrymen.[126] And there were Protestants who eventually realized that the Ukrainians' attachment to the "ritual and formalism in their worship" meant that attempts to "reform" them from without, through the medium of an "alien church," were unlikely to be successful. And that reformation of their idolatrous ways from "within" was highly "improbable."[127]

In any event, the Protestants persevered with their mission schools, mission hospitals (often the only medical service available to the farmers), and ordinations among the Ukrainians. For most of their converts these activities touched only tangentially upon their lives, showing them an alternative social organization without challenging their own attachment to Ukrainian-Canadian institutions. Thus they would attend a Protestant Sunday school in the schoolhouse, sing hymns, pick up some more English, and go back next month to the Orthodox or Catholic church for mass. They would listen to Baptist radio programs – better Baptist than no religious observance at all on Sundays – when there wasn't a service in the local Ukrainian church. At the hospitals, they would gratefully deliver their bodies into the hands of the Methodist doctor but keep their souls to themselves.

Nevertheless, a number of Ukrainians were converted, and not always as dupes of patronizing Anglo-Saxons. For one thing, there had been Protestant churches organized in the old country as part of a progressive, anticlerical movement among the intelligentsia (since the Greek Catholic church was a state-supported institution in the Austro-Hungarian empire, the venom of the radicals was directed equally towards it as to the oppressive state itself). For another, some Ukrainians in Canada, fed up with the elaborate ritual and ceremony of their own church, suspicious of its mystifications and appalled by the arrogance of priests, yet not prepared to become anti-religious turned instead to the more rational, modest, and homely atmosphere of the Protestant churches. And yet another group, disenchanted with socialist politics but constitutionally incapable of rejoining the Ukrainian church, adopted Protestantism as a decent compromise.

In 1937, the religious affiliations of the population in the Two Hills area were: 50 percent Greek Catholics, 15 percent Greek Orthodox, 10 percent Seventh Day Adventist (established in 1916). An impressive 25 percent were members of the Ukrainian Labour and Farm Temple Association (ULFTA), an affiliate of the Communist Party of Canada.[128]

These percentages reflect the facts that the majority of Ukrainian immigrants had come from the Greek Catholic territories of the Austro-Hungarian Empire and had retained their commitment to that church even after the establishment of a Ukrainian Greek Orthodox Church in Canada; that evangelical Protestantism had made inroads; and that the Communist party was a popular alternative to all of them. (Later, membership in the Greek Orthodox Church would increase as disaffected Communists returned to the fold.)

In a way, the establishment of the Ukrainian Greek Orthodox Church in Canada was as much of a political feat as the organization of the ULFTA and it remains one of the most significant accomplishments of the immigrants; its survival and growth are largely the work of the Canadian-born intelligentsia. To this day, membership in it may reflect a political stance vis-a-vis the question of Ukrainian identity.

Some history is helpful here. The Greek Catholics from Western Ukraine were members of the Uniate Church, a compromise institution established in the sixteenth century by the Roman Catholic Polish overlords of that region. In an attempt to break the back of the growing Ukrainian nationalist movement, the Poles outlawed the Greek Orthodox Church (the official church for all of the Ukraine since 988 A.D.) and organized the Uniate, in which the Greek Orthodox ceremonies and liturgy were retained but the Roman Catholic pope was recognized as infallible in matters of dogma. The assumption was that this church – "Roman to the educated priesthood but Greek to the unlettered peasantry" – would "serve as a bridge over which the adherents of the Greek Orthodox Church would ultimately be brought into the Roman Catholic fold."[129]

This, however, did not generally happen. In spite of Austrian religious repression and the subservience of the Greek Catholic bishop to the pope, the Ukrainian Greek Catholics saw their church, with its Slavonic language and familiar rituals, as an oasis of cultural identity and group strength in the desert of Polish and Austrian oppression. Damned if they would "Latinize" themselves and become Poles!

The Ukrainians emigrated without priests and when they began building churches and looking for clergy they discovered that local Roman Catholic bishops had been given authority to look after the needs of the Greek Catholics, that the Greek Catholic bishop back in Austria advised the Ukrainians in Canada to accept this aid, that the pope had decreed that no married Greek Catholic clergy could migrate to Canada (celibacy of clergy was a Polish, not Ukrainian custom) and that the local Roman Catholic priests were completely unfamiliar with the Ukrainian language and the Greek Catholic ceremonies. "There were among them (some even exist today), individuals who would want to drown our Rite in the sea of the Latin majority."[130]

Finally, the Roman Catholic bishop admitted that the work of his church was ineffective among the Ukrainians – it had reached the point where Greek Catholics were even making contact with Russian Greek Orthodox bishops in California – and in 1913 the Ruthenian (that is, Ukrainian) Greek Catholic Episcopal Corporation of Canada was incorporated, independent of the Roman Catholic bishops.

As for the priests, the first (celibate) Greek Catholic clergy arrived as early as 1902 in the persons of three Basilian fathers and four Sisters Servant. Mundare parish became the centre of their activities as they circulated from there to the local missions: Star, Wostok, New Kiew, Plain Lake, Derwent, Myrnam, Bellis, Lake Eliza, and others. Their work was basic: to build a house and a chapel, to serve at mass, to open a school, to perform weddings, baptisms and funerals. Later, came the embellishments and the disputes:

Father A. Fylypiw arrived at Mundare in January 1905. In two years of his pastoral work in Mundare and district Father Fylypiw laid the base under organized religious life. He initiated the May Devotions which were so popular and had a large attendance. He organized the Apostleship of Prayer. During his time he painted the chapel and began the construction of the belfry which in the summer months served as a chapel. People would stand outside. The large doors would be opened and one could easily follow and participate in the Holy Liturgy. Father Fylypiw survived a "strike" of the cantor, who demanded one dollar and one bushel of wheat from each farm for his services. He was given half of that amount. . . .

Father Fylypiw took part in many meetings dealing with the organizational work of parishes. On December 9th, 1905 it was passed at a meeting that half of last year's carolling donations be utilized to purchase something for the chapel. The next carolling donation was alloted to the building of the belfry. Two crosses were to be erected, one at the cemetery, and another one by the monastery. They agreed to fence off the cemetery and plant trees around it. "No unfortunate episodes befell me," comments Father Fylypiw. But all meetings were not so fortunate. During the second meeting around Moskalyk, on December 16th of that year, it was resolved that fifty cents was to be donated by each one towards the building fund of a church and the carolling donation was to be used to buy a thurible. Someone hollered out, "It is not necessary for us to build a church, because the land must be signed over to the Basilians or to the Bishop, and we don't want any of that!" Or at a meeting on December 20th near Seniuks, a motion was passed to cut the priest's and cantor's salaries. The salaries were such that there was nothing to cut. Father Filas received $176.00 for all his pastoral work in these districts. Father Fylypiw emphatically insisted, saying, "we will not settle for less and for the time being we are not demanding an increase!" His encouragement to build a church, school and reading room was rejected because "we are waiting for the title. If the title belongs to the community, we'll do everything, if not, nothing!" And Father Fylypiw makes this observation: "This meeting had a most depressing effect upon me." This was a painful blow to the idealist faced with the reality of human ignorance.[131]

The conflict over land titles – who should have it, the church or the community? – the amount of money spent on a processional cross, a bell, and a thurible, the idealism of the priests – one can see already in 1906 the provocations that would split the Ukrainian-Canadian community.

From the priest's point of view, however, his mission was strenuous, demanding and often thankless. He had miles to travel between churches, by horse and wagon, oxen and cart in every kind of weather. "Returning from Wostok on the 19th of December, Father Tymochko suffering from asthma, froze to death on the sleigh."[132] There were duties to perform that could not wait. "I am very ill. On me were placed cuppings. Afternoon I confessed the children. I am so ill I hardly finished saying the Liturgy. Then I went to Wostok."[133] As a member of a religious order, his mode of living was absolutely spartan. As the target of an increasingly skeptical community, he saw his mission work undermined. By 1935, a majority of school trustees in Mundare voted to abolish the teaching of religion in the public schools and thus began the "de-Ukrainianization of pioneer Mundare." A Mr. White, mayor and school trustee, plus his supporters among "Communist henchmen" outvoted the likes of Father Shewchuk, Mr. M. Korchinsky, Mr. P. Krezanowsky, et al, and the Ukrainian school was shifted out of the public school and into the national hall.

Typically, the Sisters meanwhile performed "feminine" tasks and social services for the community: organized an orphanage, taught young girls housekeeping skills, took care of the sick, and supervised the housekeeping of the churches.

Among the original Ukrainian immigrants had been a small number of adherents to the Russian Greek Orthodox Church. These people were served by Russian Orthodox missions established by priests from California and Alaska. Although there was little more independent Ukrainian national consciousness attached to this church than to the Uniate, it was almost identical in form and spirit with the original Greek Orthodox Church of the Ukraine and quite naturally, in Canada, attracted many members from the Greek Catholic Church who were suspicious of the Latinizing pressures of the Roman Catholics.

But there were very many Greek Catholics who felt that the Russian Orthodox church was not a meaningful answer to the grievances that were piling up. The decree against the emigration of married clergy was onerous: only three per cent of the Ukrainian Greek Catholic priests in Galicia were celibate, not enough to go around all the Ukrainians in North America.[134] Besides, the settlers were suspicious of monks: they seemed a creation of Polish Catholicism. The nationalistic intelligentsia was further appalled by a decree that placed their priests under the jurisdiction of Roman Catholic bishops. Then there was the matter of church property: wherever possible, it was incorporated under the Roman Catholic bishop of the diocese, later under the Greek Catholic bishop. Many parishioners, increasingly aware of their rights in a country without a state church, felt the property should belong to the parish, in spite of the arguments of the priests that "it was risky to have this church property signed on to the faithful because of the inexperience and unstabliness [sic] to various propaganda of the faithful."[135] Even the Greek Catholic Basilians were not above suspicion:

> The real object of these missionaries was considered to be the "Latinization" of the Greek Catholic Church, which in Galicia had meant yielding to Polish domination, hence a form of treachery. By some, the Basilian priests were dubbed "wolves in sheep's clothing!"[136]

All of these sentiments culminated finally in the establishment of the Saints Vladimir and Olga Church in Winnipeg, whose membership announced itself independent of both the Roman Catholic bishops and their own Uniate bishop in Austria. Eventually, this church became a cathedral within the Greek Catholic Episcopal Corporation and the opposition of the "independentists" subsided, but the Basilians never forgave them their hostility. Thirty years later, in 1938, Father Nil Savaryn, Basilian (and now a bishop in Edmonton), was still denouncing them: "The centre from which the black blemish emanated was the little church [Saints Vladimir and Olga] in Winnipeg. . . . It was the place of rebellion, chaos, and every kind of evil. . . . From there came the affliction to all of Canada."[137]

The affliction he is referring to is the remarkable growth of Ukrainian nationalism that would ultimately inspire the organization of a new Ukrainian church in Canada. Resentful of the Uniate church's ties with the papacy, of celibacy, of property allotment; aware that parishioners had the democratic right to debate matters of parish policy and even to disagree with the priest; impatient with the refusal of the Russian Orthodox church to recognize Ukrainian as a separate nationality, fired by events in Europe – the growth of Ukrainian nationalism and liberalism, the Bolshevik Revolution, and a breakaway Ukrainian Greek Orthodox movement in which both laity and clergy participated; infuriated by the opposition of Greek Catholic Bishop Budka to secular residential schools or institutes that the Ukrainian-Canadian intelligentsia were founding in the cities, the people were soon to demand an independent, democratically organized, Ukrainian-nationalist church in Canada.

It was the petty intelligentsia – school teachers, newspaper editors, bookstore owners, progressive priests – who first brought the nationalist message to the Ukrainian-Canadians. They founded their own paper, the *Ukrainian Voice* (its masthead: "In education and union lies our strength"), and drummed into their readers the need to use "Ukrainian" as their ethnic designation. In 1907, the Ukrainian Teachers' Association of Canada was formed, with the aims of "self-education, the cultural elevation of the Ukrainian people to the standards of other nations and material aid for teachers.'[138] Inspired by the social democratic and socialist movements in the Ukraine, they saw themselves as enlightened rationalists whose responsibility it was to banish the (foreign) forces of papacy, Polonization, Russification, and obscurantism. They were to lead their people into the New Jerusalem of ethnic cohesiveness and self-respect, individual intellectual independence and communal self-determination. As an editorial in the *Voice* put it in 1910:

> It is necessary that the people do not allow themselves to be led blindly by any kind of religion or church. . . . It is necessary that they should understand the meaning of religion as morality in life about which they can and must analyse and understand. The concern is not about religion on paper but about religion in life. Let us remember that learning and justice is the greatest religion.[139]

The fight was on. The nationalist intelligentsia accused the Basilians of being Jesuits and unpatriotic (towards the Ukraine), the French-Canadian Roman Catholic bishops of being greedy for the parishioners' property, and their church of being a "business corporation or a company like the CPR." [140] Finally, just before the

First World War, they came close to calling for the establishment of an independent church. Again the *Voice* speaks for them.

> Catholicism is as alien to us as is Muscovite Orthodoxy . . . when the *Ukrainian Voice* has in mind "Orthodoxy" then it is such an Orthodoxy which should be ours and national, and not Muscovite or any other kind.[141]

In July 1918, in the Ukrainian National Home in Saskatoon, 154 people witnessed the foundation of the Ukrainian Greek Orthodox Church of Canada. Serving on the National Committee from Alberta were three farmers, two teachers, and one medical student. The rhetoric of the proceedings underlines the association made between the new church and Ukrainian nationalism. To resist the church was to declare yourself indifferent to the idea of a separate Ukrainian identity.

> You, the People, must support the first steps of Your most enlightened sons and advance the matter of an independent church organization.
>
> It is time already and urgent to destroy the Roman Mamon and make our church a great institution, which must look after the religious, moral and educational elevation of the people.
>
> It is time already and urgent to free ourselves from the uninvited foreign guardians.
>
> It is time already and urgent to remove from our church celibacy, which is demoralizing our clergy and people.
>
> That is why it is the sacred duty of every Ukrainian to work sincerely for the organization of an independent Ukrainian Greek Orthodox Church.
>
> That is why it is the sacred duty of every Ukrainian to become a member of the Ukrainian Greek Orthodox Brotherhood.
>
> When this will be achieved then with the help of God and through the work of all of us the Ukrainian Greek Orthodox Church will become a true democratic institution which will be

working for the glory of God and the welfare of the people.[142]

The constitution of the Ukrainian Greek Orthodox Church in Canada established it, in intent at least, as the polar opposite of the Greek Catholic. Its supreme organ, the Synod, is to consist of half clergy, half laypersons. The church and its property are to be owned by "the people." The bishop and his successors must be chosen by the people themselves, and they must be "only sincere Ukrainians." Priests must be married, or single of older age. "A majority of members decide any matter. Members have the right to request another priest if the present one does not satisfy the needs according to the wishes of the people." The churches are required to be built in "our ancient style." Everything "Roman" is to be banished: "rosaries, pictures with the heart over the chest, pictures with crowns; Jesus, Mary and others, tin figures representing Christ on the cross and plaster-cast figures must be removed from the churches, as these contradict the Holy Scriptures. The Ukrainian National Church must adhere to the eastern rite and this may never change."[143]

As it turned out, even by the time the first generation had grown to adulthood, the character of this church, in its everyday, rural practice, was not always consistent with the ideals of the constitution. But the ideals were provocative and innovative, and the reaction of Greek Catholics was predictable. "The Godless Church for the Ukrainians!" "Church Subversion!" "The Black Hand of the Saskatoon Clique!" "The Ukrainian Church of Foreign Protestantism!"[144] There were charges and counter-charges, libel suits and fines. By 1924, however, the Ukrainian Greek Orthodox Church claimed seventy parishes and that, more than any rhetoric or propaganda, was the resolution of the struggle.

Shepenitz, Ispas, Mundare, Slawa, Zawale, Bruderheim, and Vilna. Thousands of Ukrainian-Canadians were raised as Greek Orthodox Christians as the churches became organized.

One day my mother visited her neighbour when a priest was there. In those days the walls were decorated, up near the ceiling with all kinds of pictures: calendars, family photos, icons. A little while earlier, a guy had gone around the district selling calendars with a picture of three Ukrainian poets: Franko, Shevchenko, Drahomaniw. Under them was a picture of a lady in white representing Ukrainian culture. This neighbour had this on her wall. The priest looked at it and said who are these *bohomazi* [idolators]? and told her to take them down. When my mother told me this – I was already teaching – that was that. I told her it just wasn't so. The local National Home had a library of Ukrainian books and in one of his sermons the local priest said we shouldn't read any of them. The priest in Saskatoon preached that those kids who were at the Mohyla Institute would go to hell. Well I took offense at that. I'm there to get an education and he tells me I'm going to hell. So I said, to hell with him and later joined the Orthodox church.

As we shall see, it was an objective of the new church, and some of the organizations it was to spawn, to provide an institution in Canada that would socialize the Ukrainian-Canadians as Ukrainians. The Methodist missionary Dr. Hunter had complained that "young and enthusiastic emissaries" of this church had hung around his mission school "to make sure we would not succeed in 'assimilating' our young charges."[145] In 1935, at a ceremony dedicating the Ukrainian Greek Orthodox Church in Vegreville, the priest assured the congregation that, thanks to this church, the Ukrainian people were now on the "right road to national uplift"[146] and the archbishop warned that Ukrainian-Canadians do not want to "become forcedly denationalized"; the proceedings ended with both *God Save the King* and the Ukrainian national anthem.

So there emerged nationalist priests as well. One who had started his ministry as a Russian Orthodox priest explains why he transferred his parish to the Ukrainian Orthodox church.

When I started to work it was a challenge, because at that time most of them came from Bukovyna. They didn't have enough understanding of who they were, they'd call themselves Russians. Because Russian priests were taking care of them. I stayed there for sixteen years and after about twelve years of hard work, I joined the Ukrainian Orthodox church. That's the place for us, and it didn't take me very much time to convince them. Of course, I did it gradually. The church is one church, but it comprises many nationalities; we are Ukrainians, then our church will become Ukrainian. We should have our own heirarchy, bishops and priests, and finally they consented. That was a battle, but I liked it. I was battling with my own people, mentally. So I began to work, we had gatherings and I used to teach them evening lessons, then we had a Ukrainian concert. I was ordained in the Russian Orthodox church but deep down in my heart I realized that we were all Ukrainians. So, I did my justice for those people.

The fuss has died down and the two churches, Catholic and Orthodox, coexist peacefully enough in the communities, often across the road from each other. Other passions divide the town now, and politically and psychologically the people have little invested in their choice of church. The ecumenical spirit moves them sometimes to attend each other's services and the fine points of a dispute sixty years ago are forgotten, if they were ever known.

Other towns like Willingdon, Myrnam, Vegreville had trouble between the two churches – the Orthodox not having anything to do with the Catholics – but we never had that kind of trouble. We'd go carolling to Orthodox homes, they'd come to ours. When I was on the church executive I used to tell the priest, "Don't you try to stir up anything. We live together good here."

When we were living in Hairy Hill there wasn't a Catholic church there so we went to the Greek Orthodox church in Shepenitz. What difference does it make? But the priest there was one of those immigrant priests and he used to thunder, "He who is not a Greek Orthodox, he is like a wolf in sheep's clothing!" My wife and I walked out right in the middle of that sermon. He'll go to hell, right down to the bottom, for talking like that. We're all just God's children, trying to eke out a living on this earth.

If there is a conflict, it's expressed privately and without much conviction – gossip about the relations between the Basilian monks and nuns and the feeling that it is "unnatural" for a man to be unmarried. The observation is made that Catholic priests were much stricter than Orthodox ones, expecially as far as raising daughters was concerned. My own observation is that resentment towards the town's elite is expressed in religious terms: "It's the Greek Orthodox who run this place." But as each new generation grows up and goes less often to any church, the antagonisms become anachronistic. There is half-hearted competition as to which church produces the most authentic "Ukrainian" citizen, but a community which celebrates its essential ethnic events together – Orthodox and Catholic priests seated together at the banquet table after the Shevchenko concert – is obviously healed of the old divisive passions and is breaking bread together, now that the passion is dead.

EIGHT

Community

Boy, I used to like dancing, waltz, fox trot, and polka. We had the hall in Royal Park. We used to go there, or to Moscow Hall and then when I worked in Vegreville there were halls in Vegreville. That was about all the social activity I had before I got married, going to the hall. There was nothing else around the place. They used to have some kind of bazaar and social basket sale. The girls would make the basket lunch and then they would sell it, auction it off, and whoever bought your basket you had lunch with him.

– Helen Hryciw

* * *

Prior to the thirties were the good times. My father bought a car in '24, a Touring Chevrolet. It had a soft top and windows like curtains. It could seat six comfortably. We went to church and weddings and parties in it. It was a luxury, we didn't use it every day. And besides the roads were all dirt roads and if you got stuck you had to get a team of horses to pull you out.

– Kay Palamaruk

* * *

Once a Jew moved here and opened a butcher shop. Sold kubassa and confectioneries. There were some guys who played poker, for money, and they ganged up on him, cheated in their games. He lasted two months. His meat turned black and he packed up and left. Ukrainians just didn't want to support him. No way did they go to his store.

– Paul Spak

* * *

Breaking and entering is the most serious crime committed around here now. Some assault cases. But there have been murders on the farms and in Morecambe there was an axe murder. And a lady teacher a few miles from here was drowned in a well. He liked her and she didn't like him so, well. . . . And it wasn't until he was dying of cancer that he confessed. The murder at Morecambe was of a grain elevator agent who was chopped up the night he was counting the money.

– Dick Geleta

* * *

I got married and I had to stay here in Two Hills because my husband had this business, the drugstore. I worked on the farm until my mother died. I had no ideas about leaving for the city to find a job, not at that time. I went to Innisfree to work for a year and then came to Two Hills. We had no money for travel. I never went to Edmonton until I was sixteen. I was scared. And I got lost there!

– Lena Geleta

Whether they grew up on a farm or in a nearby village like Two Hills, Hairy Hill, Kaleland, Morecambe, or Musidora, their community was almost exclusively Ukrainian. The exceptions tended to be the Anglo-Saxons in the white collar jobs: the elevator agent, station agent, bank manager, and, for a while, the school principal and doctor. Aside from these the community became increasingly interrelated through marriage, remained unilingually Ukrainian, and was limited geographically to the immediate area.

The roads. They defined the boundaries of a neighbourhood: if one could get somewhere in a few hours by horse and wagon, then that was still home ground, but if one had to travel overnight then he was beyond the borders of the familiar and among strangers. In 1927, the CPR finally came to Two Hills and to those who could afford the money and time, the larger towns and cities opened up. But for the rest the security and sense of real community were confined to that district accessible by buggy on a rutted dirt road. The earliest transportation routes were Indian trails but by the time the first generation was out of school these had become wagon tracks in the dirt or, when it rained, boggy sloughs; when it snowed, the way was blocked by impassable drifts. A trip to town or to neighbours was a journey. When the major roads were graded (there wouldn't be gravel until after the Second World War) and the automobile introduced, more towns and more neighbours came within the span of "home" so that while their parents had been confounded by the prospect of several days' travel back and forth to Vegreville with a load of grain, this generation would crank up the car and run into town for a dance. But one thing remained consistent: the roads and cars would still take them only as far as the next Ukrainian-Canadian settlement. It would be another generation, with six-cylinder automobiles, paved highways and cash in the wallet, that would find itself at home next door to non-Ukrainians.

The very fact that now there were towns, growing up from small nuclei of grain elevators, a post office, and a grocery store, was the second dramatic change in leisure. Until their development, the only social centre was the church (the quintessential prairie scene on a Sunday afternoon following mass: a gaggle of farmers hanging around the churchyard, gossiping, or at the farm, for a wedding or holiday dinner, or over to the national hall). With the growth of commerce in towns, however, people began to meet in the cafes and stores and beer parlours, and they saw a lot more of each other than they had ever done. They would think twice about taking off an afternoon to go down to Koziaks' place four miles away in the wagon, but they would be glad to sit with them fifteen minutes every week in the hotel cafe, between errands at the blacksmith's and the hardware.

So the town became the focal point of social life: a skating rink in the schoolyard, a baseball diamond ("We'd go by truck to

Kaleland and challenge them to a game"), school picnics, school concerts, chicken suppers at the church, political meetings, sitting around a radio in the store listening to Lux Theatre melodramas. In Two Hills, a women's sports club was active – until the churches became organized and the women split up among the ladies' auxiliaries of the churches. There were dances; the older people sat around the edges on benches, watching and talking, while the young ones waltzed. November 1932: "A hard-times dance is to be held in the Ukrainian National Hall on Friday. Low admission rates. Good lunch and good music." Now that some young working men had cars, boys would drive all the way from Willingdon and Shandro to hustle girls in Two Hills ("Two Hills had two halls. The boys would stroll from one to the other, depending on where most of the good-looking girls were") and thus began courtships and marriages of young people whose parents had never heard of each other, between farmers' daughters and the sons of Massey-Harris dealers.

During the Depression, the movies came to Two Hills.

The Town Clerk,
Two Hills, Alberta.

Dear Sir:

My partner and I have purchased a new motion-picture machine with which we intend putting on shows in suitable, progressive towns in your district. Our equipment will be showing talkies and our programmes are of the highest quality, censored by the Government, and by Church organizations. These shows will provide clean, wholesome entertainment for young and old alike and will foster a community spirit. Furthermore, as the admission price will be very low, attendance will be within the means of everyone's purse. This will attract large crowds to your town and thus increase the volume of business for the merchants.

It is our purpose to put on one of these shows a week in each of six towns, travelling from town to town by car. The shows will always go on as per schedule and there will be no disappointments.[147]

And a Madam A. Fontaine of Edmonton made enquiries to the secretary-treasurer of the municipality as to whether she would require a license to practice palmistry in Two Hills.

They organized their own cultural life. Once a church was planned, meetings had to be called to realize it. And then a choir. Parties. Ladies' handicraft evenings. On Saints Peter and Paul Day in July, a baseball game. When they needed funds for an ice rink for skating and the hockey club, they put on a carnival with queens and gambling games (who was going to stop them?) and made $2000. They built a curling rink from lumber torn from old buildings. All of it volunteer labour.

If they had a car, they could start off an evening with a baseball game in Kaleland, go to the movies in Two Hills and end up, at 2:00 A.M. at a dance in Ranfurly. They would also enjoy an upward shift in status, judging from the fact that anyone's purchase of a car was duly noted in the social columns of the Vegreville *Observer*.

Last week Peter Samoil, of the Krasne district, was seen driving a new car into Two Hills with the air of solemn importance which that particular form of activity seems to require.[148]

But the car was only as locomotive as the weather and roads allowed.

Live News From Country Points: Two Hills

Nick Kieryluk left his car on the Therioux farm for winter storage. This was as far as he could get on his way to Vegreville. Constable Ted Davies enjoyed his sleigh-ride from Vegreville as it was impossible for him to drive his car, owing to the badly drifted roads. The Ukrainian holidays in this town were "dry" as the roads were drifted to such an extent that it was impossible to get to Vegreville to the vendor's store.[149]

There was absolutely nothing remarkable about Two Hills. It was a service town like all the others growing up along the chain of Ukrainian settlement, and the fact that it was not incorporated as a village until 1928, a year after the railroad was put through, reflects its position among farms that were established by late arrivals in the 1910s. But once it got started Two Hills very quickly adopted the basic amenities of urban life, signalling the end of pioneering and the beginning of entrepreneurship. It was the first step of the Ukrainian-Canadians from the homestead to the city.

At that time there was the postmaster, the hotel, Odinsky's store, Dohaniuk, Kolisniak, Yusko; Kolisniak came as a BA bulk agent, Mr. Hrynyk had the livery barn, the high school principal was Jack Laughlin, Nick Dohaniuk (whose farm the town started on) and Kolisniak started a store, Jacob Dolynyk had a store, now the Double V, across the street was George Skakun, another storekeeper, and Peter Odinsky. All pioneers here. A fellow by the name of Flynn was at the CPR station. There was a chop mill and garages, Harasym and Nikilchuk. The Bank of Montreal was the first bank here on the same location they are now. We had a pool hall and Chow Bing had a Chinese cafe. People used to come to the market square behind all those stores. The barn couldn't handle all the horses on Thursdays and so the square was full of teams. The streets were unpaved, maybe seventy-five feet wide. The first banker I remember was Copeland, he came from outside. Laughlin came from Ontario. But almost everybody else was Ukrainian. Even the policeman. At one time, only the station agent, Porter, was a non-Ukrainian.

In 1929, a health inspector from the provincial Board of Health made a tour of inspection of the village. His report is as good a record as any of the life-style of a Ukrainian-Canadian town fifty years ago. It was, all things considered, civilized enough.

The inspector found the conditions of the water supply, from wells about forty-five feet deep, to be "good and satisfactory" and the site of the nuisance grounds "favourable." The privies were in good repair but in a couple of cases "I ordered new pits provided to replace the old pits now full." The matter of garbage. however, was not nearly so gratifying. It seems that some householders were in the habit of tossing their garbage out their doors into their backyards; and the grounds where farmers parked their horse teams were becoming "unsightly caused by deposits of manure and straw." The livery stable (Pete Hrynyk, proprietor) was brand new and clean, the meat market and slaughterhouse also clean, although "I had occasion to order the proprietor to discontinue using that portion of the premises used for the preparation of foods for human consumption, for sleeping quarters." The hotel and the laundry were also found satisfactory, and the stores, the school and the CPR depot beyond reproach. But the pool hall! "Said proprietor (Sam Balcinchi) was given his last warning in respect to maintaining his pool room in a cleaner condition in future." And the Chinese café! "These premises were found unclean and very unsatisfactory throughout. The floors of the kitchen, the tables and shelves, etc., required a thorough washing and scrubbing. A door and window were ordered to bedroom which adjoins that of the kitchen. The basement to be properly cleaned and the toilet repaired and a new pit provided to replace the old pit now full. It was my first intention to prosecute the proprietor, Tom Sing, for gross neglect to the sanitary conditions of his premises, but upon discussing the matter with the local justice of the peace, and with Mr. Skakum councillor, it was decided to give the proprietor another chance, and a notice to abate nuisance was served upon him to clean up and make conditions satisfactory within two days. Fifteen pounds of beef were seized here as unfit for human consumption."[150]

Not to worry. The town was cleaning up its act. That same year the village council passed a number of by-laws designed to discourage the most brutish behaviour and to stamp the Ukrainian-Canadian community with the same sense of propriety and circumspection as one could find in Red Deer or Grande Prairie.

By-Law No. 2: No horses, cattle or sheep the property of any person resident or non resident within the Village shall run at large or graze at any part of the Village at any time.

By-Law No. 3: Owing to the fact that many stray dogs running at large at the Village of Two Hills, and do some harm to the property and tranquillity at night Council of the said Village decided to tax all dogs at the Village, and untaxed dog may be impounded, and if unsearched within thirty-six hours, may be destroyed.

By-Law No. 4: That no person shall speedet [sic] any Auto whicle [sic] more than ten miles per hour on Central Street of the Village.

By-Law No. 5: Traders of above description (i.e. auctioneers, hawkers, pedlars and public traders) shall report themselves to the authority of the village before begin [sic] their business of any description.

By-Law No. 7: That all business places shall be closed on Sunday and holidays . . . except Cafes, Drug and Fruit Stores and Garages, Fruit stores having Groceries and other stock shall also be closed.

Temporary Regulation Notice: Tieying [sic] horses to any Electric Light and Telephone Posts, or Fences, is Strictly prohibited.[151]

Some by-laws were more easily enforced than others. A crowd got together early on a Sunday morning for a dance "noisily conducted by the attenders in spite of the village authority" right in the middle of the town.

In 1930, according to an insurance underwriter's report, there were 160 people living in a fire trap in Two Hills. Granted, the town had a small fire engine and a volunteer fire brigade of thirteen members, but only two of the members had telephones (the exchange gave only day service to boot), the fire station itself was an unheated log building, and townspeople were still disposing live ashes round and about. "Considerable defective wiring was noticed." So were the eight gallons of naphtha, five gallons of turpentine, one hundred pounds of stumping powder and one hundred caps, underground gasoline tanks and barrels of kerosene at the hardware store and garages. Buildings in the business district were of frame and metal-clad construction and the three-storey hotel was the tallest building in town. "The district is subject to serious group fires."[152] Already there had been a fire in the Imperial Oil Supply Depot and another involving five buildings. The loss from that one was $7000, proving, if nothing else, that Two Hills already had something to lose: money.

Vicissitudes and hazards. A Mr. Frank Palesky, having unlawfully erected a shack on Crown reserve land to provide a home for his children while they went to school, refused to remove it. A wind storm knocked over an oil derrick at Brosseau, scattered hay all along the Vermilion River valley and removed laundry "to parts unknown." The weather was a constant preoccupation. Two Hills was, after all, only five years off the farm; townspeople, disdaining radio weather forecasts, stood in their backyards decoding the sunrises and sunsets. The social column in the Vegreville *Observer* never failed to report on weather conditions and progress of the harvest. Alarms were raised about late rains and early frosts, thanksgiving made for heavy yields and the green buds on the caragana bushes.

By 1934, the health inspector was back. This time, order and sanitation prevailed – no offending garbage, no flies in the meat market, no filth in the pool hall – with only one jarring note: the common towel in the Chinese café. Respectable, tidy and sound. The kind of town you could bring your grandmother from Sussex to visit. The kind of town Charles Young, tourist, found so charming.

The bedlam of voices in a strange tongue in the nearest brilliantly-lit cafe, the streets thronged with the beautiful, bright-eyed Ukrainian girls who, in dress and deportment could not be distinguished from our most typical Anglo-Saxons, the more gaily costumed peasant-mothers with their low-hanging dresses and picturesque shawls, and the fine collection of motor-cars taking all the available parking space on both sides of the wide street![153]

This was the public persona, as Ukrainian-Canadian communities gradually assumed the standards and characteristics of Main Street, Canada: the self-congratulation of success stories and gentility in the English-speaking, middle-class mould.

With the coming of the railroad, Nykolai and his brother-in-law John Kolisniak built a general store, the "D and K" in Two Hills. Nykolai was a progressive businessman and a loyal citizen of Two Hills. He was instrumental in making land available at a nominal cost for the building of both the municipal and school division office buildings, the Two Hills Hospital, the high school, and other ventures. In 1943 he donated land for the first Ukrainian Orthodox Church in Two Hills. For his services to the church he was elected to the office of charter president.

In 1957 Nykolai sold the Red and White store and moved to Edmonton where he joined his son, Walter, in the construction of a shopping centre on Fulton Road. After selling this, they organized another company to undertake the building of two apartment buildings and to operate a used-car lot. In 1964 the Dow Holdings Company, in which Nykolai, his son, and his son-in-law, were shareholders, invested in the Alpine Hotel in Banff. In 1968 Nykolai sold his share and retired.[154]

As competitive and shrewd as any other good Canadian, and as esteemed. The accomplishments of local worthies were respectfully noted. The Krawchuk family leaves for a holiday to Banff, Mr. Leitch of the Bank of Montreal expects to go on vacation at the beginning of August. Miss Edith English passes her nursing exams. A.W. Shaw of Vegreville visits Two Hills on business. George Porter and family go camping. A. Calvert hosts a farewell party in honour of Ralph Smith of the Federal Grain Company. It is intriguing that a newspaper published in the heart of Ukrainian settlements scrupulously records the activity of Anglo-Saxon society (relegating the Ukrainians to sporadic notices in the social columns and to jocular references in the police court news) as though the civility of a Ukrainian-Canadian town could be measured by the number of times its English citizens celebrated weddings or entertained weekend visitors.

The town became the thin edge of the wedge of conformity. Sheepskin coats, garlic, unilingualism, and religious fervour were banished to the farms as townspeople, with their greater concentration of wealth and their accessibility (or vulnerability) to highways, radios, movies, and travelling salesmen, absorbed the styles and motivations of the majority culture "out there." It was a gradual process and a not thoroughly successful one – Ukrainian was spoken widely and major holidays of the Eastern church observed, Ukrainians married each other and worked for each other – but those of the Canadian-born generation who left the farm were the first participants in an experiment with assimilation into an urban, Anglo-American, middle-class, and very often hostile culture. As we shall see, the attempt to shape oneself accordingly very often meant laying oneself on a procrustean bed of contradictions and guilts and frustrations – but the attempt was made nonetheless. In Two Hills, they dressed from the Eaton's catalogue, read the Vegreville Observer and sometimes the Edmonton Journal, learned to serve tea in teacups and bake chiffon cakes, sent Englishmen to Parliament, put the icons in the basement and hung landscapes on the wall, believed women "of a certain class" should stay at home and keep house and men should be successful through individual effort. This was what their parents had made the trans-Atlantic trip for, had broken their backs for, had turned the other cheek for. As they broke the sod, they said their curses against black bread and homespun, sly priests and idiot bureaucrats, withered wombs and debts to the merchants. If the Anglo-Canadians had found an escape from these conditions, who were the Ukrainians to disdain imitation? They would live on respectable and comfortable streets too and someday make their way through the cities, unremarked as Galicians.

Anglo-conformity was the optimistic tendency of the town. Its subversive tendencies lay in violence, racism, poverty, and ethnicity, though poverty is difficult to document beyond the pioneer era of Ukrainian-Canadian society. Interviewees were as reticent about discussing economic distress in the 1920s and the post-war period as they were loquacious in enumerating their parents' hardships and the effects of the Depression. Pioneer struggles and Depression impoverishment are "valid" examples of economic suffering but outside of them there seems to be a tacit understanding that the standard of living in Alberta was adequate and even comfortable, as though it would be disloyal and ungrateful for a new Canadian to believe otherwise. I have exactly two references that it was otherwise. One is a statement from a man in Two Hills who told me that he had served a term on the village's Public Welfare Committee. "Had to go see the people who were needy. Mostly ladies. Married but I guess their husbands left them. They stayed on in town with their kids and needed help." And the other is a document from the archives, a letter from the secretary-treasurer of the village to the Vegreville General Hospital in 1943. The letter is written on behalf of a woman who had recently been a maternity patient. "Olga tells me that the baby has been taken away by the Child Welfare Department. Is this correct?"[155] These are the only clues I have that the economic situation of the first generation in the town was not necessarily secure, that not everyone was a character in the saga of upward mobility and that being born in Canada, going to school, and moving into town didn't always ensure that the cycle of poverty among the farming class would be broken. These two clues also hint at the probability that urban poverty, when it did exist, victimized women more than men. As long as the family unit was stable – as it was on the farms among immigrants and the first generation – women were no more vulnerable to economic disaster than men. But once the family was transferred to the town and the obligations to the homestead severed, women became vulnerable to desertion and sexual exploitation and widows were left with no source of income. Their distress was part of the hidden underbelly of an increasingly prosperous Ukrainian-Canadian town.

The same may be said for crime and violence. Charles Young, in 1930, listed assault, murder, suicide, theft, dishonesty, drunkenness, and arson as prevalent among Ukrainian-Canadians ("In the Two Hills settlement . . . two families have given the place a most unsavory reputation."[156] Significantly, violent sex crimes were almost non-existent but this may reflect more a reluctance in reporting them than of their not taking place at all. Young advances the theory that all this violence was peculiar to the Canadian-born generation rather than to the immigrants:

> The older generation of Ukrainians brought with them an inherited respect for the law. They were servile, almost abject, in their submission to the constituted authorities. One hears of incidents when Ukrainians, who were brought into the Winnipeg court in the first years of their immigration to Canada, would get on their hands and knees and crawl across the floor of the courtroom until compelled to stand on their feet.[157]

There is no end to the examples available that illustrate the apparent social "disorganization" among the Canadian-born – disorganized in the social worker's sense of being caught between the disintegrating European social mores of the parents and the segregated society of Anglo-Canadians – but the usual problem with statistics confronts us here too. Were Ukrainian-Canadians really disproportionately antisocial or did their violence just seem more sensational, erupting as it did among second-class citizens and thus confirming everybody else's prejudices? "It is true that Ukrainians in general do not enjoy good reputations as law-abiding citizens.'[158] Why? Was there a double standard of violence applied, one for the Anglo-Saxon under which much was forgiven or ignored and another for the "foreigner" whose every gesture of hostility or frustration was construed as an illegality? A survey of the inmates in the Fort Saskatchewan jail in 1932 came to the conclusion that "no other group, with the possible exception of the Poles, had as large a proportion in the gaol population in Alberta" as the Ukrainians.[159] This only begs the question: were Ukrainian-Canadians absolutely more antisocial or were they just more visible, more carefully scrutinized and less able to negotiate their way out of a conviction? Were Ukrainians more violent or were they just part of a mass of poor and thwarted people who struck out indiscriminately against their perceived tormentors? Or against themselves?

> remembering uncle pillepko
> the old railroad worker
> how his solid thighs beneath my child's
> feet felt like wood
> and maybe the way
> a corral post must have felt
> beneath his aging feet that spring day
> as he tied a baling wire around his neck
> and jumped to swing from a
> crossbar above the stockyard gate.[160]

The newspapers were full of items that supported the prevailing notion that Ukrainians were "naturally" a violent people. A violence, let it be noted, that they exercised on each other. From the Vegreville *Observer* 1932-1933:

> Alex M—, aged sixty, committed suicide by hanging himself to a tree on his homestead (near Bonnyville), his frozen body being found by the coroner and constable.

> Joe H—, W. P—, Mike and John E— were convicted for assaulting Alex S— while on the road home from a dance.

> Hired man on farm near Lavoy shot and killed a woman also working there when she refused to marry him – and she was already married. He then shot himself.

When he sentenced Nick U to two months' imprisonment

Magistrate Gore-Hickman stressed the fact that aliens coming into Canada should learn to comport themselves according to the standards of Canadian decency. The charge was laid under a morality section of the criminal code.

The reporter was amused by the image of Ukrainian-Canadians turning on each other.

George B— and Sam M— got into an argument which proceeded to physical violence, in which George won all rounds by a wide margin. Sam's face, which was not a fortune to begin with, was a total loss when George got through with it. (Fined $5 and costs.)

Dan N— was charged with purloining his neighbour's wheat. At the price of wheat, it hardly seems worthwhile to steal it but Dan took it, possibly from force of habit. Anyway, he drew down one month with hard labour at the Fort.

There was a teacher in Hairy Hill who hanged himself in his lonely teacherage, a man who fell or was pushed into a well, and deaths from gangrene, horse-throwings, accidental shootings, drownings, and collapsing wells. There was violence at ball games, and at community halls when the moonshine made the rounds.

For eighteen years, Two Hills had its own police, local men with no special training whose job was thankless. How do you reprimand or arrest your neighbour? How, on the other hand, do you keep your peace with the disorderly neighbour and still keep the town's good name?

Dear Sir:

You will kindly accept and notify Mr. Odinsky of my resignation from the duty of village police.

In respect for reason I can only say that I have had too much of the councils of the village and if they can get another individual who would police the village for nothing and get and take their dirt they are welcomed to it.

You will also, Mr. Tomyn, mail my cheque of $5.50
composed of as follows: Fine comm. of Mike W— $4.00
Cerfew [sic] ringing for Sept 1-15   1.00
Measuring the school ground   .50
                                                     $5.50 [161]

For May and June 1935, the village constable's duties included
destroying stray dogs, impounding a cow, ringing curfew (designed
to keep fractious Communists and anti-Communists off the streets
at night), and arresting a man for unlawfully consuming liquor "in a
place other than a private residence." It was not the kind of work
that endeared him to his friends and neighbours, and finally in the
late forties the RCMP detachment, whose members were moved out
every couple of years, took over the policing function. If they were
Anglo-Saxon cops, so much the better, a double indemnity from the
Ukrainians' point of view. You not only have to challenge a
uniform, you have to take on a WASP.

If the Ukrainian-Canadians were generally deferential to
Anglo-Saxons and others "whiter" than they, they were not so
considerate of Jews and Indians. "They call me the 'Jew' in this
town," says a merchant, meaning he's a popular target for curses and
complaints about prices and profits and for accusations of gouging
and hardheartedness." Adler from Vegreville tried to run a business
here but he had to pack up and go. Nobody would go to his store. I
guess it dates back to the old country where the Jews had all the
money. They had the korshma [taverns]."

While anti-Semitism was less obvious among the first
generation in Canada, there was still a series of "kneejerk" responses
to Jewish people in Ukrainian-Canadian culture: Jews are dirty, Jews
are greedy, Jews are tricky, Jews are Communists. And yet, for every
Ukrainian who refused to patronize a Jewish-owned business, there
was another who would go only to the Jew's because it felt homey,
like the old country, even though the Ukrainian grumbled all the
while about "thievery" while paying for salt and rubber boots.

In a way, anti-Semitism became formalized in Canada as a set of stereotyped attitudes that had more to do with acknowledging a historical set of relations than with actual conditions and feelings between the two peoples in Canada. The Jewish merchant or pedlar in Vegreville was neither more nor less prosperous than anybody else in the petit-bourgeoisie. This was not the point. The point was that Ukrainian-Canadians grew up on stories about the Jew in the old country village, how he snared peasants into perpetual debt by extending credit at the store and tavern, how he lent money at exorbitant interest rates and accumulated bags of gold while the peasant groaned under the weight of the landlord, how he collaborated with the Poles and sympathized with the Bolsheviks, and how he mercilessly extracted what was owed. For their part, the Ukrainians in the old country were responsible for devastating pogroms and for supporting anti-Semitic nationalist heroes and militaristic ideology. These are political rather than racial conflicts but they were popularly transmitted as anti-Semitism so that, in Canada although the Jew was no longer a money-lender or tavern-keeper, he was still despised. That Ukrainian-Canadians and Jewish-Canadians were in the same boat – objects of racial slander and prejudiced behaviour, subjects of low income, abbreviated education, and a ghetto environment – and therefore natural allies in the struggle against oppression didn't occur to anybody except the Communist party.

Attitudes towards native people were more ambivalent. On the one hand, there was a measure of sympathy among Ukrainian-Canadians who could see analogies between their situation and that of the Indians and Métis analogies uncomplicated by European memories. "We get along very well. I think one of the reasons is that the Indians have been suppressed, and so have the Ukrainians. As late as the 1940s I was called a 'bohunk' by Anglo-Saxon people, and the Indians were called 'savages.'" And there was an awareness of the Ukrainian-Canadians' complicity, along with Anglo-Canadians, in the humiliation of the native people. "People here don't give the Indians a chance. We drove them to where they are and we keep them down there." On the other hand, the Ukrainian-

Canadian as a white person was as guilty as any other of an attitude of social supremacy. The self-assigned liberal who thinks it's perfectly all right to marry anybody you want, so long as he or she is white; the woman of compassion who feels sorry for Indians because they're so backward; once they catch up with whites, they'll be admirable enough. It is the "good Indian, bad Indian" mentality.

We lived next door to Indians on the farm, you know. So, you lend them this and you lend them that and you never get it back. You have to hunt for it, you have to go for it. Alec knew every Indian, he knew what Indians were good and what Indians weren't. He seemed to have such a powerful memory. You hired them to work for awhile as everybody else was doing and as soon as you paid them, you never saw them around. However, I did have a very good girl with us for my summer work. She did the house and everything else and she was very good.

Poverty, violence, racism – these have characterized every prairie community in the transition from frontier to suburban life-style. Institutions of socialization – the schools, media, police and church – have universal application. Within a generation of living in small, urban concentrations, the Ukrainian-Canadians would have become in all likelihood indistinguishable from the mass of working class and lower middle-class Canadians had it not been for the contradictory pull of their ethnic organizations. These were subversive elements in the sense that they provided an unofficial alternative to the collectives of the dominant culture – the school, the Protestant church, the bank, the movie house; they reminded Ukrainian-Canadians that, while they may not resist the upward mobility of Anglo-Saxon attitudes, they were still by definition "other" than Anglo-Saxon. Besides, the ethnic organizations provided a welcoming, familiar, and equalizing environment for a population bruised and beleaguered by the hostility and abuses of the Anglo-Canadian establishment. "Out there" among the Anglos you were just another dumb bohunk. Inside the ethnic association you were a comrade, a sister, maybe even a big shot.

Among all the popular organizations the Ukrainian-Canadians were to establish, none was more influential or more accessible than the national hall, *narodny dim*. Every community had one and sometimes two. They were organized, erected, and administered by the community itself and ran the gamut of mere dancing halls to high-minded cultural and political centres. And they were not to be confused with the halls erected by specific interest groups, such as the churches and the socialist organizations, although they might very well make use of their resources. In the hall, all that mattered was that you were a fellow Ukrainian-Canadian interested in your ethnic condition.

The idea of a hall originated in the Ukraine where the better-educated, reform-minded individuals in a village or town gathered in "reading societies" (*chytalnia*) and discussed books and newspapers, politics and social issues (covertly, as the state repressed the outspoken). Eventually, because these societies were open to everyone, the peasants joined too, hoping to acquire there the rudiments of literacy denied them by the establishment; consequently the society's members broadened their aims to include educational work and nationalist consciousness-raising, and the society became known as a *narodny dim*.

In Canada, where there was a need to find an English equivalent for them, they were often called "National Homes." The word "national" must be interpreted to mean "awakening of the national consciousness" in the sense that much of the work of these institutions, under enlightened leadership, was directed towards awakening, among the early immigrants, of a national Ukrainian self-identification. In the decades of their existence, events such as the First World War, the rebirth of the Ukrainian state, the Bolshevik Revolution, variously influenced their work and ideals. At times, they were misunderstood and misrepresented as being nationalistic and therefore unCanadian.[162]

Quite. The national hall was not a Canadian organization in the sense that "Canadian" still meant "Anglo-Saxon." But it was profoundly Canadian in that it was an indigenous and popular institution created by Ukrainian-Canadians to fulfill needs made explicit by the experience of living as a "bohunk" in Canadian society. It was a meeting hall, a dance hall, a concert hall; it was a forum for political meetings, debates and lectures, and community business; inside it were organized plays, Ukrainian language classes, and libraries. It did, in fact, organize practically the entire social and cultural life and a large part of the political life of the Ukrainian-Canadians. And to the extent this life was carried on in the Ukrainian language, set to Ukrainian folk music, dramatized through plays set in the old country and coordinated by Ukrainian-speaking teachers and priests, it was indeed antagonistic to the assimilationist pressures of the outside world. And when it was called the Taras Shevchenko or Ivan Franko National Hall, it overtly advertised itself as an institution dedicated to inculcating national (that is, Ukrainian) pride in a people whose dignity had been seriously shaken by the political, cultural, and economic forces of Anglo-Canadian majority rule. No need to apologize. When a "Canadian" institution meant the IODE, the Orange Order, and the Chamber of Commerce (no foreigners need apply), the Ukrainian-Canadian had no choice but to define his or her "nationality" as Ukrainian. And to be congratulated for it, in the hall.

There was a hall, they built a national hall at Pruth about three or four miles from where we lived and we were active there. My mother was rather talented in some things. They put on plays, and she was a good actress, just natural, she never had any training. And then we too, as we were growing up, we'd participate in it. I used to take part in plays and they had a musical director there and they'd teach us songs and so on. These plays were written in the Ukraine, by Ukrainians. There were some by Taras Shevchenko, and there were some on his poetry and then sometimes they'd even have some of his poetry in it. I remember one very distinctly because that's the first time we had been at one. My mother was the leading character in it and it was called Machukha which was "stepmother." It was about how cruelly a stepmother treated her. It was always drama, never light-hearted. They'd portray the difficult life, and about women, that women always suffered so. And then I know that one time they had a group come from Vegreville, a concert, and they gave a very splendid concert. Everybody attended. It was a social event. It was all year round, that national hall.

If the community included someone who was well-educated in Ukrainian literature, music, and history, he was generally engaged as the director, a full-time job; and then the hall became an ambitious, almost competitive enterprise. The choral-drama club in Myrnam, for instance, made a concert tour through Derwent, Two Hills, Plain Lake, Myroslawna, and Hairy Hill (an amazing forty-two miles away). After that they congregated twice a week, once for rehearsals and once for a public performance. The director also organized lectures, the church choir, a brass band, a gymnastics club, and a picnic committee. Obviously, activities as wide-ranging as these could not be undertaken without the support and participation of almost the whole community. The hall was the vehicle for collective self-expression; for now and a little while longer, the folk music they sang and the folk dances they danced and the Ukrainian lectures they listened to (among others, officers-in-exile from the Ukrainian National Army defeated by the Red Army) were all the music, dancing, and politics they had. For this brief time, this was their very own culture.

Take, for example, the story of the "Yuriy Fedkowych Ukrainian Educational Society of Soda Lake," later called the "Yuriy Fedkowych English-Ukrainian Educational Society" of Pruth and finally, the "Yuriy Fedkowych Canadian-Ukrainian Educational Society." In a nutshell, the name changes show the changes in self-definition from an insular, undiluted Ukrainian environment to a recognition of Anglo-Saxon supremacy in Canada to a hopeful statement that "Canadian" wasn't always the same thing as "English."

In February 1921, a group of forty-four men and women met in a home near Pruth to discuss the building of a *chytalnia*.[163] They were an unusual group, a combination of radical socialist farmers and of Greek Orthodox priests, all of whom were similarly motivated in spite of the political differences. They wanted to organize an educational society that would teach the Ukrainian-Canadians in the district about Ukrainian culture and history and to teach them to be proud of it.

> The speech of the second speaker, Rev. Father John Kusey, awakened to national consciousness the lethargic Ukrainians of Soda Lake, and he too was applauded. An executive was elected and donations for a library were received. In all fifty dollars was collected. The meeting adjourned on a patriotic note, singing the Ukrainian national anthem.[164]

Men could become members for $1.00, women for 25¢ – a practical recognition of the fact that most women had no money of their own – and together they began the work of enlightening themselves by listening to readings from "Ukrainian literature of the nineteenth century" and something called "The Sinners." Apparently, not everyone was entertained. From the minutes: "If anyone has any criticism of the readings, let him first read the books."[165] In May 1921, the society posted a notice:

> The Honourable Public are hereby advised that a meeting will be held at the home of Oleksa Tkachuk, May 29, 1921, at 1:00 o'clock p.m. in the matter of building a permanent *chytalnia* and selecting a site therefor.

> Members who do not attend the meeting shall have no right to criticize.[166]

Fourteen people showed up, apparently only the most fervent of the membership, and resolved to buy a $20 acre of land. A year later they had erected a hall on it and staged nine plays to help pay the expenses.

In the ten-year period 1921 to 1931, a total of forty-three plays were staged. Lectures, readings, and debates were popular and well attended. City Life vs Country Life; Life in Canada vs Life in Austria, Uniculturalism vs Multiculturalism, were some of the issues debated. A lecture "How to Bring Up Children" receives honourable mention in the minutes. Secretarial comments indicate general enthusiasm and interest: "June 1, 1924, . . . teacher Huculak gave a very good lecture, followed by loud applause . . . January 28, 1925, . . . Hudson Bay Company agent, John Melnyk (later Ukrainian Orthodox priest) talked of his experiences among the Chukchis in Kamchatka and the Eskimos in Canada . . . December 24,1924, . . . the Christmas concert with school children participating was very good . . . February 28, 1925, . . . the play "Return from Siberia" was well received and the players deserve our thanks. It is noted that when the members sought recreation and relaxation, "the behaviour of the young people was exemplary."[167]

In the meantime, several hundred dollars were spent on buying books and newspapers (the *Ukrainian Voice*, the *Canadian Farmer* and the Vegreville *Observer*). This was, after all, a *chytalnia*.

So far, so good. In 1926, however, as just one indication that the children were not necessarily so committed to intellectual enlightenment as the parents, the Canadian-born generation successfully pressed demands for a baseball diamond. And, in 1927, a formally-written constitution stipulated that "only Ukrainian Orthodox services shall be allowed in the national home"[168] – a deviation from the original concept of a hall for the whole community. Among the remaining members a further split occurred in the thirties: many had joined the Ukrainian Labour and Farm Temple Association and voted down a proposal that the hall be incorporated into the anti-Communist, nationalist Ukrainian Self-Reliance League. By 1934, however, the ULFTA members seem to have left the hall organization altogether for it was resolved, at a general meeting, that "the Warwick Educational-Cultural Society be allowed the use of our hall for a play, provided it [the Society] is not Communist oriented."[169]

Sports events and dances were gradually replacing the more serious activities like plays and concerts. Improved travel brought mixed crowds to the dances with the resultant problem of drinking. To cope with this specific problem, the 1934 meeting resolved to lay fines from $5.00 to $25.00 for misbehaviour.

As the years pass, the records become sparser and less detailed. From 1936 to the end, only the annual meetings are recorded. The attendance gradually drops off: 1921–53; 1937–31; 1938 – 42; 1939 to 1944, no record of meetings; 1949 – 18; 1950 – 15; 1954 – 14; 1963 – 13, all descendants of the original founders: five Hills, two Lakustas, four Tkachuks, two Romaniuks.

Another change is noted as younger secretaries replace the old. The quality of writing deteriorates. Although the minutes are still written in Ukrainian, English words are frequently introduced, and English letters are used for Ukrainian ones. From 1958 on, they are written entirely in English, albeit in excellent English. In 1965 they cease altogether. Almost like an epitaph, the last item attached to the minutes is a letter dated April 4, 1967, from the Registrar of Companies, warning that the Yuriy Fedkowych Society at Pruth may be dissolved as it has failed, during a period of two years or more, to file returns required by the Statute.[170]

It was great while it lasted. But the *narodny dim* was never meant to postpone indefinitely the swallowing up of the Ukrainian-Canadians into the dominant culture. It flourished only as long as they had no choice but to develop a popular ethnic culture alongside it. As soon as they could pass as assimilated Canadians, the halls closed down.

"They helped each other. Anything you need, they help you." For the majority of homesteaders help from their neighbours was all the help they would have. They got together to build their houses and barns, their roads, churches, schools, and halls. They bought their machinery cooperatively, administered medicine to each other delivered each other's babies, and made collections of food and clothing for families left destitute by fire or foreclosure. From these spontaneous and disparate moments of mutual aid, it was not far to go to formally organized cooperatives of every description.

As early as 1901, unemployed Ukrainian workers – there was a railroad workers' strike – organized the first Ukrainian relief organization (decades before the government delivered unemployment insurance). Peter Svarich was in Edmonton at the time.

Many unemployed men then came to Edmonton from Medicine Hat, Lethbridge, and Swift Current, as there was no work for them on the railway. It was a pity to look at them, they were so exhausted and neglected, looking like so many cadavers. There were about fifty of them walking aimlessly in the town. Then I had a talk with them and found out about their pitiful plight. I went with them to the police station. The police had no way of helping the unemployed, but they told me to go with the unemployed to the land office. There the unemployed received about ten dollars each for flour.

Then I went to the editor's office of our *Bulletin*. I put an advertisement in the newspaper, saying that there were many unemployed men in our town who would be glad to do any kind of work, even at twenty-five cents a day, to earn at least enough for food. In answer to our advertisement, the unemployed were invited to split fuel wood in three places. Soon I had them organized into detachments, and these detachments went from place to place doing some kind of work, clearing bushes from the lots, digging garden plots, digging cellars, and such work.

During the two months of the railroad workers' strike the detachments of the unemployed earned together in our town about $800. . . . For all the jobs that we did we were not paid individually but deposited the earned money at the Johnson

Workers' Store which employed a Ukrainian man, Ivan Metelsky, as a clerk. There each man could buy as much food as he needed, his bill being charged against the deposited fund. Each of our unemployed men could thus buy food for himself, whether we used him for our jobs or not. The men worked at our small jobs by turns, so that all of them performed a certain amount of work, and therefore had equal rights to benefit from our earnings. If any man left a family out on a farm we shared our earnings also with those families. From time to time we sent food parcels to them.[171]

There followed cooperative stores (otherwise, produce had to be sold at prices fixed by the merchant), flour mills and elevators (the Ruthenian Elevator Company, promoted by various luminaries in Ukrainian nationalist organizations, failed soon after it got started, proving, I suppose, that farmers, not intellectuals, should run grain elevators). Ukrainians ultimately formed 10 per cent of the wheat pools in the prairie provinces, that is, 10,000 of them with a total capital investment of $5 million.[172] They organized credit unions, manufacturing cooperatives (one made gloves in Winnipeg), dairy, poultry and bakery cooperatives, and fuel cooperatives. Over 10,000 families were members.[173] Many collapsed through mismanagement, inability to compete with multinational corporations moving into the retail market, falls in prices, badmouthing from private enterprise, and lack of an umbrella structure that would coordinate all the scattered co-ops under one policy, but many survived – notably, the credit unions, again the work of the nationalist intelligentsia in the Ukrainian National Organization (one formed in Andrew in 1943) who knew what they were doing in this case.

The socialists and progressives were instrumental in the cooperative movement as well – it was a natural expression of their political principles – and in 1916 a fund for the sick was organized by the Ukrainian Social Democrat Party in Manitoba. It provided assistance to disabled workers and families, to widows and orphans, in the absence of any legislation providing for compensation to the injured and sick. This dissolved in 1918, leaving a critical vacuum. The Ukrainian Labour Temple Association, already organized as a cultural and educational society for working-class Ukrainians, expanded their role into a mutual benefit society to be called the Workers' Benevolent Association. This became as successful and popular as the credit unions. By 1920, it boasted twenty-two branches, half of them in Alberta's coal towns and mining centres, and managed not only to provide support for sick workers but to politicize them as socialists.

We used to sit in the old shacks and boarding houses, in the dim light of the coal-oil lamps, and spend countless hours in intensive discussions. It was here that many of our people first began to put the alphabet together and to make words of it. Having found the keys to a new world, they began to read. And some became avid readers of the finest literature of the time.

One of the great favourites was Upton Sinclair. His works always had deep social meaning. We read the books individually and in groups. And we always tried to get the latest in literature and to keep up with the times. So it is no wonder that ideas of organization, or unionization, and of economic and political action were in the foreground of our interests. They came up in the discussions, from the books we read, and helped to weld our generation together. And the ideas and education were all part of the background to the struggles for a better life in Canada, and to the growth of organizations like the WBA in the cities, mining camps, and rural areas.[174]

Working class consciousness was in fact formalized into the WBA constitution: "The WBA must always be a working people's organization. The WBA must never serve any organization opposed to the cause of the working people . . . ,"[175] which pitted them, ideologically, at least, not only against the capitalist structures of Anglo-Canadians but against anyone who "in any way . . . engaged in harmful anti-working class activities," including, by definition, some anti-Communist Ukrainian-Canadians. This would become explicit in the late twenties and during the thirties.

In the meantime, there was an atmosphere of general support and encouragement across the whole community for the cooperative movement. Newspaper editorialists favoured it: "Cooperative organizations . . . are the only means at the present time by which our people may expect to improve their material well-being."[176] A convention in 1920 of Alberta Ukrainians (mostly farmers) passed resolutions advocating cooperative marketing, cooperative banks, and the organization of an information bureau in connection with the United Farmers of Alberta. By way of endorsing cooperation, "D. Prystash told the gathering . . . that capitalists are organizing for the purpose of controlling the world markets." Twenty years down the road, the principles would be reiterated, if anything with more passion. Two decades of attempting collective action, in spite of doubt, timorousness and narrow self-interest within the community and contempt and arrogant individualism without, would re-inspire the next generation to unite around the ideal of ethnic solidarity.

Now I do not stand alone as I face the fate of my people, for supporting me are hundreds of thousands of disciplined and enlightened citizens. I am only a single unit among them. Individually, we might be weak; but united we shall be indeflectable.[177]

By the time these words were spoken in 1943 it would be in many ways too late. The Ukrainian-Canadian community, split along political and religious lines, with some members more successfully absorbed by the power structures than others, with some suspicious of others' motivations and goals, would experience only the false unity of race. But in the 1910s and early 1920s, the urge to cooperate was sound. All Ukrainian-Canadians were in the same position vis-a-vis the power structure – all were alienated – and all of them had only each other for a class. The "outstanding feature" of the Ukrainian communities, wrote Charles Young, "is that the Ukrainians have made such progress and have done so well with so little help."[178] With so little outside help, that is.

The fact that Ukrainian-Canadian women laboured as hard as and longer than the men does not describe the entirety of their situation in the community. They were female workers and as such experienced a status and condition peculiar to their sex. As pioneers, they did not have under Canadian law the right to a shared ownership in the homestead they helped to clear and manage, nor to the income they helped earn; for years they did not even have legal guardianship of their children. They could be, and were, deserted by their husbands with no right to support nor to the funds realized from the sale of the land. It was a commonplace observation that in the Ukrainian pioneer family "women are little better than slaves who toil laboriously at the beck and call of inconsiderate husbands. Wife-beating is common. . . ."[179] The patriarchal organization of the family was transferred intact to Canada: the father's word was authoritative, family earnings were often confiscated by him, marriages were arranged, women often did not even eat with the men but served them first and, over all such sexist transactions, the church spread its benediction. Women endured yearly childbirths and frequent child-deaths, untreated pelvic diseases, and the often fatal puerperal fever; as noted, they were more often illiterate than the men and, when educated, had a great chance of being taken out of school to marry or to care for younger siblings; as homeworkers, they tended to be much more isolated from social contacts and their participation in community activity outside the church almost unheard of.

This is not to say, however, that they did not rebel. As early as 1917 the Vegreville *Observer* reported the disappearance of a teen-age girl from her parents' home and speculated that it was "small wonder" she had struck out for herself, given that "nine times out of ten the parents take away the last cent of her earnings . . . and believe in compulsory matrimony and selling their daughters to whichever suitor can give them the best value in exchange.[180] Charles Young reported that women not infrequently asked the local doctor to abort them (in the event he refused, it is not unlikely they tried to do it for themselves, risking mutilation and death), that some women were actually taking their husbands to court on assault charges, and that daughters were refusing the marriages arranged for them.[181]

Women in Two Hills told stories of some women's experience in their own generation. Because it was a custom in the old country to marry off the older daughters first, a local woman was hastily married to an old man so her younger sister could marry the man of her choice. Another woman, married to a "brute," discovered the hired girl was pregnant by him. Confronted, the husband told her that if she didn't agree to raise this child as her own, he'd run off with the girl. She raised him as her son but, when the brute died, he bequeathed his entire inheritance to the boy, leaving his wife to manage as best she could on her old age pension. The story of a girl married off to a man she'd never seen before her peremptory wedding was related as unremarkable. As apocryphal as some of these stories may be, they are for all that the only substantial record there is of the women's point of view on local history, outside the minutes of meetings of women's organizations.

When the Ukrainians congregate, you'll find they drink and they'll start singing. The men will all sing very sentimental love songs, some of them folk songs, some of them songs popular from the thirties and forties. And there are the women, sitting hard, cold-eyed and angry. The men are sentimental slobs. They're walking around and kissing each other and each other's wives, they're saying flattering things to one another, they're gentle and tender, and the women are sitting there, steel-eyed and angry. Cold as snakes. This is very common. Their husbands oppress them all week but on weekends they get together and get very romantic and the women who have been keeping these neurotics alive all week, who probably hate them and hate themselves by now, are sitting there completely angry. That's the way my dad treated my mum. She was full of rage.

A woman who was active in the local branches of the Women's

Institute and, later, the United Farm Women of Alberta, learned in the course of many meetings and teas that most Ukrainian-Canadian farm-women had no idea they could do anything about household sanitation, the price of eggs, school bussing, tight-fisted or brutal husbands – or birth control. For one thing, she says, "they didn't at first make the connection between broad economic and political conditions and their own lives." For another, they were embarrassed. "Birth control was regarded by many as a sin. They were told the purpose of their lives was to procreate, especially by the church. But they were anxious for information and those who had some information would tell others in secret. Sometimes even do-it-yourself abortion information. They were bitter that doctors wouldn't even tell them about the rhythm method. But they never spoke up at meetings. They were afraid that if they complained openly about their family life, they would be ostracized by the community." On the face of it then, women gathered to learn about sewing, canning, and cooperative hatcheries; unofficially, they gathered in the time-honoured feminine manner to seek and exchange information through an almost underground grapevine.

The situation of women living in town was somewhat easier. They lived only blocks apart, their husbands' actions came under closer scrutiny and in many cases the wife was also a wage earner, allowing her some economic and psychological leverage in the family. And they had leisure time. The Hairy Hill Ladies' Club catered to parties and weddings, hosted baby showers and Valentine's Day teas, and welcomed new residents. The Royal Purple Club (the women's equivalent of the Elks) of Two Hills raised the money for plumbing in the new lodge. "We had teas and catered for banquets. You have no idea how hard we worked. All those pyrohy! We canvassed for money for the Crippled Children's Fund. Helped out people who were destitute or ruined. We were a big group, almost every woman in town was a member."

There is a depressing sameness to the activities of women's organizations, as though the availability of leisure time only transferred women's work from the private household to the community at large. Orthodox, Catholic, Protestant, or Communist, women cooked, raised money, beautified the church or the hall, taught Sunday school or kindergarten, made handicrafts, practiced good works, and administered social services – all of it as volunteers. Earlier, when most women were still confined to the farms, it had been the nuns who had undertaken this labour, especially educational and cultural work. Secularized, it was still done "for the love of it," and there is considerable irony in the fact that the unpaid labour of women has netted millions of dollars' worth of goods and services for almost everybody but themselves.

Such work was not without its ideological underpinnings. If the patriarchal arrangement of the family was not instruction enough in women's role, there were the folktales and narratives told exclusively from the male point of view to bolster it. Jokes about unfaithful wives, lewd references to women's sexuality, bellicose threats of abuse, and self-pitying lamentations about shrews. There were the lessons from the school primers which, derived from middle-class, Anglo-Saxon morality, were sweeter but no less stultifying: the sentimentalities, so dreadfully divorced from the realities of most women's situations, about woman as ministrating angel. And there were the priests with their benign regard for girls "reared in the Christian faith, in the love of God and the Blessed Mother and who so became more capable in the later guidance of their families and children,"[182] their exhortations to mothers to maintain a Ukrainian home and their "helping hand" when it came time to write up the constitution for the Ukrainian Catholic Women's League, for instance.

It is not surprising, then, to learn that even the Canadian-born women tended to repeat the refrains of their education, as in their speeches at the founding convention of the Ukrainian Canadian Committee in 1943. References there abounded to the "mother's duty" and "mother's responsibility" in forming a child's character – "she alone must teach it to be an obedient, thinking, toiling and useful person."[183] And there was the astonishing assertion of Mrs. N.L. Kohuska that women who refused the calling of self-effacing homemaker are "directly responsible for the degeneration of the race."[184]

It is between the lines of their reports that one glimpses another, more rebellious, purpose to the women's organizations. These are the references to heroic female figures from Kievan history – the princesses, queens, and concubines who governed, waged war, or proselytized – that reminded audiences of their antecedents in feminine actions. There are the concerts dedicated to the memory of women writers and revolutionaries and the introduction of Mother's Day to the Ukrainian-Canadian community, the speeches about "The Need of a Women's Press" and "The Role of Women in World Progress," the reading clubs, debates, and drama societies and the publication, alongside recipe collections, of literary biographies and "The Ukrainian Woman in Choreography."

The fact that, after them, came a generation of feminists is not to be wondered at. Subversives in their own way, such women passed on the word of female dignity and female legitimacy in the human collective, even as Two Hills represented it, from the subtle forum of the Hallowe'en Box Social.

NINE

Culture

I'd say we lived in a Ukrainian home. We spoke Ukrainian at all times. Christmas and Easter Ukrainian style. Mother went to church on all the holidays. She liked being with Ukrainian people, it was all she knew. She didn't have anything against the English; she didn't understand them. I have a feeling she was worried about what was going to happen to her kids once they left the farm

– Paul Spak

In Smoky Lake, I had to put on at least four big plays in a year, with the older people. But with the kids, I have once every month. Some months, concert, and some months play. It wasn't always just Easter and Christmas, it could be any time. I had a whole bunch of really good people in there. Smoky Lake stands a little higher from Edmonton in culture. We held these concerts in the national hall. We had a stage and a curtain. We only started to have the national hall in 1925 or '26, but we prepare everything in this time that we need for play. We charged admission, for about 10 cents, 15 cents. It paid for every musical that we had in there, and books for play. We had good audiences, and they were enthusiastic in this time. Nobody had a radio, and that was the reason. We'd do some comedies, some tragedies, all kinds. The most popular were comedy. Mostly plays from old country, but in that time, everybody was coming from there and knew about it. . . . At Easter we would have the *Chrisania* about our Easter, something like a passion play. We had a Christmas play too. We put on, not only Ukrainian plays but ones translated from the Polish, from Italian, from German, from

Hungarian. I don't think we ever did any plays in English. I felt that it was important that the Ukrainian heritage be preserved. If nobody do something like this, after one or two generations it would be forgotten.

– Peter Paush

* * *

There was a Ukrainian group coming from the Ukrainian Institute to perform and they sang beautifully and they danced beautifully and they played mandolins beautifully and oh, we just loved that. It was the St. John's Institute from Edmonton. It was just a little thing, and of course they always sang and played a lot of English pieces too, you know. "Springtime in the Rockies" and all that, "Ramona."

– Alice Melnyk

* * *

Before the halls, people had their weddings right on the farms; they'd build a platform to dance on or would dance in the granaries. I played for so many of those weddings, you wouldn't believe. A five-piece orchestra. I played for the Chrapkos, the Cherniowskys. They built a little platform with some benches around, and when it got dark they put up a lantern so we could keep on playing until two and three in the morning.

– Dick Galeta

* * *

I think I have to think in English and then speak in Ukrainian in my mind. I do recall that when I came back from the air force, from England, that I had a very hard time speaking Ukrainian. I knew what I wanted to say, but the words just wouldn't come out the way I wanted them. And then when I was teaching school in Willingdon, quite a lot of people were quite Ukrainian, and they'd often ask me as the school teacher to say a few words at some party or something. And I used to dread speaking if I had to say it in Ukrainian. If it was in English, good and fine, just no problem at all.

But if it was in Ukrainian, I just couldn't express myself.

– Mike Pawliuk

The culture that the Ukrainian immigrants brought with them from Europe was an agrarian and almost tribal culture. It was indigenous to the Ukraine, the upper classes having long before adopted, chameleon-like, the styles of whatever imperial state was ruling the country at the time. The customs of a villager in Galicia would have been as "quaint" to a burgher in Lviv as to an Austrian field-marshall. Of course, at the time they brought their culture over to Canada, it didn't occur to the immigrants that this was a Ukrainian or national culture; it was simply the way they lived the daily round of life at home and since they had never travelled even ten miles away they had no way of knowing that they shared common modes of cultural expression with thousands of others. Even in Canada, where people from the same community tended to settle together and even to name the new towns after their old country birthplaces, they did not necessarily see themselves as members of a "nation." This identity would develop in response to the propaganda work of the intelligentsia who, through reading and political work, did understand that Bukovynians and Galicians and Hutzuls were all scattered tribes of a formerly integrated nationstate – Ukraine – and that the folkways of the peasants were the remnants of a mass culture. This national identity would also become much more self-conscious among the first generation who did travel about Canada and who learned that children of people from Snyatyn (in southern Galicia) were raised with very much the same set of cultural habits as the children of people from Sokal (in northwestern Galicia).

But from the very first day of settlement the Ukrainian folk culture began evolving as a Ukrainian-Canadian one. In the first place, the material conditions of life in Europe could not be reproduced exactly in Canada and so cultural forms altered accordingly. Leisure time was drastically reduced: when they had to clear bush and plow virgin soil there was little time for embroidering pillow cases and rehearsing plays. The variety of tools and fabrics and dyes and instruments were not immediately available so they made do with what they had – a crude handloom, coarse hemp, dye from saskatoon berries, a Jew's harp – and created arts and crafts that were not only simpler and coarser but also different. The support structure for cultural expression – the churches, the village common, the collective get-togethers – could not be erected immediately and so artistic expression became localized and reduced to essentials: there was only so much music, dance, cooking, and sewing that one family could produce. "We learned the Ukrainian carols which we sang at home and when we got bigger we all went carolling. Mom passed along things like embroidery and egg-painting and cooking to the girls. We had *holubtsi* every Sunday, with fresh homemade bread."

In addition, the Ukrainian culture in Canada was a minority culture, an enclave of peculiarities in a vastness of Anglo-Saxon generality, and it was an inevitable and irreversible pressure that the majority culture brought to bear on the immigrants. The first instinct was to enclose oneself within the familiar forms of Ukrainianness as the "sole means of consolation in the struggle for existence."[185] Once settlement and capital accumulation were secured, once a modicum of English was learned and the children were passing through school, once Ukrainian-Canadians started congregating in towns and encountered Anglo-Saxon values, the second instinct was to open up to the brave, new, flashy, comfortable, and desirable world of the Canadian middle-class. When the radio was grafted onto the Ukrainian Christmas carol, the foxtrot onto the *kolomeyka,* and Campbell's soup onto *borshch,* the Ukrainian-Canadian culture came of age.

When the first generation was growing up, their culture was "a little bit of this, a little bit of that": an icon and a calendar picture of a blonde Miss Alberta Wheat Pool cuddling chicks; bits of embroidery and some eggs dyed simply in one bright colour; a checkered tablecloth and a chocolate Easter bunny; the spinning wheel and Eaton's catalogue; a brilliantly-coloured, hand-loomed bench cover and a Hudson's Bay blanket, grey and black; garlic in the frying pan and a can of Empress strawberry jam on the pantry shelf. Teacher said Christmas was December 25 and there was a school Christmas concert December 22; Mom and Dad said Christmas was January 6, and so you went to church and then ate like a pig.

There were, nevertheless, certain irreducible elements of the original culture that were practised for at least one more generation. In 1931, an *Alberta Farmer* reporter located, among the Ukrainian-Canadians, spinning wheels ("It seems strange to see the distaff and spindle in the hands of women who find the power washer a great convenience and who send their sons to university"), looms, tapestries, cross-stitch embroidery, quilting, rughooking, and wood carving. The tapestries had been woven by mothers and grandmothers "unconsciously seeking to escape from the dull imprisonment of routine"; the daughters didn't know how to weave. "The Ukrainian women no longer gather plants, barks and mosses to make their dyes. They find they can produce the colours they want by using commercial dyes – and who can blame them for so lightening their labours . . . ?" "The old Ukrainian embroidery is almost solid; the more modern has a lighter effect," reflected the lowered priority of embroidery in the allotment of labour time. Cotton bedspreads replace the woven "and that counts when the family washing has to be done by woman power." Concessions made to technology and the changing attitudes to what in fact constituted "recreation." Use a sewing machine and get the job done fast.

The decorated Easter egg, unlike other crafts, had no functional use. It was a decorative object and, for as long as Ukrainian-Canadians cared about such things, it was a domestic symbol of Easter, spring and rebirth; a pre-Christian symbol in fact, celebrating a sun cult (hence the motifs of the spiral, swastika, stars, and sunflowers) onto which Christian motifs were ultimately grafted: the cross, the Virgin's tears, the outline of a church. The fact that decorated eggs can be traced back to the Trypillian culture of Neolithic Ukraine may be of interest to ethnologists and archeologists. The legend of the three Marys who bribed the guards at Christ's grave with decorated eggs may have been known to some of the immigrants. But for the vast majority of Ukrainians in Canada, the preparation of coloured or designed eggs was simply an essential (though unexplained) part of celebrating Easter: they had to have some in the food basket they took to church to be blessed and they had to have them on hand to give out to visitors. If they had the time, the tools, and a good eye, they could design marvels of geometry and colour. If they didn't, they just soaked them in a bright dye and ate them for breakfast. It was the thought that counted. The next generation, bereft of the psychology and spiritual culture of the peasant, would enshrine the egg behind glass in a wood frame, the *pysanka*, as objet d'art; the exquisite ones would be the work of leisured women whose mothers had never managed more than two or three colours, a line here, a line there, and a squiggle all around.

Mother taught us girls how to decorate Easter eggs. She didn't make them too fancy, just very simple. As long as there was a line around and some leaf. You see, they believed very much in all that from the old country. The line that encircles the egg has no beginning or end so it symbolizes eternity. And a pine tree, she always made a pine tree to signify eternal youth and health. She made roosters, eternity and fulfillment of wishes and always a fish for Christianity. Mother never made reindeers, but other people did. They must have come from a different village. The dyes were all from the old country, beautiful dyes.

Of course, there were always a few farm women whose artist's pride was expressed in very refined and painstaking decorating and embroidery (especially for ornamentation in the church). But the majority, bent exhausted under a kerosene lamp with eyes half closed and hands cracked and calloused, could produce only the crudest arts.

Nothing, however, could cramp the celebration of Christmas and Easter. Traditionally, these were the occasions when the need to gather together and have a good time superceded the demands of the land and when the church's authority became more impressive than the state's. It was the same in Canada. The family's wealth was invested in food, its time in ritual observances, and its emotional vulnerability in the mass. Even the sceptics, the anti-clerics, the apostates would repeat the ancient gestures: cooking enormous amounts of food, bundling up for the sled-ride to church, inviting carollers into the house for a drink. They did it because they were Ukrainian and knew no other way – until, that is, the kids came home from school prattling about Santa Claus and Easter bunnies. Foolishness, if not blasphemy! Let Miss Jameson at the school celebrate Christmas and Easter as the joyless and overly-sensible Anglo-Saxons saw fit. In this house, the holiday mood would be an orgy of food and prayer. Two weeks before Christmas mother would start the baking – the braided breads, the buns, the honey cake – and the kids would set to with a mortar and pestle, pounding poppy seed into mush. The day before Christmas, a spruce tree or simply poplar branches would be strung with home-made decorations, nuts wrapped in foil from cigarette packages, paper chains and berries strung together – a Canadian custom – and the traditional sheaf of wheat propped in a corner. Hay, to symbolize the manger, was spread on the floor under the table and under the tablecloth. Then, finally, jubilantly, at the sighting of the first evening star, the family would eat, all twelve customary dishes if they could afford it, cabbage rolls, borsch, cooked wheat with poppy seed, two or three varieties of fish, bread, lentils, thin, sweet pancakes, cakes, till the candle in the *kolach* flared and went out and the neighbours came around to visit. Christmas Day mass was a five-hour affair. One could miss church all year except for this service. Feast and mass were repeated for Epiphany and the kids would make little crosses out of straw and stick them to the window. They stuck to the inch of ice on the inside of the pane. Throughout the season, carollers went from farm to farm, frozen from the sleigh-ride, thawed from whiskey, refrozen on the icebound sled. "January 6 would be our Christmas. We never knew there was one on December 25."

The Easter celebration was intensely religious although there was, like Christmas, the bellyful of food. Easter Thursday's mass. Easter Friday's procession around the church at midnight, men carrying an icon of Christ, girls carrying that of the Virgin Mary: three times around the little church with a band of boys playing noise-makers because the church bells could not be rung at Christ's death. Inside, a crown of thorns and a spear are "buried" in a table in front of the altar, on the altar the icon of Christ, kissed by the devout, crawling on their knees. On Sunday morning, this icon would be carried by the priest to the altar – the Resurrection – and the three huge bells in the wooden belfry in the churchyard would ring out and mass would be celebrated until two o'clock in the afternoon – "in those days nobody was in a hurry" – usually without benefit of pews or chairs. After mass, the priest would bless the food baskets of the families: a little *babka* (fruit bread) and *paska* (sweet bread), a piece of pork, raw onion, horseradish, pickled beets and, in a little bowl, cream cheese impressed with a cross of cloves. Finally, at home, the feast. Easter Monday's mass and the afternoon's "fertility rituals" when young men visited young women to throw water at them, a modification of the old country custom of actually throwing the girls into creeks and ponds.

Depending on the degree of one's devotion, one could also celebrate Epiphany and Epiphany Eve, Whitsunday, Feast of Jordan, Saints Peter and Paul Day, not to mention secular holidays commemorating various events important to old country patriots and the birthdays of the most honoured Ukrainian writers. Anything, really, to get out from behind the plough and stove and socialize like a civilized human being.

There was nothing quite so sociable as a wedding and to the extent it was exuberant and bawdy, it was more pagan than Christian. The guests laughed and got drunk and the bride cried; it was a reminder that the community's renewal through marriage was paid for by the sorrows of married women.

My oldest sister's wedding: Saturday night the bride is getting ready. Her bridesmaids came over to visit. (She was married in '26 at sixteen and he was nineteen.) Mother was getting the food ready. Sunday morning they went to church and got married. The bride and groom came home for dinner. Then he went home by himself, the bride remained in her father's house – that was the custom – until the following Sunday when we had the wedding feast, at his home and at ours at the same time. Dancing, dinner and supper. About four in the afternoon the groom comes with his attendants to get the bride who is usually in the house behind the table. She's in her wedding dress again. They take her dowry – quilts, pillows, trunk – and drive over to the groom's place where he was living with his parents. Everybody's waiting for them there and they have a supper and dance. I know that Mom and Dad met them at the gate after the church service with kolachi. The dinner: *borsch, holubtsi, nachynka,* roast chicken, jellied salads, cakes, cider. *Kolachi* but no wedding cake like now. Very elaborate with little birds and beautiful big braids.

By the time I got married it was different already. Went to the church in the morning, came back home for a dinner and had a small reception. A band played, a violin, a drum, *tsimbaly,* they played good dance music – not Ukrainian dancing though – but at my sister's wedding the men danced the *arkan* and some ladies would sing such sad, meaningful songs about the girl leaving home and not knowing what her life was going to be like. It would make you cry.

We had a small wedding at home at my mother's place. We were married in Mundare, St. Peter's church on the 12th of June. There were three couples getting married. We were all standing in a row, the bridesmaids at the back of them. I wore a white dress and veil. I had my dress made and the veil was bought and I had sort of metallic shoes on. We had made our bouquets of artificial flowers. We didn't have live ones. The groom came to pick us up and the bridesmaids and the best man came and picked me up and we drove to Mundare to church. And back from the wedding to my mother's place for dinner. In the evening we go down to the groom's place. That was sort of an old fashioned way. We didn't get very many presents, not those days. A donation was maybe a dollar or two from a couple. I think I had three presents at our place and maybe three or four over here at his place. But the rest was in cash. I got a berry bowl, a fruit bowl, towels, and a little tablecloth. Usually, in those days the mother of the bride had some stuff ready for the girl. Like the quilt, the pillows, the sheets and pillow cases, towels. The mothers really prepared for the girl. I didn't have a dowry, but I did get two cows later from my mother. They gave me two good milking cows.

Some elements were introduced as conscious adaptations of the "Canadian" way of getting married – the white dress and veil, the wedding cake, the bridesmaids, the confetti – but the overall format was strictly a Ukrainian production, as long as people got married on the farm. By contrast, a wedding in town would have to be indoors, it couldn't last more than a day (people had nine to five jobs) and the parents of the bride would pay the Ladies' Auxiliary to do the cooking that could no longer be done in the small kitchen of a town house. It remained Ukrainian so long as there were still guests who could remember the dances from the native village, remember all the verses to a song, remember the correct sequence of ritual events from the parents' blessing with the presentation of bread and salt to the "kidnapping" of the bride. Once these passed from memory and, more important, from significant meaning, the Ukrainian wedding changed character and acquired the "meaning" imprinted by loose cash (lots of presents), the automobile (all the relatives had to be invited), the electric guitar (more bunny-hops and less *kolomeykas*), and the white-collar job (the bride and groom could honeymoon in Banff).

Music and dance. For awhile, these remained spontaneous expressions of feeling and philosophy among illiterate immigrants with few other means of letting each other know what was on their minds. Songs by the railroad gang about cruel bosses; songs by women sewing together about cruel husbands. Songs at dances about romance and songs at weddings about woman's sorrow. Songs at Christmas about Bethlehem and songs at New Year's about good fortune. Lullabies and nonsense songs, *dumy;* songs about Cossacks. Songs from the caravanserai, the peasant uprisings, the anti-Soviet Ukrainian Insurgent Army. Songs from the Bolshevik Revolution and the Spanish Civil War. Songs about the weather, family history, personal misfortune, and daydreams. Hymns. This was the music of people who had not yet experienced the separation of music from everyday activity. It was unself-conscious, it was another way of speaking.

Some time ago when we were small, no matter where you went there was singing. To your neighbour's, to your aunt's, there'd be singing. Not that they were singing in four voices but they sang the songs they knew. It didn't matter if you had a voice.

With education, however, singing became more of an accomplishment, in fact, a product offered up to a passive audience by a disciplined choir with a monopoly on formal knowledge of music. Enter the musical expert, exeunt the gratuitous improvisations of the people. Intellectuals with a background in music, who could read and write musical notation and were familiar to a degree with the sophisticated forms of opera and chorale and the varieties of church music, became the musical directors of Ukrainian-Canadian communities through the halls. They harnessed the musical energy of the people by organizing choirs, producing concerts, staging operas, and rehearsing orchestras. It became important to be talented: to have a rich voice, to be able to sing in harmony with several voices, read music, and follow a conductor. In this way, because only a few members of the community at a time could fulfill the demands of the discipline, music became the privileged expression of a small group of specialists and so, by the time of the first generation's maturity, if

they knew any Ukrainian songs it was because they had studied
them. Or remembered their mothers singing at night, while darning
socks. Their songs were as likely to be English-language pop tunes as
Cossack lullabies. There were other effects of this
professionalization. For the first time, large numbers of rural
Ukrainians heard the songs originally composed for the ruling class
in the old country, the operas based on Ukrainian literature and the
masses written for urban cathedrals. And, for the first time, the
songs of the "folk" were transcribed by notation and passed on to
singers who might otherwise never have heard them.

So the making of music was gradually transferred from the
home to the public gathering place, to the hall, and to the school.
In the hall, at least, the audience was assured of being entertained
with a music of its own ethnicity even if it was based on urban
tastes; at the school, they were rather treated to the music of the
Anglo-Saxon. By popular demand, if the teacher was Ukrainian,
the concert became bicultural.

At the school where I was teaching, the students had to buy
their own mandolins, or maybe somebody's uncle and
somebody's aunt had one. Ukrainian music always lent itself to
the mandolin. We used to play half and half, you know. We
always had to have some Ukrainian songs. So I learned a few
Ukrainian pieces songs from our songbooks, and a Ukrainian
folksong, something that would lend itself to an action song.

I told you that I had a couple of very religious families there
and they didn't allow their children to play certain pieces.
Their boys were learning the violin and could pick up tunes
from the radio. So they would come to school and play us a
tune; they knew how to play some of these hillbilly pieces. It
was just tremendous what they could play, jigs and that. And of
course we were learning to play "Whispering Hope" and a few
of these nice pieces and the people clapped so hard for this
group, you know, it was a group of grade seven and eight boys,
and they clapped so hard and these two brothers from this very
religious family looked at me with one eye. Encore, I said, an

encore! The kids looked at me real hard, and the mother said, "Well, I guess that's all right, they learned it in school."

Dancing in the old country had been an uncomplicated affair. After church on Sundays, the young unmarried people would collect in an open space, someone would bring a violin and a zither, and everyone would jump and whirl around in the very basic steps of the polka and reel – there would always be some young man showing off with exaggerated kicks and leaps – that didn't take much practice or ingenuity to learn. For special occasions, more ceremonial dances would be performed by those who knew how to do them properly: dances illustrating the gathering of the harvest, flirtation and courtship, the exultation of the shepherd and the sword dances, Cossack boasts.

It wasn't until after the arrival of the dancing experts, like Vasily Avramenko, in the form of immigrant intellectuals after the First World War that Ukrainian-Canadians were exposed to dance as an "art." At this point, Ukrainian dancing became the project of the choreographers and ballet masters schooled in European cities, and the mass of Ukrainian-Canadians took up the fox trot. Now they had to be taught how to dance like a Ukrainian, an exercise reserved for special events. "My generation danced too, but only at Christmas concerts. The grade three teacher taught us."

Drama in the new country had a frankly didactic function together with the purpose (as with dance and music) of providing community entertainment, social contact and a "bulwark to protect their national identity against high-pressure 'assimilationist' policies."[186] Its use by the community didn't undergo the same transformations as did music and dance because it never came under the control of "specialists" – "the actors in real life are miners, workers on the extra gang, farmers, housewives"[187] – and because, unlike music and dance which were originally cultural forms which the whole tribe evolved together, theatre is by definition a self-conscious, intellectual, and discrete event that assumes an audience and a producer separate from one another. The plays that Ukrainian-Canadians watched (by the forties there were some 600 titles in the repertoire of Ukrainian-language theatre) were written by the educated class in the old country and were already popular there, the dramas were familiar (either they had already seen these plays a dozen times or knew the stories from other sources like folktales or the Bible or songs), and the characters celebrated, either as stock figures like the Drunk or the Jew or as heroic and tragic personages like Cossacks and medieval kings and queens or as popular stereotypes from village life like the young lovers, the mean stepmother, the wise old *kobzar* (troubadour).

In the historical dramas, the message was repeated, over and over again: "You are a common people, you are a singular nation with a heroic past; see, you should be proud, not humiliated, you should challenge the slander of the enemy Pole and Austrian and Russian." But much more often the message was more homespun. Lessons in morality: a young peasant woman is seduced by a city slicker, travels with him to the town, experiences degradation and pregnancy, comes back, ruined and contrite, to the village, is forgiven and welcomed back. A lesson in realpolitik: in "Deputies to Vienna," a comedy, two Ukrainian village hayseeds travel to Vienna to seek justice and suffer a series of tragi-comic embarrassments. A lesson in survival: the dumb *muzhik* outwits the Jew or the *pan*. A lesson in social analysis: the maiden is seduced by the wicked landlord's son, the peasant boy is drafted into the army against everybody's will, the farmer is defrauded by the magistrate. Catharsis: satire, jokes, puns, obscenities, and blasphemies.

It is obvious what function these dramas had for audiences in the Ukraine. What they provided to new world audiences, especially those born in Canada, is not so clear beyond superficial entertainment. Being able to make the analogies between European and Canadian conditions would require a certain level of political sophistication: the bank manager as the pub owner, the Anglo-Saxon foreman as the *pan,* the RCMP as Viennese bureaucrats, the travelling salesman as the profligate. Daring to make them in the form of re-written dialogue would require a certain *chutzpah* from people concerned about appearing orderly, law-abiding, and appreciative of the new life. Now and then a Canadian-situated play was written but, if anything, it would reaffirm the clichés about the good life in Canada. One should perhaps not be too cynical: in the beginning it was as necessary for the immigrant to feel there was a chance to make progress and find peace as later for the Canadian-Ukrainian to "speak bitterness" about the failed dream. On February 23, 1910, the Vegreville *Observer* printed the synopsis of such a play, which had been made available to any Anglophones who happened to be in the audience.

The Young Ruthenian Club is presenting a play "The Old and the New Country"; cast of twenty-three.

Act I:
In the old country. People gathered in front of Moshko's saloon to bid good-bye to some emigrants going to Canada. All hearts are full of grief for the separation. Young boys and girls get music ready for a dance when an alderman comes along and forbids it. Andrew is parting from his wife and Nikola (hero of the play) is soothing his sweetheart Hania and entrusts her to God, saying he will return soon with his fortune and marry her.

Act II:
In Canada. Boarding house where some Ruthenian labourers are lodging. George, laid off from work, is drinking heavily with partners. Housewife scolds them for their disorder and drinking while they are trying to please her. Meanwhile, immigrants arrive and complain of the hardships of their journey. John's wife, who is among them, learns that her husband had been killed that very day while working. Arrangements are made for the funeral.

Act III:
Nikola teaching his fellow countrymen to read and write; also handing out moral lessons. He receives a letter from Hania telling him how she is longing for his return. George, Steve and Andrew come in and make noise in the house. Andrew, who

left his wife in the old country, falls in love with Mary, housewife's cousin and tries to entice her to marry him. She objects and he is persuading her when his wife comes in having just arrived from the old country with Moshko. Seeing her husband embracing Mary, Andrew's wife gets angry and creates a scene. Andrew is badly scared and begs for forgiveness, which is duly accorded.

Act IV:
Moshko, who has robbed his people in the old country, comes to Canada to carry on the same business. Nikola warns them to avoid Moshko, who is a Jew, but some of them pay no heed to warnings and entrust their savings to Moshko, who disappears. The loss is felt very severely and while women are crying, men complaining and Nikola doing his best to smooth things over, a policeman comes in bringing Moshko. Some of the money is found on the thief and this is restored to its rightful owners. The losers get happy again and thank Nikola for what he has done. Moshko goes to jail. Nikola delivers another moral lecture and advises his countrymen to strive for education and to become good businessmen, avoiding such men as Moshko. He wants them to become independent and good honest Canadian citizens. Curtain. Directed by P. Svarich.

After the play a chorus will sing Ruthenian national songs, humorous selections and recitations in the Ruthenian language will be given. The *Observer* would advise English-speaking people to attend this entertainment, the first of its kind to be held in Vegreville.

A week later, the production was reviewed.

The Ruthenian Play
. . . proved to be an entire success from practically every point of view. . . . The town hall was crowded to the doors. . . . The entertainment closed loyally with the rendition of *God Save the King*.

The schizophrenia of the ethnic: on the one hand, there is candid reference to grievances about life in Canada, such as the unemployment, the alcoholism, the bad working conditions, the social disorganization of men outside family life, the homesickness; on the other hand, the villain is a thoroughly European character, the catastrophe is turned inside out into a farce, the only Anglo-Saxon, the policeman, is a positive character, and the moral of the piece is a marvel of Anglo-Canadian propaganda. It was to be just a matter of time before the two messages could no longer co-exist in the psyche of the community.

With the exception of post-war urban emigré productions, the dramas were makeshift. Anybody who wanted to be in a play was accepted by the local teacher cum director, whether they could speak Ukrainian or not (my father tells of directing Rumanian and English kids in plays at Hairy Hill; they learned their lines by memorizing the sounds). Rehearsals were squeezed in after school hours, winter or summer, costumes were homemade, the sets painted by a volunteer, and music provided by a spontaneously-organized orchestra of mandolins, a violin, a drum. It was do-it-yourself theatre or none at all. And, like the school concert, the Ukrainian-Canadian theatre was one of the few places where rural children could discover their ambition and exceptional aptitude, and be rewarded on the spot, even if they grew up to be farmers a quarter-mile away and forgot their lines until someone came along with a tape recorder twenty-five years later.

I could write a book about the organizations I've belonged to. I belonged to CYMK when I was young, in Myrnam. We had plays, we had concerts; oh, if I had a good part given to me now I'd still like to do that. I used to sing very well and had solos. I still think that if I was given a part today, I could take the script home and read it once, I could do it all again. Same with recitations. In two days I memorized a Shevchenko poem that took twenty minutes to say and I still remember a lot of it. I haven't said it since 1948. "O gentle region, fair Ukraine/Dear beyond every other!/Why are you plundered and despoiled/Why do you perish, Mother?"

The national or community hall tended to be the centre of all this cultural activity and as communities became wealthier, halls became better equipped; real stages and curtains, footlights and trained orchestra, authentic costumes, and a paid director. But not everyone had the same relationship to the hall and its activities as the directors and the cultural enthusiasts and not everyone had a chance to take part. Ninety-five percent of the people I interviewed had in fact something to do with it in their youth, whether it was just attending a concert or play or taking lessons or joining the choir or playing the part of an orphan in a tearjerker of a melodrama. (At the age of six, my father had a role which required him simply to cry piteously on cue.) But some, a few, felt alienated and left out, and they were never to feel as passionately convinced as did the hall members (especially true of the nationalistic intelligentsia) that re-creating European cultural forms in Canada was crucial for the development of the Ukrainian-Canadian identity, or even that the hall was a social centre, as in the case of a woman whose father would not allow his daughters to travel alone at night the eight miles to the hall.

We had no opportunity to go to those things at the hall. I was broke. We had no car and going fourteen miles by team was quite a distance. We were poor and you had to have money to go out and for them to appreciate you there; those patriots were a little bit higher class at those places and they didn't want you hanging around like a bum. I didn't really care about Taras Shevchenko; he didn't give me any help so I wasn't interested. Why should I cry for him? I was Ukrainian too and nobody helped me out.

Taras Shevchenko: he's the old man with the drooping white moustache, astrakhan hat and brooding, somewhat threatening countenance you see ubiquitously displayed in Ukrainian-Canadian social centres and in many homes. On paintings and calendars, embroidered on pillow cushions, printed on teatowels, sculpted in plaster and carved in wood. As a child, I found him only menacing but to the preceding two generations he was a kind of household god. He was a nineteenth-century Ukrainian poet, and his canonization by a mass of people just a generation ahead of illiteracy is a very interesting phenomenon, as is his cult in Canada, his incorporation into the popular culture of Ukrainian-Canadians. The closest equivalent is the commemoration of Robert Burns by all classes of Scots.

The point is that Shevchenko was not just another academic poet feted in the saloons of the wealthy and aggrandized by the paeans of the academicians. He was born a serf, and the Ukrainian-Canadians love to tell the story of his life: he came up from within their collective, ancestral misery to speak out against their condition.

Orphaned early, the starved ragamuffin was sent to school kept by the village deacon, where he led a wretched existence of hard labour, constant floggings and continued starvation. As personal valet of his master he travelled to St. Petersburg, where he was apprenticed to a painter, an uncultivated man little better than a house painter. Here by chance he fell in with a group of artists who bought his freedom and sent him to the Academy of Arts. The publication of his book, The Kobzar, instantly covered him with fame. Imprisoned for joining a group of intellectuals who aimed to improve the lot of the common people, Shevchenko lived in bitter exile for the greater part of his adult life, forbidden to write or paint. But his poetry lived on, a clarion call to his countrymen to rise against the oppression of serfdom, and gave to the Ukrainians a new national consciousness which made possible a rebirth of a people.[188]

Naturally, the intelligentsia and the middle-class in both Canada and Europe had their own reasons for enshrining such a writer. To the nationalists, Shevchenko represented the voice of a national community united against the colonialist repression of the Austrian, the Pole, the Russian. To them, Shevchenko's Ukrainian blood and his hostility to the foreigner was the essence of his poetic authority, and they accordingly extracted the appropriate poems from his opus to make their political point.

> Ah, may God pity you, my lovely country,
> Rich and luxuriant!
> Who has not marred you?
> Why must my hapless country suffer so?
> How does she merit this? Why does she perish?
> Why are her children sitting mute in chains?
> The bards have told us of our wars and quarrels,
> The years of bitter misery, the torture fierce
> Inflicted on us by the Polish rack.

To them, his importance was contained within the parameters of European experience and, in this role, he touched the imagination of only those Ukrainian-Canadians whose political consciousness had been raised around the question of liberating the Ukraine from foreign domination whether Hapsburgian or Bolshevik. To the socialists, on the other hand, Shevchenko's appeal lay in his awareness that it was the Ukrainian peasantry, that undifferentiated mass of potential revolutionaries, who held the key to the liberation of the nation. Shevchenko did not address the middle-classes, the compradors, the urban elites. To the socialists, he was much more of a class poet than a national one, and so they too quote the appropriate verse and line.

> Await no good.
> Awaited freedom do not wait –
> It is asleep: Tsar Nicholas
> Lulled it to sleep. But if you'd wake
> This sleeping freedom, all the mass
> Into its hands must hammers take
> And sharpen well the battle-axe –
> And thus start freedom to awake.

As for everybody else, outside these rarefied political circles, Shevchenko only gradually assumed significance in their emotional life. For one thing, until they learned to read Ukrainian, his writings were not accessible on a casual basis. For another, they might at first have wondered what a nineteenth century ex-serf railing against tsars and Polish gentry had to do with them, who voted in parliamentary elections, owned their own land, and never saw an Anglo-Saxon capitalist (the stand-in for the Polish gentry) from one day to the next. For yet another, it was obvious to the majority of Ukrainian-Canadians slogging away on farms and in coal mines and in restaurant kitchens, that Shevchenko was the darling of the educated class – it was they who were sending away to bookstores for his collected works, organizing the national halls and naming them after a poet, organizing Shevchenko concerts and making speeches about his life, and organizing institutes for the next generation of intellectuals.

Ruthenian Institute Successful Opening
(Shevchenko concert)

The Hall was beautifully decorated with Ruthenian flags and the Union Jack. . . . The programme of varied numbers then followed (vocal solos, a zither solo, recitations) . . . Elias Kiriak (novelist) spoke in Ruthenian giving the biography of the poet and Wm. Cory (student) followed with a similar statement in English. Translations were given in English from Shevchenko's works. . . . The concert closed by singing the Ruthenian national hymn and *God Save the King*.[189]

Nevertheless, Shevchenko eventually became their hero too. It was a question of appropriating him for themselves – never mind what all the intellectuals were saying – by coming to their own conclusions as they listened to his words at concerts and lectures, and by reading him in their own copy of *The Kobzar*. They had had a great hope that in Canada they could get some learning, that at long last they could come in touch with ideas and intellectual skills

– and here was this son of a serf telling them to "seek enlightenment!" They could tell from his language that he had profoundly identified himself with the common people and assumed their desperation as his cause. That he cared about them, cared for them, suffered for them. Where else were Ukrainian-Canadian working people to find a writer who spoke so directly and meaningfully to them – Rudyard Kipling in the school textbook? The racist H.D. in the Vegreville *Observer*? Zane Grey in a drugstore novel? Bishop Budka in the *Canadian Ruthenian*? If they read long and widely enough, and some did, they'd finally meet up with Dickens and Conrad and Sinclair, they'd subscribe to the *Western Producer* or the Edmonton *Bulletin* and make the connection between themselves and the audience of Anglophone farmers addressed by liberals and social democrats. But in the meantime, Shevchenko was to hand.

> I'll glorify
> The mute, downtrodden slaves
> And as a sentinel o'er them,
> I'll place the mighty word.

Progressive writers in other languages were addressing the ordinary Ukrainian-Canadian only by implication (in English-Canadian literature, the universal "I" was Anglo-Saxon) but Shevchenko was a blood relation. In his writings the Ukrainian-Canadians read the names of their heretofore anonymous forebears, they heard about the places their people had come from and spoke of with nostalgia, they discovered themselves marked as members of a mass of humble people suddenly taken very seriously as aggrieved and outraged and they realized that it was precisely they who were expected to do something about it.

And we, the young people, marking this anniversary [of his birth] with our older friends and comrades, should take the life of Shevchenko as an example for ourselves to follow, try to conduct our life as he did, for the benefit of the people. The

unforgettable Taras also left us this testament:
Seek enlightenment, my brothers,
Read, and reading, think. . . .
These words are a call to us to develop into conscious, cultured
people, to develop our educational facilities wherever we are, to
study ourselves and to help by teaching others. Let us mark
Shevchenko's memory with honour by carrying out his
testament and working to realize those ideals for which he
fought.[190]

It was irresistible. Compared to the outside pressures on them to
lay aside their Slavic identity, to swallow their anger about their
hardships, and smile good-naturedly at their boss, to disdain the
values of their class and imitate the styles of their "betters," reading
Shevchenko was like coming home.

The "cult of Shevchenko" was thus an altogether natural
development among Ukrainian-Canadians for as long as they read
him, as long as he made more sense about their lives than any other
writer. His picture hung in church basements and halls along with
the King and Queen, his birthday was celebrated with dances,
songs, recitations, and dramas, monuments were erected and
cornerstones laid to his memory. But just a little while later, when
the times got better and people didn't need so much consolation,
they would have to make a point of looking him up.

As with Shevchenko, so with almost the whole of the material
and spiritual culture of the Ukrainian-Canadians as they passed
from homesteading to diesel-engined farming, from the log house to
the bungalow, and the ethnic ghetto to the Anglophone "uptown."
The artifacts of the parents, which would have been familiar to
great-great-grandparents, became strange to the children, in the
same way that the poetry of a serf, which had brought tears to the
eyes of the immigrant, became an intellectual exercise for the
immigrant's son. Take, for instance, an auctioneer in Two Hills. His
father, a homesteader, had furnished his home with second-hand
castoffs; he was a junk buyer. The son, in town, sells antiques; he is
a junk seller. In one generation, the culture of the Ukrainian-

Canadian has become a roomful of curios more valuable to the city dweller who can't even name them than to the farm people who have worn them out beyond use.

At one auction sale there was an item passed to me to sell and I didn't know what it was and I was asking the people and nobody seemed to know so I asked if anybody would give me a bid on that and they laughed and said, you buy that. So I put up a bid and nobody else bid, so I had to buy it and that was how I got that item. A tobacco cutter, 1871. An Indian told me what it was.

Language

Our grammar wasn't very good and the teachers had a hard time. I'll never forget one class when the teacher made a girl run over and over again to the door. "What did you do?" "I run to the door." "No! No! You ran to the door. You ran to the door." But at home we always spoke Ukrainian because mother didn't understand English. She'd get very upset, thinking we were trying to fool her.

– Lena Galeta

* * *

I've done a lot of speaking in Ukrainian. I was MC for most of the weddings around this country for years, even at Royal Park. If there was any MCing, Mike Tomyn did it. And I tried to do it in perfect Ukrainian. And I was in politics, ran as a federal member in 1945. Also helped quite a few candidates in the provincial elections. I was a campaign agent, and I had to speak Ukrainian in some places, not Ukrainian English, I tried to speak perfect Ukrainian. I had a Ukrainian word for every English word I knew, even some words like "autonomous." I know the Ukrainian word for it. I just made up my mind to do it and I did. It's very common to use English words now. And not only that, they'll have one sentence in Ukrainian and one in English and then another one in Ukrainian and then half of the next in English and will finish up in Ukrainian. So I had pretty good Ukrainian compared to that.

– Mike Tomyn

The Ukrainian spoken by the parents of the first generation was, in the vast majority of cases, a dialect of some sort and full of grammatical and syntactical errors compared to the literary language. It was an aural, not literary, inheritance. They said "mnje" for "imja" (name), "livorucija" for "revolucija" (revolution) and "buli" for "baraboli" (potatoes). In short order, they also absorbed into their speech English words for which they knew no Ukrainian equivalent, gave them a Ukrainian pronunciation, added on the Ukrainian verb or adjective ending and used it as part of their own language. These words – garbych ken (garbage can), sipijar (CPR), ekstragyng (extra gang), zamorgicuvaty (to mortgage) – are really Ukrainian-Canadian. As are the English words which they eventually substituted for their own; no one back in the old country would ever have heard them: baksa (box), dzekrebit (jackrabbit), olrajt (all right), datsol (that's all), sanamagan (son of a gun), kenuvaty (to can food), bomuvaty (to bum).[191] The English language influenced the Ukrainian-Canadians' vocabulary for everything from names of the months to medical terms to the names of plants. This was the Ukrainian language learned by the Canadian-born; it was learned in Canada and as such was not a "foreign" language. It was part of the culture of this place.

It was also still the "mother tongue," the first one learned and the one used domestically and intimately. Most immigrant women never learned any English and the men only a "broken" English picked up like rags and bones from tortured conversations with bank clerks, elevator agents, and the postmaster.

At the time when our first pioneer settlers came here from the old country they naturally needed to buy some utensils for the house. Once a pioneer housewife went to a store to buy herself a colander. She looked all over the store but she couldn't see any colanders, and she couldn't tell the storekeeper in English what she needed. The next day she sent her husband to the store. When he came in the storekeeper asked him: "Can I help you?"

In answer, her husband said: "I like to buy a pot where the water she go, and the macaroni she stop."[192]

The oldest children went off to school speaking only Ukrainian and returned, their accumulation of English vocabulary useless in an environment where they could negotiate almost all their affairs in Ukrainian: with the priest, the shopkeepers, the neighbours, the blacksmith, and the school board. For these children, the English language was force-fed, usually by prohibiting the use of Ukrainian while at school and punishing the offenders. Most of them never did catch up with their younger siblings, all the more if they were pulled out of school after only a few years' instruction to work on the farm. Their English was learned by ear; when they wrote it they reproduced what they heard, including the Ukrainian accent. From the Lavoy post office bulletin board, 1934:

Read this Notice
Thiers one golt lost so if thiers any golt that dont belong to you then let me know please. The golt is red bay with star his forhead two years old. So if the golt is your place write to Mafty Olineck Or if youse know any place that the golt is that dont belong to them so pleace let me know or write the letter to Mafty Olinek 8 miles from Vegriville and 4 miles from Lavoy P.O.[193]

Sometimes their aural understanding of how English was literately rendered was excellent – it was the spelling that boggled them. From the minutes of a school board near Two Hills in 1938:

A spatiole meeting was held in the school howess on Juin 3 the meeting comensed at 8:30 pm the following rosalutiones were browt up as folowes 1. was mouved and sucended that on the 16 of this mont at time of Divisionel meeting the School Bowrd will be present as they have a Patation with which they wish to bring the mater up to the Divisionel School Bowrd as the People of this District wish to have the present school site changed and have to school sites in the plase of one and the

Districts amownt of children of school age is sufisundent for 2 schools.

Sometimes they were forced to write in English, even as badly as they did, and make themselves understood however imperfectly, as in a letter from an Andrew-area farmer to his brother in 1929. Obviously, either one or both of them had never learned to read and/or write Ukrainian, so for written communications English was perforce the lingua franca.

Dear Brother
Just a few lines to please you to come over to our place on November 21 and take your daughter and son with you and I would please you to go over to Harry Tomyn place and Wasyl Bilesky and Yurko Tomyn and Mike Lesakowsky and Tell them that I please them to come over because Its close to yours place and you can see them Because that makes me write to much letters and when you are comeing down come to our place on this farm where we just bought close to Andrew and tell them people the place come down and please tell them people.

Bye Bye
Yours Brother
Fred Tomyn [194]

For the younger children, learning English was not so haphazard or incomplete. Even before they went to school they had picked up a few words from older brothers and sisters and once they were going to school the had someone with whom to practice. By now, there was also perhaps a radio in the house and an English-language newspaper, and the mother as well as the father had picked up some English. The environment for these children was becoming decidedly bilingual. The parent would speak in Ukrainian, the child would answer in English and they would understand each other well enough. It would be years yet before the child would be as comfortable speaking English as Ukrainian but the trend was obvious: the longer they spent in school, the more hours they had to speak English than Ukrainian and the more frequently they associated with Anglophones, then the more fluent they became in English and the less likely they were to use Ukrainian as a tool of communication.

These were powerful forces on the first generation to adopt the English language; the irresistible one was the association between English and high status. It didn't take much analysis to see that people who spoke Ukrainian were poorer, less educated, and less respected than Anglo-Saxons, and Anglo-Saxons spoke English.

If one language is endowed with prestige, the bilingual is likely to borrow more abundantly from it as a means of displaying a higher social status, e.g., Latin words in English, or English words in Alberta Ukrainian. As the immigrant feels himself in a marginal position for a long time, he increasingly borrows from English to raise his social status, and as he gains proficiency in the new language, social pressure leads him to make a linguistic change and a complete language shift.[195]

Because of the unsuccessful struggles of their parents to establish bilingual schools in their districts, because of legislation abolishing them in Alberta, the first generation children had already understood that their "mother tongue" was disparaged by the Anglophone authorities. Once they were in school, they were punished for using it; Anglo-Canadians made jokes about it and about their Ukrainian accent. Anglophones got good jobs and made a lot of money. In other words, there were rewards in speaking English and very little in Ukrainian, except for the high regard of the priest and local Ukrainian patriot, but who cared about that? What could it deliver? The English language was seen as the way out of Two Hills County – out of farming and the menial job, out of narrow-mindedness and timidity – and into the land of the success story.

Yet, it would take a lot more than burning ambition to sound like a real Englishman. The generation was marked by its accent and its grammatical errors; in university, normal school, on the job, in the street, they were unmistakably Ukrainian-Canadian. They could change their name, join the United Church, refuse to speak anything but English, move to a "mixed" neighbourhood – but as soon as they opened their mouths and said "dis" and "dat," said Admonton for Edmonton and "I putted it in the oven," they were unmasked.

At this point of their lives (as schoolchildren) the generation was for all practical purposes between languages, losing proficiency in Ukrainian and still without fluency in English. It is not surprising then that there was an urgency in the community to provide Ukrainian-language instruction after school hours, either in the school or at the hall, by bona fide Ukrainian-speaking teachers: without it, the children would lose their capacity to communicate at all effectively in Ukrainian and would be lost to the larger world of the Anglophone. Although most of the interviewees I talked with had had several years of formal Ukrainian language instruction and could still make themselves understood in it, most felt that English "came easier." It had, after all, become their language of communication with each other almost forty years ago. When they did revert back to Ukrainian, their speech was nevertheless studded with English words and phrases, a reflection on the relative frequency of use of the two languages. The handful who felt as comfortable speaking Ukrainian as English were those who had studied it well beyond the level of after-school-hours instruction: they had been residents at an institute in Edmonton or Saskatoon or had made a study of Ukrainian literature or had been active in nationalist organizations where recent Ukrainian emigrés, with their high degree of fluency, exerted an influence. And those who were absolutely more fluent in Ukrainian than English were the priests, who were born in Europe, and the very oldest of the generation, the men and women in their seventies who had had only three or four years of English-language schooling and never lived outside a unilingual environment.

The Canadian-born are a classically transitional generation. Within their lifetimes they have experienced the change from a unilingually Ukrainian-speaking community to a practically universally Anglophone one without having moved more than fifteen miles. Under considerable pressure they redirected verbal skills from a derogated to an esteemed language and yet have almost never felt as wholly-integrated citizens of the new culture: they adopted what was necessary and what was possible from Anglo-Canadian culture and retained what was appropriate from the Ukrainian. The English they speak is often a kind of dialect, still resonant with earlier Slavic speech patterns and habits (it's only in the next generation that English will be the "mother tongue") and the Ukrainian they speak, an Anglicized variation of the original. Without access to one or another fully-developed language, they represent the payment made to transplant the immigrant peasant into the native middle-class.

TEN

Work

My father travelled. He was always a traveller. He went to B.C. and then decided to go on the land because he didn't have enough education to do something different. So he started looking around Alberta, about 1912, but every homestead he looked at was no good. It was rocky, it was sandy, so he figured he wasn't going to buy a homestead, period. He worked in the mines and ran businesses, stores. He was poor in the old country but not as poor as my mother. She came from a very poor family. They didn't worry about what they would do here because letters had come into the village from Canada saying this was a big country with a lot of room, it wasn't crowded, there's a lot of land for just a few dollars, the cities were getting bigger. So they weren't scared. They got married and Dad worked in the mines and they had a little shack. She worked to make extra money by washing the miner's clothes. By hand. She put the clothes on a bench and scrubbed them with a floor brush. They needed the money because they wanted to start something on their own. She cooked meals for workers. They had a cow. A friend of Dad's found a clucking hen with nine chicks in the bush and gave them to Mother. So when she had a hen with chicks she was rich. She was rich.

– Helen Marianych

* * *

When Dad died Mother stayed on the farm and my older brother took it over. When he got married the rest of us had to move out. In 1929 I quit school and went to work for a farmer. Did chores and field work. If I made ten bucks a month I was lucky. Milk the cows, feed the hogs, feed horses, pitch manure, haul straw, plow, seed, cut stook. I worked there two years. Save money? How? Bought myself a suit. In 1932 I came to Two Hills and my brother-in-law asked me to help in the sheet metal shop for $10 a month. I lived with them in their two-room house; they had six kids. There wasn't much business. In our business we were making pails, well buckets, pumps, troughs, chicken feeders. Seventy-five cents for a chicken fountain. Tin bathtubs. Rain barrels. During the war business picked up but we ran short of material. I went to Edmonton to work at West Steel for six months. It was tough work. You work in a big shop and hear all that big machinery going around and you come out deaf. And the smoke. Guys welding. You'd get out of there at 5 o'clock and think you were dead. I asked for a raise from 60¢ an hour but they told me I was frozen on the job. I went back to Two Hills and worked in the shop again for wages. I'm still there.

– Paul Spak

* * *

When I worked as a housekeeper, I lived right in their home, and I helped the lady with the housework, with the children and so on. I'd clean, help wash, help with a little bit of cooking, washing, ironing, scrubbing, babysitting. Most of them were English families. I think the first month I got $20 and then $25. But that was good wages when I was getting $25. There was no such thing as a day off. Sometimes I went to town for a couple of hours, but there was nothing like days off in those days. Maybe Sundays sometimes if you want to go home or to church or something. I worked right from the time I got up to the time I went to bed. I don't know, maybe I wouldn't put up with it now. I worked about four or five places during the year, for a period of two years. I didn't send the money home, I kept it for myself, spending money. Got myself some clothes. Coat, dresses, shoes, I'd never been able to do that at home. The English families always wanted a Ukrainian girl because they are harder workers. I wouldn't say I wasn't treated fairly. I never had anything to hold a grudge about. I didn't know any different, everything was good to me. They didn't look down their nose at me because I was Ukrainian, never. I think I had nice families that I worked for. If the English thought they were superior to the Ukrainians, I didn't realize it.

– Helen Hryciw

* * *

I'm a retired farmer. Quit in 1967. I'm seventy-two years old. I had a section, left it for my son. We started with one quarter from my father. We built a log house, it's still there. Made a barn myself too from logs. Granaries we had, some from logs and some from lumber. Made a chicken coop, a pigpen. My father and father-in-law each gave me two cows but they were no good because they were beef cows. I had to sell two of them to buy one milk cow. We had two kids so we needed the milk. We made cream and cheese. We had four horses, two each from my father and her father. My first year of farming one of my best horses died. You had to pay $700 for a pair of horses. We had Percherons. One sow. We bought a wagon with our wedding money. (At our wedding it was raining so hard that the crop was laid flat on the ground.) When we got our own farm we lost one crop from a frost in July. Nothing left. The wheat was just like a bran. Nothing. I got $12.40 for a boxload of it. And with two kids to feed. How do you manage? You just manage. Do what you can. You have to take it. We didn't buy the second quarter until 1948; we didn't have money until then. It was a quarter condemned by the municipality because the fellow didn't work it good, it had a lot of weeds. I had to summer fallow it. In one year I had to kill the Canada thistle, the sow thistle, the couch grass. My experience has been that if you lose a crop one year, it will put you back three years.

– Harry Verenka

* * *

I had no trouble getting a job. I don't know of anybody who didn't get a school, even those who didn't have the skills like teaching

Ukrainian or playing the mandolin or singing. I didn't care what kind of school my first one was, as long as I got a school. There weren't any roads to speak of, it was very sparsely populated, but it was bread and butter. I boarded with a farm family. I walked to school. I put on a Christmas concert and people were standing outside the windows to see it. I have pictures of that. There was a teacherage, a two-room shack whose walls you could practically see through. In the winter I woke up with ice on my eyelashes. At my next school, I was lucky because I was only seven miles from the farm and my mother would drive up to the school and bring me pyrohy and meat and potatoes. I'd go home on weekends in the summer. There was a neighbour just across the road and others just a mile away.

My first salary was $1000. The next one was $1200 because they were a richer district and sent forty-two children to the school. My salary was paid out of school taxes plus a small grant. The more populated the area the more taxes they could collect. My salary in Kraydor was also $1200. In Alberta just south of Smoky Lake I made $1375 teaching grades four to ten. They didn't like English teachers because they couldn't communicate with them. They expected you to be able to sing and play instruments and dance and work with the church choir and put on dramas – all that for free.

– Stephen Mulka

* * *

I studied five years in Belgium, finished my theological studies and came to Canada. My first parish was in Niagara Falls. I preached my first sermon to all Orthodox – Serbian, Rumanian, Bulgarian – all of them. I served about three months, and then moved to Winnipeg. In August 1962, I came to Alberta. My first parish was at Lac La Biche. I spent four years there. I built a church and a house. I had 2 1/2 members – two families and a lady. In Hyatt, Saskatchewan, I began with thirty-eight members in eight parishes. In a year, there were over one hundred and nine parishes. But this was hard work. For three years I travelled by car, day in and day out, from house to house. In Swan River, I bought the land for the church; most were young people. It was my best parish. I restored it. We sent a cheque to the consistory. They replied that there was no such parish. So I told them to set it up again because we really did exist. You see first, when I see neglect, I visit every Orthodox family, talk things over with them. I ask them: "Do you know why you are on this earth? Who gives you your crumb of bread? Do you know that people do not only live for their stomachs?" Then people begin to think. That is how I begin.

– Father Peter Zubrytsky

The Ukrainian immigrants came to Alberta to farm. They were professionals; they were farmers; they had skills and expertise. But, as homesteaders, starting from scratch, many were forced to serve several years, regressively, as unskilled labourers. It would take some time to earn a living off the quarter section but the need for money was immediate. They had to find jobs, any kind of job. They were not from the urban proletariat of Europe, schooled as tradesmen or artisans; their labouring experience there, other than on the farms, was in menial jobs in factories and mines. On the labour market in Canada they had little to sell beyond their muscle power. Unsurprisingly, they became part of the mass of overworked and underpaid wage workers who performed the dirty work of an economy industrializing and urbanizing itself. Later, when the work was done and the next generation was accruing some benefits, this labour would be seen as only a kind of down-payment paid by the illiterate and unskilled on a more secure future. No hard feelings. At the time, though, the fact that it was necessary didn't make it any less humiliating and harsh.

My father was a businessman and a very good farmer but he still felt inferior to any Anglo-Saxon, even a drunkard. *Vin anglik.* [He's still an Englishman.] He worked on the construction of the High Level Bridge in Edmonton and he walked from Ispas – ninety miles – with some bread and cottage cheese and a tent in 1911. But he often told me that the Ukrainians and Rumanians were given the real rough digging jobs for twenty-five cents an hour. What hurt them was that someone else who was supposed to be doing the very same job, a Swede or an Anglo-Saxon, was being paid thirty cents. Central Europeans were like the Chinese coolies. "Don't know nothing except how to turn a shovel over."

Some spent two years digging coal on their knees, their families housed, if at all, in a two-room company shack. While the family lived in one room, the other was given over to three or four male workers for whom the mother cooked. The pay for miners was slightly better than that for railway section workers, but night after night, loveless and homeless in the camp, they spent their pay on booze. Some cut wood and delivered it thirty miles for two dollars a load. A day's work, a day's pay. Some laid streetcar tracks and dug ditches in the city for a dollar a day. Some worked for other farmers, leaving their own harvest to be gathered by wife and children. Some had construction jobs and would walk to them, sometimes two or three hundred miles and would walk back from them, supplies for the family tied to their backs. A very many worked for the railroad laying track, for twelve hours a day under the supervision of English or German foremen. Women worked as housemaids of the middle class, ironing the dresses and combing the hair of those who had never done it for themselves.

Such labour was seasonal, lay-offs were frequent, the labour laws, such as they were, offered no protection from miserly employers, violent foremen, and dangerous working conditions. The labourers' knowledge of English was practically non-existent, their non-Slavic co-workers were often racist boors, their diet and housing left them vulnerable to typhoid and pneumonia. Building bridges, mining coal, laying track, hauling logs, digging ditches – it was mean and barely remunerative work and to say that "none were more willing to work than recently arrived Ukrainian homesteaders"[196] is only to say that they did it. It is not to say they had much choice.

Without the protection of unions or labour codes, they could be duped and maltreated with little recourse to a defense. It all depended on the luck of coming across a "good" boss who would voluntarily refrain from gross exploitation. Otherwise, it was "put up and shut up" for who was there to rally to the pathetic cause of a barefoot bohunk who couldn't even sign his name, let alone drag a boss to court?

When Wasyl and his young friends arrived in Edmonton, they met a German farmer from around Lviw who, as they discovered later, spoke Ukrainian in his home. He had brought a load of hogs to Edmonton and informed the young men that he needed labourers. He promised them seventy-five cents a day, but they had to sleep in the loft of his barn and cover themselves with horse blankets. Though they worked hard, brushing and uprooting trees in preparing the land for plowing, they were not even provided with soap and had to wash themselves in the horse trough. After two weeks of this kind of life, they informed their German employer one Sunday that they wished to go home. He refused to pay them their wages and threatened them with a shotgun. Though they had each earned ten dollars and fifty cents, he paid them only eight dollars, and then only when they threatened that they would complain to the authorities.[197]

Mines and railroads. It was rare that a Ukrainian immigrant, or even an immigrant's son, did not work on them at some time in his life. After the turn of the century, mines were opening up all over the Rockies and southern Alberta, and there were employers who in fact preferred the immigrant as employee: he was so manageable. The manager of the War Eagle Consolidated Mining and Development Company in Rossland, for instance, thought so.

In all the lower grades of labour and especially in smelter labour it is necessary to have a mixture of races which includes a number of illiterates who are first class workmen. They are the strength of an employer, and the weakness of the Union. How to head off a strike of muckers or labourers for higher wages without the aid of Italian labour I do not know.[198]

Eventually, the Ukrainian miner would be unionized and the object of as much obloquy as the English and Scots union organizers – he would come of age as a proletarian – but it would take some years of disaster and despair for the glue of class camaraderie to stick. As in the case of Peter Kyforuk,[199] it would take jobs like digging basements with a pick axe and shovel for twenty-five cents an hour, laying track in wintertime and getting one month's wages for four months' work when the contractor went bankrupt, digging coal for forty cents a ton and hammering away at a stone quarry; it would take the experience of seeing an out-of-work family live on bush rabbits, of being chased out of town by the RCMP for demanding sick benefits from the mining company, of learning that three miners had been killed while trying to organize a union, and of wiling away the evening hours by reading *Rabochi Narod (Working People)* before Kyforuk finally became convinced of the necessity of organizing the mass of unskilled workers. Without such organization, the Ukrainian miner had perforce to submit to foul working conditions for as long as he could stand it or for as long as he was alive. The Hillcrest Mine explosion of 1914 killed more than two hundred miners. In 1921, Mike Olshaski, age thirty-one, had his ribs broken by a falling beam at the CPR coalmine in Lethbridge; T. Werechuk, twenty-four, was fatally burned and Pete Chemuk, thirty-three, smothered to death by a cave-in at the Mountain Park coal mine (the board of directors, living in Edmonton, had names like Mitchell, Robinson, and Scott). Most victims are nameless and barely remembered. With the last of the memories goes their memorial.

Suddenly, a tremendous explosion shook the mine. Concussion knocked me down, unconscious. The next thing I remember were the unearthly and inhuman cries of terror, pain, and the agony of death. It was difficult to breathe; there seemed to be

no air. An intense heat hit me like a blast from a furnace. The
force of the blast had extinguished the lamps. It was pitch dark.
Cries of panic and pain were heard from all sides. Voices in
various languages beseeched God for salvation and pleaded for
help. . . . My horse lurched to its feet and began laboriously to
walk along the track in the darkness. I grabbed its mane and
half walked, half dragged myself along. I shouted to the others
to follow. Along the way, I recognized the voice of Budzynsky, a
countryman, begging to be killed. Both of his legs were crushed.
What could I tell him? What could I do? Hanging on to the
horse, I was barely alive myself, with foaming spittle running
from my mouth, dripping on my bare arms. All my hope was in
the horse. So long as it was alive and able to move along, I
could hang on. Its instincts were better than mine, and I felt it
could find the way out better than a human in the darkness. But
it swayed; it emitted sounds that I had never heard from any
animal before. I feared it was nearing its end.

And all the while, the pitiful cries of human survivors
continued: pleading for help, asking that last messages be
delivered to thier [sic] loved ones, making peace with their
Maker.[200]

Railroad work was another way of dying, sometimes suddenly,
sometimes by slow degrees with the attrition of the body and soul.
A worker would pay a contractor's agent a dollar for the dubious
privilege of being signed up for the "extra gang" and would be
shipped out to the work site in a box car. The work on roadbeds and
tunnels and trestle bridges was done with picks and shovels and
muscles. It was dangerous – "an army of 4,207 slain and 13,368
injured on the CPR and GTR"[201] over a twenty-year period – and
inhospitable.

The common labourers were for the most part Ukrainians.
These naive, trustful, bearded giants worked like elephants,
laughed like children, and asked no questions. They were
shamelessly exploited. At the time the labour laws in Canada

and America, especially for immigrants, were made chiefly for the benefit of the contractor. . . . As timekeeper in charge of sales and books, I was agent for the robbers. True enough, the lowliest of labourers got three dollars a day, a bunk with vermin-infested blanket and pillow, and free grub. But the food doled out in meagre rations was barely edible. In my commissary the labourers could buy bacon, flour and canned goods of tolerable quality, but for prices that New York clubs would be ashamed to ask. Those who didn't like it could get out (at their own expense), for there was a never-ending stream of new serfs, shanghaied by the mass procurement agencies of the East.[202]

Compared to this, the work of breaking and cultivating the homestead was a joy. At least there were no foremen about, the family was intact, neighbours were friendly and there was lots to eat. But it was tedious and risky, for all that. Back and forth, back and forth across the acres of roots, stumps and rocks, disciplining animals and dragging them around this side of collapse and disease; living through nightmares of hail and early frost; and hauling the grain a wagonload at a time to the elevators thirty-five miles away, back and forth, back and forth between home and a livery stable where "we slept on planks on which we put bundles of hay and some bedding. If there was no more room on the planks, we'd sleep on the floor."

In the meantime, the other half of the homestead economy was managed by women – at least half, considering they did field work as well – on whom the responsibility fell to keep the family alive and well no matter what. No matter hail and early frosts, crippled draft animals, absentee husband and older sons, or, for that matter, mine explosions and anti-union violence. As sensational as the suffering of male workers was, it was the everyday banality of women's work that sustained the Ukrainian-Canadians as a community. Housework created homelife. And homelife meant settlement and relationship.

Their ingenuity and productivity were prodigious. While

waiting for the garden to produce and for the husband to show up again with wages, they picked wild mushrooms and berries, snared rabbits and shot game birds, trapped muskrats, skinned them, and sold the pelts. Leaving the older children alone and carrying the baby on their backs, they got jobs in the neighbourhood hoeing gardens, pulling roots, and digging potatoes (payment was a percentage of what was dug). "They walked twice a day to work through five miles of bush. It was a backbreaking job and for lunch they were given raw carrots out of the garden."[203] They walked to town to sweep out the boxcars on the sidings for whatever grain was left on the floor. They spun and wove their own wool, ground grain for flour, pressed their own oil, wove rope from hemp, and made their own soap. If a cow died, they skinned it and tanned the hide. If a child got sick, they concocted herbal medicines. Not to mention pasturing and milking the cow, weeding the garden, cooking meals, doing laundry, knitting, sewing and mending, making bread, cheese and sauerkraut, washing dishes, and ironing clothes. In addition, of course, to rearing the children.

It isn't the sort of labour that has been commemorated on cairns or in folk ballads, it did not have propaganda value for the rising swell of ethnic and class consciousness nor was it ever accurately appreciated for its economic contribution to an expanding prairie wealth; but without it no continuous communal life among the Ukrainian-Canadians would have been possible. In their housework, women tended and nurtured men and reinvigorated them for their labour; in their childcare, they reared the next generation of workers. And in their farmwork, they often made the difference between mere subsistence and security.

Memories: cheese and sauerkraut put up in wooden barrels, peas, stringbeans, broadbeans and berries dried and sacked, homemade doughnuts sparkling with sugar. Mother in the middle of the enormous garden, reigning there as custodian of the well-fed. Mother at the woodburning stove, sweat running into her eyes as she did the canning. Mother getting up at four in the morning to do embroidery. Kids' work: weeding the garden, fetching the cow,

watering the horses, driving the tractor, washing and ironing, babysitting. When the daughters married farmers, they did more of the
same. Unpaid.

Years back, when I worked in a grocery store it was just so sad,
to see some women – they're looking after the house, they're
looking after the children, they're helping, especially when they
live on the farm, most of them help the men out with work –
get bawled out when they were buying something. Their
husbands say, "Why are you spending that money? I gave you
ten dollars already." And you would think, the poor wife, isn't
she worth that? He's got money and he's just dishing out five
dollars or ten dollars and that's all. And he can go and spend his
money wherever he wants and whatever he wants to do with it,
but because you are a wife, you are supposed to just need a little
bit and that's it. There was one farmer and he says to me, "Well,
you're lucky that you work. You've got extra money." I says to
him, "Your wife doesn't work?" He says, "No, I'll have to get rid
of her!" "She works on the farm, she keeps all the stock, she
sells chickens, she sells eggs," I says. "You figure out how much
that's worth and you see whether your wife works or not." Isn't
that the attitude of everybody? That you can work your head off
in the house or on the farm, but if you don't get a cheque, you
are not working.

The labour of the immigrant generation (and their children as
unpaid help) was meant not only just to keep body and soul
together but also, of course, (this ambition is almost a mystique) to
release the Canadian-born generation from menial work forever.
They were more or less successful. According to the 1961 census, 24
per cent of Ukrainian-Canadians in the labour forces were
"craftsmen and tradesmen," 12.6 per cent were in "services and
recreation" and 11 per cent in "clerical occupations." Almost half,
in other words, had made it into waged work. An accomplishment
not to be sniffed at. However, one should not be misled by the
occupational designations. They include not only mechanics,

tailors, policemen, artists, and bookkeepers but also janitors, waitresses, trackmen, and typists, all of them waged but some with a lot less wages than others. (Of the 12.6 per cent in "services and recreation" for instance, 8.8 per cent are classed as "janitors, waitresses, barbers, kitchen help and others.") As for the other half in the labour force, 21.1 per cent are listed as "farmers and farm workers" (compared to 10 per cent for the national average). As businessmen and professionals, however, Ukrainian-Canadians were in exactly the opposite relationship to the rest of the population. Only 5.9 per cent of Ukrainian-Canadians were employed as "managers and proprietors" compared to 8.3 per cent for the national average, and 6.5 per cent as "professional and technical" compared to 9.7 per cent for the national average. As for the professionals, they are top heavy with teachers – a third of them were so employed – and almost non-existent among physicists, computer programmers, and judges. "The general conclusion which can be drawn is that in 1961, the Ukrainians were not fully integrated into Canadian life if integration is measured by their educational levels and occupational status."[204]

More or less successful. What seems to have happened is that the majority of Ukrainian-Canadian working people simply made the same shift as the economy as a whole: as the dirty work moved from the farm to the factory/shop/office, so did the Ukrainian-Canadians. A few managed a university education or specialized training but most ended up performing the same level of services for an industrialized economy as their parents did for an agricultural one. One has only to ask about individual job experiences:

The grocery store hired me and I worked for them. For eighteen years. But not until my children were in school. That was all I could get. As a matter of fact, I kind of needed a job. I wasn't working at the time, so I put the children in school, and I thought to work for just a little while when I started, but then I got used to the job. It wasn't an interesting job but there was a cheque every month. Better than being a cashier. You go to the cafe, wait on tables, you go to the hospital, work on the floor or cleaning lady. Not much more I could do. I worked eight hours every day, five and one-half days a week. Meanwhile I was keeping a house and having a garden. I honestly don't think my daughter would grow a garden, freeze the stuff or make pickles or do all that and look after children. I don't think she'd do that, and keep a job. She would say it's too much.

I got the Co-op job in Hairy Hill in 1940 and batched in the living quarters behind the store. I did everything. I'm surprised I'm still living, I did so much. I ordered stuff, I sold stuff, I priced stuff, I did the books and then on Wednesday and Thursday I'd run down to the stockyard to buy livestock. I started at forty-five dollars a month. It was considered low but there weren't many jobs. I worked like hell, day and night, even on Sundays, when I'd catch up with my books. Seven years I did that.

I stayed here until I was eighteen, I had been working for other farmers too. In 1921 I left home completely. I worked a whole summer on a CPR gang west of Calgary. There was five hundred of us, lifting track and putting new ties under. I still remember the foreman. His name was Simon but he was Ukrainian. He was rough, I'm telling you. I was a kid. Whenever I registered at the employment offices, I said I was a spiker, but I was no spiker at all. The first day I was working with a spiker from Drumheller, Alec Boretsky – see, I still remember the names – and he was sore at me because he had to do a lot of extra work for me. Ten hours with that hammer. I was just about played out. Just a kid. We were very hard-working but sometimes the foreman treated us like a dog treats a cat. I also worked for neighbours. I worked for Sikolsky for thirty-five dollars a month cutting brush. Seven in the morning to nine at night without lunch. This was not a prosperous farm. It was mostly bush and timber and we had only three horses. It took a whole summer, with a pick and axe, to clear a couple of acres.

Building granaries for $1.75 a day. Waitressing for ten-cent tips – "it was still money" – and working at the switchboard and taking in laundry. Restaurant cook. Sorting mail in the post office. Pantryman on a CNR dining car: filling water glasses and cutting up butter. Sales clerk. Dishwasher.

These are the jobs that Charles Young, in 1931, described as "indicative of the amazing specialization which has occurred, and of the progress [the Ukrainians] have made in adapting [themselves] to the ramifications of our highly industrialized society."[205] It is a specialization of sorts when a peasant class produces a generation of cooks, waitresses, grain buyers, cashiers, spikers, meat-packers, and housekeepers. But there wasn't much specialization in the wages – twelve dollars a week in the packing plant, eighteen dollars on the railway, ten dollars behind a cash register – and even less in status. It was all unskilled or semi-skilled work that one performed for the pay-cheque and not for the love of it or for the more refined rewards of respect and admiration. Careers and "self-expression" were the luxuries of the better educated and the salaried middle-class. These were the people most Ukrainian-Canadians worked for or under, and the "progress" Young refers to was the shift from self-employed to employee, from farm to cafe. "While their sons and daughters might be asked to work long hard hours for little pay," says J.G. MacGregor about servant-girls in *Vilni Zemli*, "nevertheless their employers treated them more or less as equals, who ate at the same table with them. This example of absence of class consciousness in the West was something new in Ukrainian experience."[206] The employer may very well have been a decent person who was not so arrogant as to banish the "help" to the kitchen table; but that is hardly the point. When the daughter of an immigrant makes her living by doing chores for the middle-class Anglo-Saxon, when her father walks fifty miles to the city to collect her wages so the family can buy another pair of shoes, when she is hired so that the able-bodied children of the family can take summer trips and piano lessons, then class distinctions are operative whether one is conscious of them or not. The only thing that was new about this was that the *pan* was no longer a Polish martinet brandishing dueling pistols but a benign bourgeois profferring compliments on the ten-cents-an-hour wax job on the floors. When they went out to work, the Ukrainian-Canadian generation had few illusions about the advance they were about to make as hired hands. Someday, more well-off and relaxed, they might see their earlier working lives as a kind of boot camp for middle-class security.

In 1921, when I was fourteen, I went as a dishwasher in a lumber camp in Vilncourt just west of Edmonton. Used to be a lot of bush there. Very sad my situation, you know. I had a suitcase but I had no money. See, the fall had come and I was supposed to get my wages from the farmer I'd been working for but when the time came he couldn't pay me up because he didn't have the money. So, with the few dollars that I had collected, I bought myself a suitcase and a blanket and whatnot. So I land in this employment office in Edmonton and they tell me so-and-so time the train goes and I had to have so much money to pay the fare. But I had already spent my money, you know, young and not realizing things. So I turned around and went to this Jew's store and I traded in my suitcase and a few other things, valuables that I had. He advanced me enough money to buy the fare, and I had to wait another day, but I didn't have the money to buy a meal. So I just loaf around and wait till next day to go to the camp. I put in all winter there. The grub was good, but the accommodation I wouldn't say was the best. We just had hay mattresses. But you had a few blankets. There was all kinds of racial origins up there. Of course, I was one of the youngest and they used to kid me around, but I got along well. They treat me awfully well, but when the spring came, everything closed and I got on the railroad. I went in as a flunkey, as a dishwasher and assistant cook. That was promotion. I was experienced. Put in a summer there and next winter I go back to the bush. And after two winters of bush, I was getting up to seventeen or eighteen years of age, so I went into the mine. I went to Kimberley ore mine.

And when I landed in the mine, well, I stayed. It was an underground mine. You go down in a shaft about hundred and fifty feet. You go into the mountain. They build a little railroad, about two foot wide tracks, and you drive in with that through tunnels. So when you get in there, you have to shovel about forty tons of that ore. Ten hour shift and sometimes ten and a half, because at that time there was no unions. And when they blast, one blasting would give you at least from forty to fifty tons of that loose rock. So you gotta move all that in one shift, and you gotta build more tracks and you have to extend the pipe for to get in air. They used to drive these jackhammers with air. Oh, was it ever deafening! And you get seven, eight, nine hours of it right at the face and the dust. We wore ordinary caps and carbide lamp on our head. That was the only means of lighting so you could see what you're doing. You had a shovel, you had to load up the cars. But I didn't do that long. I ran about five, six months and then I got a chance to go in a shop. Sharpening the steel that they use. And I was doing all right at that. I saved enough money to buy a farm.

Ironic, that. To decide to be a farmer after all. Their parents had no choice but the kids did and maybe if the working conditions off the farm had been more humane and the pay ten times what it was and the chances for promotion more reasonable, they would have kissed the countryside good-bye. Or maybe, God knows, they wanted to farm. It was becoming a profession of sorts by the late twenties, no longer a grub hoe and oxen operation. It was a subject of study at the colleges and universities. The agricultural experts, disdained or ignored by the immigrants, were listened to with interest by the Canadian-born who took themselves seriously as farm managers. It wasn't good enough, financially, just to be able to make a crop grow or a cow give milk or a chicken survive the winter to lay another egg. In 1916, when the first Ukrainian-Canadian entered the Vermilion School of Agriculture, it was the thin edge of the wedge. More and more Ukrainian-speaking agents of the Departments of Agriculture and Health descended upon the communities and propagandized on behalf of new strains of disease-resistant wheat, new breeds of milk cows, new, fattening chicken feed. Their efforts paid off well. By 1930, the Ukrainian-settled area of Norma won first prize in a "Competition of Community Progress" which evaluated rural municipalities on the basis of their progress in farming, in community life, and in cultural development indicating, if nothing else, that Ukrainian-Canadian farmers, contrary to popular opinion, were not amateurs. They went on to win several awards for champion oats and barley, "Master Farmer" awards, and government positions as agronomists. None of this could have been accomplished without the decision to choose farming as one's profession.

Unfortunately, many made the decision precisely when the Depression struck and were not to realize any security until after the Second World War. But the late twenties were a bonanza and anybody farming at least half a section was prosperous for awhile. If you could hold your own for the next ten years, you would live to be a farmer again another day. As risky as the business was, there was something to be said for not dying of silicosis or not living on charity after the kitchen staff got laid off. It was a question of sticking it out and believing that an honest day's work would earn its reward.

> I am farming four quarters. I am in a little better position now than I was twenty years ago, but that's not because I made money by raising crops. I saved a little money by not buying my wife mink coats like other people did. It's not that other farmers don't know how to save, but they didn't get enough for what they were doing to be able to make a living and maybe save a few bucks for a rainy day. There wasn't enough left. My machinery is a little older. My combine is a 1959, swather, self-propelled. My newest tractor is ten years old, and one is still older. But I do all my repairing alone. I do everything for myself.
>
> We lived in a two-room house on the farm, built out of logs. I built it. We had about thirty-five head of cattle, we didn't have enough water in the well, so my wife drove them to a lake,

about mile and a half to water them, and I felt it was too hard for her. That's when we got rid of the livestock and went into straight grain. The log house is still there. I built it just the way my father built his house with mud plaster, whitewashed inside. I can build a house out of logs now.

There were times that I had hoped to have been something else. Because it was hard work on the farm, always hard work. At night when your arms ache, you hope you would quit farming and do something else. But I stuck it out. I'm not sorry that I was farming, but to date I feel that the farmer is not getting the deal that he should be getting on his product. He doesn't have the bargaining power, he doesn't set prices on his product and that's his trouble. If I could accomplish that one thing, I'd be satisfied. I wanted to quit farming this last spring, but my wife thought we should farm another year or two. Oh, maybe next year I'll quit.

The boarding house in Edmonton or Vegreville, owned by a Ukrainian, operated by his Ukrainian wife and specializing in (crowded) accommodation for single men recently arrived from the Ukraine or the farm may have been the first example of independent Ukrainian business in Alberta. A man with disposable capital need not work as a coolie for richer men; he could invest in a business and make a profit from servicing a captive clientele: his fellow Ukrainians. Few others would patronize him but the Ukrainians would be glad of a chance to do business with somebody in their own language and in the style to which both were accustomed. Mutual self-service. Why subject oneself to the disdain and malpractice of the "whites" when one could be treated with respect and sympathy by a Ukrainian grocer, barman, mechanic, hairdresser, carpenter, insurance agent, and tailor? Besides, the argument went, if you "support your own businessmen whenever possible, this in turn will assure us of a solid foundation and there will be no need for us to beg favours from others. . . ."[207] Liberation through private enterprise – a mythology apparently no less compelling for Ukrainian-Canadians than for anybody else. And when appeals to ethnic loyalty were attached to it, the message became irresistible to all but the most cynical and stubborn. The pressure was on the Ukrainian-Canadian consumers to identify the merchant's cause as their own: what's good for Babiuk's Red and White Store – or, for that matter, what's good for the Co-op – is good for you too. In the early 1900s the Vegreville Co-op (Ukrainian-managed) printed slogans on the paper shopping bags.

Sviy do svoho
Ne idit' bil'she do chuzhoho.
V Russkim shtori vse kupuyte,
I chuzhentsiv ne huduyte.

(Rough translation: Let's stick together/Stop going to the foreigner's, [i.e. non-Ukrainians]/Do all your shopping at the Ukrainian's store/Let the foreign bastards starve.)

Trouble was, in the case of this Co-op at least, the consumer didn't necessarily always feel treated with consideration. Very often the prices were higher than the competitor's but to go across the street to the "Jew's" was regarded as an act of bad faith. Adding insult to injury, the Co-op managers, self-styled intelligentsia and ethnic progressives, sometimes behaved arrogantly and superciliously towards their "sheepskin" customers, who must have, eventually, come to the sour conclusion that a profiteer is a profiteer is a profiteer.

There were, however, many businessmen who were neither more nor less educated or politicized than their clientele and whose profits were no more startling than the income of a successful farmer or tradesman. When no one else would dream of setting up a business in Hairy Hill or Two Hills or Musidora, they filled the gap and when others, more ambitious or greedy, would take their profits and move to the city, they stayed on, almost as a community service. "Ethnic loyalty" worked both ways. A consumer could appeal to it when it was time to pay a bill or ask for more credit. And a mean or mercenary merchant, even if one had no choice but to go to his store could be socially ostracized. As jobs went, it wasn't the securest way of earning a living: whenever the community was short of capital, sales took a nosedive; whenever the banks' credit policy tightened, expansion was forestalled; when the roads were paved, business was siphoned off to the larger towns. As jobs went, though, it didn't break your back. And you might even strike it rich. A general store. A barber shop. A bit of real estate or used cars. Repairs. Services.

> I worked for an electrician in Edmonton for a year and then I went into business with a couple of others but I was in the shop from nine in the morning to eleven at night and I thought life was too short for that kind of a life. The electrician here in Two Hills was bugging me to come and work with him. Then he quit, I bought him out and I took over. He was starving in this business. I'm not sorry I made the move but I'm sorry I never moved to a larger town later. You get into a rut. There are many disadvantages to having a business where you know everybody. "Come on, Sam, give it to me cheaper." "We've been friends for so long. You're not going to charge me all that for that transistor. I know the mark-up." I point out to them that when they get their wages they don't tell the boss they'll take five dollars less. Everybody thinks the electrician has money up to here. But it's not true.

In the old country, one of the very few people to get an education was the priest, an education variable in quality but still more than that of any other Ukrainian; and if he was venerated, it was as much for his "professional" accomplishment as for his spiritual authority. Until the Ukrainian-Canadians began graduating in their handfuls from the normal schools and universities, the priest was one of the two or three people in the community with specialized training and learning, and on him fell a whole range of responsibilities deemed appropriate if not imperative to his status. Naturally, not every priest could live up to them – the profession was not free of mediocrities, sloths, and frauds – and eventually he was superceded in status by doctors and lawyers, and even teachers, who made more money if not more sense. But for the most part the priests were hard workers and poorly paid for their commitment. The discrepancy between their sophisticated education and their mundane parish work wearied some; the contradiction between their old country status and their parishioners' hostility embittered others; the conflict between the goal of selflessness and the need for material security overtook them all. They were professionals often living at the economic level of poor farmers, experts in questions of less and less interest to parishioners and lonely prophets of ethnic doom in a land of swelling Anglo-conformity. Without much choice but to "keep on keeping on," they grew old and fatigued and watched the next generation of priests either settle happily into mediocrity or give in guiltily to melancholia. Lucky the priest with his passion unrebuffed and his kids in winter coats! A living twice over. Most priests had to make do with one living, more or less skimpy.

I was ordained in Chicago, Illinois on July 12, 1926 and I was sent to Shepenitz to serve eight or nine parishes. In Shepenitz, I travelled by buggy and cart, because they didn't have good roads. They were such roads that I wouldn't be able to go by car, I'd have to ride trains for long distances. It took me about three or four hours to get to Myrnam by horse. We didn't have any telephones. People came to see me when there was a sickness in the family. A child died in the winter time; it was cold, no medical attention and the child passed away. But they helped themselves all they could. Pioneer days were hard days. But they didn't seem to mind, they worked and did their best.

And you know, at that time, there was some kind of communistic trend. They used to call the priests all big shots, they said we wouldn't work. But I came and helped them for so many days, five, six days working just like that, and they liked me. And at the end of threshing, they had a little gathering. I had my supper and I came in and they said, hey, here is our "little father." I had to serve each Sunday, and every day after four I used to go to schools and teach them catechism and Ukrainian history, and make them understand who they are. I taught them in Ukrainian and at that time most of them did understand Ukrainian and English. But certain terms that they couldn't understand in Ukrainian; well, it means that I had to use English. Just like now.

In church, we didn't have a choir. So being musical, I taught them how to sing. We had concerts. I organized a choir, and it was a pleasure, it was a joy. First, in the beginning, we had Mother's Day concerts, and then we had some concerts and some plays, and then when March came, we used to have Taras Shevchenko concert. As they do have now. Everything was new for them, they didn't know those things at that time. They didn't have a chance to learn them; didn't know much about the Orthodox church or about Ukrainian history; who Ukrainian people are. I started gradually and they just loved it. They were proud of their church. And then I did complete my mission.

When Ukrainian-Canadians talk about themselves in the professions, they like to refer to the lawyers, doctors, dentists, and academicians among them. But the fact is that the overwhelming majority of Ukrainian-Canadians educated beyond high school were people who had decided to become teachers. In 1941, as in 1961, teachers made up the largest category of "professionals" in the Dominion census (clergymen were second). One thousand, two hundred and thirteen teachers and two hundred and two public service workers. The disparity in numbers reflects not so much that Ukrainian-Canadians of that generation were uniformly pedagogical zealots or that schoolteaching delivered rewards that a post office job didn't, but that work in the public service (not to mention high status jobs in the private sector) "was considered a privilege reserved for certain nationalities and the access to which for Ukrainians was only accidental."[208] But there was no objection to Ukrainian-Canadians holding a teaching job in a one-room rural school among Ukrainian-Canadian farm families – in 1940 there were exactly two teachers of Ukrainian origin in the Edmonton Public School system – and so inevitably most educated Ukrainian-Canadians became teachers.

Some, of course, really wanted to teach. They had, like priests, a sense of vocation. "Some of my teachers really fascinated me. They had discipline and order, they got results. So I felt that I wanted to contribute to the younger people something of what these teachers had given me. It was hero worship. They were my idols." Some were motivated by community spirit and happily assumed all the responsibilities expected by the school boards of their employees: a Ukrainian-Canadian hired by Ukrainian-Canadians was expected to provide leadership in cultural and political work for the whole community; was expected, in other words, to return to his or her people the surplus profits of education.

> Our intelligentsia in Canada must be in close contact with the rest of the population of the community. Our progress in Canada will depend mainly on the following factor: the length of time it will take to create a large number of our own intelligentsia with all attributes for leadership in our national (ethnic) life and which will not break away from the people, forming a cast of *paniv* (upper class)....[209]

This at least was the hope, more or less fulfilled. Less, by the lazy and dull-witted who faded away into mediocrity, and by the personally ambitious who soon enough deserted the rural classrooms and communities for more lucrative and high-status positions in administration and politics (and soon enough the "pany" were reborn). More, by those committed to teach under the community's conditions, assuming responsibility for hockey and softball clubs and paperwork for the Elks' and Lions' clubs: if not, they would be asked to move along.

Looking back on the early days of the profession, a teacher now would have to say that such local regard and such symbolic emblems of status were a kind of compensation for the bad pay and working conditions – no school library or gymnasium, make-shift equipment, fifty-six students in a class, dreary loneliness, and a draughty shack for home. It would be another kind of worker mentality that would organize collectively against these conditions; at the time, this generation put up with them. They feared losing their jobs if they made a fuss (it was a buyer's market) and besides, compared to the majority of Ukrainian-Canadians, their jobs represented one foot in the door of the middle-class. If it was a choice between money and "professionalism," the money could wait.

In the Ukrainian-Canadian pantheon of professionals, lawyers have always occupied a highly-esteemed position – the mystique, perhaps, of a seeming power to manipulate laws to one's own advantage – a shocking proposition to Austro-Hungarian subjects and other second-class citizens – but even so it was a relative esteem based on the degree to which the Ukrainian-Canadian community would give business to one of their "own." In this respect, the lawyer was in the same relationship to the people as the merchant and the teacher: only tolerated (at best) by the majority of Anglo-Canadians, he derived his power from the ghettoized mentality of "ethnics" who knew they could not expect a fair deal from non-Ukrainian merchants/teachers/lawyers and believed they could get it from their own. In turn, he was expected to make his expertise available to the people who needed it most. If he didn't, who would? The "English" lawyer was working for Them. If the Ukrainian-Canadian lawyer, thanks to this bond of trust and mutual interest, made a lot of money and quickly forged a place within the elite of the ethnic community (together with the doctor, dentist and, maybe, the secretary-treasurer of the county), it was considered only natural. He had, after all, risen above the vulgar destiny of the mass of Ukrainian-Canadians; he had shown Them what a bohunk was capable of and had returned to his fellows to provide an important service. Never mind that he had little choice, or that much of his status derived from the money he was able to collect from people with problems or that there were many who were instinctively suspicious of a lawyer's "wiles" and "tricks" – he was a brother for all that, and expected to act with authority for those unable to act for themselves. In return, he had a ready-made clientele.

We have clients all the way from Myrnam, and then some from Vermilion and north of Two Hills, and Willingdon and Hairy Hill, Andrew and Lamont, and Holden and up to Viking and east to Mannville even, which is close to Vermilion. I've been in the area for twenty years and I've had repeat customers and people who have been sticking with me over the last twenty years.

I had a general practice in Two Hills. It was everything from estate administration, wills and criminal matters, domestic relations, conveyancing, land transactions, mortgages and things of this type. When they were purchasing lands, or when they were borrowing moneys, or entering into contracts on purchases of equipment, or having difficulties with machinery suppliers, things of this type. Or sometimes, the preparation of leases, farm leases, or difficulties between land owner and tenant and not accounting for share of crops. Or sometimes, even such things as boundary and fence disputes or cattle going out from pastures into grain crops and damage actions. And there were also motor vehicle accident cases and then a number of criminal matters. Somebody charged with impaired driving or ordinary criminal assault, things of this type, or thefts. There wasn't all that much criminal activity, but no community is immune from these things. But there were no murders, no serious or aggravated assaults. There may be a barroom fight or something, and minor things of this type. Every once in a while domestic disputes or separation agreements and there was an odd divorce, but very few of those. In Two Hills, I'd say the people are quite rigid in their principles and their morality is on a very high level. Well, things have changed now, but at that time, divorce was unheard of.

I'd say it has helped to be Ukrainian. Especially for the Ukrainian clients. I think, slowly, it's coming where it doesn't matter whether you speak Ukrainian or not, as the older generation fades away and the younger ones come in, and we haven't got the large immigrant population that there had been in the past. And I think people look to service more than anything else these days. But I still would say that all things being equal, and suppose there are two law firms providing equal type of service and if there's a Ukrainian, some of the Ukrainians, especially the older ones will go to *nash* [ours].

Ask them what they wanted to be when they grew up. The farmer wanted to be a rancher, the stenographer a nurse, the parish priest an academic, the cashier a teacher, the teacher a principal, and the principal a professor. They grew up and found they had already gone as far as they were going to go. For many that was good enough, and as good as they felt they deserved. For others, as for me, listening to them, the compromise felt more like a forfeiture of who they might have been if they hadn't been Ukrainian-Canadians fresh off the farms at a time when to be Anglo-Saxon from a high school in the city was to be everything.

ELEVEN

Depression

My wife and I worked two years for my father before we got our own farm and only sixty-two acres were cleared. The rest, we had to break ourselves. The year after was the early frost and the third year was dried out. This was in 1927. And by 1930 the prices started to go down. Instead of selling some wheat at $1.30 I stored it to sell the next year at $1.50. Instead, it went down to 60¢ and I had to pay storage. Why didn't we quit? How? Go where? With what?

– Harry Verenka

* * *

There was no crop insurance for frost – another time the crops got frozen by an early frost on August 2 – and the kids would get sick and somebody would need an operation, there were doctor's bills. To send kids to school you needed clothes and it was hard to get clothes. You needed money for that. Prices were too low to bother trying to sell milk and butter and eggs. The work wasn't worth it. But we didn't lose anything. We kept what we had. Dad sold the pigs to pay the mortgage with compound interest. He was very nervous. He said he had thought it was going to be a good life but that things were turning against him.

– Kay Palamaruk

* * *

In '35 all kinds of businesses were going broke. We drove through all kinds of towns checking to see what was for sale. So we bought a store for sale in Myrnam and stocked it with $1,200 worth of drygoods. My family lived in two rooms in the back and my brother-in-law set up a cot right inside the store. I knew nothing about business. One evening, an old man came in and told me that we were selling our cattle salt blocks for $1.05 and the store across the street was selling for 85¢. We'd run short of goods because we didn't buy in bulk. When I got a chance to pick up the International Harvester dealership I became just a silent partner in the store.

It was tough trying to make a go of business in those years. In '35 when we came into that area the crops froze. In '36 we were hailed out and I couldn't sell any amount of machinery to speak of. So my brother-in-law and I organized a band – I played the sax and violin and he played a car horn attached to a kazoo and he had a good voice – one boy played a banjo and somebody else a drum and we played at dances in the halls for 25¢ or 50¢ a night. We played in Mannville, Clandonald, Two Hills, country points. I audited books – livestock books, hospital books, for $10. We were much worse off than when I had been teaching. Spring of '37 was dry. I sold maybe one seed drill and one disk. I tried to look for another school. But then it started to rain and it rained for three days and even while it was raining farmers came in putting in orders for a binder or a plough or a disk. So it looked like it might be a promising year. In May I became secretary of the village for $75 a year. I decided to stick it out for another year. That fall I sold nine binders. And I became the secretary of the hospital for $150 and sold hail insurance. So we stuck out 1937.

– Stephen Mulka

* * *

After school in Vegreville I worked in my relative's store and then I'd do homework. Sometimes I went skating. But I never took out a girl while I was in high school. There was no money. Two bits was as big as the rear wheel of a wagon. In Edmonton I could have gone to the Gem Theatre for a nickel but I didn't have a nickel. My uncle in Edmonton used to work in a brickyard and in winter they'd be laid off. He didn't have money to buy coal to heat his house, so we went digging in the river bank for coal. You had to make do and you did. How could you have a revolution? When you didn't have a nickel for the movies, how could you buy a gun?

– Paul Spak

* * *

During the hard times Dad was travelling all around having meetings to tell people not to sell eggs for 4¢ and not to sell their grain for 30¢ a bushel. He went to farms and halls and schools and put up notices about the meetings. This wasn't just a Communist movement because my parents were never Communists. A bunch of fellows a mile from our farm, they were Christians and churchgoers, and yet they tipped a box of wheat into the snow. They said to the guy, "You cannot take the wheat to the elevator. Understand?" and he said, "No, I'm taking it." He was breaking the strike. They tipped over his wagon and told him to go home. He went. The same thing happened with a woman who had a can of cream. She brought it to the station and they told her to take it home. She said, "No." They said, "Take it home." She said, "No." So they opened the can up and spilled it on the ground. It did some good, but not much.

– Helen Marianych

* * *

There must have been three, four thousand people at the Hunger March in Edmonton. But it was no good, Premier Brownlee didn't even come out to meet us. That's what most defeated us. I mean, a lot of us understood that he couldn't do too much, but we figured since it's a farmers' government, least he can do is to come out and explain. But they wouldn't let us near the Parliament Building. They got Mounties on horseback and they just plowed right through us. Well, we didn't come there with the clubs to fight. We came peacefully, demanding the moratorium on debts and so forth. And actually, at that session before spring, he did pass that legislation. But he was so ignorant that he didn't come out, or Minister Reid of Agriculture. He wouldn't come out and tell us what could be done and what couldn't be done. Instead, they sent

234

an army or police force of about three hundred, and so you can see
the resentment in the farmers' attitude.

– Jack Malenka

————

The Ukrainian-Canadian generation's coming to maturity during
the Depression marked them for the rest of their lives. Not just in
terms of their attitudes towards personal security, the work ethic,
and the following generation of hedonists, but also in terms of the
maturation of their politics. I'm not simply speaking of who joined
what political party and why, or just of the fact that the miseries of
the period provoked widespread, organized protest – not all were
lambs to the slaughter! – but more generally of the profound
alteration in consciousness that occurred in many Ukrainian-
Canadians. If subscription to the mystique of private enterprise and
the mythologies of sacrifice and reward, assimilation and
advancement had served many of them as psychological cushions
during the preceding period of settlement and education, the abrupt
bankruptcy of these notions left them naked to the winds.

Their economic vulnerability was the first shock: in 1937,
"probably 75 per cent of the holdings in the entire [Ukrainian-
Canadian] block are 160 acre farms"[210] and the dismally low prices
for agricultural products in the thirties meant that the average
quarter section could no longer provide more than subsistence
living. Teachers' salaries were cut, goods mouldered on store
shelves, municipalities failed to raise enough taxes for roads and
relief and mortgage companies foreclosed on debts. So much for the
fantasy of securing a foothold, through hard labour and frugality, on
the cliff face of Canadian capitalism: "only them what already had a
lot will stay steady." The second shock, like thunder after the
lightning, was that the dream of the immigrants for their liberation
from the material and mental culture of serfdom was passed on to
their children as prickly shards of illusion. So much for the pride of
race and posture of loyalty: in the thirties, as everlastingly before,
the Ukrainians were grist in the mills of privilege, power, and
politics. (More specifically, those Ukrainian-Canadians involved in

socialist, Communist, or just plain populist political activities – "troublemakers" – found themselves exposed again to the baneful hostility of racists and assorted conservatives, and once again the cry was heard in Canada to deport or otherwise silence "foreigners," public charges, and agitators. A kind of psychological pogrom, this hostility revealed to Ukrainian-Canadians the anti-libertarian tendency of the Anglo-Canadian establishment and soured them about advertisements of Canadian democracy and decency.) Their pride and dignity turned out to be of little import to the forces that shaped their success or failure; the dream to be the creature of nobody's imagination but their own.

These were the provocations – economic and psychological disruption – shared by them all; but the responses, the ways of coping, varied considerably. Along with non-Ukrainians, many Ukrainian-Canadians accepted their situation as inevitable, "toughed it out," and believed that no decent democratic government would actually let them be irreversibly ruined. Others felt the appeal of agrarian populism and joined the CCF or Social Credit in the belief that if one kind of political party had botched things, another, different kind could clean up the mess. Some didn't, couldn't, wait for somebody else to act on their behalf – the wheels of parliamentary democracy turn slowly, slowly – and spontaneously organized local protest marches and strikes. Some saw the hardships as just another example of the inherent injustices of monopoly capitalism and accordingly joined the Communist party. Of course, some suffered less than others – even a cut-back salary was still a guaranteed income; and farmers with a lot of cultivated land and several good years behind them could afford to carry losses for awhile – and such people did not have to reexamine so attentively their assumptions about their situation: the "system" and its logic still worked for them, however creakily. From their point of view, the Depression was a temporary malfunction of a process that would eventually pay off and the important thing was not to lose heart nor to give way to cynicism nor to attempt foolishly a revolutionary overhaul. As the status of Ukrainian-

Canadians was ambiguous at best, protest could only make matters worse. On the other hand, there were all those who, suffering more, felt betrayed and abandoned by a "system" whose promises of abundance and just reward were withdrawn unexpectedly. They survived, but at the expense of their hope and good will. The cleavage between them and their more optimistic and forgiving neighbours in the Ukrainian-Canadian community found its most sensational expression in political activity and destroyed forever the illusion of cohesion through ethnic sameness. It may have appeared that the Depression affected them all the same way but when it was all over it was obvious that there was more than one, sanguine, way of looking at one's Ukrainian-Canadian position in the world.

Most Ukrainian-Canadians in the thirties were still on the farm, either their own or their parents'; and so to describe the Depression from a farmer's perspective is to describe it for almost everyone. (From the child's point of view, circumscribed as it was by lack of transportation and minimal communication with the outside world, the Depression never did have greater significance than what was happening to the immediate family on the farm: hand-me-down clothes, meatless suppers, fewer or no Christmas presents and the strained expressions on the faces of Mom and Dad.) The story of the Depression is the story of what happened on the farm and once you've heard one you've heard them all almost. There were important differences – clear title vs. mortgage, good soil vs. bad, health vs. sickness, one hundred acres cleared vs. fifty, honest grain buyers vs. cheats – that explained some families' relative security but, nevertheless, there is an archetypal Depression story.

When I came here in '28 I bought one quarter of land with fifteen hundred dollars down and the balance to pay in annual installments. In '28 there was no homesteads. You bought from other land speculators or neighbours. Anyways, I bought it in a boom. 1928-29 was a boom year. I bought this one quarter for around $5000, just about sixty acres cultivation and no buildings or anything. And then I got married. I stayed with her father until spring. And then in spring I built a two-room shack on the farm, starting from scratch. I figured at that time the farming looked prosperous; reasonable good prices. But then, no sooner I get settled on the farm when in 1930 we got the Dirty Thirties, Depression or recession or whatever you want to call it.

In 1929, I still got $1.25 a bushel for wheat which was considered good price at that time. And in 1930 I got only 50¢ a bushel. And I was fortunate to get even that because those days, you see, there was no marketing board. It was strictly a grain exchange, open market. So today you take say a load of wheat and maybe you listen on the radio and in the morning it'll be $1, and you come to the elevator and the elevator tells you it's already 80¢. So you decide well, I couldn't sell for eighty, I'm going to starve. You wait another week and it goes down to 70¢. You had thirty days to make up your mind. Well, it was all right if it stayed the same or if it went up, but if it was going down? Pretty soon you figured, well, you are going to lose everything.

I was just starting out and I had certain commitments already made. Those days you bought the machinery not through the finance company or through the bank, you bought it direct from the agent and the company. You signed the notes, and you paid your annual installments to the company. You paid maybe 25 per cent down on seed drill, which I acquired, and binder and plow. The interest rate was about 7 per cent. But if you didn't make your payment, there was a clause in the agreement that said they give you thirty days grace and if you didn't meet in thirty days this payment, they had the full right to repossess that machine, it didn't matter what. I had three commitments. I had the seed drill, I had the plow and the binder.

And although the price was not big, when you compare these three commitments with the wheat down already to 50¢, and I didn't have that much wheat, either, then I figured out that unless I sell and meet these commitments, I'll lose everything. Should I not sell this wheat at 50¢, I figured I'll lose everything, so I sold it. And people that held on, they finally sold it for 19¢. The oats went for 7¢ and the barley about 10¢, and it used to cost us about 7¢ a bushel just to thresh it. Let alone the cost of your seed, let alone your stook and twine. Not to mention your labour. There was about five or six different elevator companies, but it didn't matter, still you had the same deal from them all. And you still got a worse deal because the agent would come out and he would grade everything number four, because that's the only room he had.

And I had lovely wheat. It had been stooked, it was well sheltered, wasn't wet, it was good and the field was reasonably clean. But so either I give it for four or take it home. Are you going to take it ten, fifteen miles home? Farmers would haul three, four thousand bushels of wheat, and had quite an expense, and then they had to sell it for 19¢. I couldn't make very much money up until 1935. It got so bad, because unemployment was so bad, and every cent that I'd earned in three years working hard in the mine and the smelter I'd sunk into the farm. You know, I never paid up the land until I quit farming.

Variations on the theme. One couple operated the post office as well as their farm, which brought in an extra ninety dollars a year; this was translated into a bed and buggy. They never drank, they never smoked. "Some people were partying too much, having a good time, so they didn't have enough money to pay their bills. That's the difference between them and us." Survival is this side of a pack of tobacco. Or an insurance policy cashed in to pay the interest on a loan. Or a relative well-off enough to hire help at harvest time. Large or small yields, the price paid per bushel or animal represented only a fraction of the costs of mortgages and loans; every family endured the heartbreak and chagrin of delivering up to the buyer a wagonload of wheat or a couple of pigs for a fistful of loose change.

And with this handful, a variety of essential expenses had still to be met. Food and clothing, taxes, interest on borrowings, domestic and farmyard provisions. The bare minimum of needs. The simple satisfaction of physical survival. Early in the decade you had learned to withdraw expectations of material progress – each year more comfortable than the one before, last year a radio, this year a car – and now you measured success by being no worse off today than yesterday. Or by observing that a neighbour was a lot more desperate than you. You should, perhaps, consider yourself lucky. There were widows' families with one pair of shoes for seven children and ragged clothes hardly covering their nakedness. Families with bread and jam for dinner. Farmers with more debts than their land was worth and others who lost their land to the municipality because they could not meet their taxes three years in a row.

The pride in not-going-under was the thing, the refusal to depend on assistance and the insistence on finding one's own solutions. In a lot of cases, this mentality depended on accepting the common view that, no matter how dreadful the situation, one was still obliged to fulfill one's end of the bargain with banks and creditors, even though they were manifestly prospering amid the general deprivation; and to view the failure to keep this bargain as a failure of character. A man signing himself "Debtor Farmer" wrote a letter to the editor of the Vegreville *Observer* in 1933 expressing this mentality. Those who couldn't "cut" it, who succumbed to failure and defaulted on their financial obligations, were a disgrace to the conscientious poor, and gave them all a bad name.

I happen to be one of those farmers who has a mortgage and I cannot keep up my payments. Yet my relations with my mortgage company are most pleasant. I look upon them as a buttress, knowing that if I am reasonable, they will not only grant liberal extensions, but will come to my assistance in a case of emergency.

I am doing the best I can. I farm as economically as

possible, and only expect a very little from my crop for living expenses. Practically the whole proceeds after paying for threshing, twine and grist, and providing for seed and feed, goes to my creditors and the living comes from the cows, pigs, chickens and the garden, which any practical farmer knows is possible.

I do believe the great majority of us farmers would feel disgraced if we deliberately evaded the payment of our debts. The maintaining or perhaps I should say the restoration of our credit is vital. Honest men are entitled to some credit and during these times, they are entitled to protection against harsh creditors, who are a menace to a country, but don't forget the dishonest and lazy debtor is in exactly the same class. Let our laws look after the honest hardworking debtor, also the honest creditor, both of whom pay taxes and are the backbone of the state, and set up some other kind of machinery to look after the undesirables.[211]

The "undesirables." Presumably he means people like Helen C — whose mother's allowance the Municipal District of Sobor wanted to cancel in 1929. A superintendent from the Department of Neglected Children reported on her situation:

I beg to inform you that Helen C—has no property whatever. Last year they had a crop in on a rented farm at Musidora, there were only thirty acres under cultivation. They received two-thirds of the crop for their share but the crop was frozen so their share did not amount to much. Her son John who is about nineteen years of age purchased S.W. 1-51-10-4 last fall for twenty-two dollars an acre paying one hundred dollars in cash and agreeing to pay the balance in time. This farm lies five miles north of Minburn and has one hundred acres under cultivation. John had four horses, a plow, wagon, harrow and seed drill and one cow. John is a sturdy young man and appears to have the right attitude towards life and is likely to make a success of this venture.

I believe her allowance of twenty dollars a month should be continued.[212]

The undesirables. The families, abandoning their dried-out farms in Saskatchewan for homesteads in Peace River, travelled by hayrack along the highway, stoves and mattresses piled up, cows following behind. The men on the boxcars, going west to east and back again in search of work, came begging at a house for a bowl of soup. The widows and deserted women collected five dollars a month in mother's allowance and, to make it go further, mixed weeds in the porridge.

As bad as it was on the farms, families could grow their own food, milk a cow, and sit tight on the one quarter section; at least that was paid for. People in town were "sitting ducks": employers laid off workers, landlords evicted tenants, and merchants cut off credit. For these people, the humiliation of going on the "dole" was the clear and present possibility against which they organized all their remaining resources and kept a step and a half ahead of the application forms, chits, and supervisors' reports that rained upon them once they went on relief. Besides, applying for relief meant draining the municipal budget of funds that had been collected from friends and neighbours not much better off than themselves – "The government had to take over a lot of municipalities because they couldn't collect any more taxes, there was no road work being done and the town couldn't feed nobody" – and meant publicly acknowledging that they had given up while those around them were still putting up a fight. The least they could do was hang in to the bitter end.

There were five of us kids. Mother was completely out of her tree. My older brother knew that my father couldn't cope, my mother wasn't coping, but he could. He was big and he was very strong. He was very wild. He'd hang around the stockyards and he'd unload cattle from the cars and he'd get thirty, forty cents from Mr. Woods who was very humane. Old man Woods. He'd unload about ten boxcars of cattle, loading them from the stockyards into the car, prodding them up the chutes. And closing gates, opening gates. And he'd get some money and he'd have fifteen cents for the movie house Friday night and he'd buy himself some bars and some sandwiches and he'd survive. And he'd always give money to Mother too. So we go to the store and get credit from the storekeeper who was quite humane. You could sit there and have Orange Crush, a roll of kubasa and white bread. We loved white bread. It was like cake to us. On pig day, Wednesday, we would take the stock to the stockyard and get a little money and go to the store; it was always embarrassing to go there and say, "Could you put it on the bill, please?" But he didn't mind because my dad had made a deal with him. He had sold him our house for about one hundred dollars.

The newspaper for 1933: a year in the life of the Depression. Petty theft is on the increase. The school fair in Vegreville is cancelled because no grant is forthcoming from the Department of Agriculture. Special notice to farmers! We have reduced the price of milling to 22 1/2 ¢ a bushel! Teachers' minimum salaries were cut from $840 to $600. There is a sale of village property under the Tax Recovery Act. Wheat acreage remains the same.

Two Hills News: One member of the community who is evidently undaunted by the Depression is Nick Dowhaniuk. That gentleman has in the course of construction a large and somewhat imposing residence; larger in fact than any other in this fair village. This is interesting from another angle, as it suggests that Nick is not expecting a Communistic regime to prevail here in the immediate future.[213]

Dowhaniuk had earlier sold forty acres of land to the CPR and now owned the general store – "Businessmen didn't do too badly. Like the groceryman. Food was essential. You had to buy" – and so may have been forgiven his rather ostentatious optimism in the future by those with less money at the time. Judging from what's left in the archives, they were an absolute majority.

From the Vegreville General Hospital to the secretary-treasurer of the Municipality of Plain Lake: a woman from Two Hills "who appears to be an indigent of your Municipality" is admitted to the maternity ward, her case certified to be one of "urgent and sudden necessity," which is to say she has no money and the rate-payers will have to pay the bill. From the village of Two Hills to the Department of Public Works: "I have been requested to write to your Dept. and ask for the removal of a shack which is owned by Frank P— of Two Hills and is located on your property. . . . At the present time neither the Village or School District are getting any taxes from it. Therefore they would like it moved to some other property." From the village of Two Hills to the Department of Municipal Affairs: "Mr. Philip L— and Wife have moved into our village off the farm. . . . Now as far as I can find out they have no visible means of support. And I expect it will only be a short time before they apply for relief. They rented a house here and gave a waggin [sic] in payment for eight months' rent. Would it not be up to the municipality they came from to look after them?" From the judicial offices of the government of the Province of Alberta to a resident of Two Hills:

> I am informed by the solicitors for the plaintiff that you were in to their office yesterday with a view to settling this matter [of an unpaid bill]. I am setting out below the amount still owing on this claim and all details showing how the balance is arrived at. Upon receipt by me of this amount I am prepared to release the seizure of the car.[214]

From the Department of Municipal Affairs to all municipalities:

> In view of the improved crop conditions in some parts of your district, it would be appreciated if your Council will have the relief situation in the district reviewed with a view to having all recipients of relief who have mature gardens and cows milking, and are otherwise able to provide for themselves, cut off relief.

Farmers who have suffered crop damage due to hail, grasshoppers or drought may require further aid.

From a woman in Edmonton to the secretary-treasurer of the Municipality of Sobor, asking for the tax notice on her farm:

> You have a beautiful country all around there. If you ever saw the land that the farmers west of Wetaskiwin were trying to make a living on you would appreciate your land more.[215]

Appreciated or not, the land was not providing much of a living for anybody, neither for the farmer, nor the town merchants who depended on the farmers' purchasing power, nor for the municipality which needed taxes to provide services and jobs, nor for the labourers who needed the jobs, and housewives and children the wages, nor for churches which depended on donations and community organizations on fees. An application for relief meant that, for one person after another, this complicated and integrated economic system had come to a grinding halt. Not a single dollar more could be extracted and the only solution left was to appeal for help from fuller coffers than those of poor, depleted, and debt-ridden Two Hills.

> You were allowed to go out on road work to a maximum of $10. But you weren't paid this in wages, you were given a tax credit. The municipality needed to build roads and repair roads and install culverts and it got this done by free labour really. We needed money to pay for sanitorium patients and indigent patients and mother's allowance and old age pension. The municipality was thousands of dollars in debt.

December 1935, a married couple in their forties apply for relief in the town of Two Hills. They have four children, a "small, poor" garden, a house they rent for $15 a month, no "relatives able to help" and no car: "Income previous 12 months: $172.00." "Cause of distress and reason for which relief is asked: Unemployment." They read and sign: "I am destitute and not able to provide for myself and

245

dependents from my own resources, and I have no income or property of any nature whatsoever other than that set forth in this declaration."[216] Relief is granted and the wife gets a form letter addressed to the grocery store listing the ten dollars' worth of groceries she is entitled to receive per month:

Flour (the cheaper varieties only, and no bread), rice, beans, ground meal, oatmeal, 4 lbs. sugar per person per month, salt, tea or coffee, salt bacon only (not export varieties), boiling beef or pot roast (not to exceed 10¢ per lb.), a limited quantity of cane syrup, limited quantities of: yeast cakes, soap (not toilet), coal oil, prunes, lard, matches, baking powder or soda; vegetables, when applicant can satisfy the issuing authority that he was unable to produce same. Potatoes have not been included, but can be purchased by destitutes in drought areas. Made in Canada goods, and Alberta goods, if possible.[217]

Two months' back rent, however, is not covered, and the husband writes the municipality:

I had expected to get work at the Post Office during the Christmas rush and did not pay the rent, letting this go in arrears rather than the grocery bills expecting to pay the rent when I got in the Post Office. The job didn't materialize however and the owners are after us pretty hard.

I could have applied for relief a month before I did as we had no money at the end of November but I refrainded [sic] from doing this expecting to get work. I don't like asking for relief and know you have your own troubles and for this reason ask as little as we can possibly get along on.[218]

A year later he wrote again.

I had an application for a job at a mine but am sorry to say this has not materialized to date. I also had an application in for an extra at the Post Office during the rush but these extras had already been appointed.

I let the November and December rents go behind in the hope that some position would be forthcoming. I would ask you to kindly pay these and would state that as soon as I get work you will be informed.[219]

It is possible that the man never did get his back rent paid for by the municipality; as early as April 1933, the Relief Branch of the provincial government had urged communities to remove as many people from the relief rolls as was decently possible. But the demands for assistance from desperate people continued. From the Office of Civic Relief, City of Edmonton, to the secretary-treasurer of the village of Two Hills, February 16, 1934:

Mrs. Jessie M— and four children were, I understand, residents of Two Hills for four years. She was deserted by her husband some time ago, and was obliged to rent her house and garage there at the end of August. She is in receipt of $18.30 per month from the premises described, but this is not sufficient to maintain herself and four children.

She has got by so far by disposing of a car she owned and some articles of furniture, but now is at the end of her resources and is asking for assistance.

This woman's residence is clearly established at Two Hills and as such I would ask you to make some provision for her, or arrange for her accommodation at Two Hills.

Mr. John L— has a lease on the premises described for eighteen months, from August 1st 1933. The garage is being used, I understand, as a Public Hall for dancing.

From the secretary-treasurer to the Office of Civic Relief, February 20, 1934:

I took this up with the new elected councillors and they will furnish her and family with Food and Clothing here but not in the city. I was informed that she put her husband out about two years ago and has held the property in her own name ever since they come to Two Hills. I have written to her telling her to come back to Two Hills.

From Mrs. M—'s landlord in Edmonton to the secretary-treasurer, February 23,1934:

She applied for relief here and they said that she belongs to Two Hills and that they are responsible for her. I would like to know if you will pay for her rent. She owes us for one month, $16.00.

From the secretary-treasurer of Two Hills to the Department of Municipal Affairs, Edmonton, February 23, 1934:

There is a party by the name of Mrs. Jessie M–– and four children who used to live here. She made life so miserable that her husband left her about two years ago and he gave her all the property here. Now last August she made a sale and sold off all the repairs which she had on hand in the garage and rented the garage and her residence to John L— for 1 1/2 years at $18.30 per month. Then she moved to Edmonton and spent all her money and all she has coming in now is her rent. Now she applied to the city of Edmonton for relief. They told her to apply to Two Hills for relief. She wrote here and wants us to send her relief. Kindly let me know what is the proper procedure to follow.

From Jessie M— to the secretary-treasurer, February 28, 1934:

Will you please cancel those [relief application] papers that I signed on Monday as I do not want to live in that old shack across the track.

From the supervisor of Charity and Relief, Department of Municipal Affairs, to the secretary-treasurer, March 7, 1934:

We regret that your letter of the 23rd ultimo has not been replied to before this but we have had some difficulty in tracing the above named.

We now find that this woman was remanded on the 5th of this month for sentence on the charge of corrupting her four young children. We have also been informed that the two daughters who are sick with whooping-cough have been removed to the hospital and the two boys have been taken to the children's shelter.

P.S. Since writing above I see by a report in the Edmonton *Bulletin* newspaper that this woman was sentenced to two months in jail, having pleaded guilty to the charge of corrupting her children, and that the children are now in the care of the Department of Neglected Children.

From the secretary-treasurer to the Department of Neglected Children, March 9, 1934:

Re Jessie M—— I understand that at the present time she is serving time at Fort Saskatchewan and that your Dept. are looking after her children. She has property here in this village and I believe is trying to sell it either to A.I. H or John L—. In the event of a sale would it be possible for your Dept. to look after the money for the benefit of the children and herself, as she is a very poor manager. The property is valued about $100 now but it cost them over $2500.

From the Department of Neglected Children to the secretary-treasurer, March 13, 1934:

As to her property at Two Hills, while I cannot give you any legal advice I might suggest that if she proposes disposing of same you might be wise to have a caveat placed on the property, as these children will be charges of yours, the mother having been sentenced to two months imprisonment for immoral conduct in the home of her children. The children are being brought before the Juvenile Court here and will in all likelihood be made your responsibility, hence my suggestion, which I am giving you for what it is worth.

File closed. Prostitution or relief, take your pick.

Salaried workers did not have to make such a desperate choice but teachers, for example, did have to choose between a cutback in wages or unemployment. Of course, they accepted the cutback, and then scrambled to make the ends, moving off in opposite directions, meet. Cashed-in life insurance policies from a more prosperous decade to pay for room and board. Borrowed and begged money to be able to go home for Christmas. Spent summer holidays, free, on the family farm. Paid out of their own pockets for cocoa and soup to feed kids worse off than they. Spent night after night in the teacherage, surrounded by total darkness and the howl of wolves outside, because it cost too much to have a cup of coffee in the town. Sometimes they went over the line of propriety. And sometimes they survived only because of another's generosity.

I remember when Father couldn't get a job. He had been fired because he remained adamantly Ukrainian. He never tried to polish his accent although he had made a study of grammar since he was a child because he delighted in Latin grammar. He liked to correct fellow teachers on the English grammar and say they didn't know anything about it. He would say, "Don't you know the difference between I and me? You don't know which one is the object of the verb and which is not, and you're arguing with me? The commonest idiot in Germany or Ukraine or Russia knows the difference between I and me. And you don't know it, and you pretend to be a teacher?" So some of them wrote a letter of complaint to the Minister of Education, complaining my father was incompetent as a principal. He was fired in mid-term and he couldn't get a job. He went out looking for a job and he didn't get a job for about six months, so he ran up credit. This was about 1937. So Harry Kostash, his best friend and a superintendent, says, "Wally, the first opening I've got I'll give it to you, but there are none. There are people who are offering me money, they're offering bribes." He never took any bribes, give credit to Harry. A lot of superintendents did. Or the board men all did, school board chairman, these small district boards. Your first pay-cheque was a standard bribe. So anyway, Harry couldn't find a job for Dad so instead, he created a high school for Dad and called it the Arrow High School. And it was the living room of a farmhouse near the Saddle Lake Reserve. There was a small Ukrainian enclave there next to the Indians. He created a school for him and the superintendent in Edmonton was furious because he said they had no equipment there. They had no blackboards, nothing. It was horrible. But my dad's life was saved.

In 1926, the School District of Two Hills was operating on a surplus budget; not an astounding surplus – $91.12 – but a margin against bankruptcy if worse came to worst. They were able to pay for two boxes of Japanese oranges, twelve cords of woods, labour costs for oiling the school floor and carpentry, and for three teachers' salaries and still have a surplus. By 1931, just about all the ratepayers were in arrears for taxes, and in 1933 several appealed for a revision in their tax assessment and all were granted a reduction. Even taxes on Sheldon Burden Ltd. – an oil-prospecting company whose venture in the district was considered a failure – had to be written off. By 1934, at the annual ratepayers' meeting:

> Due to the fact that the amount of outstanding taxes was becoming greater every year and that there seemed to be no apparent effort on the part of the ratepayers to reduce same, it was moved and seconded that ways and means be devised to enforce the collection of arrears. This motion was carried by a unanimous majority.

It was further moved and seconded that:

> a resolution be forwarded to the Alberta Trustees' Association requesting them to take up with the Department of Education the possibility of having the Department supply all pupils with the various instruction books required free of charge up to and including grade eight. The reason for this being that many

parents and guardians were unable to finance the cost of sending their children to school.

The budget for 1934, with $5500 in outstanding taxes not collected, showed a deficit of $5417.26. In March 1934, a group of local businessmen showed up at the board meeting, arguing that the tax on their stock in trade was not "a fair tax in that it did not provide for a reasonable tax against those who were unfortunately carrying a large 'dead stock' on their shelves or warehouses." By 1936, the school district's expenditures were pared to a minimum standard of upkeep: coal, show-shovelling, chimney sweep, four tin pails, and the premium on accident insurance.

By Christmas of 1930 the Depression had set in and that's when they started cutting into the salaries of the teachers. I came into South Kotzman School at $1375 and they wanted to cut it to $900. Before that happened I got another job at $1200 by replacing a teacher who had been suspended because his students had been caught copying during the exams. So they were pretty desperate for a teacher. The trustees didn't want to let me go but it was the wishes of the majority of ratepayers to lower my salary. They wanted me because within four months I had organized a mandolin festival, my grade ten students were doing well and the choir had won second prize at a festival. But it was a question of money. The next teacher who came in got $900. But salaries kept going down every year until the point when the government said no teacher could be paid less than $640. But schoolboards who hired teachers for that said the teacher also had to be the janitor: wash the blackboards, get the fire going, sweep the floors. And there were districts that had an under-the-table agreement that the teacher was supposed to refund $200 of that $640.

A "Communist" in those days was not necessarily a member of the Communist party (if not, they preferred to call themselves "progressives") but someone associated with a range of activity from simple picket lines at the railroad crossing, to campaign work for the Communist (later, the Progressive Labour) party or CCF candidate in an election, to membership in a hall affiliated with the Ukrainian Labour and Farm Temple Association. Memories are long and today these people are still referred to, more or less slyly, as "Reds" or, if they have rejoined the church, as "former Reds." The serenity and orderliness of life in Two Hills in 1976 belie the fact that the district was once a scene of tumultuous, not to say violent, political activity, some of it more anarchic and spontaneous than that associated with election campaigns, invited lecturers, and May Day concerts. Some people still carry the disgust and passion of the thirties with them, relating their experiences with a conviction more appropriate to past conditions of gross economic privation and of the sense of outrage than to present security and mollification; some speak of those days with nostalgic indulgence; and others with sour disapproval. But no one has forgotten how it was and what happened and no one has grown indifferent to their younger selves who were touched and moved and prodded and jolted by events that almost severed their generation's attachment to the national conceits of peace and good government.

Not that mass protest was an entirely revolutionary idea to the Ukrainian-Canadian community in the thirties: back in 1910, a mass meeting in Winnipeg protested the murder of a Ukrainian student killed in a scuffle between Polish and Ukrainian students in Lviv; in 1914, a cross-section of the community organized spontaneously to protest Bishop Budka's pastoral letter (urging Ukrainian-Canadians to join the Austrian army); and in 1915-16, various organizations struggled around the question of bilingual schooling.[220] But it was the Depression, with its unusual effects and commonality of shared (unhappy) experience, its time-span across the youth of the Canadian-born generation and their identity as natives and citizens by birth ("How dare this happen to us?") and its arrival on the heels of political agitation following the world war and the Winnipeg General Strike, that for the first time provoked Ukrainian-Canadians en masse into prolonged and thoughtful protest against their general condition as working people in Canada. This was hardly a single-issue campaign or a denunciation of some distant calamity in Western Ukraine or even just a series of instances of bloody-mindedness. Mass protest during the Depression was the result of Ukrainian-Canadians finally seeing themselves as part of a class whose function and purpose were explicit: always to be the scapegoat for the vagaries of capitalism and to bear the responsibility of economic and political change.

Only the theoreticians among them explained the situation in such terms but when thousands of farmers and their sympathizers organized marches, drew up demands, organized boycotts, and made speeches, they amounted to the same thing: analysts of the Canadian political economy. From their own lives they knew what was going on. Twenty-five cents a bushel for wheat in 1932. Wages and mothers' allowances cut. Foreclosures, evictions, and tax sales. Pictures in the newspapers of the jobless in the cities marching with banners down Main Street. Pictures of policemen on horseback and policemen with batons charging into the crowd. Name-calling: "Communist stooges," "savages." Publicity, favourable and otherwise, given the progressive point of view:

> The capitalists were heartless men, only too eager to order the use of truncheons and tear gas on people who, through no fault of their own, had no jobs and no prospects of getting any in the foreseeable future. Brute force decided the outcome of riots, while "class justice" prevailed in the courtroom where rioters were fined or sentenced to short terms of imprisonment. Canada, the argument went on, was becoming a fascist state.[221]

For the people near and in Two Hills, the chance to take direct action against these provocations came in December 1932, with the organization of a Hunger March to Edmonton. Farmers from Myrnam, Slawa, Spedden, Mundare, Vegreville, and other towns had announced their intention of joining the march, great quantities of food were being donated, and "for days on end, women cooked, baked and prepared food, expecting to feed upwards of

3,000 for several days if necessary."[222]

The Farmer's Unity League, responsible for organizing all this along with the Workers' Unity League, was distributing pamphlets which demanded, on behalf of all farmers, a minimum income of $1000 for every farmer, free education and medical care for the poor, old age pensions at sixty years of age, and – for good measure – workers' control of the state.[223] The idea behind the march was to present Premier Brownlee with a set of minimal demands – he was, after all, head of the United Farmers of Alberta party – and a display of collective strength. As a brother farmer, how could he not but accept the justice of cancellation of debts, exemption from taxation of small farmers, cessation of sheriff's sales and grain seizures for tax arrears and cash relief? The excitement around these preparations was palpable.

Unfortunately, everything went wrong. A heavy snowfall a week before the set date, December 20, made many roads impassable to out-of-town marchers. Many didn't have enough money or warm clothes for the trip. Application for the right to march to the Legislative Building was turned down by the premier although permission was given for a mass assembly in the market square. The media were hostile.

> Groups of "Hunger Marchers" left on Monday for Edmonton to invade the offices of Prime Minister Brownlee and lay before him their preposterous "demands." At the moment of writing, we do not know what the outcome has been, but we surmise that the Hunger Marchers will find themselves in the same predicament as the King of Spain, "who marched right up a hill and marched right down again."
>
> But why "Hunger Marchers" from this district?
>
> If there is one thing in this world which this district has in superabundance it is foodstuffs in every variety. It seems impossible that any farmer should lack the requisite amount of food. He doubtless lacks money; he may be ill-clothed; he may be buried under a mountain of debt; his land may be in danger from a tax sale; but how in Heaven's name, can he be hungry?

The fact is, of course, that most of these people brought their troubles on themselves, by poor management, by improvident living, by reckless expenditure in good times, by sheer, downright laziness. Now, they expect the public to care for them, not only care for them but supply them with a better living than the public itself can hope to enjoy. [224]

Special squads of police were detailed to prevent the march and

it was learned via the grapevine that RCMP would be posted at certain country points to turn back, on any excuse whatsoever, groups of people obviously heading for the Hunger March in Edmonton. The word soon spread around. A truckful of farmers from Lavoy fell into the police trap four miles west of Mundare. After they were threatened with arrest unless they turned back, they back-tracked, then learning of a safer route, continued on their way.[225]

In spite of these obstacles, people kept coming in, from Willingdon, Two Hills, Mundare, Smoky Lake, Radway and gathered at the Labour Temple ready to start marching on the afternoon of the 20th. Just before noon, adding insult to injury, the hall was raided by seventy policemen, ostensibly searching for the firearms such a grisly group of revolutionaries must be hiding. "No arms were found. What they did find was a group of women cooking turkey."[226]

Finally, at 2:30 P.M., about 10,000 people had gathered in the market square, some ready to march, some waiting to see what would happen next. It was obvious that a confrontation between marchers and police was inevitable. Machine guns were posted on the roof of the post office building, a phalanx of mounted police were lined up across the street and behind them police on foot, including 150 RCMP brought in from Regina, were poised with batons. It was scary, but no marcher worth his or her salt would retreat now. The order was given to begin marching.

Carrying slogans and banners, the demonstrators surged forward with loud cheers. Immediately, the foot policemen, swinging their clubs, barred the way. They grabbed at the banners and tore them down but the crowd closed in around them and passed on. The Mounted Police who had been waiting on the sidelines then came galloping into the milling crowd, trampling all those who stood in their way. Reinforcements of foot police rushed in after them, their batons cracking against skulls and bones, drawing blood as they went.

Caught in the police rush, many of the injured screamed. The mood of the crowd changed suddenly. Curses and loud shouts escaped from a thousand throats. A roar of anger swept across the square as unarmed demonstrators near a bunch of Christmas trees, tore off the branches and rushed towards their attackers. But few could withstand the organized attack by the police. In the confusion that followed, the ranks broke. The marchers had advanced only a half block before they were forced to disperse. At 3:05 the Hunger March was over.[227]

Of thirty marchers originally arrested, only seven were ultimately convicted of unlawful assembly. Along the way to trial, cases had been dismissed for lack of evidence, technical errors, poor health, hearsay evidence, and a judgment that merely being at a meeting did not constitute unlawful assembly. Not a very spectacular denouement to a police riot. It was assumed, however, that the state's case had been made. Mass displays of popular dissent would not be tolerated. "It was impossible. Some of the things we asked was impossible to expect." Two years later, the farmers were at it again.

There was a grain strike that started at Myrnam (which had a very strong progressive movement). Wheat was eighteen cents a bushel and when the idea of a strike was proposed the idea spread like wildfire. I was on the picket line with lots of my neighbours right on the road near Lavoy and Vegreville. There was the odd fellow who tried to break through and I understand that there were picketers who took in their grain late at night, after the pickets were down, but we proved ourselves. We showed that people had to fight for their rights.

The picket lines had been thrown up on the roads to prevent farmers from delivering grain to the elevator: the local elevator agent had been grading everybody's shipment as "tough." It took several weeks of picketing (it could have been shorter, had everyone respected the pickets and turned back) to win but win they did, at least technically.

The Myrnam farmers who have been on strike against their local elevators for several weeks tallied a win last week when one of their main contentions was granted, this being the removal of the present elevator agents there and their replacing by a new set of agents. Whether this will bring about any change in the grading of their wheat is something for the future to tell.[228]

It would have been longer had farmers in other districts not gone out on "sympathy strikes" and thus tied up deliveries to branch elevators along the line. Mass meetings in Ranfurly and Stubno passed strike resolutions with "100 percent unanimity" in support of the actions in Myrnam.

Later that same year, a number of Mundare area farmers decided to mount a strike against conditions at local elevators: they were angry about the lack of cleaning equipment which meant they were being docked unnecessarily severely for weeds and were paid for artificially low grades. They issued a set of demands that were considerably more far-reaching than those of the Myrnam farmers: immediate installation of cleaners, more definite and equitable grading, and establishment of a minimum price for grain equivalent to cost of production.[229] A picket committee was organized and delegates from other districts committed themselves to organize their own localities in sympathy. A day later, it was obvious this was not going to be a tea-party of a strike. Ten picketers from Mundare overturned a wagon of grain that was on its way to the elevator—

under police escort – and were summarily arrested and charged with intimidation with violence, wilful destruction of property and obstruction of police. The trial was set for November 19. The community was appalled.

> While the first uproar created by the farm strike at Mundare has subsided, the farmers in various other districts have also threatened to go on strike and it is possible, or probable, that the movement has already extended or will extend in the near future, to Warwick, Fitzallen, Hairy Hill, Two Hills and other points north. At the south, at Inland, Haight, Holden, a policy of watchful, but sympathetic, waiting seems to prevail.
>
> It is not likely that any serious clashes will arise hereafter with the non-striking farmers or with the RCMP. The return of the Grain Commissioners within a week or ten days is being awaited with anxiety, although no one expects the Commissioners to meet all the demands made by the Strike Committee.[230]

It all depends on what one means by "clash." Murder and mayhem, no. Self-defense against scabs and assorted other adversaries, yes. Success, however, was equivocal.

On November 19, 1934, the "Mundare Ten" went to trial. Three had charges against them dropped, leaving seven as defendants: Peter Kleparchuk (a Communist and secretary of the strike committee), William Zaseybida, Metro Ulan, Sam Ulan, Peter Beresiuk, Fred Yaniw, and Joe Osinchuk. The prosecution was conducted by an RCMP sergeant, himself a defendant in another case brought by a Mundare striker, alleging he was struck by the sergeant while being questioned. Lawyers for the defendants were from Edmonton and soundly respectable: Fred C. Jackson and W.R. Howson, MLA. Examination and cross-examination revolved around the question of the overturned wagon. The police presented evidence that "the grain wagon had been pushed, sideways, bit by bit, into the ditch, and cited ridges in the gravel surface to support this view." This evidence was confirmed by an engineering graduate. All of the defendants, however, "denied having touched the wagon or the horses. . . . It went into the ditch, they claimed, because Const. Graves drove it too close to the shoulder of the road." The judge's summation, however, situated the act where it belonged: in the provocative area of civil disobedience.

"In Canada," the bench said, "every citizen has the right to work out his own salvation in his own way. John Lamash had the right to market the products of his labour, and no one had any right to interfere with him by use of violence or threats.

"Picketing itself is no crime, provided it is carried out in an orderly manner, without force. Under our law there is nothing wrong in asking a man not to go to work, or not to deliver grain. But where force enters, the law steps in.

"Violence of this kind will beget violence. It is serious to start violence because no one knows where it will lead, and it is up to this court to prevent it. . . ."[231]

Guilty as charged. The back of the strike was broken. The same evening as the trial, a meeting of Vegreville farmers, organized by Hairy Hill strikers, failed even to move a resolution that district farmers go on strike. The arguments supporting the idea were among the more political and sophisticated of the whole campaign but they fell on deaf (frightened? suspicious?) ears. "If the strike is to be effective it must embrace all farmers." "Farmers are unable to obtain a proper return for our labour. The only way to obtain redress is by direct action for ourselves." "Big companies and corporations stick together. So should the farmers." "We must get our own rights. Others won't do it for us." "Farmers crossing our lines should be completely ostracized." "People in town understand our interests are their interests. Why shouldn't they back us?" Even the presence of George Palmer, a Communist organizer tarred and feathered in Innisfree a week earlier, even his denunciation of "police scab-herders and strike breakers," could not change the mood of resignation. "The chairman then called for a resolution from a Vegreville farmer that the Vegreville district should go on strike.

None was forthcoming."[232] On December 12, the *Observer* noted that "Mike Dedinski's truck is once more engaged in hauling grain to Two Hills."

The Vegreville farmers' reluctance to associate themselves with the strike (and hostile neighbours and police and court appearances and fines) is not so mysterious, given that this was 1934 and the "anti-progressive" elements of the area were themselves well organized by this time. Given, too, that many erstwhile sympathizers were exhausted. Carrying on a strike in the middle of winter, standing frozen to the bones at railroad crossings, feeling betrayed and dishonoured by neighbours crossing the picket line, and realizing that dumping a can of cream into a ditch was only an irritating prick in the hide of the "system" forced many to withdraw their support. Many who sympathized with the idea of a strike distrusted the Communist leadership. There were those, of course, who bore ill-will towards the strikers but there were others who just couldn't sustain a fever pitch of indignation and excitement months on end. Besides, they were scared.

Back in 1931, the Vegreville Chamber of Commerce had passed a resolution which revived memories of abuse at the hands of the Anglo-Canadian establishment only fourteen years earlier. Given "existing conditions," they recommended deportation of people not Canadian citizens who were in jail, who "have been, *or may become* [italics mine], convicted of criminal offences" and who "may be guilty of making seditious utterances, or who are engaged in attempting to create distrust in, or disrespect for Canadian institutions."[233] This point of view may have been merely tedious if it weren't for the fact that once again immigrants were being singled out, in a time of social crisis, and in an ill-defined manner, as partly responsible for the problem, and for the fact it was seriously debated. An editorial in the *Observer*, for instance, managed simultaneously to disapprove and encourage the Chamber in its resolution. On the one hand, "deportation of undesirable aliens" is a "drastic remedy and not always effective" and "even if all the undesirable aliens are rounded up and deported, our troubles are not over. There are quite as many naturalized Canadians who are agitators and general nuisances." On the other hand, "Canada is now paying, more or less, the penalty of its own folly in encouraging, or at least permitting, certain classes of immigrants to enter the country. . . . The policy of deportation should be carried out much more vigorously by the Dominion Government. . . . Possibly the only thing wrong with [the resolution] is that it requires re-drafting in some particulars. . . ."[234]

This argument would have been merely sophistical, and exclusive to the faint-hearted who imagined hordes of Ukrainian-Canadians brandishing fists, if it weren't for the personalities with more clout and a bigger audience who were saying the same thing. Charlotte Whitton in 1932, a social worker, presented a report to the Prime Minister's Office on "Unemployment and Relief in Western Canada"; on the face of it, she wrote objectively and merely descriptively.

> The number of single men, foreigners on relief, is unduly large, and in several centres, officials reported them as among their troublesome clients. Language differences, their tendency to segregate, their corporate loyalties, their susceptibility to seditious propaganda, their known proclivity to hoard money, and the consequent difficulty of ascertaining their actual need of relief, all greatly complicate an already difficult problem in these cities.[235]

Between the lines she is confirming what a lot of Anglo-Canadians believed to be true: that foreigners were unreliable and devious, disloyal and lazy; and that if there weren't any around, there wouldn't be a Depression or Bolshevism or government handouts.

By the thirties, however, it wasn't just Anglo-Canadians who responded with misgivings and animosity to the "troublesome" foreigner; by this time there was among the Ukrainian-Canadians themselves a class of people whose interests were closer to those of the non-Ukrainian establishment than to those of the agitators, the unemployed, the striking farmers. The Ukrainian-Canadian merchant, lawyer, doctor, and large farmer formed an economic and social elite which, although not so wealthy and powerful as its Anglo-Saxon counterpart, was manifestly better off and more influential than Ukrainian-Canadian teachers, tinsmiths, and debtor farmers. Influential in two ways: within their own community and in relationship to the outside establishment. They now "spoke for" the Ukrainian-Canadians as a group, explained and interpreted them and, in a crunch, assumed the responsibility of defusing the "troublemakers" who caused the Anglo-Canadian establishment such anxiety. There was also a group, popularly called the "nationalists," who were ideologically committed to anti-Communism and pro-Ukrainianism (the notion of strength through ethnic pride), and who found themselves very often in agreement with the economic elite in its confrontations with the "progressives," even though they may have been as poor and disdained as any Ukrainian-Canadian on relief. The "nationalists" and the "bourgeoisie" had a common cause, the repression of political dissent from the left; the former were motivated by their repugnance towards any idea or activity that suggested sympathy with Bolshevist ideals, the latter by their vested interest in the status quo of private enterprise. Backed by the church, the school board, and the mainstream media, they were an impressive force respected and deferred to by most other Ukrainian-Canadians. To challenge them would take a large measure of confidence, boldness, and group support, not to mention the willingness to run the risk of being "Red-baited" and ostracized. To many "ordinary" Ukrainian-Canadians outside the charmed circle, it just wasn't worth it.

While the church spoke for the virtues of humility and piety, the nationalist intelligentsia spoke for the values of patriotism and political conformity. By 1933, there was already established in Two Hills a group of Ukrainian-Canadians known as the "United Loyalists of Canada" (Defenders of Canada and the British Empire) who assumed the responsibility of propagandizing in the community the government's case against the "Reds."

By the forties, Father had citations from Prime Minister R.B.

Bennett for having fought the Communist-inspired farmers' strike. My father was in a bad position. He agreed that they should strike, but he was afraid, because people came to him and said, "We'll have to get something organized against the Ukrainian Communist farmers in your area because it could go very badly for Ukrainians." They wanted to deport a lot of them before World War II, for being Communists. "And if you don't do something to oppose this Communism, it's going to go very badly for your people, we'll still deport them." And my father felt a little bit ashamed that they were getting a bad name with the authorities so he went around organizing meetings against the Communists who were encouraging the farmers' strike. And he was a paid government agent for the federal government of Canada to go around as a strike fighter.

Unsurprisingly, then, by the time of the hunger marches and farmers' strikes, the community was divided in its politics, and the marchers' and strikers' failure to sustain a long campaign of protest was as much the result of resistance within the Ukrainian-Canadian community as opposition from without. In one issue of the Observer alone four news items recorded the extent of anti-strike sentiment. The mayor of Mundare, Harry White, knowing "full well the parties responsible for [the Mundare strike] and how little they represent the real feeling of the farmers" called a public meeting of "citizens" to discuss ways of handling the situation. (There is no indication in the report of just how broadly representative these "citizens" were.) The meeting determined to swear in special police and to send a request for assistance to the RCMP in Vegreville.

> The strike has been effective at Mundare for a month and has paralysed business men to such an extent that the merchants of the town, together with the farmers who oppose the strike, resolved to put an end to it.[236]

In the Willingdon National Hall, a group of district farmers discussed how best to conduct the strike along "legitimate lines" and without relying on present "Communistic leadership." They resolved "that the farmers of the Willingdon district form a farmers' union to be absolutely non-Communistic and non-political, to act in cooperation with all recognized farm unions in parts of Canada not affiliated with any political party."[237] An editorial in the *Observer* interpreted this example of farmers' caution as a sign that the "strike is not by any means approved by the majority of farmers." It seems to me that they did not so much oppose the idea of a strike as support the pipedream of a gentlemanly one. If it was true – and it was – that some farmers, after "whooping it up" at a meeting "went home and delivered their own grain as fast as they could to elevators at points where there was no strike but where conditions were exactly the same as at picketed points," this does not "prove" that the tactic of striking was misconceived. It shows rather that the organizers had not done their political education work very well. Otherwise, how could the "bulk of the farmers decide that they intend to market their own grain in their own way at their own time"[238] and believe anything would ever change for them? And in Myrnam, where it had all started a few weeks earlier,

> several loads of grain brought through picket lines Thursday were greeted in town by a parade of Nationalists with the Union Jack flying and the marchers singing *God Save the King* while several hundred Nationalists and Communists gathered in town for an auction looked on.
>
> Only one load was held up but constables were on hand and no trouble ensued.[239]

In 1935, six months after the strikes but still inside the vortex of the Depression, a farmer from Innisfree wrote a letter to the editor summing it all up. Unlike many farmers, strikers, and non-strikers alike, he was able to see beyond the end of his own bloody nose to the complex configuration of economics, politics, and police power that stood between the farmers' grievances and their transfiguration into a cohesive resistance movement. Unlike them, he was not despairing. Angry, yes, caustic and impassioned, but also serene in his confidence that critical lessons had been learned and, who knows, a revolution of sorts underway.

In 1932 the farmers throughout this province were badly hit by the Depression; 90 percent of them were down and out. They decided to organize and march into Edmonton – our Capital City – and there stage a peaceful demonstration. They considered this would be the best way to present their grievances before the government.

What happened to these farmers upon their arrival in Edmonton? Yes, indeed, the Brownlee farmer government got right behind these poor farmers – but they did it with RCMP. The reception these poverty stricken victims of the Depression received was that of swinging police clubs. . . .

As a result of the grain strike last November at Mundare, some farmers were arrested. They were imprisoned for seven months, in Fort Saskatchewan Jail. When I was in Edmonton early in Feb. this year, I visited the Farmers' Unity League office, and there I saw a delegation that had been sent to visit these imprisoned strikers. They reported that the Warden at the Jail would not, at first, give them permission to see the jailed farmers, but after a long argument he had very sharply and gruffly said that they would be allowed fifteen minutes only. When they did let these visitors in they placed benches between them and the prisoners so that they could not come closer than ten feet. What the farmers would like to ask Mr. Reid [UFA Minister of Agriculture] is whether he was elected by farmers or jail wardens?

The farmers' struggle for better grades and against excessive dockage was fought by the "farmer" government. They sent in the RCM Police to break the struggle. After putting the farmers in jail they set up an "investigation" by the Grain Commissioner, and he turns in the type of report one would expect from a servant of such a government – "the strike was groundless." In the rottenest display of discrimination ever pulled on farmers this government ranked itself alongside the profit-making elevator companies. They know their kind.

However the farmers have learned that organized struggle does benefit them – for it can be proved that grain graded No. 5 tough, before the strike, graded No. 4 dry afterwards. Does that look as though the strike were groundless and that the elevator companies were in the right?

These thoughts are well to keep in mind as election nears. Fortunately we farmers also have memories.[240]

TWELVE

Politics

I was a little bit depressed financially and I started to think and do some reading. Shevchenko, Franko. And that's what convinced me to go to some political meetings and do more reading. Shevchenko said that if you have a little bit of knowledge you must share it with your brother who has none. Raise him up! You can learn a lot of things from those guys, draw your own conclusions, think for yourself. I became more class conscious, of which class I belonged to. So when the Depression came I was already prepared.

– Tom Horon

* * *

Of 230 miners that were killed in the Hillcrest mine disaster, the worst in history, my brother-in-law's dad was one of the four or five survivors. His rib cage was smashed. The mining company decided to get some good doctors to save the surviving miners but some were unconscious from gas poisoning and they died anyway. In Estevan, Saskatchewan, the miners were all Ukrainian and they were all unionized and organized and they were very political, extremely politicized, very sharp, and they went on strike and all marched to the outskirts of town and joined the farmers and marched back again. And the police shot at them. And how many guys crawled away with bullets in their guts we'll never know, because a lot of men weren't going to go and report they were wounded by the RCMP. Christ, they didn't want any more trouble.

– Oleh Kupchenko

* * *

My dad was a member of the United Farmers of Alberta, so I as his son was with the UFA too. And then, when I was on my own, I was paying my membership to the Farmers' Union of Alberta. The farmers would go to conventions and pass resolutions asking government to do things, but nobody ever did anything for the farmers. All we did in the years and years that I remember of passing resolutions, that's all we did was pass resolutions. But nothing came of them. Some of the people who were quite left-wing had some good ideas, others expected a little too much. They wanted forgiven loans and stuff like that. And I, at that time, being a postmaster, I had to stay out of it. I was expected to be a loyal Canadian citizen. The RCMP would come and check the post office for *Farmers Life* newspapers. It was a newspaper out of Winnipeg and it was leaning to the left a little bit I'd say. So the police were checking the names, the subscribers, and during the war, some of these people were watched in case they were disloyal.

– Metro Shipansky

* * *

We got permission from the police before we marched. When we marched we wanted to have the Union Jack, but they wouldn't allow it. They said, "It's a shame for the country and for the Union Jack that you are demonstrating in this country." So we carried the other flag, we made our own. The flag had the hammer and sickle on it. The sickle, that stands for farmers, the hammer stands for labour. The farmers and labour united together. But it was mostly farmers in the march. I wasn't actually involved in the organizing but afterwards, they called me over. They were scared to take the lead and they asked me to take a lead. I didn't care, I'm very big and tall, I would go. Maybe they were afraid that they would be arrested but the march was very peaceful. There was a couple of guys that tried to make trouble, but the police told them to quiet down. So we came up and had a meeting and speeches and carrying signs demanding better prices for our products. After, everybody went home.

– Matt Hnydyk

* * *

When I was teaching, I had a fight in Hairy Hill with the Communists. They were against anything that was nationalistic. They hated these things. They weren't nationalistic, they were Russians. They had a strong organization there at that time, they had the hall and they were writing letters against me. I was fighting Communism; myself and John Kupchenko, who was also teaching. We had meetings in the towns, in Two Hills which was just born; public meetings against Communism. Once in Two Hills he was giving a lecture and said that anybody who was a Communist must have some Tartar blood! Their centres were Vegreville, Hairy Hill, north of Innisfree, Plain Lake, Kiew. Hairy Hill still votes NDP because they have no other place to go. They ran their own candidate here and we had to live this down. Now they have only a few hundred votes when they used to have thousands. Because the young people left it; fingers were pointed at them and so they quit. A Communist from Two Hills became secretary of the church. I asked the Metropolitan if it would be all right for us to bury church members in that Two Hills cemetery where the Communists are buried and he said a Christian shouldn't be afraid to see the Devil himself!

We called ourselves the "United Empire Loyalists of the West" because we were true blue, true blue Canadians. Whereas the Communists were here to upset the government. Their business then, the object of their party, was to start revolution all over the world.

– Peter Shevchook

* * *

I had been urged for some time to consider standing for nomination for the CCF. I did not take it seriously until I saw the futility of the farmers go begging cap in hand, to governments – most of the time a deaf ear was turned. Therefore I became involved in politics. I had no doubt which political party I was attuned to. It was the

Canadian Commonwealth Federation. My experience was that after my nomination was confirmed, many people avoided meeting me on the street, avoided being associated with me in public, some would only admit their support confidentially. – CCF seemed to be a dirty word. Many did not like the idea of a woman candidate and possibly MP. Some of them said openly, "We are not going to have a woman represent us." In fact, some said, "If she gets elected she will not treat us to drinks." The worst reaction I had was in our local town, Vegreville. One man tried to intimidate my husband by saying, "If your wife gets elected she will be in Ottawa only to service the male MPs." There were many other insults. Tricks were played. Often our posters were torn down or defaced. Our opponents spread a rumor that our meeting was cancelled. In one community, we could not rent a hall and in another the caretaker conveniently went home with the hall keys. In another, the power was cut off. We also experienced hecklers with a low intelligence level. But the most insidious thing was when the other candidates, at their own meetings, would frighten some folks about a CCF government curtailing their freedoms and even confiscating their land. They would cast doubts in peoples' minds. It was woe to a minority political party with ideas for progressive change. But who really is the enemy? It is not only the hostile sovereign state, violating the natural rights of man. Is it not also the man who believes in his own helplessness and actually worships it? He tries to convince others that there is nothing they can do. Isn't it the one who has a total willingness to delegate his worries about the world to officialdom, not accepting his responsibility to be informed and the need to act? Isn't it the man in government who fears criticism if he speaks up, when he sees grave injustices whereby injury can be caused to human beings? Isn't it the one who professes helplessness, and doesn't helplessness lead to hopelessness? At a time when the fate of man is in jeopardy, it may help to know the face of the enemy.

– Nancy Zaseybida

The politics of the Ukrainian-Canadians in all their wonderful variety and remarkable refinement (joke: put two Ukrainians together and you'll get three political parties), came of age in the thirties and prematurely withered in the fifties, but it was not as though these politics had arrived full-blown in any given year. There had been a lengthy and half-conscious preparation for them in the public and private lives of the generation during the preceding decade, and if one includes the political culture of the immigrants as another antecedent, then the Ukrainian-Canadians of the thirties can trace the sources of their political consciousness back to the turbulent events that took place in turn-of-the-century Western Ukraine.

The fact is that Ukrainian-Canadians come from a tradition of violence and insurrection including anarchic peasant uprisings and Robin Hood-like banditry, underground terrorist organizations, insurgent armies, illegal revolutionary and nationalist groups and martyred heroes, as well as legitimate populist and social democratic parties, all of whom were at one time or another the repository of the collective aspiration for social and political justice of the Ukrainian people. Naturally, there were some Ukrainians who, at the turn of the century, identified more closely with this tradition than others – those who had lived in the towns and cities of the Ukraine as students, petty bureaucrats or labourers and who had made contact with anti-Polish demonstrations, police riots, election fracases, the political press, political and civic organizations, and the cultural work of the enlightened intelligentsia. Whether or not these activities touched meaningfully on the lives of the majority, the land-bound, village-bound peasant, is debatable, to judge from histories of the period. Ivan L. Rudnytsky writes about the "dense and ever-expanding network of economic, educational and gymnastic associations, branching out to every village" that covered Galicia and through which the "peasant masses . . . became deeply imbued with the nationalist spirit."[241] Arthur E. Adams, on the other hand, rejects the image of a Ukrainian countryside rumbling with nascent national revolution before 1917 but argues, rather, that the Ukrainian peasantry was not so much inflamed with the political consciousness of nationalism (in the manner of the intellectuals) as with "hatred of the unbearable tyranny of foreigners and a lust for land."[242] Thus the peasants paid their taxes, served in the army, registered births, marriages, and deaths with the church and otherwise minded their own business, except for sudden and devastating uprisings which subsided, usually because of irresolute leadership, into the gloomy and brutish daily round from which they had exploded.

At first it seemed that life in Canada would be conducted much the same way. One's society was no broader than the homestead, the neighbours, and the nearest town – most of them Ukrainian-speaking – which entailed responsibilities no more complicated than taxes (again), the Homestead Act, and donations to the church. One could live out a whole life never having more than this to do with government. Except that, unlike in the old country, roads and schools had to be built, post offices staffed, school boards and village councils elected, priests' salaries paid for, community halls organized, and government regulations about sanitation, weed-control, and water supply followed. Suddenly, it was as if one's whole life was impinged on by politics: everywhere you turned was a government department to consult, an act or by-law to carry out, a position to be filled through a defined procedure and decisions to be made as a group. Not to mention the political education acquired through dealing with the clauses and conditions of naturalization, mortgage, and the labour codes. Gradually the Ukrainian-Canadians became conscious of the fact that not only did government act in many large and petty ways upon their lives but also that self-government was a useful and necessary process by which they could do things for themselves (election of school trustees, organization of a church board, appointment of a hall director, collecting for an institute, funding for a newspaper). Consequently, one need not accept everything that was dished out by authorities in the manner of a Galician peasant accepting the kick-in-the-pants from a Polish landlord.

This level of consciousness was retroactive; once they had acquired it, they could train it back on what had already happened to them and come to certain conclusions about their status and position within the whole of Anglo-Canadian society. From dealings with a superintendent of education about a specific board of trustees in a single school district, for example, they could extrapolate a hostile tendency of the majority culture surrounding them. From their own experiences of trying to make a living off a mediocre quarter section – dealing with banks, grain buyers, and implement dealers – they could begin to see the rationale behind government-sponsored immigration and settlement. In a conversation with me, Winston Gereluk, formerly an NDP organizer in the Vegreville area, described the process of coming-to-consciousness this way:

> Let's look for the very basis of protest in the conditions under which they were brought over: large groups of people, divested of whatever money they had on the way, are settled into large blocs and told to produce or starve. Some of them protested the first day they got here – sit-down strikes in the immigration halls. They realized they had been lied to. Led to mosquito-infested swamps and told to make a go of it. Finding it expedient to keep on talking Ukrainian and to maintain their culture and find that the *apparatchiks*, the overlords, were all English-speaking – in that you can see more of the basis of protest. "This guy is not one of us but we are forced to speak to him in his language and idiom, adopt his way of thinking because he is the boss."

Less dramatically, the next generation was affected by the same process of gradual awareness. Although bilingual, it understood, from the school teachers, from the press, from Anglo-Canadian contacts, that the Ukrainian language and culture were devalued relative to the Anglo-Saxon ones. In many cases, they grew up in homes where an atmosphere of "free-thinking" prevailed, where parents were outspoken, welcomed questions, and encouraged speaking out against injustice. "When Dad was helping organize the grain strike in our area, he made us all sit around the table and listen to him tell why he was doing it and what had happened to him that day." In the minds of the listeners, such conversations (and simple narratives of personal experience) became the basis of many a future protester's attacks on social injustice. As did reading newspapers: a host of Ukrainian-language papers were published in Edmonton alone, most of them during the twenties but some as early as 1911. Their names bespeak the temperament of the critic: *The Whip, Our Progress, People's Truth, The Warning, Farmer's Word.* From Winnipeg: *Voice of Labour, Our Strength, Working People.* Charles Young took an issue of *Truth and Liberty* (for February 20, 1929) and made an inventory of its contents. From pages one and two:

Page one: Polish government oppresses Ukrainian peasants.
Polish emigrants leaving for Canada.
Memorial of Shevchenko in Detroit.
Lindbergh married!

Page two: Editorial as to whether it would be wise to have Ukrainian political party in Canada; better in the interest of the Ukrainians and Canada to join the established parties.
Novel.
American delegates to Russia on their return report as they were told to report.[243]

These were the contents of a politically moderate paper but even so a reader could come to his or her own conclusions about the state of the economy, the situation of the farmer, the development of Ukrainian-Canadian ethnicity and the significance of events in the Soviet Union.

Another factor, rich in implications, in the politicization of the generation was the impact of the Depression. Not only did Ukrainian-Canadians witness the loss of farms to tax debts and mortgage foreclosures and the sporadic but passionate activities of "hunger marchers" and grain strikers but also many were forced to look for work hundreds of miles away from the farm which brought them in touch with strikes, union organizers, and radical literature. The realization that industrial workers were in the same leaky boat as the farmers was all that some Ukrainian-Canadians needed to put together a politics of protest against, not only what banks did to farmers at Two Hills, but also what a whole class of industrialists (with help from the police) could do to a whole class of working people. If they worked at the Monarch mine in Drumheller, they might have been beaten up by a group of returned veterans, angered by the red flag waved by "foreign" strikers.[244] They might have been accused of getting their ideas from subversive literature smuggled in from Russia and of being gullible to the agitation of wild-eyed radicals from the One Big Union movement.

The "ethnic" worker on strike was a problem for everybody, for the Anglo-Canadian establishment suspicious of Bolshevist subversion and for the Anglo-Canadian workers themselves, afraid that "aliens" would settle for company terms a lot faster and more willingly than a Canadian. But if one looks at the history of union-organizing in the West, as did Charles Lipton in The Trade Union Movement in Canada, one faces the fact that "Again and again . . . it was the immigrants – Scots, English, Ukrainians, Jews, Russians – who took the lead in building the unions in the mines, lumber camps and factories."[245] The coming-to-consciousness of the Ukrainian-Canadian worker was the best thing that happened to the Canadian worker; working conditions changed largely because "aliens" were willing to make a fuss.

But these – strikes and marches, radical literature, rhetoric – were the overt routes to politicization. There were subtle ones as well, isolated moments which, when recollected, become educational. For one person, it's the times he or she was called "bohunk" or "dumb farmer." For another, it was a teacher who taught his students the "Internationale." For a third, it was the hired hand, a man good at carpentry, who one day left to join the international brigades fighting in Spain's civil war. More typically, it would come from reading the Ukrainian poets, Taras Shevchenko and Ivan Franko. This was the first broadly literate generation and it took to books and newspapers like a prison inmate to a hole in a barbed-wire fence. Self-taught, a farmer who became active in the local ULFTA hall listed the *Ukrainian Voice*, *Workers' News*, Lenin, Stalin, and Shevchenko as the sources of his political education. Another farmer studied the works of Shevchenko because "Taras wrote for the working people. He wrote simple so people would understand. Like Jesus, who went among the fishermen." A teacher, and anti-Communist propagandist, read Shevchenko, Franko and Wasyl Stefanyk (a short-story writer and a radical in the Western Ukrainian parliament) for their evocation of Ukrainian history, Ukrainian landscape, Ukrainian traditions, and Ukrainian nationalist consciousness. A restaurant cook was familiar with Shevchenko because "he stood up for us women."

A quarter mile away from the Shepenitz Greek Orthodox church is the Ivan Franko Ukrainian National Home. The church is tidy and sturdy still but the hall is a dilapidated, weedy derelict, its usefulness superseded by the social events in town. No one goes there anymore. But you can still read the painted sign that tells you that the people who lived near here once honoured the memory of a poet by organizing their concerts, debates, lectures, and classes in his name. He was a hero. He was an inspiration.

I thought of the new human brotherhood's birth,
And wondered: how soon will it come to this earth?
I saw in a vision the vast, fertile fields
Worked jointly, providing magnificent yields,
Supporting the people in freedom and bounty.
Can this the Ukraine be, my own native country,
Which once was forsaken, the conqueror's prey?
Yes, that is indeed the Ukraine, new and free!
I gazed, and the ache in my heart ebbed away.[246]

It would be misleading, however, to say that all Ukrainian-

Canadians who read this were inspired in the same way. Take, for example, two separate collections of selected poems translated into English. One is published *by Ukrainska Knyha,* a leftist house, and introduced and edited by John Weir, a Ukrainian-Canadian Communist; the other is published by The Philosophical Library in New York, is introduced by Percival Cundy, a Presbyterian minister from Manitoba, and edited by Clarence Manning, academic at Columbia University. The two books share exactly two poems in common, called, in the one case, "Pavers of the Way" and "The Spirit of Revolt" and, in the other, "The Pioneers" and "Hymn." The same stanza from "Spirit of Revolt"/"Hymn" may be compared. Here is Weir's version.

> Bright it burns in human hearts!
> Ages since the spark was lighted,
> Now a world-wide fire's ignited –
> Revolution's on the march!
> Loud and clear the call is sounding,
> Over all the Earth resounding:
> Working folk, from sleep awaken,
> Rise to meet the dawn that's breaking!
> Masses hear and they rejoice,
> Many millions heed the voice.[247]

And here is Percival Cundy's.

> It is not dead – this very hour
> 'Tis more alive. Though it saw light
> A thousand years since, yet in might
> It onward moves by its own power.
> In growing strength, without delay
> It hastens where it sees the day.
> It sounds a trumpet to awake
> Mankind to follow in its wake,
> And millions gladly join its train
> Whene'er they hear that thrilling strain.[248]

Note the difference between "working folk" and "mankind" and the absence of "revolution" in the second version. The Ukrainian original uses the word "millions" and the literal translation of the fourth line is, "And by its own power it goes." As to the rest of the poems in each book, if one did not know Franko had written them all, it would take a leap of imagination to construe a single writer. In Weir's collection are poems called "The Spirit of Revolt," "From the Prisoner's Dock," "Decree Against Famine," and "The Constitution for Pigs." In Manning's, "Hymn," "Spring Song," "Christ and the Cross," "Thine Eyes," "The Poet's Task," etc. To read one collection and not the other would give you only half the man. The poet who wrote

> And also tell the reason why
> That social system we'd transform:
> Because there wealthy people rule,
> The poor are servants, nothing more;
> Because there honest labour is
> Despised, degraded and oppressed,
> Although the system as a whole
> By labour's fed, on labour rests[249]

also wrote:

> Thine eyes are like a deep, deep well,
> To the bottom crystal clear;
> And like a star in heaven's depths
> Hope is shining there, my dear.[250]

The point is that each editor was simply reproducing his own particular ideology in the form of an apparently arbitrary, even casual, selection of Franko's poetry, and making the assumption that his audience was similarly biased. Obviously, Franko's poetry meant one thing to a debtor farmer, say, critical of the power of "bosses" and another thing to a lawyer, interested in cultivating literary taste. Thus, Weir says, "Ivan Franko was a socialist. He was the first Ukrainian writer and one of the first writers in the world to write novels of the life and class struggle of the industrial workers,"[251] while Manning has him simply "sympathizing with socialist ideals."[252] Thus, Manning mentions the "harmonious relationship of the poet with all classes of his fellow-Ukrainians"[253] while Weir says that Franko "rejected loyalty . . . to the Ukrainian upper strata that were riding on the backs of the workers and peasants. . . . Franko poured vials of wrath and contempt on those 'patriots' who love the Ukraine 'like beer and a hunk of pork fat.'"[254] Weir claims Franko "not only envisioned the future of Galicia in reunion with Ukraine but the future of Ukraine in re-unification with Russia."[255] Manning, for his part, speaks of the "iron curtain" which has "descended more tightly over the heads of the Ukrainian people"[256] and the need to heed the "calm, clear, strong voice of Ivan Franko" during these times (1948) when an "unspeakable brutality is being let loose,"[257] namely, Soviet Communism.

It's another, separate study to determine who the "real" Franko was and what he really said. The point here is to show the contradictory interpretation the Ukrainian-Canadians have made of the same poetical source and their need to have confirmed for them, in the sanctified stanzas of a national hero, their own particular worldview. In other words, the reading of poetry may yield not one but at least two kinds of political stance and Franko had as much to do with the formation of the consciousness of a Ukrainian-Canadian "progressive" as of the "nationalist."

The debate around Taras Shevchenko has been more problematic if only because his reputation approaches that of a saint among the Ukrainian-Canadians. Critics and commentators may deviate from the consensus of Shevchenko as liberator – Franko called him a "Great Power in the Commonwealth of human culture"[258] – in emphasis, not in substance. Everybody who read even a smattering of his *Kobzar* knew that Shevchenko spoke for the oppressed and unhappy Ukrainian masses, that he celebrated Cossack history (that is, the people's freedom-loving past) and suffered his own trials at the hands of tsarist authorities. One didn't have to read him to know that he represented the group's longing for a figure as passionate and courageous as they were often dispirited and afraid.

That was the consensus. The refinements on it were picked up at the halls, the Shevchenko Day concerts, in the newspapers and in lessons at *Ridna Shkola* (Ukrainian-language school). Those who went to a ULFTA hall heard him spoken of as an international champion of the working classes, a man himself risen from benighted serfdom who never compromised his hatred of the exploiter, be it the Polish regime, the Ukrainian gentry, the priest, the tsar. At a concert organized by the cultural wing of the Communist party, they heard the Soviet Ukraine described as the fulfillment of Shevchenko's dream for a classless Ukraine; in the left-wing newspapers they read that "the Ukrainian Social Democratic Party see in Shevchenko a great poet, who with his inspired and prophetic words carried to the Ukrainian community the good news of political independence and social justice for the Ukraine."[259]

> Ukraine is weeping, groaningly she weeps
> As to the dust head follows after head,
> And the oppressor rages without ceasing;
> Meanwhile the Polish priest with rabid tongue
> Vociferates: *Te Deum! Hallelujah!*
> And thus it was, O Pole, my dearest friend,
> That greedy priests with greedy magnates joined
> To set us all at variance and divide us
> And otherwise, we'd live today as friends.[260]

On the other hand, those who went to the national hall heard of Shevchenko as a great poet who associated with the intelligentsia and literati of St. Petersburg and Ukraine, who was admired by Charles Dickens and whose life represents the struggle against ignorance and enslavement and the achievement of genius and patriotism. At a concert organized by the membership of the Greek Orthodox parish, they heard him described as a devout Orthodox Christian and an anti-Russian who, if he were still alive, would use

his flaming pen again to denounce the tyranny of Communism over
his people; in the "nationalist" press they read that Shevchenko
wanted all Ukrainians to be "agreeable with each other and let
neither borders, nor parties, nor social status, nor governments, nor
wealth separate us."[261]

> Meanwhile let renegades grow up
> To give our foes relief,
> To help the Moscovites to rule
> Ukraine's broad acres black,
> To strip their mother's last parched shirt
> From off her bleeding back![262]

Everyone agreed, in other words, that Shevchenko was a foe of
the enemies of human liberty but no one agreed on just who the
"enemy" was and just how that liberty was to be ensured. A
"progressive" was suspicious of the tendency to turn Shevchenko
into a national hero for all Ukrainians instead of seeing him as a
"people's poet who hated all slavery – whether it be in feudal Russia
or capitalist America."[263] A "nationalist" was suspicious of the
tendency to interpret Shevchenko's radical utterances as a
revolutionary manifesto: "Just as it may not be taken that
Shevchenko was irreligious . . . neither is it to be deduced from
certain passages in his works that he was rabidly anti-this or anti-
that."[264] It all depended on what served one's own interests best.

As for the thousands who simply revered him, without
developing a political analysis as to why, they knew their favourite
poems by heart, they hung his picture, and at the Shevchenko Day
Concert, packed cheek-by-jowl with their neighbours, they stood
up, as if in church, and respectfully, prayerfully, wistfully intoned
the words to "My Legacy":

> When I shall die, pray let my bones
> High on a mound remain
> Amid the steppeland's vast expanse
> In my belov'd Ukraine;

. . .

Bury me thus – and then arise!
From fetters set you free!
And with your foes' unholy blood
Baptize your liberty!
And when in freedom, 'mid your kin,
From battle you ungird,
Forget not to remember me
With a warm, gentle word![265]

In each person there, year after year, the words meant this much at least: I come from slavery and grief, I go, hopefully, to liberation and joy. And Taras marks my way.

The Depression was the crucible of Ukrainian-Canadian politics in Alberta. What had been impressionistic, tentative, and speculative, through reading, conversation, workaday experience, now solidified as ideology from the pressure of concrete and mass misfortune and the widespread publicity of protest activity. Even though one might not choose to become directly involved in a party or organization, it was almost impossible not to identify with one side or the other of the ideological "either-ors": "either you support the struggle of the Canadian working people against the capitalist state or you join the forces of oppression"; or, conversely, "either you support the elected government of Canada and the due powers of law or you join the Communist outlaws." Granted that these propositions were emotional more often than political realities and that many political shades could be found on the spectrum between the extremes, the fact was that politics during the Depression polarized Ukrainian-Canadians as had never happened before and hasn't happened since.

None of this may be understood without an appreciation of the role of the Communist Party of Canada. And the CPC itself, as far as its work among Ukrainian-Canadians is concerned, may only be understood in terms of its antecedants. As was pointed out, not all Ukrainians arrived in Canada as political virgins; there were, in particular, members of the intelligentsia and semi-intelligentsia who had been members of, or participated in, one or another Ukrainian radical party or organization and who, in Canada, became involved in newspaper publishing, Shevchenko literary societies, lectures, and fundraising for political groups back in Western Ukraine. Soon enough they were also organizing Ukrainian branches of the Socialist Party of Canada and in 1907, in Winnipeg, a totally autonomous Ukrainian Social Democratic Party of Canada. "The Ukrainian Social Democrats comprised a very peculiar collection of utopian socialists, agrarian radicals, Marxian scientific socialists, populists, romantic nationalists, religious visionaries, proletarian internationalists, professional revolutionaries, and ordinary sincere humanitarians,"[266] who were as critical of the values and behaviour of the Canadian capitalist ruling class and the liberal Ukrainian-Canadian professional elite as they were of Austro-Hungarian imperialism and Ukrainian Catholic doctrine. From a membership of less than two hundred in 1908 they had expanded by 1918 to fifteen branches and 1500 active members, among them the miners at the Hillcrest camp in Alberta.

After 1910, the leadership of the USDP passed into the hands of its younger and more radical elements, the Marxian or "scientific" socialists who attempted to refine an ideology that spoke not only to the cultural and national aspirations of the Ukrainian-Canadian workers but to their incipient proletarian internationalism as well. Thus, their newspaper, *Robotchi Narod* (Working People) "took extra care to identify the Ukrainian people's national struggle with the class struggle in general, extolled the insurrectionary tradition of the Ukrainian people, and bitterly condemned all manifestations of 'spineless plebianism, boot-licking and submissive creeping' by Ukrainian community leaders anxious to win 'favours' for their people from the government."[267] This was not the last time that Ukrainian radicals would struggle with the apparent contradictions between class and national consciousness and eventually the contradiction would break the back of the Ukrainian-Canadian left. In the meantime, they attracted as members those who could neither resign themselves to exploitation nor accept that they had come to Canada just to make their own, individual fortunes.

In 1910, the USDP merged with non-Ukrainian socialists to form the Social Democratic Party of Canada. Anglo-Canadians dominated the executive while the rank-and-file remained predominantly Ukrainian. The coming of war and the 1918 ban on the party and its newspapers effectively terminated SDP activity and by 1922 most of the Ukrainian membership had gone over to the newly-formed Communist party and/or to the Ukrainian Labour and Farmer Temple Association. Both newer organizations were to find support among Ukrainian-Canadians for the same reasons the USDP had found it: the Ukrainian in Canada felt screwed.

Ukrainian farmers and farmhands in the prairies, Ukrainian and Jewish workers, artisans and others in Montreal, Toronto and Winnipeg, Finnish miners and lumberjacks in isolated Ontario and B.C. communities, Ukrainian miners in Alberta, all shared a common disappointment in Canada. Their high expectations of life and riches in the New World vanished in the face of reality: the lack of attractive opportunities in Canada for many East Europeans in the 1920s, which would decrease even more in the 1930s. Unable to speak English and without many opportunities to learn it properly, lacking either technical skills or money to help them up the social ladder, working for employers who were eager to maximize profits, many of these semi-literate East Europeans gravitated towards the CPC at one time or another.[268]

Although the Communist Party of Canada originated in Toronto (in 1921, as the Workers' Party of Canada), Ukrainian input was considerable: pro-Bolshevik Marxists like John Boychuk and Matthew Popovich were among the delegates to the organizing conference, and next to the Finns, Ukrainians were the largest group in the membership. As miners and lumber camp workers, as railroad workers and ditch-diggers, they were impressed with the CPC's broadside attack on the evil conditions of their lives. Who else was there to agitate against wage reductions and arbitrary lay-offs, against dangerous work practices and the use of troops against strikers? Who else was prepared to campaign militantly for unionization of the unskilled and the right to peaceful picketing, for minimum wage laws and unemployment insurance? Who else was imaginative enough to demand nationalization without compensation of banks, mines, and the CPR, workers' control of industry, the repeal of the BNA Act, and, to top it off, a workers' and farmers' government over all?

Communist-led unions within the Workers' Unity League helped to organize 100,000 workers in previously unorganized industries and 109 out of 189 strikes that took place in 1934.[269] In the case of the Estevan strike in 1931, their spilled blood fertilized the militant consciousness of thousands of Ukrainian-Canadians, among them members of the Workers' Benevolent Association who retell the tale as it has become: a working-class legend.

This coal field in southern Saskatchewan employed six hundred miners during the winter months. There was little work in the summer. The pay was the lowest on the continent. Miners were paid twenty-five cents a ton for coal, and it wasn't unusual for fifteen-year-old boys to work for ten hours for two dollars. The company deducted costs of doctor, hospital care, rent, lights and other payments from the small monthly earnings of the workers. The miners were also compelled to purchase food and merchandise from the company stores where they were grossly over-charged.

The miners joined the Mine Workers Union of Canada, an affiliate of the WUL, with the majority in its ranks by August 1931. They immediately asked the mine operators to recognize the MWUC and to negotiate an agreement. They demanded the eight-hour day, a minimum of $5.40 a day for underground work, and union recognition. The companies refused to negotiate and the union decided to strike. The miners walked off the job on September 8 and manned the picket lines.

There were about four hundred federal police in the

Bienfait and Estevan region at the time. Peter Gembey, one of the strikers, describes the situation that developed. "In order to intimidate the miners and force them back to work, the RCMP rode with two of their number in the cab, and another two with machine guns in the back of each truck. They would make two and three trips daily through the camps and repeat the procedure during the night. In order to put an end to this harassment, the strikers decided to see the members of the town council and to protest the use of mounties armed with machine guns.

"The miners began gathering at the Ukrainian Labour Temple in Bienfait at noon on September 29. By two o'clock that afternoon they had joined their fellow workers at the Crescent Mine. More than six hundred boarded trucks and almost a hundred cars of sympathetic farmers formed the parade to Estevan. There were many without transportation who went on foot. As we approached the town hall on 4th Street, we saw a column of mounted police and another of town police. They stopped the trucks.

"Without warning, two mounted police seized one of the leading committee members off the truck and took him to jail. Soon other police were doing the same to other committee members. The strikers went to the aid of their leaders, and the police retreated before the angry crowd of miners. The fire brigade was brought into action and attempted to disperse the strikers with blasts of water. When this proved futile, the firemen abandoned their trucks and disappeared."

Mike Moroz of Estevan, who was a participant in the demonstration, recalls the brutal killings and violence that followed.

"We got off our truck and ran towards the town hall. The fire trucks were already there. Nick Nargan and I were standing a slight distance away. Nick suddenly made a move towards the fire hose. I will never know what he intended to do. I do know that McCutcheon, a policeman, immediately drew his revolver and shot him dead. Nick dropped right there.

"At first the police resorted to clubbing the demonstrators. And then, with their backs to the town hall, they started shooting. Blood flowed on that street in Estevan on that particular Tuesday . . . Nick Nargan died instantly with a bullet through his heart. Julian Gryshko died ten minutes after being shot in the chest. Peter Markunas died of a bullet wound in his stomach. Because he was refused medical aid, as were many others, he was driven sixty miles to the Weyburn Hospital where he died the next day. . . ."

The funeral of the three murdered miners was held in the Ukrainian Labour Temple in Bienfait. Fifteen hundred miners, war veterans and farmers from miles around came to pay their last respects. The mandolin orchestra of the ULFTA in Moose Jaw was invited to render several musical selections at the service. On their way to Bienfait, they were followed by the police the whole distance from Weyburn. John Weir from Winnipeg, in the name of the Canadian Labour Defence League, delivered the eulogy. The funeral procession to the cemetery was a mile long, the largest ever seen in that part of the country.[270]

Besides the possibility of being shot at and killed, a Communist risked arrest for sedition and deportation, raids on party offices, the confiscation of damaging literature and documents and betrayal by informers, the forfeiture of party property to the Crown, and the general high-handedness of the police.

Detectives, acting on instructions from the Police Commission, insisted that speeches at indoor Communist meetings should be delivered in English, even if the majority of the audience consisted of unassimilated East Europeans. When speakers declined to cooperate, they were hauled from the platform.[271]

For these reasons, perhaps, and because the CPC program

appealed more directly to the urban worker than to the farmer, the majority of Communist sympathizers among the Ukrainian-Canadians in Alberta were to be found in the ULFTA, a party affiliate, rather than in the party itself. The ULFTA had the great advantage of being most of all a cultural and recreational organization that provided a congenial social environment for rural people who rejected the organizations of anti-Communist and church-affiliated Ukrainians but yet who were not prepared to subscribe as party members to overt political activity. By 1938, there were 15,000 members involved in the ULFTA,[272] including women's and youth sections, seventy-five mandolin orchestras, choral and dramatic clubs and children's language classes. Its constitution claimed it was non-political and non-sectarian and dedicated to the promotion of cultural and educational activities but this was not the whole story. Their claim that "wherever in Canada progressive Ukrainians form part of the population . . . there you will find a branch of the association"[273] hinted at the fact that the ULFTA was organized precisely because a large number of Ukrainian-Canadians no longer felt at home within the politics of the "nationalists" and the conventional political parties. Matthew Shatulsky, secretary of the Central Executive Committee of the ULFTA, outlined the objective of the association at its 1931 convention:

> To transform the ULFTA and its sections into a powerful means of class enlightenment for the Ukrainian workers and destitute farmers and a medium for the mobilization of the working masses of this country for the revolutionary struggle of liberation.[274]

A group does not arrive at such political positions merely through mandolin concerts and poetry readings. ULFTA halls hosted speakers from the Communist party, produced plays by socialist writers and distributed Marxist literature. Ideally, according to the convention,

> The cultural-educational work should at last be put on the right

class track. . . . All the bourgeois-urban trash, in drama as well as in song, should be thrown out from our labour farmer stage . . . . Dramatic works, as well as song and music, should be selected for class content.[275]

The ULFTA published a newspaper, *Ukrainian Labour News*, which in the space of two years (1919-1921) went from this kind of language

Now you Ukrainian labourers and farmers, consider what is going on around you. Observe and reflect upon your hardships, because you are like those bees who are busy on flowers day by day, from daylight till dark, always working, and you never think, and do not like to hear a voice telling you: "Look at the drone bees, how they destroy your work."

to this:

will we ever celebrate (as in Soviet republics) the first of May? . . . Yes we will. . . . The ranks of our proletarian fighters are increasing every day . . . we will accept their call, as the proletariats did in Russia accept their call to overthrow despotic Czarism . . . the struggle will be a hard one, but all our lives have been hard.[276]

Matthew Popovich, addressing the founding convention of the CPC, said the ULFTA was "in sympathy with the call to form a national open revolutionary party."[277] And at the 1931 convention of the association,

Reports from all parts of the Dominion showed increased activity by the branches in the general labour movement in Canada as well as in that among the impoverished farmers. This activity, it was pointed out, is shown in concrete and increased support to the Workers' Unity League, the Farmers' Unity League, the Canadian Labour Defence League, and to the general political aims of the Communist party.[278]

One can assume then that in all probability a member of the ULFTA hall in the Two Hills area in the twenties and thirties was a Communist party sympathizer – eventually, if not initially. Initially, a hall was organized as a social centre; eventually it became a political centre as well, as the political and economic events of the time impinged upon the members' lives, and they decided to take a stand.

But it was the social and cultural activities of the association that brought them in, providing as they did "a modicum of welfare, entertainment, information and companionship for people vegetating on the fringe of an Anglo-Saxon society which seemed to need them only for menial tasks and on election day."[279] The halls were used to accommodate the unemployed, collect food for marchers and strikers and rehearse choirs and orchestras for Shevchenko Day concerts and May Day rallies. The Lanuke hall orchestra, for example, played at an election rally in Two Hills for the local Communist candidate in 1935. While the CPC leadership may have frowned upon this Ukrainian "peculiarity" of a segregated social life that placed a greater premium on mandolin orchestras than on lectures about the class struggle, the ULFTA rank-and-file knew it was on to a good thing: just because they wanted to organize a revolution didn't mean they couldn't go to a dance and fall in love, under a portrait of Joseph Stalin.

The intensest left-wing activity in the Two Hills area took place during the Depression. The twenties, with its forming and re-forming of political parties, appearance and disappearance of newspapers, and organization of ULFTA halls, proved to be a dress rehearsal for the passionate and purposeful rhetoric and confrontations of the thirties. The radicals got down to business. God knows there was a fearful amount of work to be done, from making speeches to throwing out the Bennett government; but for awhile at least it looked like the whole capitalist house of cards could be flattened by the collective huffing and puffing of progressive people. The Ukrainian-Canadian communities of northeastern Alberta were just such a collective; radicals could usefully work among them, among their desperate and angry farmers, and, to a certain extent, among their intelligentsia, the teachers.

In January 1931, Carl Axelson of the Farmers' Unity League (an educational organization formed on the initiative of the CPC executive) gave a speech in the Vegreville ULFTA hall outlining the aims of the FUL. To the farmers in the audience, these aims must have sounded like music:

1. No evictions for non-payment of mortgage indebtedness, rent or arrears of taxes.
2. Organized resistance against foreclosures and evictions
3. Boycott of sheriff's auctions
4. Cancellation of arrears of taxes
5. Complete control of grading of all farm products in the hands of the farmers.
6. An income of not less than $1000 per year to be guaranteed to all farmers by the state, this money to be raised by a tax on the profits of banks, mortgage firms, railroads, farm implement and oil companies and other similar corporations.

Following the address questions were asked for and the folks obliged with a barrage of them. These dealt mostly with conditions in Soviet Russia where socialism is being given its trial. All information which was not for the benefit of the Soviet, the speaker scored as anti-socialist propaganda.[280]

As for conditions in Two Hills itself, the farmers took the advice of the FUL.

The hunger march in 1931 was done by farmers, when everybody was so poor, you had to do something. Prices were so low that a lot of people were selling their farms for the taxes. So we organized the farmers to come down to an auction and tell everybody not to buy. The auctioneer would be there, auctioning off a quarter of land being sold for arrears. But not a soul would give one cent for it. "How much am I bid?" Nobody would give nothing. They stood and waited, nobody making a bid, because, they said, "You're selling him today and tomorrow you're going to sell me. There's no buyers, there's nobody wants to buy it, no use, go away." So the auctioneer would have to close the sale and go home and leave the quarter alone. If somebody wanted to sell off his land, willingly himself, nobody ever said anything. But if the mortgage company or sheriff was throwing the man out, well, that was different. There was by Innisfree a mortgage company throwing a man out and the farmers came down and burned all the buildings. So the mortgage company got nothing. Another place an old lady got thrown out and the fellow that bought that land at the sheriff's sale, well, he seeded it a couple of years but he never took a crop off. His fences were always cut, cattle wandered all in his grain and he just gave up and left.

A year later, in 1932, the tension was palpable whenever the radicals convened. The language of the newspaper reporter covering the events had become decidedly sarcastic, violence was anticipated, and, in retaliation, the tone of the meetings was defiant. The bitterness in the confrontations between "Reds" and their opponents was escalating.

A feeling of tenseness was in the air in the ULF Temple on Sunday night when the local Communists attended a meeting held in memory of Lenin, Liebniecht and Luxemburg, all martyrs to the "cause." The feeling of tension was due to the memories of the night of Feb 25 last, when the hall was smashed up during a meeting of the Reds. Several selections were given by the mandolin orchestra and Comrade Stewart of Calgary was then called upon to give an address. At the conclusion of the address there were no questions asked or any disturbance created.

A short playlet was given, following some further selections by the orchestra. The concluding item was an address in Ukrainian by "Tovarish" Pete Kassian.[281]

In May 1934, people from thirteen localities held a "mass, open-air anti-war meeting" featuring a war veteran as the main speaker and the Vegreville Mandolin Orchestra as the entertainment.[282] Later that year, the Farmers' Unity League was in the newspaper again, this time demanding not only larger relief benefits to farmers and the establishment of trade and diplomatic relations with the USSR but also that charges of unlawful assembly against a FUL member, who had been arrested for his part in the famous hunger march to Edmonton two years earlier, be dropped. Otherwise, the FUL warned, "mass rallies and demonstrations of protest" would be held at Smoky Lake, Two Hills, Thorhild, and Rocky Mountain House until he was released.

In April 1935, there was a mass meeting in Two Hills – not a demonstration, however, but an election rally. The speaker, an Anglo-Saxon Communist from Edmonton, attacked Social Credit theories, Adolf Hitler, and "the capitalist order of society" and concluded by urging the audience of two hundred to vote for Mike Nowakowsky, Communist party candidate from Mundare.

Local delegates were named to attend a Youth Conference Against War and Fascism in Edmonton. In July 1935, the ponderously-titled United Anti-Capitalist Front Nominating Convention (127 delegates from twelve workers' and farmers' organizations in eighty-four polling divisions)

adopted a Communist election program and unanimously declared Matthew Popowich, (Communist leader who served over 2 years in Kingston Penitentiary for working class activities) as a United Front Communist candidate for Vegreville Federal Constituency.

The executive of the Vegreville Federal Constituency Political Association of the UFA and M. Luchkovich, the sitting member, invited to join the united front and take part in the conference, refused to attend, disregarding all other farmers' organizations, and called their own nominating convention for next Saturday at Willingdon. Farmers are indignant at this attempt at splitting their votes.[283]

Popovich's appeal to the electors followed in October. Those were, indeed, the days when the rhetoric of class struggle and the righteous indignation of the "masses" were still fresh and outrageous and thrilling. Who, that was impoverished and humiliated and questioning, would not be moved?

If I am elected, I pledge myself to fight in Parliament for the needs of the common people and stand uncompromisingly against war and fascism. I shall consider it my duty to fight for the immediate needs of the people of this constituency as outlined in our election manifesto and pledge myself to be with you in every struggle you will have to carry in defence of your interests, and attend to all your grievances that may come to my knowledge, irrespective of the differences that may exist in our views on political, national, religious or other questions.

Yours for

A mighty United Anti-Capitalist front and for a better life of the toiling masses,

Matthew Popovich.[284]

He was not elected and the Front disappeared. There were many, as it turned out, who had not been moved by the rhetoric. The Two Hills area was the scene of right-wing politics as passionate and single-minded as the left. The clashes between the two groups of adherents were often nasty and grotesque, and the history of them is more readily found in the archives than in the memories of the participants, as though it were shameful now to recall them. But the shrill antagonism to and decisive repudiation of radical ideology were very real in the thirties. It is obvious that much more than a "point of view" was at stake here. In the minds of the anti-Communists, the principles and actions of the radicals were a clear and present threat to their way of life. This was only reasonable, given the intent of Communism and revolutionary organizations. The right-wingers were not naively persuaded by the propaganda about the Communists' respect for law and order and democracy. Neither, for that matter, were the Communists, in spite of their proclamations. Everyone knew what the real game was – insurrection – and anybody who had much to lose, or thought he or she did, at the hands of the "rebels" fought back.

The Ukrainians who had a glimpse of middle-class existence like my dad, who had left the mud-floored huts, all opted for a conservative political point of view. These few had a chance to "make it" so they became very right-wing. And the pious ones, who blamed themselves for everything, were told by the church that Marxists were the Anti Christ. The leftists were the ones who had remained poor, but not necessarily uneducated, because you'll find that a lot of them are extremely bright, thoughtful people. Those who were exploited, who suffered, the ones who worked in the mining camps and the railroad gangs, they were really screwed and they knew it. They had a hard, bitter life and the Communists offered them a better thing. A chance, at least, at vengeance, of revenge against the ruling class.

The irony was that by no stretch of the imagination could the Ukrainian-Canadian anti-Communists, reactionaries though they were, be construed as the "ruling class." The radicals' quarrel was with the governments, the corporations, and the financial institutions, yet time and time again this class struggle was acted out as a fracas between poor and not-so-poor Ukrainian-Canadians. Granted, that even though they themselves were by no means well-off and were known as "bohunks" along with the rest of the Ukrainian population, many conservatives adopted the political values of the Anglo-Saxon middle-class. Granted, that among the right-wingers was a sprinkling of comfortably middle-class entrepreneurs and professionals who had more in common, culturally and economically, with middle-class Anglo-Canadians than with Ukrainian-Canadian farmers. Granted, that because this was true the radicals correctly analysed these hostile compatriots as "enemies." Nevertheless, it also remains true that the right-left conflict among the Ukrainian-Canadians was partially fratricidal. As long as the "have-nots" pick off each other, the "haves" can eat their dinner in peace.

In any event, the anti-Communists had their reasons for their politics. Some were bitter about the chance of Ukrainian national independence lost to the advancing Red Army and the Bolshevik cadres after 1917 – "My dad wanted to tear their eyes out" – and some misconstrued the definition of Communism, believing, for instance, it meant sexual licentiousness, prohibition of private belongings and "working like a slave for the commune." Some, experiencing the hostility of neighbours and friends, the ostracization from the church, intimidation at the hands of the RCMP, retreated from their earlier militancy, conscious as they were that in the minds of many Anglo-Canadians being Ukrainian was synonymous with being pro-Bolshevik. Some despised the left-wing's tendency to self-righteousness and its gullibility to Soviet propaganda and some were simply irritated by the radicals' preference for the "Internationale" rather than the Ukrainian national anthem. And there are those who were once activists in an anti-Soviet underground and never lost their combat preparedness.

> Biographical information I give to no one. The matter is thus: you see, I come from under Russia. I have some relatives there – two sisters. I was one of Russia's greatest enemies. For that reason I do not wish any publicity. There are some priests like myself, we want to lie low – don't need to tell you why. The Herald [official organ of the Ukrainian Orthodox Church] for two years gave the biographies of the priests. But when Father Sawchuk came to me, I said no. I say nothing to anyone.

Among the politically uncommitted or cautious, it was difficult not to become anti-Communist: the point of view of political conservatives was speedily and ubiquitously provided through the press and radio, the schools and churches and the utterances of the courts, the governments, and the business community. One would have to make a special effort to seek out the alternative point of view, an effort *ipso facto* considered suspicious. One's patriotism, piety, and common decency could all be impugned by an expressed sympathy for the agitators and rabble-rousers. Police, police informers, and reactionary hooligans could crack your skull. The Communists themselves could be frightening, with their wild-eyed and inflammatory rhetoric, their wrath and menaces, and their disregard for the vulnerability of all Ukrainian-Canadians once the Anglo-Canadian establishment was aroused by the provocations of a minority. As a Slav, one was presumed guilty of pro-Bolshevism until proved otherwise and one might have to go some, apologetic, length to get that approval. And, besides, things may have been bad for the moment in Canada but someday they'd get better and then all this fuss about changing the "system" and overthrowing the "capitalist exploiters" would become inappropriate.

There was, then, an atmosphere and mentality among many Ukrainian-Canadians not unfriendly to the development of right-wing extremism. Not everyone interpreted the conditions of the Depression as the death-rattle of capitalism; indeed, for many the problem was not with capitalism but with the sworn enemies of capitalism who were making life so difficult for even the most law-abiding Ukrainian-Canadian citizen. Fist fights, rotten tomatoes, police surveillance, Anglo-Saxon scorn – who needed it?

In January 1931, in Willingdon, Carl Axelson, Farmers' Unity League organizer, was prevented from addressing a meeting of local farmers.

The lights were switched off on two different occasions, and when the meeting finally broke up and the delegates and Axelson refused to sing *God Save the King*, the fun began.

The lights went out and missles [sic] began to drift through the air. The men on the platform were under the impression that they were being snow-balled by the audience, but when the lights were turned on they found that they were being bombarded with anything but snow balls. Eggs, ripe and juicy eggs, were scattered here and there and yon. The meeting broke up in disorder and the delegates from Mundare and Axelson got into a car and sought refuge in the railway station which was besieged at once.[285]

No arrests were made. The next evening, in Two Hills, at a similar meeting, the scene was quieter. "Police were watching the crowd." In an editorial, the *Observer* rather presumptuously spoke for the Ukrainian-Canadians: "Mr. Axelson himself isn't such a bad scout at all, but his Communistic views are anathema to most Canadian citizens, including the Ukrainian-Canadians."[286] A week later, in Mundare, a mass meeting of Greek Catholics chaired by George Szkwarok, local lawyer, not only dissociated themselves from the "Reds" but also anticipated Anglo-Canadian reaction. In effect, they were prepared to act as policemen of the elite against their own community.

We, the loyal citizens of Canada, of Ukrainian race, assembled to the number of about 700 people at a mass meeting at the Ukrainian Catholic Hall, at Mundare, Alberta, this 8th day of February 1931, for the purpose of protesting against the propaganda of Bolshevism and Communism among our people in Canada, hereby register our most vigorous protest against the agitation of paid Communist agents and their efforts to undermine our confidence in Canadian democratic institutions, and call to our brethren in Canada to demonstrate their loyalty to this our adopted land, by similar protests and active support of all our Canadian institutions.

Furthermore, we petition the government of our province of Alberta and the government of the Dominion of Canada, to prohibit the publication in Canada of all the Bolshevistic revolutionary literature and cause the deportation of all those foreigners and to suspend the naturalization of all those citizens of foreign birth who propagate and who follow the radical teachings intended for the destruction of our democratic system of government.[287]

An identically-worded resolution was passed two weeks later by a meeting of Andrew-area residents who had assembled to hear a debate, "Resolved that Bolshevism is a menace to society." The four speakers, "leading educationalists [i.e. teachers] of the Ukrainian people, none of whom are Bolsheviks," had conceived the idea of the debate "in order to disabuse the minds of the public from thinking that the Ukrainian people were largely holding Bolshevik views. . . ." Those who were, were styled by the *Observer* as the "rag-tag and bob-tail of the Ukrainians, who are cordially despised by their Ukrainian fellow-citizens."[288]

Although the Anglo-Saxon editorialist dismissed the influence of Communist ideology on Ukrainian-Canadians as merely the agitation of "windbags preying on the credulity of ignorant people,"[289] the anti-Communist Ukrainian-Canadians understood that the threat was more serious than that. Far from being ignoramuses, the Communist sympathizers were developing a sophisticated and knowledgeable critique of Canadian society through studied comparisons with the Soviet Union. The way to deal with this sophistication was not to laugh it off but to challenge it, debate it, expose it, and refute it. For example, the United Loyalists of Canada, meeting in Two Hills in April 1931, argued that the "liberty and justice which all Canadians enjoy in the Dominion under the British flag . . . was little in evidence under the Soviet regime." A second speaker, V. Kupchenko, appealed to fellow Ukrainian-Canadians to unite against the few who were disloyal and fractious.

> Although Mr. Kupchenko vouched for this loyalty of the majority of his own race, yet he urgently appealed to the small percentage to judge fairly of the situation themselves; not to be swayed by the smooth-tongued agitators who depicted Russia under the Soviet government as a land of Paradise, and in so

doing showed conclusively an utter disregard for the truth.

Substantiating his argument, he pointed out that the "marital laws" (presumably divorce laws) of the Soviet Union "disrupted the whole morale of society," jeopardizing the "family unit as the essential basic factor of any moral nation."[290] Resorting to moralizing to make a political point is not so strange as it seems – the stated purposes of the United Loyalists of Canada were not only to promote "loyalty and patriotism among all citizens of Canada" and to insure "the integrity and maintain the honour of our country" but also to be active in "establishing a pure and noble citizenship throughout the Dominion."[291] "Purity" and "nobility" are notoriously relative concepts having as much to do with the mind of the beholder as with the objective behaviour of the beholdee. Nevertheless it is to be noted that, by declaring such an objective, the United Loyalists intended to focus their debate with the Communists outside the sphere of economics and politics altogether. Nowhere in the notions of "patriotism," "integrity," "honour," and "purity" is there a response to the Communists' attacks on unemployment, labour laws, marketing, banking, and profiteering. I can only conclude that either they had no response to make or they believed no response was necessary: it was as though radical criticism of the Canadian status quo was by definition disloyal and dishonourable.

I also conclude that for the conservatives the objective of refuting Communist theory was secondary to the real issue: protecting the mass of Ukrainian-Canadians from the exasperation of the ruling class. The painful lessons of Ukrainian-Canadian history had showed them all just how vulnerable the "alien" was in times of social and economic stress to the aggressiveness of the elite. Unlike the leftists, who examined the economic and political basis of that vulnerability, the rightists sought to deflect the aggression from "good" Ukrainians to "bad" ones. I doubt very much that the Loyalists really were prepared to promote the "loyalty" and "nobility" of all Canadians – a defensive and apologetic ethnic is in

no position to challenge the morality of the Anglo-Canadian boss –
but were fully prepared to take on the responsibility of supervising
the morality of their own fellow Ukrainians. In all fairness, they
argued, the agitators should be isolated from the rest of the
community and disciplined; the Loyalists should then be left in
peace.

The right-wing Ukrainian-Canadians and the Anglo-Canadian
establishment, then, shared the same interpretation of events. If
there was massive trouble in Canada, it was largely the fault of the
agitators. Silence them and the trouble might go away. Efforts to do
just that were strenuous.

Exaggerations notwithstanding, it was a fact that the radicals
were more often the victims of violence than the perpetrators of it –
in the *Observer* copies I read, I came across only the instance of
heckling as an example of Communist "aggression" – unless, of
course, one considers inflammatory speeches, petitions for
signatures, grain strikes, and hunger marches to be examples of
violent activity. As the thirties, and the Depression, ground on,
however, the emphasis of their detractors changed from personal
attacks on "fly-by-night windbags" who should be handled by
"hunting up some lonely island off the British Columbia coast and
dumping them on it to sink or swim"[292] to general attacks on the
Soviet Union and its "agents" in Canada. This signalled a tactical
switch as well. Rather than taking on each separate case of local
agitation, the rightists hoped to discredit the very basis of the
movement by denouncing the policies of the Soviet Union. The
assumption they made was that Ukrainian-Canadian agitators were
getting their ideas, not from an analysis of their own environment,
but from outside sources. If Soviet policies could be demonstrated to
be perverse, then local Communists would lose all credibility,
especially as those policies affected Ukrainians. Just as the events of
the Depression were the fuel for left-wing arguments, so were the
events in Russia the fuel for the right-wing.

On Sunday, Nov. 5th, 1933, the Ukrainian National Hall in
Willingdon was packed to capacity with the Ukrainian people

of Willingdon and the surrounding territory. The following speakers denounced the Bolshevik regime in no uncertain terms: Mr. Yanda, Mr. P. Miskew and Mr. Lazarowich of Edmonton and Mr. Piruchney and Dr. Boykovich of Willingdon. The speakers painted a true picture of the Communistic rule with all of its horrible results. Hundreds and thousands of Ukrainian people are being starved to death in the once productive Ukraine. In the meantime the Soviets blind the eyes of the world with their successful five year plan. At the close of the meeting Mr. Luchkovich addressed the meeting declaring that the eyes of the civilized world should be turned to the unfortunate situation that now exists in the Ukraine. Four strong resolutions were passed, condemning the work of the Communists in the Ukraine and in Canada.[293]

In their resolutions to protest the deliberate policy of famine and the forcible deportation of Ukrainians to eastern Russia, to recommend to Ukrainians in the USSR that they form an independent state and to denounce Ukrainian-Canadian leftist newspapers as subversive, this audience, and many others, made their choice between the struggle against Soviet imperialism and the struggle against Canadian capitalism. Obviously, the left had not succeeded in synthesizing the either-or into a credible ideology that would convince the mass of Ukrainian-Canadians that their desire for an autonomous national identity went hand in hand with the radical restructuring of Canadian society. Instead, the right had been able to polarize the debate as a confrontation of mutually exclusive options so that, by 1935, in the throes of Depression, a speaker at Miroslawna could equate the hunger marches and grain strikes of northeastern Alberta with the aims of the Communist Third International.[294]

The right-wing was, as usual, aided and abetted by the mistakes and occasional idiocies of the left itself. By the thirties, the ongoing assimilation of the Canadian-born into the Anglo-Canadian system of values was a fact of life. When those, anxious about the future integrity of the Ukrainian-Canadian community, asked the question: "Which is more important, the class struggle or the preservation of the ethnic community?" they were answered, on the one hand, by a well-organized, highly-respected, nationalist leadership which spoke directly and articulately to their desire for a collective identity and, on the other, by an unrespectable and inflammatory left which "denounces the nationalists as capitalists, enemies of the workers and as propagandists of fascism. They point to the Soviet Ukraine as the logical answer to the nationalist demands for a Ukrainian state."[295] This was not what they wanted to hear. Nor was it, by the late thirties, credible. The Stalinist rule of terror in the Soviet Union was being publicized and as the horror stories were disclosed – the brutal purges of the Communist party, the terrorization of the peasantry through collectivization of the agricultural lands, the secret trials and gross fabrications of the secret police against nationalist intellectuals, the Russification of Ukrainian culture, the destruction of the All-Ukrainian Marx and Lenin Institute as well as the Ukrainian Orthodox Church. The non-Communist Ukrainian-Canadians were confirmed in their repudiation, not only of Stalinism, but of the CPC as well, especially as it did not immediately have anything to say in response to the news beyond pious and platitudinous "explanations."

Of course, it was one thing to disbelieve the right-wing extremists and quite another to subscribe to revolution. Between the two the majority of Ukrainian-Canadians around Two Hills found their political position. For several years they elected United Farmers of Alberta candidates and took an enormous amount of pride in the fact that the election of the UFA candidate from Vegreville, Michael Luchkovich, in 1926, put a Ukrainian into Parliament for the first time in the history of the Commonwealth. With the advent of the populist parties, Social Credit and CCF, and the organization of the CPC, political preferences were further diversified. The candidates tended to be teachers and farmers, with a sprinkling of lawyers, pharmacists, and civil servants. They also tended to be Ukrainian-Canadian, a fact which caused some concern among the Anglo-Canadians who speculated that, since more than half the electors were of Ukrainian descent, no non-Ukrainian had a chance of being elected. The Ukrainians would stick to their "own," the political platform being of little consequence. This was simplistic. It's true enough, for example, that when Peter Svarich ran as an Independent Liberal in 1913, he announced publicly that "my chances for election in this contest are based upon the fact that I will get every Ruthenian vote and the Ruthenians comprise some 45 percent of the electorate in this district."[296] But he had entered the contest in the first place because the Conservative nominating convention had deliberately ignored the Ukrainian-speaking delegates' wish for a Ukrainian nominee. "A nominating committee was appointed and in due course this committee reported, placing only one name, that of F.A. Morrison, before the convention." In the second place, Svarich lost. So much for ethnic solidarity. "The result was to be expected. Mr. Svarich has excellent qualities even if he is a little fond of saying, look at me! but an Independent Liberal, nominated by a strong-arm squad of nationalist Ruthenians at a Conservative convention was a combination little likely to captivate the public mind."[297]

By the thirties it had become commonplace for Ukrainian-Canadians representing several political parties to contest an election in the same constituency and so the electors had perforce to vote on the basis of politics, not nationality. In 1935, for instance, the very popular Michael Luchkovich lost out to the Social Credit candidate, an Anglo-Saxon, as did Matthew Popovich. The *Observer* was surprised: a year earlier it had editorialized that "Within recent years, the Ukrainians have developed a 'race' consciousness. . . . Mr. Luchkovich's re-election in 1930 gave additional warning of the fact that the Ukrainians knew their strength and intended to use it."[298] Given that Luchkovich was a UFA candidate, one could just as easily argue he was elected on the basis of "farmer" consciousness; given that he was later defeated by a Social Credit candidate, one can argue that Ukrainian-Canadians were developing "anti-business" consciousness; given that the Socreds lost out eventually to the

Diefenbaker-Conservative sweep, one can additionally argue that Ukrainian-Canadians ultimately evolved "western" consciousness. And so on. Certainly, any candidate who could speak Ukrainian at a rally, who had relatives in the area and went to the local Ukrainian church was a "known quantity"; one felt comfortable around such a person. But such persons were to be found all across the political spectrum – political, not race, consciousness informed the electorate.

Because the Ukrainians had immigrated under the auspices of a Liberal government, they tended first to vote for that party – the Conservatives were never very popular as the party which had disfranchised and interned them and then ushered in the Depression – but the advent of the thirties and hard times convinced the farmers, at least, that the UFA might better serve their interests. It talked tough without sounding revolutionary, it stood up for the "little guy" and was not ashamed to solicit the support of Ukrainians. On a speaking tour through the Ukrainian district, Premier Brownlee brought them the good news:

> "We are now going thru hard times," the premier stated. "Do you think any government wants hard times? No." As the principal part of the audience were Ukrainian people, the speaker went on to say, "No good will be accomplished by obeying some who are coming among you asking you to refuse to obey the laws, trying to raise disturbances, by introducing untried methods, and trying at this time to cause unrest among you. . . ." The premier went on to state emphatically that he and his government were in perfect sympathy with the Ukrainian people and would allow no discrimination, and would as heartily shake hands with any of them and do them any good equal with any other citizen in the province.[299]

Four years later he was out, defeated by scandal, the worsening Depression, his treatment of the hunger marchers in Edmonton, and the twenty-five dollar promise of Social Credit.

By April 1935, Two Hills community had formed a Social

Credit Association. The *Observer*, for one, sarcastically suggested that Social Credit candidates were opportunistically willing to run because it was the party of the moment – *God Save the King* and the *Internationale* sound much alike to some folk under such circumstances"[300] – and that the "sincerity" of the electors "will be out to a severe trial" by the adoption of the Social Credit program, but the electors felt otherwise. Social Credit representatives were sent to Edmonton and Ottawa.

In some ways, Social Crediters were the institutional wing of the right-wing "nationalists," taking up the cause of anti-Communism and anti-socialism and spreading the word among non-Ukrainians as well as Ukrainian-Canadians. As an official party with broad support, Social Credit had an authority and presence the United Loyalists, for example, could never muster and, unlike the Loyalists, was prepared to address itself to the economic issues bedevilling the farmers. The campaign literature of Michael Ponich, Socred MLA, urged voters to remember that: "Alberta Social Credit protected you from exploitation and foreclosure; paid cash for every mile of public road it built; believes that the people should have more power than the government; Big International Financiers support Socialism because under centralized Socialism they will have a still greater control over the lives of the people." By 1944, this approach had escalated to a vehement and dismal attack on the "doctrine of the supreme state"; the annual report of the Social Credit board in Edmonton predicted that "socialism would finish the job, already far advanced by the present financial dictatorship, of completely enslaving mankind. Creation of a world slave state is the ultimate objective of both."[301] This was not only thinly-disguised anti-Semitism (*vide* the *Protocols of Zion*) but also a transparent attack on the CCF, by that time already the government of Saskatchewan. Yet the two parties had much the same appeal.

Aberhart and the CCF spokesmen in Saskatchewan spoke a more appealing language to many farmers than *The Furrow* with its references to *kulaks* (rich peasants), "social fascists" and "toiling farmers." The CCF program seemed radical enough to those who wanted major changes but saw no need for a "Soviet Canada" or a class struggle in the Canadian countryside.[302]

Assailed, on the one hand, by ultra-leftists denouncing "reformism" and, on the other, by conservatives fantasizing the "slave state," the CCF made its precarious way among the Ukrainian-Canadians. It took on the tricky assignment of simultaneously championing the people's cause and affirming the democratic, non-violent path to socialism. In the 1935 federal election, the Vegreville association described the CCF as a party which "is not beholden to 'Big Interests' for their campaign funds, but who derive their funds from the rank-and-file of the common people. (He who pays the fiddler calls the tune)," a party "pledged to end the economic injustices suffered by the great mass of the people" and a party committed to "consistent, cohesive and prolonged effort" – beware the fraudulent lure of the putsch artists! "The way is long and listening to the political sirens that line the economic beaches will only postpone the time of achievement."

Trouble was, the Ukrainian-Canadian community was anything but politically cohesive. From right to left, there were the ultra-right "nationalists," Social Credit, a sprinkling of Liberals and Conservatives, the "progressives," the ULFTA members, and the Communists. Rejecting the extremes, the CCF looked for its support among the "progressives" and the disenchanted moderates, the farmers, teachers and working people, and housewives in the towns who could be counted on not to confuse democratic socialism with either "free-enterprise" or "Bolshevism."

By the thirties I was quite disillusioned with the conditions in the country and I was tired of doing without conveniences. I began to realize hard work and economy were only part of the answer. The system was unjust, was the problem. Farmers couldn't afford to buy machinery to work the land. Tractors stood still because gasoline cost too much. So I became active in one organization after another. The Women's Institute of Alberta was the first one. It was interested in things like sanitation and health and handicrafts. After the meetings we had a social hour which for us farm women was really important. We never saw each other anywhere else. Then I moved on to the Women Farmers' Union of Alberta which was more militant and progressive. I organized branches in a thirty-square mile area. A lot of women came to the meetings but it was hard to get them involved. They said, "This is the way it's always been. There's nothing we can do about it." It seemed farfetched to them to be talking about electricity and running water and bathtubs on the farm, bussing children to school. But there were some eager ones who wanted to leave the confines of their homes and find answers. As for politics, my husband was going to a lot of meetings and when he returned I'd ply him with questions. When Social Credit seemed to be getting a foothold, I decided it was time to join the CCF.

For some the decision to support the CCF was inevitable once they had determined that (peaceful) change was necessary, but the rest of the community was scandalized. Pamphlets in Ukrainian and English allegedly printed up by the Communist party, were circulated at CCF organizing meetings accusing the CCF and Brownlee's UFA government (which had sent the police against the hunger marchers in 1932) of being one and the same; and accusing the CCF of naively believing that want and poverty could be voted out of existence. A CCF organizer was accused by a Greek Catholic priest, by Social Crediters, Greek Orthodox parishioners, the dentist, high school principal, and secretary-treasurer of the municipality, of being a Communist.

The political history of these Ukrainian-Canadians is rich, then, with episodes of struggle and it becomes impossible to view them as an undifferentiated mass of "ethnics" who, peacefully and untroubled, made their orderly progress from homesteading to urbanity, from servility to the Progressive Conservative party and from pioneering enthusiasm to middle-class security. Their progress was often thwarted, often stymied, often revoked and their ethnic collectivity shattered by divided class loyalties. They could not, as a community, seek to acquire the privileges of Anglo-Canadian middle-class society and expect to remain a cohesive political unit: there is only the sentimental loyalty of "blood" between the poor farmer and the merchant. They could not produce a group of intelligentsia, professionals, and businessmen (even on a modest scale) and expect them to refuse an investment in the status quo. The internecine political confrontations were the inevitable result of class differentiation within the community. To expect a unified response to the conditions of the Depression and the rhetoric of protest, say, just because they were all of Ukrainian descent, is naive. It was just as much a waste of time for the leftists to denounce the machinations of the church and some school teachers as for the rightists to deplore the Bolshevism of the farmers. There was no way, by the thirties, for a grain striker, infuriated by the exploitative system of elevators, railways, grain buyers, and mortgage companies, to share the conviction of a hotel owner about the benignity of the "system." For the upwardly-mobile Ukrainian-Canadian, with the privileges and security of the middle-class just around the corner, political conservatism and social stability were of the essence; to the devastated farmer and worker, agitation and militancy were the only useful postures. It was no surprise, then, that when the protester "spoke bitterness," the conservative heard "treachery" and vigorously defended what the other sought to destroy. Although one may be disgusted, in retrospect, with the conservatives' failure to support their blood brothers' and sisters' skirmishes with Canadian capitalism, it is romantic to believe they could have done otherwise. In spite of the superficial similarities of a common ethnicity, the Ukrainian-Canadians were no longer all huddled together at the bottom of the socio-economic ladder. Those who were on their way up naturally viewed the approbation of the Canadian middle-class as a necessity and the defense of the Ukrainian-Canadian farmer and worker as a luxury, if not a liability to their status.

The ethnic apologists, then, sought to minimize the importance of radicalization among the Ukrainian-Canadians by ascribing it to "indoctrination," and "efficient propaganda machines," "hypocrisy" and "false propaganda"[303] rather than, as farmers and workers themselves explain it, to a credible and useful analysis of their problems and a blueprint for change. "The times were ripe for a change," they explain, "and people would grasp at anything out of desperation, out of believing that Communism was a better alternative than the way we were going – downhill. When a speaker came to the hall to say that coal miners were being robbed by the bosses, everybody was there to hear it." Then came Stalin and it seemed to the Canadian rank-and-file that maybe their class interests, their security and well-being and dignity were better served after all by the liberalism of capitalist institutions than by the authoritarianism of Soviet ones, and so they too took their chance with the status quo. As for the progressives themselves, no regrets. "We didn't get much done in Canada but over the whole world people like us made a lot of big changes. And someday that change is coming here too." The speaker knows he speaks into the probable future.

> mrs. krasniansky mourning
> she remembers the end
>   of the second world war
> their being very poor
> and in need of something better
>   to call home
> remembers how she her husband
>   and two small kids
> protested outside the regina
>   legislature building
> and she still treasures
>   the faded news photograph:
> she and her husband
> and the kids
> smileless

each with the right arm proudly flexed
with a fist
tightly formed
and personifying proletarian power
the ultimate pride in protest

they believed in no religion or god
yet recently
digging through his old things
she found his hidden litany
he wrote giving thanks to the virgin mary
after the new house was built
and she copies it now
over and over again
imitating his spidery slavic calligraphy
and thus learns how to write
                              in her 70th year[304]

THIRTEEN

World War II

I was called up for the army during the Second World War but I was disqualified because I have flat feet. I wasn't disappointed. Not exactly. I don't know what they were fighting for. There wasn't much talk about going over to free the Ukraine. These wars are such a mix-up and a lot of people just wanted to stay out of it. A lot of them when they came back were cursing it up and down. Some enlisted because they didn't have jobs and thought they could get enough to eat, some went because they wanted to see some action, some never came back, some came back injured and sick, no foot, no hand.

– Walter Kitt

* * *

Men had to go to the army; they had no choice. A lot of guys didn't have any work or place to stay, nothing to eat, so they were compelled to volunteer. When the war broke out all the men at the soup kitchens took off to the army. It was good pay compared to relief. So I wouldn't say they volunteered out of patriotic reasons!

– Paul Spak

* * *

When Poland and Hungary were attacked and the Germans kept on moving and moving, the Ukrainians were very much against these invasions and quite a number became volunteers. And Ukrainian people felt that Canada had given them the freedom, the opportunity to get ahead, the education, and now Canada was at war. We Ukrainians felt it our duty for what Canada gave us that we send our young people to fight for what Canada thought was right. So I'd say it was Canadianism. Families were very proud to say a son had signed up, especially when he came back. I think the Ukrainian people have their own way of thinking about this. Our history. When the mother blessed a son to go and fight, I think that meant a lot. A lot of our mothers felt that when the cause is there they don't spare their own children.

– Stephen Mulka

* * *

Enlisting was a traumatic experience. I felt so alone and so out of place because I'd never been away among strangers for such a long time. The first two or three weeks were, oh, I think I wanted to break down a lot of times and cry. Well, let's put it this way, we were good boys and girls in such days. We heard no rough language and so on, but when I got to the depot and heard some of the language that these boys used, it just shocked me. They were city boys, they were all kinds of boys. Some from Toronto, some from Winnipeg, some from Edmonton, and of course, this was the Commonwealth Air Training scheme, and we had boys from all over the world. But a lot of them were just youngsters who had a little more experience in the world than I did anyway, and a lot braver. I don't think I ever thought about being killed. I don't think anybody thought about it. I don't think I ever thought about it even as I made my operational flights. You just don't think about it. It's a strange thing, but you don't.

– Mike Pawliuk

* * *

There's one thing that makes me proud of being Ukrainian-Canadian: that a lot of us had an analysis of the war and weren't going to be stampeded. There were Ukrainians who spent the war years in the bush being fed by their families because they were hiding from the RCMP and weren't going to "serve." They had an idea of where their loyalties lay and their relationship to such ideas as patriotism. Their idea of loyalty was to keep body and soul together and not spill their blood to fight an imperialist war. They knew enough about their own history to know that the Ukrainians had been battered back and forth among four or five different sides in a war. They knew how Hitler had expanded and why he was being opposed. They were Communists and knew that fascism was capitalism with its mask taken off and that there weren't many fascists worse than the Americans and the British. They had just lived through a depression and were now being asked to be patriotic to this rotten system which suddenly found unlimited amounts of money to produce jeeps and guns. So a lot of them simply decided, "Hell no, we won't go" and took to the bush.

– Winston Gereluk

The outbreak of war in 1939 put a new twist in the politics of the Ukrainian-Canadian community around Two Hills. The Depression, which many had feared would last another ten years, softened, as prices on farm products increased. Militant protest against the state of affairs lost its edge of urgency. Money began circulating again, farmers could buy new tractors; bills were paid, merchants could increase their stock; taxes in arrears were collected and the municipality could begin new roadwork. A revolution no longer seemed necessary. The rural unemployed returned to the farms; there was work to do again for the war effort. Leisure time for politicking and organizing and debating was scarce and people were tired.

It began to look like a futile fight for the CCF. I had worked for elections about four or five times and then finally I said, for better or worse, rightly or wrongly, now I shall start working for myself for a change. The children were growing up; politics is one thing but my children needed training, university and whatnot. I had to work for them too. Sometimes politics can ruin a fellow. It's ruined quite a few people. You lose the election, you are defeated, and you haven't got a job anymore, no money, flat broke, well. . . . I just looked after myself.

There were new troubles to deal with that made the struggle against capitalism seem academic: European relatives were being bombed; Canadian ones conscripted; coal for heating was rationed and consumer goods scarce. War certificates, not petitions, were publicized; war bonds not strike funds funnelled off the spare change. There was a danger the army would appropriate the community's essential workers. More ominously, anti-foreign, especially anti-German, sentiment was revived, with a new respectability. In a war, xenophobia is patriotic – "I remember a fellow in Hairy Hill, he was a German, born in Germany, and he had to report to the police quite often because they thought he might have been pro-Nazi" – and, as had happened during the First World War, Ukrainian-Canadians could be "it" again. Better watch your tongue.

In all these communities like Radway, Bellis, etc., people had German neighbours who were in trouble. And they were scared shitless, the Communists were. They knew that eventually, their time would come to get locked up too.

Beyond the immediate community, political events were taking place that had repercussions on the political attitudes of Two Hills. The ethnic press reported on the defection of some Ukrainian-Canadians from the Communist party who reconsidered their support of Stalin's policies in the Soviet Ukraine. This was a stunning event: the anti-Stalinist diatribe of "nationalists" was one (expected) thing, the disillusioned confessions of a "progressive" quite another. Was the righteous indignation of the Communists not all that it seemed?

The existence of anti-Communist Ukrainians, who were and remain more critical of the USSR than any Anglo-Saxon organization in Canada, must be borne in mind if one is to preserve a sense of proportion about Ukrainian support for the Communist movement.[305]

When it came to the crunch, one was perhaps more "Ukrainian" than "Red" after all. Especially since the Communist party leadership seemed unconcerned that innocent Ukrainians were being murdered by Stalin.

> A former secretary of the Ukrainian Agitprop Committee of the CPC complained about Soviet policies in the Ukraine. T. Kobzey and his associates were expelled from the CPC and denounced in the party press.[306]

If this sort of thing created consternation and soul-searching among the left, it added fat to the fire of the anti-Communists and convinced those caught between that more than ever holding pro-Communist points of view could get you into trouble. I was told of an avowed Communist who was advised by the school board that he'd never be principal of the school because of his politics. I was told of the RCMP, following local Communists to their hall and crawling on hands and knees around the parked cars and trucks, "reading" the license plate numbers with their fingers.

> Being a Ukrainian was a very political thing. There was something positively Communist about being a Ukrainian in those days. That changed for awhile when the Soviet Union became an ally, but other than that, people hated the Russians and Ukrainians were too close to being "Russian" for comfort. You knew that the RCMP would be watching you. They'd been watching Ukrainians ever since the days of moonshining and growing hemp [cannabis plant used for making fibre] and so they were symbols of repression. There were some Ukrainian communities where the RCMP didn't dare appear in uniform. Like Estevan in Saskatchewan. The tombstone of the Ukrainian strikers says, "Murdered by the RCMP." So most Ukrainians wanted to keep their noses clean.

By 1939 the Communists were doubly unpopular, to the authorities and a majority of Ukrainian-Canadians, because of their anti-war agitation. People distributing anti-war literature were arrested and jailed. Organizers of anti-war meetings found it more and more difficult to rent halls. In 1940, with the country under the War Measures Act, the federal government issued an order-in-council banning not only pro-Nazi organizations but also the CPC and Communist newspapers in English and Ukrainian, placing a seal on ULFTA property and allowing for the arrest and internment of Communist leaders. As a result, thirty-six Ukrainian-Canadian Communists were interned – they probably saw it coming, remembering their World War I experiences – including Matthew Popovich, John Boychuk, Matthew Shatulsky, and the editorial staffs of the newspapers.

The halls were raided, books and documents destroyed. Some of the halls were given to the nationalists, some sold to private individuals, some just padlocked and abandoned. In 1940, the ULFTA owned 113 buildings worth about $1,000,000 and printing equipment valued at $60,000.

The printshop of the *People's Gazette* was confiscated and sold to *New Pathway*, the nationalist paper. Books were burned or shredded for no other reason than that they had been printed in the USSR. Among the books so destroyed were: Shevchenko's *Kobzar*, *Eugene Onegin* by Pushkin, *War and Peace* by Leo Tolstoy, *King Lear* by William Shakespeare, *Oliver Twist* by Charles Dickens, and many others.

The only left-wing Ukrainian organization not banned was the Worker's Benevolent Association.[307]

The WBA, for its part, described the internees as "political prisoners," whose anti-war activities had been used as an excuse by the authorities to "attempt to behead the leadership of the militant political and cultural working class organizations."[308] To head off, that is, the possibility of political disorder and class confrontations within Canada by isolating the most notorious of the subversives. This is not unlikely. The CPC had been a thorn in the government's side for years; under the banner of the "war effort," arbitrary repression of left-wing agitators would appear less provocative than under normal conditions of peace. Officially, the CPC et al were banned for their refusal to support the "effort" but it is interesting that the right-wing Ukrainian-Canadian organizations which were virulently anti-Soviet (and thus pro-fascist in some cases) were untouched by the ban. It was then, not so much the pacifism of the Communists that was threatening as their on-going radicalism. As Paul Yuzyk describes it,

> The ULFTA together with the Communist Party of Canada, openly attacked Canada's war effort and advocated a soviet revolution in Canada. Seditious activities increased to such a proportion that the Canadian government was forced to suppress the ULFTA in June 1940, and to confiscate its 108 halls and property.[309]

It is debatable, however, whether the government was "forced" to do any such thing or whether it merely found it expedient to do so. From the Communists' point of view, the Ukrainian-Canadian radicals were clearly the victims of the ruling class's offensive manoeuvres.

> While Canada was officially at war with Nazi Germany, there were still illusions in high places both here and elsewhere, that Hitler would eventually turn the full force of his war machine against the Soviet Union. So that the "foreigners" in the country, and particularly the Slavs with socialist convictions, were regarded as the main danger to internal security, they became the target of hysterical excesses and persecution. The Ukrainians were never fully accepted by the Anglo-Canadian core society and the establishment found it relatively simple to cast them in the role of villains and a menace to national security.[310]

Meanwhile, back in Two Hills, the situation was clear enough: there's a war going on and who's going to go fight it? The answer was not "instant, unquestioning and unquestioned."[311] The population may have become increasingly skeptical of leftist propaganda and their own youthful expectations of immediate social and economic change but this did not mean they were prepared to make ill-considered sacrifices just because the government asked. They would have to have their own reasons.

They went to liberate the Ukraine from the Soviet Union. They went for "pride of country," believing there was a just cause they had been called upon to champion. They went out of hatred for Nazis. They went to become heroes, beloved by the weak and helpless for their sacrifice. They went because the incessant propaganda could not be ignored and because they would win and come back home.

For others, there was no triumph in the enterprise, it was merely inevitable. "Everybody in the town was very sad about the war. Nobody knew what the outcome was going to be. The young boys were going away. Would we ever see them again? When the war stopped, *that* was happiness." The boys were signing up or being drafted and leaving, because there was no way out of it. As full of chagrin and fear as the hearts of the soldiers and their families may have been, all were agreed that the sacrifice was their "duty." "I don't think my mother ever felt I shouldn't go but I do think she wished I didn't have to." Perhaps, even more so, as "ethnic" Canadians; what could prove their loyalty more than enlistment in the name of King and Country? "Sure some people complained about us 'foreigners' but when it comes to defending the country during the Second World War, who was in the army? All of us who they said weren't loyal. All us boys went to defend our country." Between 35,000 and 50,000 Ukrainian-Canadians served in the army alone. Out of duty, out of loyalty, out of despair.

I don't think they joined out of being so much patriotic as because there was unemployment and no security and they felt they might as well join up with the rest of the rank-and-file. And the people that had the least security, the least to fight for, was the first to be called up. I know two families that were on relief in our community. They were barely existing and them boys were the first to be called up to defend this country. And they had the least to defend because if the country had not made the provision to give them a living, what is it worth to defend? For who?

There were those, however, who were rather more enthusiastic. While not discounting the sincerity of individual anti-Nazi sentiment and the voluntary commitment made by thousands of Ukrainian-Canadians to the struggle against the German war machine, the argument may be made that so much of what appeared to be the spontaneous fervour of a united community in a collective revulsion against the fascist beast was really the enthusiasm of an elite. As a group, this elite shared a motive – their individual commitment is not the question here – and a double-headed one at that. As notables of the community and under the spotlight of publicity, they took on the job, on the one hand, of allaying suspicions that Ukrainian-Canadians were secretly sympathetic to the Nazi cause because of Hitler's alleged support of Ukrainian independence movements and, on the other, of refuting charges that Ukrainian-Canadians were secretly sympathetic to the Bolshevik cause (this was before Hitler's invasion of the Soviet Union) because of the Allied war-mongering against the international working class. In other words, the job of presenting to Anglo-Canadian view a "united front" among Ukrainian-Canadians when there was in reality disunity and cross-purposes. As an up-and-coming establishment in its own right, the Ukrainian-Canadian elite in the forties had much to lose should their compatriots fail to act as "good Canadians": the carrot at the end of the stick of "unity" was the approbation of the Anglo-Canadian establishment and, presumably, an invitation into its class precincts.

It was an Anglo-Canadian academic, Watson Kirkconnell, who wrote,

Both Canada and the United States entered the present war with a sociological problem on their hands. This was the presence of very large numbers of newly acquired citizens who, while predominantly well-disposed in their New World citizenship, still thought in old world patterns and were unduly susceptible to old world propaganda.[312]

He went on to point out the strategic importance of the mines, shipyards, and factories to the war effort, the preponderance of workers of "recent European origin" in them and the consequent need of a "fervent solidarity among such workers in support of the war on behalf of their new country. . . . The same is true of their attitude towards military service."[313] In another article, he referred to Anglo-Canadian anxiety about the number of Ukrainian-language newspapers in Canada (they had doubled in fifteen years while German-language newspapers had declined), the variety of Ukrainian cultural organizations whose "aim is the perpetuation of their ancestral language and culture" and the alleged failure of Ukrainian-Canadians to vote for the moderate political parties.[314] Both Kirkconnell and Yuzyk argued that the anxiety was without basis. By 1941 the Canadian-born Ukrainians constituted 65 percent of the Ukrainian-Canadian population. "A second generation was growing up which regarded itself primarily Canadian although its background was Ukrainian.[315] Kirkconnell pointed out that Ukrainian enlistments were well above proportion to population, that leaders of the Ukrainian churches "were emphatic in commending the Canadian cause,"[316] that, in a Manitoba constituency, non-Communist voters had united and "transferred their weight of several thousand votes to the Liberal candidate in order to demonstrate their enthusiastic support of the Government's war policy"[317] and that "the Ukrainian settlement of Myrnam, Alberta, has alone sent in several carloads of scrap metal and rubber."[318] Yuzyk pointed out that although "the Ukrainians have no really rich among them . . . they are mostly farmers and industrial workers, and their purchasing power is quite limited," they nevertheless oversubscribed their quota in the Victory Loan campaigns: subscriptions in Smoky Lake averaged 136.8 percent of their quota, in Vegreville, 121.3 percent.[319] More conclusively, "while the total loss for the whole of the Canadian expedition to Hong Kong amounted to about 15 percent, the Ukrainian loss amounted to 34 percent.'[320]

If all this were true, one may well ask why, then, "early in 1940 the federal Department of National War Services after consultation with the Department of External Affairs, took steps to achieve unity among the Ukrainian Canadians?"[321] Were there still doubts about the solidarity of Ukrainian-Canadians behind the war effort? Were the arguments to the contrary unconvincing? The answer is, perhaps, the lingering nervousness about the Ukrainian-Canadian left: "Only the Ukrainian Labour Farmer Temple Association [sic], a small group, which espoused the Communist cause of the Soviet Union, at first opposed Canada's participation in the war. . . ."[322] "The wild men on the wings . . . are particularly liable to listen to the loud and irresponsible promises of the Communist agitator and his incendiary press."[323] All this begs the question: how could a "small group" of "wild men" and "incendiaries" be simultaneously negligible in influence and so threatening to "unity?" Because, they were neither negligible nor the moderates so united. Although the CPC and the ULFTA had been banned, their combined thousands of Ukrainian-Canadian members did not *ipso facto* cease thinking and feeling as they had hitherto done. Although banned, their ideology did not cease being a provocation to the government. "The attacks of [Tim Buck] and [the Communist Ukrainians'] one, scurrilous newspaper . . . is a constant and pernicious scandal."[324] Although the moderates – the farmers and townspeople of Two Hills, Myrnam, Hairy Hill, Bellis – went in their thousands to the armed services, they often did so reluctantly, fatalistically, and cynically. As we shall see, a number refused to go at all. Something had to be done about this equivocation. Someone had to get the faint-hearted and cynical into line and soothe the anxieties of the authorities. Someone, too, had to try to forestall abuse of the loyal Ukrainian-Canadians as had occurred during the First World War.

Enter the Ukrainian Canadian Committee. "One of the *raisons d'etre* of the Ukrainian Canadian Committee was to unite the

Ukrainian Canadians behind the war effort. This was the prime consideration in the minds of the government authorities."[325] It is misleading to assume all Ukrainian-Canadians were represented: the left had been outlawed so the UCC never did speak for it. But, through its representation from church groups, veterans' associations and middle-of-the-road nationalist organizations, and its Anglo-Canadian advisors, it did officially represent the opinion of Ukrainian-Canadians not of the left and received the government's mandate to organize their communities behind the war effort and make their views known to the government.

Enter, also, the Committee on Cooperation in Canadian Citizenship, Communities of Recent European Origin; also known as the "Nationalities Branch." In the persons of Professor G.W. Simpson, Professor Watson Kirkconnell, Mrs. R.F. McWilliams, Major J.S.A. Bois et al, it supported the UCC, "recommended promising volunteers from ethnic groups for officer training," "drew attention of Canadian newspapers to heroic war deeds of members of these groups," and supplied the foreign language press with a "regular war news service reflecting a Canadian point of view."[326] The extent of such propagandizing on behalf of "good ethnics" and the UCC's campaigns of mobilization are a measure both of the public's lack of conviction and the Ukrainian-Canadian community's own lack of resolve.

An example of the efforts made to bolster enthusiasm was a banquet and dance in Edmonton in 1942, sponsored by the Ukrainian platoon of the 2nd Battalion, Edmonton Regiment. Significantly, the event, "arranged primarily for the purpose of rallying more young men to enlist," was held in the unbanned national hall and featured *holubtsi*, waitresses dressed in Ukrainian costume, and an address by the ubiquitous V. Kupchenko. "Any able-bodied young man should be ashamed of wearing civilian clothing at this stage of the war," he said. "The freedom we are enjoying in Canada is too precious to be lost through complacency on our part." A Lt. Col. Hale complimented the youth of "Ukrainian extraction" who had already signed up; W. Kossar, president of the National Ukrainian Federation, appealed to the Ukrainian-Canadians to enlist because "we know what it means to lose freedom," an allusion to the political condition of European Ukrainians repeated by a William Dorosh who argued that the "only chance the 50,000,000 Ukrainians in Europe have for enjoying freedom is if every person of Ukrainian stock in Canada does his utmost to win the war for the cause of democracy."[327] These were, calculatedly appeals launched in the face of Communist statements that there was precious little "democracy" in Canada to defend and, conversely, that since the Ukrainians in the Soviet Union already enjoyed the "freedom" of socialism it was illogical to support a war on the basis of "liberating" them from Nazi imperialism only to deliver them into the hands of the "capitalist bosses."

Many Ukrainian-Canadian servicemen were, in fact, aware of the ideological conflict behind their simple resolution to fight overseas. The act of enlisting was interpreted as a repudiation not only of Hitler's designs against peace and freedom but also of the Ukrainian-Canadian Communists' arguments that the Canadian soldiers were being manipulated by the enemies of the Soviet Union. (The pro-Communists' explanation of the Soviet-German Non-Aggression Pact of 1939 referred to the "need to buy time in a situation in which the main thrust of a Nazi war would be against the Soviet Union with the connivance of other imperialist powers" and their description of the first two years of the war emphasized that "even at this point in Hitler's open drive for world conquest there were desperate efforts to divert the Nazi juggernaut to the east."[328]) The president of the Ukrainian Canadian Servicemen's Association on Active Service Overseas wrote to Kirkconnell:

> We who have left our homes to come here and to every theatre of war, left with one aim and only one aim in mind, to help rid the world of that Nazi scourge so that we and our children and our children's children may be able to live in peace and freedom, that freedom that made Canada so dear to us. We resent and oppose most strongly the policies pursued by such

papers as *Ukrayinska Zhittia* [published by the CPC], and are most glad that you and your fellow-members on the Federal Committee can defend our rights in our absence. The Empire is our Country and Canada our Home. That's why we're here.[329]

As late as 1943, the loyalty of the mass of Ukrainian Canadians was still under discussion: the *Star Weekly* sent a writer out to Alberta to reconfirm that the people there were supporting the war effort. A priest was interviewed:

To hear my father talk Canada is next thing to heaven, for he realizes that in the place from which he came he could never have done what he did here. And his sons and daughters know, too, that if he had stayed in the Ukraine we would probably be poor peasants ourselves. Can we help being patriotic Canadians?[330]

There follows a long list of Ukrainian-Canadian success stories – legislators, doctors, servicemen, master farmers – and the author's own comments on the reliability of the community: by their works ye shall know them as good Canadians.

When a Toronto reporter arrives in a Ukrainian-Canadian settlement east of Edmonton and observes the friendly, orderly, and eye-twinkling natives going about their unremarkable business, I am reminded of Catherine the Great's visits to her Russian villages: behind the facade, erected for the occasion, of tidiness and prosperity which she observed with satisfaction lay the real and wretched life of her people. What the *Star Weekly* writer could not see was that beyond the self-confident and patriotic front of the community lay dissension and confrontation. All was not at all well with the war effort. While the readers of the newspapers may have been finally persuaded that the "ethnics" were indeed united enthusiastically in support of the pursuit of war, the community itself continued to be ambivalent. Perhaps, after all, the persuasion itself was the point. The contradictions would take care of themselves.

A man openly admits today that he, and many others stayed on the farm or returned to it "because that's what kept us out of the army." Enlistees went AWOL. Pacifists went underground. Families of men who refused to enlist received white chicken feathers in the mail. Army deserters took to the bush and lived in dugouts in the banks of the creeks, and were fed by their families. Pacifists wore the big red badge on their uniforms that made them "zombies." Protesters taunted police and beat up informers.

I think there was an ideological commitment to pacifism. I think that these people had no use for the military officials who will screw you, and they knew it. The peasantry the world over knows that anyone who's urban is probably out to get you, whoever wears a suit is a shit. They're suspicious of all authority and hated all authority.

Alongside this naive disobedience went, as always, the critiques and remonstrances of the Communists and their sympathizers. As early as 1934 there had been an antifascist demonstration in Two Hills – "We were protesting against war, we didn't want another war, we went up and down the streets protesting against war and Nazism" – and by 1939 there was cynicism about the motives behind the hostilities in Europe. Not to mention resentment against the War Measures Act.

During the war, people like Boychuk and Popovich were put in concentration camps for four or five years. We were not allowed to have public gatherings of any kind. And that's democracy?

In 1940, the argument was made that "Canadian capitalism, not German capitalism, is our main enemy"[331] and that the "Canadian people are more interested in early peace than in the prosecution of the war."[332] For some Ukrainian-Canadians this was accurate enough.

Lots of people said, "You go and fight the enemy." Well, what kind of enemy was it that we never seen him? Fighting our own brother. I got two cousins in Ukraine. If I go in the army and they're fighting against me and I'm going to fight against them, we would be killing each other. The governments conscripted manpower, why didn't they conscript wealth? Never did. Why didn't they do it? That Depression was purposely set up to prepare for war. The poor fellows starving, so when the war starts, they all go and join because they're going to have a little money and have a place to eat and sleep. Otherwise they'll be on trains, riding boxcars the rest of their lives.

But for others, as the CPC was forced to admit, the appeals to "unite to defeat the imperialists on both sides of the imperialist war" fell fallow. "It would be an exaggeration to say that the slogan of the Communist Party of Canada, 'Withdraw Canada from the Imperialist War' has become the slogan of the masses." Tim Buck, in 1940.[333]

In 1941, with Hitler's attack on the Soviet Union, the acquisition of the USSR as an ally, and the CPC's *volte face* on the nature of the war from "imperialist" to "holy," the agitation from the left did not subside, but only shifted gear. The ULFTA halls, because of the "early hysteria of the war," were still locked up; Watson Kirkconnell was under attack as the "patron, defender and 'fuehrer'" of the Ukrainian-Canadian "fascists."[334] Vegreville M.P. Anthony Hlynka, Social Crediter, was exposed as a "Ukrainian fascist" and, in a published letter to his fiancee, Michael Fedirchyk, ULFTA member and "enlightened anti-fascist," explained the difference between his war and "their" war.

Along with thousands of other boys, I do not want to die . . . I only wish that if I must die, I will die in such a way that will make you proud of me . . . I have chosen my path and I must follow it. I am proud to have been given my chance to strike a blow for freedom. I am not fighting for England or for Canada. I fight for the right of freedom which we are all born to. No one must take this heritage from us.[335]

The end of the war did not immediately reconcile the right and the left. The CCF warned of the Labour Progressive Party's intentions of imposing "a Communist dictatorship on the Canadian people," the Ukrainian-Canadian Veterans' Association was organized to "protect the Ukrainian communities and Canada in general from subversive elements, to be good citizens, and to set the pace for others,"[336] and, although the ULFTA halls were restored to their owners, it was said that the members had not really experienced any change of heart.

As the result of their treason to Canada and their seditious opposition to Canada's war effort in 1939-40, the Canadian government suppressed the ULFTA halls, but restored them to their Communist owners after 1941 when Hitler attacked Russia and the latter became our "ally." There are no indications, however of any changes – since 1939 – in the attitude of Communists, and among them Ukrainian-Canadian Communists, toward Christianity and democratic institutions in general.[337]

As for the left, the LPP ran Ukrainian-Canadian candidates from Vegreville, Redwater, Vermilion, Grouard, Beaver River, Willingdon, and Edmonton in the provincial election of 1944 and pledged itself to "a square deal for our veterans of the People's War" and to "unite all Alberta democrats, regardless of party or philosophy, for the conquest of poverty and unemployment, ruined farms and broken homes." They reorganized their halls but fewer and fewer people came. "During the war, there were high prices for farmers and a lot of guys made extra dollars and they said they had no more time to spare for the progressive movement. They thought they were secure without it."

The end of the war felt like a good time to consolidate resources, not to risk them in a political poker game.

The Ukrainian-Canadians won their independence by serving in that war. One of my cousins came back with one shot-up eye and one foot in plaster, gold joints in it. He said, "Now, goddamn it, we've paid for our legitimacy in Canada, we're no longer European bastards, we're Canadians because we've paid for this in our blood." So they came back and demanded their constitutional rights as Canadians. And a lot of the veterans who had no high school were given every opportunity to finish their grade twelve, and others went on to university from these little grade twelve schools that popped up all over. One veteran here in town, a teacher who had been in combat, was really going overboard getting them through university. He was grabbing professors who were flunking them and saying, "Goddamn you, so-and-so was with the tank corps, all his buddies died in battle, pass him, you son-of-a-bitch!" He was collaring them in the halls and beating them up if they didn't pass his veteran buddies. So that was how they all joined the middle-class, and respectability.

It is the good and simple things a community remembers and memorializes, the unconditional actions and unproblematic events. Such were the collective horror of Naziism, the shared pathos of the brothers and sisters overseas, the courage of volunteers at the front. The names of the dead are cut into the stone of the cenotaph and the living retell a simple and sympathetic story of how was done what had to be done. But for every one of these stories there is another between the lines for which there is little or no public commemoration because it is somehow shameful or too complicated or burdened with misrepresentation. But these uncommemorated stories – of agitators and resisters, draft-dodgers and prisoners – belong to the community in the same way the shadow belongs to the cenotaph in the little square across from the Co-op store.

FOURTEEN

Nationalism

Between 1918 and 1921, my father was in the Ukrainian nationalist army. Between the capitulation of the Austrian Empire and 1921, for three years, he was in the Ukrainian army. And it was just chaos, pure chaos. The Ukrainians formed a small independent nation for about four years. They survived for four years and they were destroyed mainly by highly trained assassins. They were impotent, they couldn't move, they couldn't plan anything because within their own ranks, there were very highly devoted Marxist agents. So it fell apart. My dad got into trouble with the authorities in 1919 when he was organizing, he was with a propaganda group that was going around the community and, first of all, fighting Rumanian annexation. The Treaty of Versailles had given Bukovyna to the Rumanians. The Rumanian Orthodox church took it upon itself to send the clerics out to Bukovyna and tell the people that they were Rumanian. And some of the peasantry probably accepted it. So my father's group was going around telling Ukrainians not to listen to these Rumanians. So they formed the counter-propaganda group and an archbishop of the Rumanian church got a warrant out for my father's arrest and they finally caught him and he was in prison for about nine months in 1920. The Rumanians had occupied the Ukraine, there were bands of Tzarist White Army troops still hanging around, the Red Army had a lot of Ukrainian Communists, there were Russian agents in the Communist party. It was real chaos in this transition zone. Really, it was a bloody mess. And a lot of the peasants got sick of all parties and said a pox on all your houses, to hell with all of you. So when they came to Canada, these immigrants were already split up.

– Oleh Kupchenko

* * *

When people first came over from the old country Ukrainian wasn't even a common word; we were called Ruthenian, Galician, Austrian, Bukovynian. When I got to the Ukrainian Institute in Saskatoon they told me, "Never say you are Ruthenian. You are a Ukrainian." You see, a lot of these immigrants, especially the ones who came earlier, didn't have much, if any, education. And they didn't know who they were. The Ukrainians in the old country only started to awaken with Shevchenko and Franko; before that they were in slavery under the Russian or Polish regime. So some of our parents said, "Well, I am a Hutzul," or some said, "I am Polish," because they were Roman Catholic, though they didn't speak a word of Polish. So this is what the Institute gave us: the feeling we all belonged to one nation.

– Stephen Mulka

* * *

My parents weren't interested in nationalism. They believed in the church and that's about it. But I certainly think it's important for us Ukrainians in Canada to remember the old country. I've never been there but I think of it as my *ridna zymlya* [motherland].

– Harry Verenka

———

For the record: the last time there was an independent Ukrainian state of any duration was the Kievan Empire in the thirteenth century. Ukrainian history after that point is a dreary and woeful catalogue of everlasting violence and despair, characterized by a series of plunderers and despots, rapists and torturers, thieves and slave-drivers, martyrs and vassals, traitors, desperadoes, and luckless champions of lost causes. The good times were known by their relief from such catastrophes, periods when mere effete landlords, churlish bureaucrats, and bullying priests held sway. Given that, over the course of several centuries of foreign occupation troops, foreign clergy, foreign suzerains, academicians, and tax-collectors, the historical reality of an ancient and relatively sophisticated Ukrainian culture receded behind the smoke of burned-out memory, it is astonishing that in 1900 there were sparks of national consciousness in an otherwise devastated people reduced to simple clannishness. The political and cultural allegiances of the overwhelming majority of Ukrainians went no further than the last cottage at the rim of the village and the last surviving great-grandparent. One was not born in a country, one was born in a village; one did not have compatriots, one had relatives. The actions and postures and tools of everyday life were believed unique to each rural enclave and the sense of "otherness" from the foreign master had no extension beyond the local landlord and priest. From time to time, out of this pool of benighted rusticity emerged exceptional personalities – a rebel serf, a runaway Cossack, a crafty soldier, a poet, a conspiratorial concubine, a prophetic monk or nun – who synthesized the disparate and singular experiences of the common people into notions of shared class and cultural identity. But their brief clamour in uprisings and warfare, verses, visions, and schemes subsided quickly under the better-organized retaliation of the enemy and the scattered millions retreated back into servility and silence.

In the nineteenth century, however, in Western Ukraine, upon the abolition of serfdom, the growth of cities, the slight expansion of literacy and electoral politics, the Hapsburgian experiments with cultural autonomy, not to mention the development of transportation systems, cheap printing presses, industrialization and proletarianization, and nationalist movements "abroad," there emerged a nationalist consciousness that stuck. Its propagandists were members of the local intelligentsia and anybody who came in contact with and was aroused by their rhetoric. (Since the local gentry tended to be Polonized or Russified or Germanicized beyond recall to their Ukrainian origins, the nationalists' message was necessarily directed towards all the other Ukrainians who at least still spoke the language, practiced the customs and took some measure of pride in their resistance to assimilation.) Through this intelligentsia's works, their manifestos and pamphleteering, their plays, operas and poems, their research into history, linguistics and economics, the idea of a Ukrainian nation with an autonomous culture and the right to self-determination was sustained and strengthened among the rebellious, the vengeful, the alienated, and the imaginative.

The nationalists were apparently cohesive, united by a shared vision of a future Ukraine free of foreign domination and alien cultures and organized around an enlightened and productive peasantry. In 1917, however, upon the collapse of Russian czarism in the March Revolution, all hell broke loose. Over the turbulent course of events of the next seven years – the declaration of a Ukrainian National Republic in Eastern Ukraine, the invasion of Eastern Ukraine by the Red Army, the counter-invasion of the German army, the installation of a puppet Hetman state, the re-establishment of the UNR, the declaration of a Western Ukrainian Republic, the invasion of Western Ukraine by the Polish army, the unification on January 22, 1919, of the WUR and the UNR, ("This creation of a unified and independent Ukrainian state is considered by the Ukrainian nationalists as the manifestation of the supreme will of the Ukrainian nation"[338]), the capitulation of the new state two years later to the encircling forces of the Polish, Rumanian, White, and Bolshevik armies, the re-partition of the Ukraine, and the restoration by 1924 of Polish, Rumanian, and Russian hegemony over the dismembered country – the nationalists found themselves in a variety of competing camps. There were those who supported the Bolshevik Revolution and the ideal of a socialist Ukraine, those who favoured a democratic republic in the Western European mould, those who hoped for a constitutional monarchy, and even those who fancied a patriarchal-aristocratic arrangement in the manner of feudal, Cossack Ukraine. Clearly, their common nationalist consciousness had obscured their political incompatibilities and now there was no going back. World War II only exacerbated them. Another round of invasions, counter-invasions, puppet governments, fratricidal underground resistance groups, broken treaties, and false pledges while nationalist support was thrown behind now one and then another hopeless cause and contradictory strategy. Republicans vs. monarchists. Pro-Germans vs. anti-Germans. Anti-Russians and anti-Germans vs. pro-Russians. Fascists vs. Bolsheviks. Nationalists vs. internationalists. The Second International vs. the Comintern. And so on, down to the last ordinary Ukrainian trying to keep alive in the crossfire.

Naturally, these extraordinary events were followed closely by the Ukrainian-Canadians, who were neither so emotionally exiled from their recent homeland nor so securely identified with Anglo-Canadian society as to be indifferent to the fate of the people "back home." And so the same ideological competitions and political diversities were reflected among them too. If it hadn't been for the horrendous policies of the Soviet Union under Stalin, with its purges and deportations and artificial famines and Russification committed against the Ukraine, which united at least the centre and right-wing of Ukrainian-Canadian nationalists; and if it hadn't been for the slow and reluctant absorption of Ukrainian-Canadians into the Canadian mainstream, the various nationalist factions might long ago have cancelled each other out.

For all their bitter infighting, however, the nationalist factions shared the same hostile regard for the "internationalists" (those Ukrainian-Canadians who believed the troubles of the Ukrainian people, both in Canada and in Europe, were rooted in class warfare rather than in foreign domination) and the "melting pot" enthusiasts (those who believed that rapid and good-humoured assimilation into Anglo-Canadian society was an ethnic's obligation). Their nationalism came in two basic versions, the imported and the home-grown, and evolved not only in relationship to the political events of the Ukraine but in response to their Canadian experiences as well. Among the original immigrants were progressively-minded individuals who had been influenced by nationalist ideas back in Galicia and who carried the word among Ukrainian communities in Canada. In 1913, Peter Svarich, speaking for his self-designated constituency, informed the Vegreville *Observer* that "all men (including editors) are asked to take notice that there is no nation in the whole world which can properly be called 'Galician.' It is high time for our Canadian friends to learn that. We are not Galicians, Bukowinians, Austrians, Russians but we are once and forever Ruthenians, a nationality which with our brethren, the Ukrainians, in Russia, comprise a nation of 34 million people."[339] He is here making a distinction between the eastern Ukrainians who lived within the Russian empire and the western Ukrainians, or "Ruthenians," who lived within Austria-Hungary. Two years after this letter, my father, Svarich's nephew, in answer to his teacher's question about his nationality, replied "Ukrainian." Neither knew how to spell it in English. Two years after that, in 1917, he recalls it was common for all the Ukrainians in the area, whether from Eastern or Western Ukraine or otherwise, to refer to themselves as such.

The fact that Svarich is addressing the newspaper's readers at all is an indication that the reality of Ukrainian national identity was considered, by the Ukrainian-Canadians, as important to establish in the Anglo-Canadian community as within the ethnic one. Similarly, in 1919, when a representative of the Western Ukraine National Republic, Ivan Bobersky, visited Canada, he not only spoke with members of the Ukrainian-Canadian communities but also appealed to the Canadian government for diplomatic recognition of the WUNR. (In 1922, the first Ukrainian-Canadian protest demonstration of large proportions took place in Winnipeg when 10,000 people demanded "justice for the Ukrainian nation" and protested against the "terroristic politics of the Polish government on western Ukrainian territory."[340] This need to be validated in their national identity as Ukrainians, not Canadians, suggests that the hostility of the Anglo-Canadians towards the immigrants' "foreignness" was forcing many Ukrainian-Canadians to seek consolation, not in the anonymity of assimilated

"Canadianness" (for the immigrants and the first generation this was impossible anyway), but in the assertiveness of racial pride. A defensive strategy, to be sure, but the only one available, short of collective guilt, self-disgust and inertia. Admittedly, there were individual Ukrainian-Canadians for whom the re-awakening of nationalist consciousness was far more relevant to the political struggles in Europe than to their citizenship in Canada – the man with murdered relatives and a score to settle with the Polish secret police, the intellectual with a master-plan for the Ukraine, the priest who felt "banished" to Canada by the Red Army – and others for whom it represented the opportunity to complete old and unfinished business.

The Poles and Ukrainians have invariably settled in the same districts in the West, and in one of these, northeast of Oakburn, Manitoba, the Polish priest had a cross built at a crossroads after the fashion of the old land. This aroused the ire of the Ukrainians who contended that the priest was trying to Polonize the country, so they cut it down. The Poles put it up again, but it met the same fate. They put it up a third time, and this time left some of their number in ambush in the vicinity – and that night one of the Ukrainians was shot in the hand.[341]

But to make the claim that J.G. MacGregor does, that the "recollection of their old wounds and of their one-time national pride" led to their "dreaming of resurrecting a new Ukraine in this land"[342] is preposterous. Creating a Ukrainian nation is one thing. Scrounging for the bits and pieces of pride and passion and ambition – an Alberta village is named "Myrnam" (Peace be with us), a hall is dedicated to Franko, a WASP teacher is resisted, an Educational-Economic Congress of Ukrainians in Canada is organized, the Ukrainian national anthem is sung – that make up a psychic point of security and fraternity from which the racist slanders of the ruling class may be resisted, is another thing altogether. One could capitulate, yes, and try through apology for and contempt of one's sources and one's singularity to please the master. One could hope for solidarity across racial lines and within class, in spite of the misgivings of the Anglo-Canadian working class and the vigilance of the police. Or one could insist on the distinction of one's inheritance and the integrity of one's patriotism as the basis of self-respect and social action. Who else was there to guarantee these things? Who else gave a damn? As the man said, at the First Ukrainian-Canadian Congress in 1943,

> You are not alone; you need not attempt to solve any particular problem with your own individual strength and through your own individual will. No, you are only one of hundreds of thousands. Your will is merely a fraction of the concerted will of hundreds of thousands of other individuals of your people.[343]

This was the ideal. The ideal of racial unity so that the community's centre would hold against the onslaughts of bigotry, discrimination, assimilation, and persecution. Trouble was, the conflicts within the community as often as not were responsible for the failure of a "common front." Leaving aside the ideological and *de facto* resistance of the left to whom the notion of "unity" across class lines was a spurious ideal, the nationalists themselves represented a gamut of political positions and religious convictions that became impossible to reconcile. And so, very quickly, a plethora of organizations arose, each competing for membership, funds, and publicity; in the heat of competition very often the original argument with the Anglo-Canadian majority was set aside as energies became absorbed by the internecine struggle for ideological supremacy.

The Canadian Sitch Organization was the first to be organized in 1924 (renamed the United Hetman Organization in 1934). Decidedly right-wing in its politics, it derived its inspiration from the person of Pavlo Skoropadsky, the puppet-governor of Eastern Ukraine, propped up by the Germans in 1918 and forced to flee the country when the Germans retreated. The Sitch favoured physical training, their own uniforms, military discipline, and the ideals of "One path, one Hetman, one flag, work and order." As this motto, if translated into English, may have offended the democratic sentiments of Anglo-Canadians, the English-language version read, "One God, One King, one flag, one Empire,"[344] a not altogether sincere rendition of the original. In 1928, in fact, men of the First Yorkton Regiment and the 16th Canadian Light Horse objected violently to the behaviour of the Sitch in that community.

> The situation arose over members of the Ukrainian Sitch wearing uniforms resembling those of the German army, with officers, tunics, side-arms and Sam Browns.
>
> Objection was taken by the men of the First Yorkton Regiment and the 16th Canadian Light Horse when members of the Sitch paraded Sunday. The Union Jack at the head of the parade caused the militiamen to look towards St. Joseph's college, and there no Union Jack could be seen, but several Sitch flags were floating from poles.
>
> It [the Sitch charter] also contains a clause permitting the teaching of the Ukrainian language in the schools. This information soon got to the ears of the military men, and about 7 o'clock on Sunday night about 70 men gathered at the college and threatened to break up the Sitch organization.[345]

In 1927, the Ukrainian Self-Reliance League, a creation of the Ukrainian-Canadians much more than of recent immigrants, was organized, with its roots in the institutes, the national halls, and the newly-formed Ukrainian Greek Orthodox Church; that is, an indigenous Canadian formation. This was middle-of-the-road nationalism, repudiating both right- and left-wing extremism and supporting the ideal of Canadian patriotism. It is written in its constitution that,

> bearing in mind that Canada is the new and adopted homeland of the Ukrainians, the USRL appeals strongly to the Ukrainians that as citizens of this country they take a most active part in all matters concerning this state, at the same time benefiting from their rights and privileges as citizens, but at the same time,

carrying out their obligations as such.[346]

By its motto, however – "Self-respect, self-reliance, self-help" – it revealed a certain skepticism regarding the immediate possibility of Ukrainian-Canadians becoming wholly integrated into Canadian society and therefore propounded an alternative process: the organization of purely ethnic structures to "foster the spiritual development of its members" and to "advance the economic and cultural progress of Ukrainians."[347] If, individually, Ukrainian-Canadians could not "make it" within Anglo-Canadian society, then they would be encouraged to "develop" and "advance" within their own communities.

The USRL was organized primarily to serve the interests of the emerging, and frustrated, Ukrainian-Canadian elite of professionals, businessmen, and intelligentsia who were denied a place in the Anglo-Canadian middle-class. As "leaders" of their own people, they could simultaneously encourage "dignified Ukrainianism" in their constituency and convince the Anglo-Canadian establishment of their own competence, sobriety, and propriety.

This posture of conciliation and reasonableness was rejected by a number of recently immigrated Ukrainians who were much more agitated by the position of the Ukraine in Europe than by the status of Ukrainian-Canadians. Accordingly, they formed, in 1932, the Ukrainian National Federation, in effect a branch of a Western Ukrainian organization, the underground Organization of Ukrainian Nationalists, dedicated to the liberation of the Ukraine from Poland and the Soviet Union. Their partisans tended to be condescending about the Ukrainian-Canadians' abilities to take care of their own interests, ascribing to them a susceptibility to "various kinds of propaganda which was dangerous to themselves and to Canada," irreconcilable religious differences, "danger of moral deterioration" and general disunity.[348] An Anglo-Canadian writer, T.C. Byrne, characterized the typical UNF member in 1937 as:

usually a veteran of the Ukrainian struggle in Europe. He has been baptized in the national cause . . . and is quite sure that he is destined to lead the national movement in Canada. Filled with strong feeling for the Ukrainian homeland he was impatient with, as it seemed to him, the lukewarm nationalism of the Ukrainian with a Canadian viewpoint. The result has been the addition of another organization by these ultra-patriots to the already overcrowded Ukrainian picture.[349]

Although the Greek Catholic church had been regarded by many "nationalists" as less devoted to Ukrainianism than to Catholicism it spawned several "ethnic" organizations, more or less committed to the development of ethnic identity. The Ukrainian Catholic Brotherhood, for instance, organized in 1932 by a group of teachers, farmers, and a priest, believed that the "Catholic religion was the guide and helm of life from which there emerged cultural and spiritual values of the nation not to be destroyed even by the passage of time.'"[350] At the same time, the ideologists of the Brotherhood argued that devotion to "Catholic action," while it may have disallowed concerted action with non-Catholic Ukrainian nationalists, in no way prevented Ukrainian Catholics from being patriotic Canadians.

We are not exiles here, nor seasoned labourers whom fate has forced to seek employment here in order to make a living, but masters and owners of this land. Therefore the army is our army, Canada's laws are our laws, her government is our government.[351]

By 1938, however, after the wave of immigration from Europe, the Ukrainian Catholics, like the Orthodox, experienced an invasion of their ranks by nationalists ideologically committed to the restoration of an independent Ukrainian state – a commitment exclusive of political action within Canadian political structures – and the revival of semi-mystical Ukrainian fraternities and the pursuit of Ukrainian cultural indoctrination. Take the youth organization, *Plast*, for instance. The organization has a patron saint, an emblem, a peculiar form of salutation, uniforms, language and history classes, calisthenics classes, and a hymn.

Hey Plast members! Hey Youthful Ones!
We are children of the sun and spring.
We are children of mother nature.
To us the green forest murmurs,
Go to thy woods, fields and hills;
To the bright stars and serene waters.[352]

The first generation Ukrainian-Canadian Catholics may well have wondered what any of this had to do with their own time and place.

Years before the European immigrants had brought the "word" of Ukrainian nationalism, the clerical community of Mundare had assumed the responsibility of raising the national consciousness of the parishioners, on the two fronts of identification with ongoing Ukrainian political affairs and support of local institutions of enlightenment and recreation. The latter front had a longer life. While there were isolated moments of action taken on behalf of the Ukraine – fundraising for the Ukrainian National Republic in 1919, meetings with representatives from the Ukrainian government-in-exile and various intellectuals, relief committees formed to send aid to Galician flood victims – "the Bolshevik occupation in recent years can be compared to the nail that seals the coffin and tore away that life line between Mundare and the Ukrainian nation."[353] And that was the end of any public and collective manifestation of involvement in Ukrainian politics. The communal life, however, flourished within an extravaganza of community-based organizations. The national hall, of course, (for Ukrainian Catholics only), the drama club, choir, brass band, *Ridna Shkola*, and dancing club. The Brotherhood of Ukrainian Catholics (of which all hall members became *de facto* members), the Ukrainian Catholic Women's League, Ukrainian Catholic Youth, the Apostleship of Prayer, the Brotherhood of the Living Rosary, the Association for a Good Death, the Sodality of the Blessed Virgin Mary, the Knights of Columbus, etc., formalized and institutionalized practically every significant moment, private and public, in a Ukrainian Catholic life, with the emphasis on Catholic. Catholic or Greek Orthodox, however, they organized Ukrainian schools and celebrated national festivals, exhibited folk crafts and decorated the church, ate, dressed, sang, and danced. The ideological conflict of whose Ukrainianism was purer, sounder, and more antiquated was a struggle for bishops and intelligentsia. The people themselves carried on as they had more or less always done – Catholics, Orthodox, Communist – according to the ways they knew. Their "nationalism" and that of the intellectual and social elite are not to be confused.

Thus, when one hears of the chronic failure among Ukrainian-Canadian nationalists to unify around their supposedly common cause of establishing a national identity, one is hearing the complaints of an elite who forever disagreed on the finer points of ideological patriotism (and dragged their membership and sympathizers along with them into the squabble) and not the voice of the populace who were working out the question of identity in the daily round of community life. In the late thirties, the *Ukrainian Voice* addressed itself to this discrepancy.

As the Ukrainian groups in Canada have disagreed on old country questions and not on local, practical ones which emerge from our life here, what is the sense then to perpetuate without end these differences? Why couldn't the various groups get together sometime to discuss their mutual problems and why shouldn't they not agree on issues on which in reality they do not differ? We live in Canada, and what ails one, ails the other, what is solace for one, is solace for the other. Why shouldn't we come to an understanding amongst ourselves and say to ourselves at least this: up to that and that point we are in accord, beyond that, our paths are divided.[354]

But there were conflicts and disunity that could not be wished away. They were not mere quirks and perversities of character or indulgences in intellectual curiosities or even evidence of bad faith. They were symptomatic of a more fundamental disharmony within the community that was as inevitable as the development of social, economic, and cultural differences among them. One may have deplored the "existence of violent disharmonies" as a "serious obstacle not only to the Ukrainian ideal of national independence in Europe but also to the harmonious integration of the Ukrainians into the national life of Canada."[355] But this ignores the reality that by the thirties the Ukrainian-Canadians were not a homogeneous group that could be lumped together under the catch-all phrase "Ukrainian" and therefore absorbed holus-bolus into the Canadian mainstream like a lump of fat into a vegetable stew. It is in fact a patronizing attitude, close to "all Ukrainians look the same," which does not allow for the socio-economic and political stratifications among "ethnics" which it allows everywhere in discussions of Anglo-Canadian society. The Ukrainian-Canadians themselves are as guilty of this naiveté as anyone.

> The various Ukrainian groups have been parochial in their attitude to one another, and have emphasized their particular party interests above the general good of the whole Ukrainian community in Canada. Too long have they emphasized those issues that divide them rather than those issues that would unite them.[356]

The question is: was there any more a "general good" universally beneficent? Were there any more unifying issues other than the most basic and inarguable? Surely none among the factions and sects argued against the "common good" of collective self-respect, racial pride, and an even break. But beyond these shared assumptions, how were the fascist monarchist and liberal democrat to unify; how were the interests of an ambitious professional intent on assimilation into the Anglo-Canadian middle class and those of a unilingually Ukrainian farmer worried by the next generation's loss of spiritual values to coalesce; how were the Orthodox church member, convinced this church was a beacon of racial consciousness, and the Catholic parishioner, equally convinced that Christian charity was more important a value than nationalism, to agree; how were the members of the various Ladies' Auxiliaries, perpetually under obligation to cook, serve tea, raise money, and collect old clothes, to share the enthusiasm of a "leadership" holding elections for provisional Ukrainian governments; how were the mass of farmers and working people, absorbed by the quotidian demands of bills to pay, mouths to feed and chores to complete, to share the same sense of urgency as the intelligentsia and wealthier classes about the preservation and perpetuation of the national traditions of the Ukrainians.

Not many of them could, of course, and so the disunity of nationalist organizations must be accepted as a fact of political life. There is nothing unnatural or seditious about conflicts between opposing world-views, whether of religious, cultural, or political character. Rather, it is unnatural to believe they can be reconciled, except around the most generalized tenets.

But the attempt was made. During the Second World War the government of Canada was troubled not only by the unpatriotic disruptions of the ethnic left but by the factionalism of the centre and right-wing as well. It was Watson Kirkconnell who proposed an answer.

If these Slavic citizens of Canada show obvious appreciation of liberty and democracy here, and a willingness to cooperate in maintaining Canadian unity in a time of great national stress, it will all be counted to them for righteousness when they plead the cause of their European kinsfolk. If on the other hand they remain hopelessly disrupted by political dissension and if the chief characteristic of their nationalism seems to be hatred for other national groups, then they will do a fatal disservice to the cause they seek to serve, for they will persuade the Canadian nation that the Ukrainian has not yet reached political maturity.[357]

What was meant by "political maturity" became obvious as the

Ukrainian Canadian Committee, organized in 1940 under Kirkconnell's direction at the behest of the Canadian government, undertook its obligations. Composed of representatives from the Ukrainian National Federation, the Brotherhood of Ukrainian Catholics, the United Hetman Organization, the Ukrainian Self Reliance League and the League of Ukrainian Organizations (secessionists from the ULFTA), its structure satisfied the government, and the committee members, that an opportunity had been given to "the middle-of-the-road organizations and, in general to the Canadian-born, to gain some control and to promulgate values and goals more oriented to integration into the fabric of Canadian society."[358] In due course, the UCC issued statements about their "unswerving belief in liberal democracy" and their loyalty to the "great country of their adoption" and to the "British flag,"[359] presented briefs to the government arguing against legalization of the Communist party[360] and presumably stood behind Kirkconnell's claim that

> All of these groups have supported the war from the beginning, and all are mortal enemies of the ULFTA and its conspiracies. Some 99% of their members are strongly religious and detest the Communist group for its attempts to destroy Christianity among the Ukrainian Canadians. They would as soon sleep with a rattlesnake as admit the atheistic revolutionaries to their councils.[361]

And, under the auspices of the UCC, the First Congress of Ukrainian Canadians was convened in Winnipeg in 1943. It was a strange affair, from the perspective of the seventies. One is accustomed nowadays to the self-confident rhetoric and proud, if not boastful, image of the organized Ukrainian-Canadian elite. Such styles were just emerging in 1943, awkwardly but passionately, and one reads the account of the Congress with a combination of embarrassment and sympathy. Embarrassment at such exaggerated and self-serving phrases as: "the excellence of the address delivered," "their rhetorical eloquence," "their depth of thought."[362]

And sympathy for the attempt made to write optimistically and lovingly of one's origins; and, in spite of the obvious manipulations of the Canadian government behind the scenes of the UCC and its efforts to control the Ukrainian-Canadian community through officially-approved leadership, sympathy for the attempt of the delegates to evolve their own ethos, however mystical or sentimental:

> Emanating out of the external manifestations of the Congress, those of us who were present felt that slowly but majestically, – seemingly from the very innermost depths of the Ukrainian motherlands, and from the prayers, the endeavours and the sacrifices of numberless generations, we were receiving our beauty and strength. We seemed to be witnesses of the birth of a new belief in the future progress of our members, and this belief seemed to be crowned by our love of the Ukraine and the Ukrainian people. We seemed to hear an age-old and yet an ever-new melody embracing us all, capturing our feelings in their entirety, and welding the Ukrainians scattered across Canada into the one and only multi-thousand choir of the Ukrainian Canadians.[363]

There one's sympathies end, however, or rather, become conditional. Considering that the UCC was a creation of the government, the Congress made some rather bold statements about the life conditions and attitudes of the Ukrainian-Canadians it presumed to speak for.

> Wherever they live, and that is true even of Canada, the Ukrainians experience more unfavourable and more unfortunate circumstances of life than any other single people in the world.[364]

A dubious claim, to be sure – the Chinese at the time, the peon in Latin America, the North American Indian were demonstrably worse off – but at least it was a departure from the smug and dishonest statements of other times that Ukrainian-Canadians were a prosperous and satisfied folk.

> On the soil which till this very day they have been fertilizing with their sweat and their blood, these people endure primitive privations, suffer constantly from wilful discrimination, and are given no recognition for their labours and sacrifices; nevertheless, these same people, as a whole, constantly demonstrate their passionate desire for cultural growth, and for a more equitable standard of living.[365]

Considering the nationalists' repudiation of Communism and socialism during the thirties, this kind of language comes as a surprise. The Congress goes on to demand "work and fair wages for all," "for a fair day's work there should be just remuneration," "a new order based on social justice," distribution of "a larger share of the national income . . . among labourers and farmers so as to result in a just increase of wages and farm prices and a program of post-war works, the balancing of the budget, a program of social security for all citizens, the development and the extension of labour unions, public ownership or at least increased public control of essential utilities. . . ."[366] Can this be the Ukrainian Greek Orthodox church speaking, the Ukrainian Catholic Brotherhood, the United Hetmans? Or is it the mass of delegates, the farmers and residents of Myrnam and Radway and Vegreville, the Ukrainian Women's Association of Lesia Ukrainka (Ukrainian poet and freedom-fighter) of Kossiw, Manitoba, the Ukrainian Shevchenko Association of Chipman, Alberta, the Workers' Union, Branch 266 of Toronto, and the Ukrainian Educational Association of St. Martins, Manitoba?

However, this manifesto only stole the thunder of the left. The Congress, in spite of its grandiose reference to the "one and only multi-thousand choir of the Ukrainian Canadians," in spite of its complaints about social injustice and its demands for a new order had nothing more to offer as a strategic program than the homilies normally served up by those who need more to be agreeable than right. Thus, as a remedy for the "mania for power and profit" abroad in the land, the Congress recommended the "application of Christian principles in a political, social and economic order" for these principles "denounce in no uncertain terms any social order based on economical abuse and profit."[367] A naive observation considering the age-old coexistence of the church and social abuse and subverted in any case by the Congress's commitment to "safeguard free enterprise as the basis of an economic system which can bring stability, prosperity and justice"[368] when free enterprise had manifestly failed to provide any of these things at several points of Ukrainian-Canadian history. "We reiterate our unshakeable loyalty to His Majesty, King George V1"[369] and "our political principles are identical with the political principles of every honest Canadian patriot."[370] These statements are more than formalities: they are reassurances that one's voiced dissatisfactions and one's self-conscious identity as a Ukrainian, are not revolutionary statements. They may have demanded a new order based on social justice but they would settle for the familiar political contract tarted up with exemptions for those who have "thus far demonstrated both their industry and their love for the democratic freedoms and for the British institutions."[371]

The other side of pro-Canadianism was anti-Communism, the unconditional point of unity among the nationalists. They may have waged bitter ideological struggles around the questions of the form of the future Ukrainian nation and the role of the church within the Ukrainian-Canadian community and the appropriateness of segregated cultural institutions but they all agreed that Communism was a menace, to Ukrainian-Canadians as well as to Soviet Ukrainians. Undoubtedly, they abhorred it for its own sake, particularly for its brutal opposition to Ukrainian national independence, but they had other reasons to repudiate it as a group. When Anglo-Canadians tended to think all Ukrainian-Canadians were, or were about to be, Communists, when Watson Kirkconnell wrote darkly of "our large masses of recent immigration especially from Central and Eastern Europe, whose deeply engrained

European habits of thought make them more susceptible to alien propaganda,"[372] when the exigencies of war might have reactivated anti-foreign terrorism, it was time enough for the anti-Communist loyalists to unite and be counted.

> On behalf of the Ukrainian Self-Reliance League of Canada, we are happy to be able to assure everyone that all those many thousands of Canadian citizens of Ukrainian descent who are members or who are in sympathy with the League and its affiliated organizations . . . have never, at any time, wavered in their loyalty and devotion to the British Crown or to Canada and in their faith in democratic institutions and that, therefore, all of them will without hesitation respond to the earnest appeal of their King and their Government and will faithfully serve and defend the vital interests of Canada and the British Empire side by side with other citizens by all means at their disposal and in every manner which may be demanded of them.[373]

With the banning of Ukrainian Communist organizations, however, the anti-Communists' energy was free for the task of denouncing the machinations of the Soviet Union and in this their vigilance was extraordinary. They assumed, of course, that they were behaving as any good Canadian might but it is to be wondered if in fact non-Ukrainian-Canadians cared half as much. In their most zealous moments, the anti-Communists were on their own. For example, who, in Canada, besides the Ukrainian Catholics, would be outraged that in Western Ukraine in 1945, "strong pressure is being exerted on priests and people to abjure their allegiance to the Holy See and to enter the Orthodox Church, under the ecclesiastical jurisdiction of the Patriarch of Moscow"?[374]

Not that Anglo-Canadians were "soft" on Communism, but as long as anti-Communist nationalists based their position almost exclusively on historical and current events in Europe and as long as they refused to discuss the possibility of a socialist route to national independence (à la Yugoslavia) and to curtail their lunatic fringe, they found little support outside their own circle and the King government. Their intransigence on the subject of the perils of Communism forced the Ukrainian Communists to harden an eventually discredited Stalinist line, the Anglo-Canadians to a wariness of nationalist motives in general and the politically uncommitted Ukrainian-Canadians to impatience and retreat.

The Ukrainian Communists had amalgamated their disparate organizations into the Association of United Ukrainian Canadians and had immediately denounced the formation of the UCC as undemocratic, pro-fascist, and pro-Nazi.[375] Understandably, they could not accept the UCC's claim of its "all-inclusive character" when the AUUC membership was excluded; Kirkconnell's about-face on the character of the Ukrainian National Federation from "markedly anti-democratic" in 1939 to "radical and republican" a year later,[376] and such imprudent claims (considering that the UCC was the brain-child of the Canadian government) as Yuzyk's that "the Committee regards itself as the spokesman for the aspirations of the 45,000,000 Ukrainians" in Europe[377] further discredited the UCC. It was a war of statistics and phrase-mongering between the Communists and nationalists. They disputed each other's figures regarding membership of their respective organizations, they denied each other's legitimacy to represent the community, and abused each other's intentions. The Communist press characterized Tracy Phillips (member of the British Secret Service, European adviser to the Canadian government, and a liaison person with the UCC) as a "fascist"[378] while Kirkconnell described him as the "son of a distinguished old English family" with ancestors buried in Westminster Abbey.[379] The Ukrainian-Canadian Communists repeated Soviet charges that the UCC was composed of "traitors and pro-German Ukrainian separatists"[380] while a sympathizer speaks of the UCC's commitment to "democratic principles and the maintenance and development of British institutions."[381] Kirkconnell called the ULFTA a "Judas" to the "Apostles" of the Ukrainian-Canadian community.[382] And so on.

But the critiques of the "progressives" were more complicated than the mere "yelping" of a "seditious organization."[383] Undoubtedly, much of their anti-nationalist and anti-UCC sentiment was fuelled by their own loss of legal status and their relative obscurity once the UCC was launched.

UCC slander against the USSR gave fuel for a more fundamental opposition to the "nationalists." Because Communist ideology has its roots in a class analysis of society and because the Communist Party of Canada has almost never deviated from the pronunciamentos of the Communist Party of the Soviet Union, the Ukrainian-Canadian Communists and their sympathizers neither accepted the nationalists' priority of national liberation of the Ukraine (preceding, if at all, the liberation of the working class) nor had the opportunity, except for a few imaginative individuals, to analyse alternatives to Russian chauvinism and Stalinist "nationalities" policies. Once the pick-axe had smashed Leon Trotsky's skull, for instance, the majority of CPC and ULFTA members repudiated as deviationist anathema such analyses of the position of Soviet Ukrainians as this:

> But in the Ukraine matters were further complicated by the massacre of national hopes. Nowhere did restrictions, purges, repressions, and in general all forms of bureaucratic hooliganism assume such murderous sweep as they did in the Ukraine in the struggle against the powerful, deeply rooted longings of the Ukrainian masses for greater freedom and independence. To the totalitarian bureaucracy, Soviet Ukraine became an administrative division of an economic unit and a military base of the USSR. To be sure, the Stalin bureaucracy erects statues to Shevchenko but only in order more thoroughly to crush the Ukrainian people under their weight and to force it to chant paeans in the language of the *Kobzar* to the rapist clique in the Kremlin. . . .
>
> A clear and definite slogan is necessary that corresponds to the new situation. In my opinion there can be at the present time only one such slogan: *A united, free and independent workers' and peasants' Soviet Ukraine.*[384]

As a result, Ukrainian-Canadian Communists were in no position to refute the anti-Sovietism and Russophobia of the nationalists except through more and more bizarre and desperate defenses of the Soviet Union in the face of mounting evidence of a massive terrorist campaign being waged against various Ukrainian "deviates." ULFTA members deported to the USSR and emigrants from Canada in the thirties were executed or deported to Siberia during the great purges of 1937-38 and the minister of education in the Ukraine committed suicide in 1933 "in protest against the reign of terror."[385] To believe such "lies" and "distortions" as printed in the nationalist press was, in their minds, to give comfort to the enemies of the socialist experiment in the Soviet Union. Except for the brief war-time period when the Soviet Union was an ally, the notion of unity with the nationalists was untenable: the nationalists' anti-Communism and bourgeois proclivities were repellant even to those Communists who might have otherwise supported the campaign for a "free and independent Ukraine." And when, after the war, the nationalist organizations were fortified by an influx of anti-Soviet refugees and immigrants, the "progressives" and "nationalists" were polarized as they had not been even when their debates had centred on the question of social justice for Ukrainians in Canada.

The self-conscious abstractions of the nationalist intelligentsia and the tendentious, hostile jargon of the Communists were, for everybody else in the community, a choice between the devil and the deep blue sea. Neither one vision nor the other seemed to have much to do with the mundane realities of the farm and the town – who, on his tractor in the northeast quarter or behind her cash register in the Co-op store could care much about the dream for a Cossack fiefdom halfway around the world? Or the excruciating debates around the difference between an "imperialist" war and an "anti-fascist" one? In fact, subscribing to either vision could make life difficult, and who needed that? Declaiming loud and long on the subject of Ukrainian independence could make a person seem like a "loud-mouth foreign meddler" who should go back where he or she came from. On the other hand, sneering at ethnic pride and the celebration of folk arts and religious practices could make a person look like a bootlicker, agreeing with Anglo-Saxons that Ukrainian-Canadians were slightly nauseating in their Ukrainianness. It was a positive thing that some of the nationalists were making such a fuss about Ukrainian culture then, and telling their fellow Ukrainian-Canadians not to be ashamed. But really, who but the "big shots" in the community, with their committees and speeches and letters to the editors, had much invested in persuading the Anglo-Saxons out there that "the preservation of Ukrainian culture is not only helping to enrich the culture of Canada, but it is also paving the way for harmonious relations between Canadians of Ukrainian and Anglo-Saxon origins"?[386] It was all very well for the local nationalists to call for "unity" of all Ukrainian-Canadians and the collective need to "emerge from our concealment and . . . enter unto the wider fields of public endeavour"[387] but there was often the suspicion that they were really talking about *their* need to get ahead – to get elected to the House of Commons or called to the bar or appointed as a school inspector – and *their* frustration at being blocked as bohunks; forget the poetry!

"We were good Ukrainians because we were exposed to it everywhere we went. We took it for granted." Is that not the preservation of Ukrainian culture and the declaration of ethnic self-acceptance? The people of Two Hills could not be anything but Ukrainian-Canadians as they spoke Ukrainian, ate Ukrainian, sang and danced Ukrainian, prayed Ukrainian as a matter of course; there was nothing either remarkably wonderful or notably wretched about it. And since there were few Anglo-Saxons in the area, and those that were, were friendly neighbours, the problem of establishing "harmonious relations" with Anglo-Canadians was not their problem. Nor was the establishment of an independent Ukrainian state – talk to them instead about the miserable budget of the Municipal District of Two Hills.

Not that one wouldn't go to the hall and hear what one of

those "patrioty" had to say; it could be very entertaining, what with the *bandura* orchestra, the decorated stage, and the exuberant speaker, tearing at his clothes as he spoke of the Ukrainian soul. But could such men be trusted? There's the story of a nationalist group that came to Two Hills collecting money, and the next one heard of them, they had bought an apartment block in Miami! Could ordinary people afford them? Money for this, money for that, a Shevchenko monument, a bursary, a banquet for the bishop, a newspaper! Could one live up to their expectations?

Not that the "Reds" made much more sense. One grew quickly tired of their bitter harangues against everything that one had respected – the church, the priest, the old ways of *baba* and *dido*, yes, even the "professors" – and even if there were doubts at times about the sense of liberating the Ukraine, one thing was certain: there was no more a "free" Ukraine under Stalin than there had been under the czars and there was a lot of heartache knowing that so much blood had been shed in the struggle for a liberation that always seemed to slip through the fingers of the Ukrainians.

The nationalists wanted to talk about Mother Ukraine but not about unemployment and fair prices. The "Reds" wanted to talk about capitalist bosses but not about the pride of being Ukrainian. A plague on both their houses.

Letter from my father:

Not all nationalists were self-seekers, dupes of the imperialist establishment, rogues or worse. They were, during World War II, like me, compelled by force of circumstances to make a choice: back our authorities, even if it had to be in the form of the UCC, or stand up and be counted as "peace lovers," "anti-fascists," "saviours of the Socialist Fatherland." Even if we were not asked to stand up, we had to make the choice in our own consciences.

I think that the nationalist leaders (moderate and extreme) were less concerned about the possibility of Communist overthrow of the Canadian government than by the defeat of the Ukrainian liberation armies by the Reds. Consequently, they went along with the WASP "persecution" of the Communists in Canada. You know how hysteria builds up in a crisis.

Granted. The fact remains, however, that the nationalists were still committed, not to the reorganization of Canadian society so that the economic, social, and cultural rights of all citizens would be guaranteed, but to the "opening up" of capitalist structures to competition among all persons, regardless of ethnic origin. "They expressed no desire to re-appraise the values at the basis of a socio-economic system where production was carried on for profit. . . ."[388] And it was through the nationalist institutions that Ukrainian-Canadians could be mobilized for this competition.

The nationalist institution was a two-way street. On the one hand it provided cultural and social continuity for a generation, stranded between the two communities, who might otherwise have presented an unmanageable "sociological problem." On the other, it represented the collecting place where this generation could most efficaciously and mildly be enlisted into the projects of the Anglo-Canadian middle-class. But not all Anglo-Canadians could see this, distracted as they were by the institutions' ethnocentrism.

English businessmen in Ukrainian towns suspect the nationalists of undermining their business. The Protestant and Roman Catholic clergy decry the activities of the nationalists as defeating their efforts among Ukrainians. The nationalist is accused of self-seeking opportunism. He is accused of disloyalty to Canada, of hindering assimilation, of increasing the whole racial problem. These accusations are partly true and partly misconceptions. Nevertheless the nationalist stands indicted on one serious charge that he is doing very little to assist his people to merge into the Canadian nation.[389]

It may be argued, from the nationalists' point of view, that neither for that matter had the Anglo-Canadians themselves done much to assist the Ukrainian-Canadians. Falling back on their own resources, Ukrainian-Canadians made of their nationalist organizations a kind of "hot-house" in which an ethnic middle-class could be nurtured before the transplant into the larger community. In any event, by 1945, it was still the case that the nationalists were having less effect on the thinking of Anglo-Canadians than the other way around. Anthony Hlynka's suggestion in the House of Commons, that the UCC be permitted to send delegates to the San Francisco Conference as representatives of the "submerged nation" of the Ukraine, was treated as a scandal.

> "Fantastic" is the only adjective which can describe this proposal. The Ukraine has been a recognized division of Russia for nearly 300 years, and its people have been universally regarded as Russian citizens. It is as much a part of Russia as Ontario or Alberta is of Canada. . . . It is time the Ukrainian nationalists and similar groups stopped trying to involve Canada in the racial and political feuds of eastern Europe.[390]

Clearly, the nationalists had failed even to establish the elementary fact of the difference between a Ukrainian and a Russian.

> In view of the remarkable service they [the Ukrainians] have been rendering to Soviet defense, it is impossible to believe that they regard their own interests as differing from those of the Soviet Union as a whole or would approve of the attitude taken by Mr. Hlynka in the Ottawa debate. In fact it would seem to the impartial observer that dissension among Ukrainians only exists outside of the Ukrainian republic and that it only exists among Ukrainians here in Canada because it is carefully cultivated by interested persons who would receive short shrift from their fellow Ukrainians in the Soviet Union if they were to attempt such tactics in their native land as they do here in Canada.[391]

An interesting variation on the theme of "foreign agitators," the editorial was remarkably unsympathetic to a basic tenet of Ukrainian-Canadian nationalism: that Ukrainians had the right to national self-determination. Because the editorial goes on to recommend "proper respect for a brave ally," i.e. the Soviet Union, it seems that in the minds of many Anglo-Canadians support of Ukrainian nationalism was a sign of unpatriotic equivocation in the pursuit of war. Because it so complacently assumed that all Ukrainians were pro-Soviet, I can only conclude that, to the average Anglo-Canadian, the safeguarding of decorous politics in Canada was more urgent than the investigation into the nature of Soviet imperialism in Europe. By 1950, the nationalists were criticized not for their anti-Sovietism (this was now the Cold War) but, again, for their un-Ukrainian-Canadianism. Again, the nationalists had failed to clarify a basic argument of their politics: that support of Ukrainian national independence and behaviour becoming a decent Canadian were not necessarily (they could be, but not necessarily) mutually exclusive.

The main argument of our editorial was that Ukrainians in Canada should concentrate on being good Canadians, and that their effectiveness as citizens of this nation was diminished to the extent that they preoccupied themselves with the affairs of the Ukraine itself.

When a man comes to Canada from another land and takes up Canadian citizenship, he solemnly declares that henceforth his first and only loyalty is to Canada. No man can serve God and Mammon, and no man can preserve his loyalty whole if he is giving part of it and part of this social energy, to another country [392]

When it had reached the point where the Ukraine was the "mammon" to Canada's "god," then surely the Ukrainian-Canadian nationalists had seriously miscalculated the readiness and willingness of Anglo-Canadians to accept the value of a citizenship rooted in the pride and dignity of one's own Ukrainian self. This was to be then a message for the tribe alone. Within the ethnic collective, reminders of where the people had come from and who they had been would remain an introspective if not covert act. A series of ritualized encounters – dance, song, poetry, speeches – in the church basement or national hall with none but themselves as witnesses and consumers. The fact that the rituals were mysterious to outsiders was the essence of the act – they may, after all, have been hostile! – and the exclusive use of the Ukrainian language until the death of the generation was evidence of that introversion. Who could blame them? Once they had turned their backs on organizing proletarian revolution and had failed thus far to secure an invitation to the great Canadian middle-class tea party, it was the only way to feel at home.

FIFTEEN

Assimilation

Father had a chance either to go farming or into the Methodist ministry, and the reason he went to the ministry was because even a few days before he died, he kept saying, "Remember, be good Canadians. I brought you from a land where you had no future so you be good Canadians." Not good Ukrainians, good Canadians. He didn't care whether we learned the Ukrainian language too well. That's not how we were going to be living. So, our upbringing was altogether different. We were not amongst the Ukrainians so much as we were with the English folks, because of the church. Because of Mother, we learned how to eat and to cook Ukrainian but when it came to other old country ways. . . . If you were a Methodist and a strong Methodist, you wouldn't repeat the old stories. There was an old lady in Radway that used to come and tell us these old folk tales and Mother said, "Those stories should remain on the other side of the Atlantic." They were so full of superstition and against the Bible. I went to a wedding in Musidora when I taught there, and told my parents I had seen something very unusual. People would take a drink and throw it over their head. And Father said, "Those are the customs they had and they brought them over here into Canada. Don't you think we deserve something better than that? They should change and be more up-to-date. Imagine carrying on such a custom that only the lowest type of person practiced in the old country!"

– Alice Melnyk

* * *

People in this area generally frowned upon a mixed marriage. "He's taken an English girl. What's the matter with him?" I think I would have disappointed my parents had I not married a Ukrainian girl. The Anglo-Saxon people here in town were the bank manager, the station agent, the teachers. They held important positions. Almost without exception these people's wives were lazy. They'd hire people to weed their radishes! They'd devote too much of their time to leisure. They became stereotyped by our people. But you could count on a Ukrainian girl to work hard, keep a clean house, cook for you. That's why so many of the Anglo-Saxons liked to have Ukrainian cleaning ladies. They'd earn every penny. There was an inkling of the feeling among us that Ukrainians who married non-Ukrainians were a bit like social climbers.

– Nick Olinyk

* * *

Take, for example, the Seventh Day Adventists. The pastor is a Negro. I spoke to the Ukrainian member. "Tell me, Brother. What will the Negro teach you in that church? Our church not only teaches the gospel. It teaches you about your people, your heritage, your language, your country. What can the Negro tell you about Ukraine?" They also had a German pastor. What could he tell them about Ukraine? I tell them, if there were no Ukrainian Orthodox church in Canada, there would be no Ukrainians in Canada.

– Father Peter Zubrytsky

* * *

The young people aren't interested in these old things at all. Maybe one in a hundred. All they're interested in is drinking a lot, as far as I'm concerned. They're not interested in history, all they want is a car to drive around in. I just can't see how they're going to make a living. If they lost a can opener they'd starve. If things keep on going the way they are now, in twenty-five years, that's it. There won't be anybody around who will remember the past. You try to speak Ukrainian to these young people and they won't listen.

– Walter Kitt

Assimilation is the process by which the Ukrainian-Canadian community got from the Ukraine to Canada, from nineteenth-century folk culture to twentieth-century computer culture, from homestead to city, from *baba* to me. Irresistible and inevitable, it was a process that interfered, without exception, with every inheritance of the first Canadian-born generation, from language and religious practices to clothing styles and eating habits. Assimilating, one learned not only how to behave like a Canadian. One also learned how Canadian society was structured and stratified, how economic rewards were distributed, and how the individual psyche was shaped to fit in. One learned, in other words, that the process of assimilation was the sweep of the long arm of Anglo-Canadian political power.

The Anglo-Saxons, by historical accident the resident ruling class, were in a position to define themselves as the real Canadians and their Britishness as the standard against which the newcomers were forced to measure their own approximation to the cultural ideal. Naturally, the failure to be Protestant or English-speaking or urban or half-way educated, the failure to be emotionally attached to the symbols of British imperialism, the failure to be detached from the security of old-country social and cultural styles were all interpreted as a gross unwillingness to become a decent Canadian citizen. A double bind! At the same time, of course, it had been made clear that they should know their place and keep to it. It was, to say the least, unfair to expect that a much maligned and patronized group of second-class citizens would not gather together in their own, culturally self-determined institutions to get in from the cold.

For my part I don't think they will become assimilated any quicker than they can possibly help; for the reason that they settle in agglomerations, hang on to their mother tongue, marry strictly among themselves and very naturally crowd around their national church. I may be mistaken, but I can with difficulty conceive the idea of a people speaking and thinking in English and imbued with British ideals and customs while belonging to the Orthodox Greek Church and going on strike a couple of days a week in honour of one or another Big Sunday.[393]

Even the more sympathetic Anglo-Canadians, while acknowledging the need of Ukrainians to hang on for awhile at least to their old habits, tended to view these habits as uncouth and forlorn, and their practitioners as pathetic rustics about whom the best that could be said is that one felt sorry for them. Clearly, this was not the stuff of which Canadianism could be easily manufactured.

By the First World War, however, with its confused European politics, the emergence of liberated nationalities and homelands, and the celebration of British imperial prowess, the need to assimilate the foreigners in Canada became emphatic. Not only had the supremacy of Anglo-Saxon culture been confirmed, but there were trouble and restlessness brewing among the unassimilated who unconscionably still identified with the fate of the Ukrainian nation and the status of Ukrainian culture, and who dreamed of restituting both through nationalist consciousness-raising among the Ukrainian-Canadians. Instead of assimilating unconditionally into the Anglo-Canadian version of Canadian society, they were reviving their exiled identity and calling it the missing half of their new one.

> This country is big enough, broad enough and good enough to demand from its citizens unequivocally that they drop this hyphenated stuff entirely and become Canadians only. Either that or get out.[394]

What the Vegreville *Observer* neglected to mention, of course, was that the Canadian authorities themselves had, during the war, redefined the immigrants as Austro-Hungarians and Germans, had disenfranchised them, suppressed many of their Canadian-born organizations, and interned their alleged disloyalists. Thus, the irony of the *Observer's* statement that "the war has taught the people . . . that hyphenated citizenship is a rotten foundation on which to construct an enduring nationality" is probably unintentional. To the disaffected Ukrainian-Canadians, it was certainly "rotten" that the "Canadian" side of the hyphen had counted for very little.

No amount of Anglo-Canadian agitation, threat, or reasoned persuasion, however, could make Ukrainian immigrants into Anglo-Saxons in the end. They lived out their lives in Ukrainian-speaking communities, fulfilled their spiritual obligations and social needs in customary institutions and worked, in isolation from the Anglo-Canadian majority, at the foundations of the economy. But their children were a different proposition. Canadian-born, educated in Anglophone schools, accessible to the media, consumers of Canadian-made artifacts, and workers not without ambition, they were incipient "common citizens" to whom friendship and confidence could be extended if ethnic institutions and nationalist propaganda didn't get to them first and twist their identity around the excruciating hyphen.

When the generation was growing up, 1920-1940, "Canadianization" and "Anglicization" were interchangeable notions, the first being a more liberal and covert version of the second. Since one of the characteristics of being a Canadian was the expressed admiration for what was then called British civilization and positive identification with the mission of spreading it around among those deprived of its benefits, it followed that "Canadianizing" the Ukrainian-Canadians meant making them British patriots. Through the schools, the newspapers, the radio, the public meeting, the Veterans' Day parade, the commemoration, jubilee and civic holiday, the Ukrainian-Canadians were educated in the symbols, self-image, and content of British patriotism and learned to think of it as their own, voluntarily-adopted inheritance. They were part of the crowd that stood "thoroughly chilled" in the school grounds in Vegreville, listening to Professor Corbett deliver a "stirring address" on the occasion of George V's twenty-fifth anniversary as King. They sang O *Canada* and *Land of Hope and Glory*, watched the parade of the colours of the Alberta Mounted Rifles, and applauded the dignitaries on the platform, Inspector Scott, Mayor Holden, Major Fane, Sister Josephine, etc.

In Myrnam, they celebrated the jubilee with a day-long program, (it was also St. George's Day, one of the more popular Ukrainian holidays), and prayed for the continued health of His Imperial Majesty, King George V. In the evening there was an "unforgettable" jubilee concert at the national hall.

Students lived in residences and boarding schools where they took courses in Canadian citizenship and "Modern Problems of Political Ideologues." Take St. Joseph's Greek Catholic College in Yorkton, Saskatchewan, in 1943:

> Framed on the wall of the boys' library is an illustrated history of the Union Jack and the meaning of the flag. Also prominently displayed are Churchill's "A Briton's Creed"; a quotation from Churchill's speech of July 1940, beginning "But all depends upon the whole life style of the British race in every part of the world"; and quotations from Churchill's speech beginning "Come then, let us to the task." In the corridors are pictures of the Royal family, Premier King, Prime Minister Churchill, and President Roosevelt.[395]

They made speeches. (They were forever making speeches.) They stood in front of Anglo-Canadian audiences and were hyperbolic with admiration.

> In my opinion the British commonwealth of nations is still the most outstanding example of political organization that the world has ever seen.[396]

They addressed Ukrainian-Canadian audiences and spoke of how they had come by their patriotism naturally.

Members of the school of thought that believes in the building of the Canadian nation on the pattern of British culture only – fearing that to do otherwise would sever our connection with the British Empire – should visit any one of the country schools situated in a non-Anglo-Saxon community. If they heard the spirit with which those children sing *God Save the King*, if they saw the enthusiasm with which these students wave the Union Jack, they would realize how misconceived their analysis of Canadian nationhood is. When these children sing *God Save the King* with such fervour or wave the Union Jack with such enthusiasm, they do so not because they have been brought up in the British cultural background; they do so because they believe in the principles for which the Union Jack stands.[397]

They sat glued to the radio during the Second World War and, thirty years later, can still quote Churchill's speeches. They joined the army in proud defense of King and Country. They had Shakespeare on their book shelf, Westminster Abbey on a calendar, and the Union Jack on a cookie tin. They knew the verses to Anglican hymns, the patron saints of England, Scotland, Ireland, and Wales, and the difference between a Constable and a Turner. They admired English gardens and wept when Edward VIII abdicated. They agreed they lived in a democracy, that democracy was a British institution, and that British institutions were the best there was. They agreed that they were lucky to live in the British institution of Canada. They agreed it would be dreadful to be in the Ukraine. They were, in short, the creatures of Anglicization. They were learning to see themselves as the natural progeny, not of Slavic serfs and Cossacks, but of British parliamentarians and poets. They were learning where most appropriately to place their faith and loyalty. They were vindicating those Anglo-Canadians who had believed they could be good Canadians given half a chance and an Englishman to imitate.

Yet, in general, the Ukrainian-Canadian community, while unavoidably metamorphosing from the cultural pressures of the surrounding society, was still able and willing to sustain a parallel cultural environment distinctively its own. The halls, the churches, the *Ridna Shkola,* the holidays and celebrations, the language, the press, the nationalist organizations all co-existed with Anglo-Canadian cultural intrusions. The community itself seemed comfortable enough with the compromise: two Christmases, one with Santa Claus and the other with midnight mass; Ukrainian spoken at home, English at school; Shevchenko and the King of England side by side in the hall; Red Roses flour for making pumpkin pie and *kolachi;* the waltz and the *arkan* at a wedding dance; debates on Greek Orthodox church history and the Social Credit party platform at meetings of the Ukrainian Self Reliance League.

But the Anglo-Canadian observers of this cultural dualism often felt uneasy. In the late thirties, T.C. Byrne in his travels through the community, was nonplussed by the general failure he perceived of the Canadian-born to be satisfactorily assimilated. He acknowledged the schools as the "spearhead of the advance of Canadian ideas" but deplored the "home environment" which cancelled the influence of the school. He noted that English language newspapers and the radio – "The rural Ukrainian-Canadian rarely owns a radio. He regards it as an English luxury" – were rarities in the homes. He theorized that "block settlement" of Ukrainian-Canadians, their ethnically homogeneous communities, retarded assimilation. And he criticized the nationalist organizations for being deliberately subversive of the assimilationist ideal:

> If Ukrainian youth, through an appeal to national pride can be aroused over a matter remote from Canadian interests, they are far from being assimilated.[398]

Curiously, a few years earlier, Charles Young had made the same tour and come to different conclusions. He made a note of the disappearance of the skill of embroidery among the Canadian-born women and, rather than rejoicing in this evidence of cultural forgetfulness, regretted it.

It is all the more regrettable because the loss of this art must be placed at our door. The younger generation of Ukrainians can hardly be expected to cherish the old customs and crafts when they hear of nothing but the excellence and superiority of things Anglo-Saxon. Nothing could be more distasteful than to go into a rural school in one of their settlements, as we have done, and find a bright Ukrainian girl teaching a class predominantly Ukrainian, embroidery and tatting after our Canadian patterns, while both she and her class were absolutely ignorant of the patterns of their own people.[399]

Two sides of the same coin. The Ukrainian-Canadians themselves were experiencing both tendencies – the conservationist and the assimilationist – and each person had to come to terms with the apparent contradiction of living in two separate cultural milieu. In fact, they straddled it. Ukrainian Christmas, for instance, was still observed but family-by-family; publicly it had become a Canadian affair, with English carols, Christmas cards, tree decorations, and closed businesses for December 25. They went to the hall for entertainment as long as there was nothing better to do. There were plays and music and dance just as long as somebody was willing to invest his or her energy in an uphill struggle against the local movie house and "Amos and Andy." Sometimes they had to leave the community altogether and go to the city and mingle with the self-conscious nationalists, the intellectuals, there to keep a hold on the culture. They recognized tunes but no longer knew the words. They would agree to take part in a concert but felt stiff and unnatural – "What has the story of gypsies and Jewish innkeepers got to do with me?" – and would agree to go to the performance only if bribed with a free pass to the dance afterwards. Except for those who lived awhile at an Institute, there was nothing systematic about these attempts at cultural retention. One held on to what was convenient and what one had no choice about in any case and discarded or forgot what no longer applied or seemed troublesome. Fragments of the parents' culture. Memories and hand-me-downs wearing thin.

Even facility in the Ukrainian language, the key to continuous access to the culture, was no longer inevitable. The lost battle over bilingual schooling and the introduction of unilingual Anglo-Canadian teachers into the schools had institutionalized the English language as the crucial instrument of assimilation and although there had been those who believed that "the longer they continue to know two languages, i.e., a knowledge of their mother tongue as well as English, the more readily can they be called intelligent and better educated,"[400] the fact was that the better they learned English the worse they spoke Ukrainian. In 1941 only 5.1 percent of Ukrainian-Canadians could not speak Ukrainian; in 1951 this had increased to 10.6 percent.[401] When, in 1961, the definition of mother tongue was not of language spoken but of "the language a person first learned in childhood and still understands" (by this definition 70 percent of Ukrainian-Canadians on the prairies listed Ukrainian as the mother tongue),[402] then one has to ask if a language which the person may not even be able to speak or read or write can conceivably be a "mother tongue."

Nevertheless, it was the first language spoken by the generation, and they retained it with varying degrees of success. For one thing, compared to the level of Ukrainian vocabulary and grammar that they heard at home, their level of English was soon superior; for another, in 99 percent of the cases they read and wrote English far more easily than Ukrainian. Inevitably, then, it was easier to make themselves understood in the assimilated language. Perhaps even more decisively, the language was undermined by the conflict within the community between well-educated and not-so-well-educated speakers. It was not only a question of whose language was "better" but also of one's politics. A high degree of fluency in the Ukrainian language was associated with nationalist consciousness, Ukrainian patriotism, racial pride, and spokesmanship, not to mention "hi-falutin" pretentions and snobbish overbearingness. This was particularly true of the recently-arrived immigrants with their disdain of the semi-literate, partially-Anglicized, and de-Ukrainianized Ukrainian-Canadian culture and their sense of mission as "real" Ukrainians among the backsliders. Some of the Canadian-born were unimpressed and managed to be phlegmatic about the changes the original culture had undergone.

I think communities like Two Hills are still close to the original spirit. Look, we still go regularly to church. And there is still quite a bit of Ukrainian spoken, even though it's Anglicized. *Ya pishov na farmu i fiksovav fants.* [I went out on the farm and fixed the fence.] You say that to a fellow just recently from the old country and he'll wonder what you're talking about. But we understand. It's our language now.

But for many others, the conflict was traumatizing and alienating. They went to church but couldn't follow the priest's sophisticated speech. They went to hear speakers at the hall but recoiled at the vehemence of the language and sentiment of "ultra-Ukrainians." They hung around the Institute to get in on the dancing and singing but deserted under the fire of language purists and elitists.

See, I shouldn't even be talking English with you. I'm supposed to speak Ukrainian all the time to improve it. My husband's family speaks it very well and they make me feel I have to catch up. When we got married, they called me a *Zhydivka* [Jewess] because I spoke it so badly. I won't even open my mouth around those "patrioty" from Edmonton.

They couldn't, in the end, rise to the occasion of hyper-Ukrainianism. And, in the absence of any self-conscious collective pride and righteousness in their Ukrainian-Canadian place and the way they lived and talked there, they gave in to linguistic assimilation. Bought a radio, subscribed to *Reader's Digest,* spoke English at the bridge party and Ukrainian only when they had to and as best they could.

"I knew I was Ukrainian because I went to a Ukrainian church." Never mind language difficulties, ideological differences and class antagonisms, the Catholic or Orthodox church was still the place where a Ukrainian-Canadian could make an unequivocal, unmistakable statement about his or her identity. The church was an institution peculiarly impregnable to Anglicization. Not a word of English spoken, not a single concession made to Protestant iconography; in the Orthodox church not a revision made to the Julian calendar, not a shift in doctrine since the seventeenth century. A veritable colossus of conservation. It was the nationalist rallying-post for all those who deplored the encroachment of the school, the media, and the highway and railway on the Ukrainian consciousness of the Canadian-born; more simply, for those who needed a point of familiarity and continuity with their forebears and neighbours, it was available, dependable, and comfortable. One did not need to be a religious fanatic to make use of it and to be loyal to it. The priests may have had a different view of this in their self-appointed roles as cultural custodians but to the average parishioner one or two masses a month, marriage, baptism, and funerals at the hands of a priest, and a few dollars in donations were an ample commitment to Ukrainian self-respect.

Refusal to become Protestant, however, did not mean that the Ukrainian churches would hold the allegiance of the community forever. The Canadian-born, much more at ease than their parents with Anglo-Canadian society and adept at communicating and doing business with it, obviously required the cultural consolation of the church less and less. Besides, much more than their parents, they were in touch with the skepticism, the hedonism, and even the atheism abroad in the land of Anglo-Canadians and by 1930, the Greek Catholic priests in Mundare were complaining that

> people, more and more, are indifferent toward the church. On holy days, instead of going to church, they go to the market. Once at a youth meeting in *Narodny Dim*, Father Shewchuk preached to the youth and the older people smirked.[403]

By the thirties, the young generation no longer depended on the church as a place to socialize; now they had community dances and movies and pool halls and taverns. There were stories told of young people who went to church with their parents but remained outside the church during the service. Clearly, whatever was going on inside was not of much interest, if one was neither very pious nor very nationalistic.

It seemed that every priest that came over was an old priest who couldn't speak English, who didn't seem to care about our own Canada or about the English language. But rather he cared much more about instilling the Ukrainian language. Now to me, it didn't seem to make much sense. I realize the value of it, I know that there is a lot of value but they turned me off because they didn't seem to want to learn our Canadian ways.

Since the generation's experiences were entirely Canadian in orientation, many were simply bored by and impatient with the church's scrupulous attention to age-old tradition and doctrine and its consistent equation of Ukrainian-Canadian identity with an emotional and spiritual attachment to the forms and systems of an institution evolved in a country they had never seen. Some never received much of a religious or nationalist education at home in the first place – some parents were avowed unbelievers, some were still attached to the Russian Orthodox faith, some went to church only out of a sense of obligation – and this, combined with the decidedly secular tone of their Anglophone schooling, made them feel that "the priest no longer has the upper hand as formerly in Europe. They become suspicious of their priest and openly disregard his admonitions."[404] Besides, when all the imagery and public representation of ordinary religiousness in Canada portrayed a decorous Protestantism in which parishioners wore white gloves and business suits, ministers stood at lecterns and the church itself looked like a modest bank building, the Ukrainian churches seemed embarrassingly, annoyingly, unacceptably lurid. All that incense and dirge-like music and flashy vestments, the genuflecting and woeful countenances of a hundred saints, and old women in babushkas kissing the floor. It was no wonder, then, that many Ukrainian-Canadians simply crossed the street and joined the United Church.

I think if there had been some young priests who had more Canadian ways, they probably would have persuaded me that I should stay with the Orthodox church. But at that time, I had so little to do with these priests and it didn't seem that I could understand what they were trying to tell me in church. And when I went to the United Church, I felt that I understood what they said. It was a shorter service and more Canadian as far as I was concerned.

And there, in the Protestant church, one never heard another word about Ukrainianism and the responsibilities of national identity. By 1961, only 58.5 percent of Ukrainian-Canadians were still members of the two "mother churches."

As for the faithful, they carried on, making those adaptations to the old Slavic ways of being that were possible outside the purview of the priest and the unnegotiable principles of nationalist extremists and conservative diehards. Given the trends of the world that surrounded the wood-frame church with the bulb on top and the little graveyard facing east (last burial, 1938), these adaptations were inevitable.

Now at Christmas we avoid things like hay in the house because of the rugs. Back on the farm it was a dirt floor. No *kutya* on the ceiling either; you couldn't wash it off. The church service is shorter now and the men and women stand together. Only the bigger church holidays are observed now. People just don't go to church the way they used to. If you have a store you're not going to close it down and lose business just to go to church. Churches are being centralized like schools, the smaller ones are being closed down except maybe for *Provoda* [ceremony at the graveyard]. At Ispas there are only two or three families left in the district, the Musidora families have signed up with our church. There is also a shortage of priests. The priest at Myrnam used to serve eight different churches. Now he's gone.

To the casual observer, the ethnically "solid bloc" of a Ukrainian-Canadian community seemed like a monolithic, inward-looking fortress whose inhabitants were self-sufficient, like-minded, and old-fashioned. "Permeated with the atmosphere of the old world," said Charles Young, "and composed of members knit together by the common recollection of neighbourly associations in the past, [they] are inimical to the assimilation of these people."[405] In 1931, he should have known better. By 1931, the Ukrainian-Canadian community included a whole new generation who had no "common recollection" of the old country and had in fact been influenced in a rich miscellany of ways by the "outside" world. A community which had some telephones and radios, graded roads and a CPR line, tractors and cars, cooperative associations and a municipal council, normal school graduates and MLAs was not an island unto itself. It was as Canadian in its style as Ukrainian: good riddance to manual labour from dawn to dusk, to bowing and scraping before authorities, to handmade tools and a monotonous diet, to draughts through the mud-plastered walls and vermin in the bedding. Maybe the old folks had that "far-off look" in their eyes as they sat in their "quaint" Carpathian outfits spinning wool and dreaming lugubriously about the village they had once been glad enough to leave behind. But the next generation was anxious to get on with the business of making it in Canada, of finding out just how far they could get up and out of the ghetto.

Back in 1920, a convention of Ukrainian-Canadian farmers in Edmonton, the majority of them the immigrant generation, had concluded their proceedings with an announcement that "efforts will also be made to enlighten Ukrainian farmers sufficiently to enable them to cooperate with Britishers."[406] A decade later, the Canadian-born would not subscribe so ingenuously to such humility. They were finishing high school and getting "good jobs," they were dressing better, building larger homes, and buying sophisticated machinery. Among them were doctors and lawyers. In their dealings with Anglo-Canadians they experienced some respect. The community was socially stratified, a vertical organization committed, whether one was at the bottom or top of the ladder, to the Canadian values of "private enterprise," "competition," and "individual rights." It was not always a homogeneous, tightly-knit, or fraternal organization. While, to the outside world, the leadership may have presented a united front of Ukrainian-Canadians seeking status and legitimacy *en masse*, within the community itself, there was frustration among the businessmen and professionals that, not being able to

> earn a living among English people, they are forced to turn to their own people. . . . Ukrainian-Canadians are quick to resent the fact that, although their numbers are great, few are employed in the civil service. They resent the discrimination against Ukrainian teachers. . . . No Ukrainian-Canadian has ever been appointed to the judiciary.[407]

They had assimilated psychologically as competitive Canadians but were denied the material fruits of that apprenticeship. The effects of this frustration on the rest of the community were divisive. The farmers and working people, feeling the loss of that "ethnic camaraderie" which had characterized their dealings with the professionals in the good old days, now saw them as a class of "nouveau riche": ostentatious, materialistically minded and, as expected, egotistical.[408]

The irony of having, in good faith, assimilated the values of good Canadian burghers, of being proud of one's industriousness and orderly behaviour and agreeable speech, of being consumers and voters and clients, and then being turned away from ordinary, middle-class citizenship by the very people who had made such assimilation a requirement of acceptance, was painful and embittering. Not just for the Ukrainian-Canadian elite, in their banishment from affluence and respectability, but for everybody else too, in their banishment from ordinariness.

I remember walking into a barracks one time in Winnipeg. I was looking for a friend and mistakenly I walked into another barracks, and a guy asked my name and I said, "Pawliuk." And he said, "Oh, a bohunk." That's what he said, right off the bat. And I said, well, what could I say? I was just one among the whole barracks full of them. But I recall little things like that very clearly, because it did hurt me. I felt, gee, I am as much Canadian as anybody else. I spoke no other kind of language except English, I did all the things that everybody else did, and why should I be called something different?

This Canadian-born generation, rebuffed by the "outside" world of the Anglo-Canadian – "You will go this far and no further" – socially and economically, was also emotionally, psychologically, culturally, set adrift from the "inner" world of their parents. The generation gap of the ethnic. To the natural and inevitable drift between two generations separated by peculiar but overlapping experience was added the yawning alienation between two mentalities formed under utterly different circumstances. The points of contingency were so few! Formally, they were there. The two generations cohabited, they ate and worked and played and prayed together in a shared milieu; they conversed together in a common language and repeated the same proverbs and prejudices. But, in terms of personality and style, it was as though the Ukrainian-Canadian was a character built from scratch. There was no picking up where the preceding generation had left off, for the immigrants' habits and perspectives and sensibility were buried with their bones. It was up to the Canadian-born to evolve the culture and character that referred only to the given of their experience: Canadian society. Responses and values derived from the cumulative effect of centuries-old economic and social patterns in a Ukrainian village obviously no longer applied. The parent could feed, clothe and house you, introduce you to a Byzantine God, enrich you with Slavic folk-arts, and pass on homilies of peasant wisdom. Beyond that, you were on your own in the uncharted territory of the Canadians. And no amount of Ukrainian education was going to protect you from their pervasive and irresistible cultural biases.

Not that no one tried, or was alarmed. Either because they simply knew no other way of living or because they had intellectualized and politicized their identity as Ukrainians and working people, most parents resisted the assimilation of their children as best they could. It was a losing battle, not the least because they simultaneously encouraged the children's economic assimilation. The almost universal emphasis on educational accomplishment and a job away from the farm was proof of this. The Ukrainian-Canadians, then, were in an impossible situation. On the one hand, they were expected by their parents to "get ahead," to live other than as Ukrainian farmers. On the other, they were also expected to keep faith with their elders' mentality. It is not, however, possible to be both places at once and so the generation gap widened and wounded. The parents' campaigns of resistance to assimilation were skirmishes in a lost cause. They could agitate against unilingual schooling, organize nationalist societies, defy Protestant missionaries, celebrate working-class and peasant heroes, and keep a tight rein on their children's behaviour at home but, once the children finished grade eight and looked for a job in the post office, they were on their way out of the village.

But there were ways in which the parents acted to forestall the disintegration of familiar and time-tested mores. Take, for instance, the question of whom to marry. "We were fortunate," said one woman, "that all us boys and girls in the family married Ukrainians. My parents preferred it that way. So did we. We were lucky that almost everybody around us was Ukrainian and so we had a good choice." Not everybody in the generation felt so agreeable – those raised on or converted to a Protestant church were indifferent to the issue of the pitfalls of intermarriage – but they generally went along with their parents' wish, if only for their own reasons. In a way, it was an academic issue. "When I was younger, I don't think I even knew any English people." But it was considered and discussed at length and the theoretical possibility of marrying an Anglo-Saxon was refuted in a list of attendant horrors.

I was warned jokingly about mixed marriage. By my parents and sisters. "You enjoy *holubtsi* so much. Just wait until you marry a Scotch girl! You'll be eating haggis." And I'll admit I didn't feel as much at ease with one of those gals as with one of ours. I don't know why. I was introverted and shy and many of these Anglo-Saxons had high positions. It struck me that the Ukrainian girls were more serious about things in life. The others struck me as giddy. Very probably because they didn't have to work so hard to get what they wanted.

An Anglo-Saxon mate would lure you from the Ukrainian church, cause you to abandon Ukrainian customs, and give you children who wouldn't be able to speak to *baba*. You'd have to change your name, stop seeing your relatives, and live far away.

In 1927 in Alberta, 7 percent of Ukrainian-Canadian men were marrying non-Ukrainian women; in 1935, 10 percent. As for Ukrainian-Canadian women, their percentages were 10 percent and 18 percent for the same years. "The higher percentages [for the women] is probably explained by the fact that there are obviously fewer obstacles to such a union."[409] Meaning, a woman acquires the status of her husband. By 1961, 62 percent of the Ukrainian-Canadians were still marrying each other; 15 percent of the men were married to "British" women (Statistics Canada does not measure how many women had intermarried), one of the lowest intermarriage rates of the British in Canada. T.C. Byrne in 1937 admitted "English Canadians of the middle class frown on such an alliance"[410] and Charles Young, in 1931, explained the same phenomenon by the Ukrainian-Canadians' lower standard of living, but expected that continued economic progress, educational accomplishment, and ambitions for higher status "would tend to increase the rate of intermarriage with those of British stock."[411] As long as the majority of the community was still living within Ukrainian-Canadian enclaves, socializing with each other in ethnic societies, and experiencing the disapproval of Anglo-Canadians, they met and married each other. Assimilation through marriage was the prerogative of those who left home early, or who didn't much care about their "Ukrainian" identity, or who were not particularly impressed by another's "British" one.

In almost every other part of their life, however, the Canadian-born were on a collision course with their parents. Young women who went into the towns and cities to work as domestics in middle-class homes returned to the farm with tales of fashions, etiquette, cuisine, and speech as practiced by genteel society. Young men came back with experiences of paycheques, union-organizing, and technology. In both cases, they tended to admire Anglo-Canadian society, saw it as a model for their own behaviour and began to view their parents' household and habits as uncouth and backward. They went to school and absorbed the conceits of the Anglo-Saxon, they returned home and were confirmed, by their parents' cynicism and reproaches, in their own cultural inferiority. "So you are turning your back on your parents' ways, so we're not good enough for you anymore, so you think you're as good as an Englishman!" etc. As they grew up, the Canadian-born spoke English better and better and more and more often, imitated Anglo-Canadian household styles in their furniture, decoration, food preparation, and entertainment, and through reading and the radio participated intellectually in the political and cultural issues that concerned the Anglo-Canadians. Vera Lysenko, speaking from the generation of the forties, admitted that the pioneers before them had "admirable qualities" but

> the younger generation could not help but see that their life was narrow, constricted, ridden with ignorance and superstition.
>
> First of all, we of the second generation, children of Ukrainian immigrant parents, were intensely "American" in our speech and manners. There were no evil spirits in our world. We had studied chemistry at school: physics, biology. We had moved with the times, much more rapidly than had our parents. What to them had been the mysterious workings of nature became the abc's of school textbooks. For all our modernity, we were keenly conscious of our complex social and national

background. About three generations back (1861) our ancestors had been serfs. That slavish psychology – instilled by decades of bowing before Russian and Polish *pans* – the psychology of hunted and persecuted races – we saw it cropping up in ourselves, and it was galling to us.[412]

It was no simple or easy thing to identify positively with one's Ukrainian origins. It was not a foregone conclusion that one would "respect" one's parents. "Due to the patriarchal set-up of the family in the old country, our parents had the feeling that their word was supreme, consequently, no comradeship was possible between parents and children."[413] It appeared to them that Anglo-Canadian families behaved differently. The wives had more status and a public life, the husbands were far less authoritarian and the children were raised more liberally. In the Ukrainian-Canadian home, such liberalism was rare. Traditionally, the wife had no more status than the cow and probably less than her own sons, the husband was a dour and judgemental presence, and the children were obedient, respectful, and hard-working. Given these expectations there was inevitable conflict when a son refused to go to church and spent Saturday night at a dance hall, when a daughter refused an arranged marriage and went to Edmonton for a job. The parents complained that their children showed so little interest in community activities, that they took material comfort for granted, didn't truly appreciate the hard work that built it up, and sneered at traditions. They got themselves into debt, spent money frivolously, cut their ties with neighbours and relatives, and preferred a baseball game to a play in the hall. The parents saw these trends as a slap in the face of respect. The children viewed them as the only appropriate way to live as Canadians. This conflict between loyalties Lysenko calls "second generation blues," the pain there is in feeling ashamed of the old identity and the thin disguise of the new.

In the confusion, an ever-increasing number of young people attempt to cast off what they consider to be the useless and impractical Ukrainian culture of their fathers, by changing their

names, by refusing to speak Ukrainian, and by avoiding
Ukrainian activities. They often profess to be English or just
Canadian, even though their features, some of their manners,
and often their accent betray their Ukrainian identity. In
reality, these people are not whole-heartedly accepted in
Anglo-Saxon circles. Thus this "marginal" man finds himself in
a sort of No Man's Land.[414]

Confusion, conflict, fear, guilt, resentment, and bedevilment, yes.
But whether this psychological commotion amounted to the
"disorganization," "demoralization," "mental and moral
deterioration," and "moral anarchy" of the community, as several
writers charge, is debatable. From the perspective of the seventies,
the Ukrainian-Canadian communities seem to have endured with
remarkable stability and cohesiveness, the painful generational
battles having been resolved in the course of time as the immigrant
generation died or retired and the Canadian-born one replaced
them in power, authority, and influence. In their lives, the
Ukrainian-Canadians seem to have been no more and no less than
other Canadians and one wonders now what all the fuss was about.
Both Ukrainian- and Anglo-Canadian writers at the time, and even
as recently as 1953, voiced considerable alarm about the
implications of the generation gap, concluding it was symptomatic
of a profound and potentially dangerous disorientation among the
new generation loose and vagrant in the broad daylight of society.
Their evidence and theoretical speculations only beg the question.

As evidence of the disorientation, Watson Kirkconnell cites
"scorn for the language and tradition of their parents" and
concludes that this "would tend to break down those sanctions of
authority and tradition by which the conduct of youth is most
effectively regulated."[415] Charles Young was more specific.
Differences in language, customs, and attitudes between the two
generations were

making for maladjustment and disorganization in the Ukrainian
family. The result is . . . misbehaviour among large numbers of

the younger generation. . . . In many cases, they have made a sorry mess of things. By staging wild parties, forming gangs, getting mixed up with the lawyers in the settlements, etc., they are giving the Ukrainian settlements a reputation for lawlessness and disorder.[416]

T.C. Byrne observed that

frequently the Ukrainian youth rejects home standards without replacing them with Canadian ideas. He loses respect for all authority. Lacking a definite, assured basis of behaviour the young Ukrainian-Canadian is more likely to commit offenses against the law.[417]

Ukrainian-Canadians agreed. Piniuta talked about the "moral aspect" of assimilation.

By discarding the cultural values of their parents and adopting new ways which actually have little meaning to them, such children break with the old but do not acquire the new. As a result, they deteriorate mentally and morally.[418]

And Paul Yuzyk deplored the generation's

inferiority complex and anti-social attitudes. The loss of a set of values, which is not firmly replaced by another set, causes demoralization of the individual and disorganization in the communities. The emotional conflict in such persons often leads to an undue tendency to commit crime.[419]

In the first place, it is interesting that they all, Ukrainian- and Anglo-Canadian alike, agree that loss of respect for authority is a social problem, whether it's patriarchal or liberal authority. Except for Lysenko, there is no analysis of why the generation repudiated that parental one (except for the sweeping generalization of cultural maladjustment) or why they allegedly failed to take up with the new. They all agree that this, somehow, no one really explains how, leads to criminal behaviour. Their assumptions seem to be that rejection of authority equals anarchy, that the youth could only reject it on perverse and neurotic grounds and that the struggle for an identity which is free of the cultural absolutes of either Ukrainianism or Anglicization is invariably debilitating. These are extraordinarily conservative assumptions. They do not allow for the fact that in their "moral anarchy," the Ukrainian-Canadians were working out a new relationship to authority that was neither sycophantic nor nihilistic, that they had valid political and economic reasons for resisting both an anachronistic patriarchal Slavic authority and a racist, capitalist Canadian one and that their experiments with hyphenated culture were as creative and sensible as they were difficult. In the second place, it is patronizing to conclude that a person who is neither Ukrainian nor Anglo-Saxon by culture is no one at all. Anglo-Canadian chauvinists said it first: "The presence of alien and unassimilated elements has aggravated the difficulty and tended to retard the development of a sense of community fellowship or corporate responsibility, and of devotion to a social ideal,"[420] as though none but the British may have them. In the third place, it is unreasonable to assert that a person suffering from "foreign psychosis" has only his or her own "weak thinking" to blame, criticisms of Anglo-Canadian society and its biases being "unrational." In the fourth place, it is simply absurd to claim that the modes of Canadian society "actually have little meaning" to a generation born, educated, employed, politicized, and socialized within them.

Given the conservative nature of their Ukrainian nationalism and their mistrust of Anglo-Canadian values and attitudes, the intelligentsia's description of the process of assimilation among the Ukrainian-Canadians was understandably alarmist. With so little faith in the ordinary person's capacity to make sense of both cultures and come up with a workable compromise, with so much elitist readiness to assume that only degeneration and anarchy could accompany the transition from one culture to another, the Ukrainian-Canadian intellectual consequently developed rather specious and untenable arguments which, if the mass of Ukrainian-Canadians were to take seriously, would put them in an impossible psychological position: the disavowal of their real and present Canadian experience and the attachment to a Ukrainian myth. Ironically, even as the intellectual was formulating the anti-assimilationist argument, he himself along with the rest of the community was being systematically assimilated: perfection of the English language, adoption of the bourgeois values of Anglo-Canadian society (the work ethic, status through money and education, accumulation of status symbols, etc.), and the acceptance of the world-view of the establishment (anti-Communism, monarchism, capitalism, and secularism).

It was perceptive of Paul Yuzyk, for instance, to describe assimilation as "brain washing"[421] – the means by which politicians, clergymen, and sociologists invalidated the "natural traits" of the Ukrainians and replaced them with their own "social and psychological patterns" – especially if one understands assimilation as the work of the political establishment's propaganda. But it is romantic and reactionary cant to characterize the process among Ukrainian-Canadians as "degeneration," "perversion of the soul," and "negation and denial of the cultural values of their fathers."[422] How the cultural values of a people adapting to twentieth-century Anglo-American political realities are more degenerate, perverted, and negative than those of a people who had adapted to feudalistic, brutalizing East European realities is a mystery to me. While it may be true that "psychology and sociology gradually reveal the tragic results of the assimilating processes" (Yuzyk gives delinquency and crime as examples), this describes not the assimilation process itself (one could emigrate to Samoa, say, and have a very pleasant assimilation experience!) but the particular society into which Ukrainian-Canadians were inserting themselves. And to imply that the culture from which their parents had voluntarily extracted themselves was free of crime and degeneration, was altogether harmonious and soul-satisfying; to assert that the repudiation of their parents' patriarchal, pre-literate, and colonialized values was tantamount to a loss of "faith in self-reliance"; and to hope to counteract the results of a wholly Canadian set of experiences by the retention of so-called "national characteristics such as language, customs, art, literature and history"[423] – as if the national traits of Ukrainians were fixed and immutable – all seem to me to be misconstrued and patronizing arguments.

Yet another critic justifiably dismissed as "undemocratic" the assimilationist tendency to make all "foreigners" into Englishmen but his fear of the "melting pot," that "no one knows what the final result might be. . . . it might mean the lowering of present, known standards,"[424] strikes me as elitist (while objecting to becoming an Englishman, is he also worried about becoming a "nigger"?). And his support of the theory of "unity not uniformity" through the preservation of "various cultural heritages but not the political loyalties"[425] ignores the fallacy of a cultural heritage surviving apart from its political context.

The arguments are specious because they assume assimilation can somehow be avoided or forestalled. They are reactionary because they refer back to a culture which was moribund and inoperative. The culture of the immigrant had been agrarian, closed within the in-group, and practised by every member. By contrast, the Ukrainian-Canadians were becoming urbanized, making contacts outside the community, and leaving the Ukrainian culture in the hands of specialists. In the mind of the immigrant, "details of the old country [folklore] complex remain intact"; in that of the Ukrainian-Canadian, the "specifics . . . are forgotten, unknown or blurred."[426] In the old days, the culture had "varied and numerous" functions; in the new, they are "limited in number to two or three: to entertain and to promote ethnic identification and economic prosperity."[427] The culture had been transmitted orally and interpersonally; now it tended to be passed on institutionally and mechanically (concerts, formal instruction, records, and books). The attempt of a "new Canadian" to re-enact the old forms was bound to be strenuous, if not absurd.

It is sometimes ridiculous to see a young professional man or woman, trained in all the advances of scientific thought, insist that his children celebrate the old pagan Christmas and Easter customs, whose origins go back far into the most primitive kind of pagan life. For older people, living on the land, these customs had significance – they were connected with their life on the soil, with the harvest and planting. In the new country, these customs were the only link they had with life in the old country. But for the younger generation, a sort of romantic nostalgia coupled with the stigma of the word "foreigner" sometimes causes them to take refuge in a narrow nationalism whose pride is the perpetuation of the old culture. . . . Nevertheless, for most of the younger generation, these customs belong on the stage, in books, not in everyday practice.[428]

Even though institutionalized and mechanical, fragments of the old country culture were naturally and universally inherited. How to keep them alive and well in the Ukrainian-Canadian consciousness alongside the assimilated habits and attitudes of Anglo-Canada was the problem the self-conscious members of the generation addressed. Wanting neither to slough off like an old coat the European inheritance nor to huddle defensively within it, they struggled with theoretical compromises. S.W. Frolick, making a speech in 1943 on "The Future of Ukrainian Youth in Canada," counted on the family, the church, Ukrainian schools, youth organizations, and educational institutes to generate the hyphenated consciousness of the future.[429] Theoretically, then, it would be possible to live domestically, spiritually, and linguistically as a Ukrainian and intellectually, socially, and politically as a Canadian. J.R. Solomon, deploring the feeling that "if a Ukrainian-Canadian wanted to be a loyal citizen, he would have to suffer all the abuses rallied against him without raising his voice in self-defense,"[430] proposed that instead "we should build our Canadian nation through the incorporation into its culture of the first qualities of each of these groups that are to form the component parts of this fair nation of ours."431 There should be a way then, to retain bits of Ukrainianism as vital elements of a cosmopolitan Canadianism.

The next twenty years would tell if these theoretical possibilities would be realized. As theories, however, they already contained the germs of future dilemmas. Would it be humanly possible to sustain the oasis of Ukrainian homelife within the vast and expanding spaciousness of Anglo-Canadian society? (What is a Ukrainian homelife anyway? Only Ukrainian spoken here? *Holubtsi* for dinner? The apotheosis of the patriarch? Listening to the "Ukrainian Hour" together at the hearthside?) Would the Ukrainian churches be capable of responding to the existential conscience of the Canadian-born? Could "fortresses" of Ukrainian culture avoid becoming isolated posts of navel-gazing purists? Would an incorporated Ukrainian culture be long recognizable as such within a Canadian culture wedded to the class interests of an Americanized bourgeoisie? Would the entertainment value of picturesque ethnics be convincing non-conformity for very long? In other words, could the Ukrainian-Canadians have it both ways: the social and economic success of a Canadian in-group, the sentimental and stylistic behaviour of ethnic outsiders? It was Michael Luchkovich, MP, who ruefully quoted an Irish politician: "Don't worry about the foreigner. He's all right. In about ten years he'll be out of the skinned class into the skinners' class and he'll then be as patriotic as any of us."

In the midst of all this theorizing, the people of the Ukrainian-Canadian community lived daily with the pressures of newly-assimilated practices and the counter-pressures of long-implanted attitudes and reflexes. The two were in balance for only a short time; by the time the Canadian-born had left school, they had already received more and were continually receiving more cultural input from the society surrounding them than from the frozen, truncated cultural corpus of their parents. With each succeeding generation, this core of Ukrainian inheritance would shrink and shrivel but for as long as it was there at all the generation would be collaborators in a hyphenated culture. It may not have been the fastidiously faithful replica of the original Ukrainian one the purists had wished for nor the slavishly imitative one the Anglo-Saxon chauvinists required but it was derivative of both and said more and better about the psychological and political spaces the Ukrainian-Canadians inhabited than did either extreme.

Their language was an amalgam of both influences, their home life a reflection of traditional exercises easily repeated and of the convenient, labour-saving, and necessary Anglo-Canadian culture to hand. Their religious life was a compromise between Byzantine forms and Canadian conformity, their celebrations a commemoration of both cultures' epiphanic events. Their arts became a pursuit of the expedient and accessible; a bit of this and a bit of that: some embroidery, some egg-painting, some petit-point, some cake-decorating, a stanza of Shevchenko, a stanza of Shakespeare, and country and western music with Ukrainian lyrics. Their settlement was a bicultural stand-off, the church and the bank, the hall and the cinema, the farmers' market and the grain elevator. Their values comprised a casserole of what could not be shaken off and what could not be deflected: from their parents an inheritance of familial centredness, communal togetherness, and ethnic loyalty; from the Anglo-Canadian outsiders, individualism, upward mobility, and Anglo-conformity.

Ideally, the two sets of inputs could be balanced as complementary cultural data. In reality, they were often in conflict, if only subconsciously; or, as one sociologist, Charles Hobart, described it, they could produce a feeling of alienation: "powerlessness, normlessness, meaninglessness, isolation from others, and self-estrangement."[432] An ethnic is alienated when he or she feels at the mercy of the dominant group, personally unworthy as a Ukrainian, anxious about the future, unsure of who to trust and unable to feel identified as either a Ukrainian or a Canadian. Integration, on the other hand, is defined as "his awareness of the opportunities that do exist, the better life he can make with his abilities, ambitions and willingness to work long hours and to save frugally."[433] Hobart then went to Willingdon, Thorhild, Lamont, and Edmonton and measured the "adjustment" of Ukrainian-Canadians there. He discovered that opposition to intermarriage, commitment to support of Ukrainian schools, low educational level, low-status jobs, membership in a Ukrainian church, Ukrainian chauvinism, and being female are associated with alienation. Conversely,

> there is evidence that the integrated or non-alienated subjects tend to identify with work success values and to repudiate Ukrainianism. . . . Indicators of upward mobility, of intimate interaction with non-Ukrainians and of participation in voluntary associations are associated with low alienation scores, that is with integration.[434]

It is understood that alienation is a bad thing, integration is good.

To be "integrated" then, was to be successfully and contentedly assimilated into Anglo-Canadian society. More than that, it meant unambivalent acceptance of Anglo-Canadian myths and mystifications. To be assimilated was to believe that hard work and frugality led to economic success, that abilities would be recognized and rewarded, that it was within the individual's control to make a better life; assimilation was socializing with Anglo-Canadians, admiring and emulating their culture and working within their institutions; assimilation was repudiating Ukrainianism, discarding ethnic traits, and rejecting ethnic community. Assimilation was integration into the Anglo-Canadian political machine, consenting to its order, its function, its control, and its perpetuation. The ultimate ingestion of that unknown quantity, the outsider. Alienation, however, was the condition of the majority of the generation by these terms. The majority did not intermarry, did support *Ridna Shkola,* did go to a Ukrainian church or the ULFTA hall; the majority had no high school education, no affluence, and no bourgeois status; half were women and doubly alienated from sexist, class-stratified Canadian society. Whenever and wherever the Ukrainian-Canadian felt oppressed, humiliated, cheated, and spurned, there the myths could not stick nor the machine indulged. Whenever and wherever the Ukrainian-Canadian still used and renewed the fragments of Ukrainian culture available, there the long arm of Anglo-Canadian political power had failed to reach. To this extent, such as it was, the Ukrainian-Canadian remained unconvinced of the alleged beneficence of that power and the inevitability of the control. To this extent, the alienated, unintegrated, unassimilated consciousness was subversive. The Ukrainian-Canadian as mutineer, for awhile.

> The culture I was raised in is being bid off at the auction sales. They bid $25 for a sieve but there's no way they would want the life that that sieve represents. It's as though you can acquire or hold in your hands a piece of the past, without having to live there anymore. What's happened to the culture I was raised in – the paintings and icons and borders on the wall – is that it was supplanted by Anglo-American culture so now we have North American paintings and pictures and trimmings. Quite simply, the greater force of one culture forced the other one out. So when I express regret it's not really that I feel that some vital part of myself has been lost but that I wonder how it happened that many people told us that our culture was not worth having and would have to be supplanted. It was economic and political power that allowed them to do this.

It does not necessarily follow that to be unassimilated was a form of mental and social disease. It may in fact have been a sign of intellectual and political clarity and a strategy of self-defense. But neither does it follow that the Ukrainian-Canadians could go back to where they came from. The road back home to the village had disappeared under the weeds of blurry memory and second-hand history. They would have to take their chances with the highway out of Two Hills.

SIXTEEN

Mythologies

It never occurred to me that we were anything but Canadians of Ukrainian origin. We were taught by English teachers, we studied English and Canadian history and when you became a teacher you took an oath to the King. We were taught not to be ashamed of anything Ukrainian but to go ahead and learn the English language first of all. Our parents, knowing they could get an education for their children and had the freedom to buy and sell wherever, never thought we weren't Canadians.

– Stephen Mulka

* * *

Still somehow this Ukrainian blood is left in us but due to certain circumstances we lost our identity and now we are living in some other situation. The Ukrainian language was prohibited even to use in the school yard and, not a long time ago, when you spoke on the bus in Ukrainian, the bus driver was mad at you. Now we get more recognition and maybe that is a renaissance. We are a sentimental people. And if our people are not lost it is only due to the guidance of the church. Still it will come, this renaissance. We are more recognized now than before, we have our representatives, even though high society is still Anglo-Saxon. But our representatives have talked even with Trudeau, so we are not unknown. I am a Canadian citizen but still my origin is Ukrainian and I want my children who are of this origin to have esteem for this nation. Nobody wants to build a Ukrainian Canada but we do have the privilege to preserve our ethnic identity. I think it is my duty to help my people to be proud of their origin, not to have a minority, inferiority complex.

– Father Peter Lytwyn

* * *

Our parents were happier than we are. We're making double, triple the money, but that means nothing. When I was just a young shaver, people at that time used to get together with a bottle of whiskey or moonshine, "Mountain Dew" in other words; they'd sit for a whole day and sing and laugh. Now a bottle of whiskey, two men sit and drink it and fight in ten minutes. They were happy, they got along. See, people now are envious as far as I'm concerned. We have more money, but what's the use of that?

– Mike Kindrake

* * *

Ukrainian-Canadian urban culture is in fact something incredibly crass and sterile. But if a group of Ukrainian-Canadian peasants – and there still are some who burn their grass every spring – were to present their culture to the outside world (you can call it that because you have to get off the dirt road onto the gravelled road then onto the oiled road to get to the pavement that goes to Vegreville) it would be very rough-hewn, but it wouldn't be crass.

– Winston Gereluk

———

Once the generation had served its time in the correctional institutions of Ukrainian nationalism and Anglo-Canadian chauvinism, providing they didn't get stuck in either, its members emerged, parolled, as the ethnics. Ethnic identity was recognition of the fact that there were stability and reliability enough in a consciousness dancing between cultural absolutes, as long as certain primary Canadian loyalties were served and certain Ukrainian ones renounced. Here was reluctant acknowledgement that a person who was neither Ukrainian nor Anglo-Saxon was perhaps a Canadian;

the ethnic as first Canadian. After all, there had to be some designation other than "British" or "alien" for the person who could say: "I know that I'm Ukrainian and I have no hard feelings about that and I know that I'm a Canadian, too. I was born here. I've often thought it would be nice to go and see the place where my parents came from but I wouldn't want to live there."

When talking to them, one senses the satisfaction of the generation in having settled on a compromise for an identity. To the unhyphenated outsider, the compromise may seem like a neutralized and attenuated substitute for a real name but to the ethnic it was the only alternative to the fantasy of Ukrainianism and the trauma of Anglicization. By means of the compromise, the contradictions could be contained and the neurotic equivocation between two sets of opposed expectations stilled.

> My generation has wanted to preserve itself as Ukrainian but we still think we're Canadian. At one time, we all thought we were just Ukrainians. Then the teachers started talking about how we were all Canadians. Well, that made sense. We were born here. So now I'm a Ukrainian-Canadian or Canadian-Ukrainian – I always get that mixed up. The point is, I still have Ukrainian blood in me. But I'm as good a Canadian as anybody else.

The compromise was also tangible evidence that the generation had progressed in consciousness from their parents' values without abandoning them altogether in an excess of the neophyte's zeal. They report that their parents rarely propagandized one loyalty or the other, either out of indifference, nonchalance, or circumspection. The parents had made a clean break with the old country when they made the decision to emigrate; they made few references to past history or to relatives left behind; they understood themselves to be displaced Galicians with the unremarkable biographies of people who just worked, worked, worked and who had emigrated to work some more. They were unmoved by the defiant racial pride of the intelligentsia and mystified by the struggles of their children to define Canadianism.

The next generation emerged with a radically different psychological perspective. Canadian identity was their birthright, Ukrainian loyalty a learned response. For that matter, given the generally low level of nationalist consciousness among most of the immigrants, loyalty to one's Ukrainian origins was an ideal of the following generation as much as was the concept of Canadian membership. It was the Canadian-born who attached ideological and sentimental importance to Ukrainian-bred behaviours. The parents were Ukrainians. The children paid homage to them by declaring they were too. "I am very proud to be Ukrainian and I will always be what my mother and father were. I'll carry on what they gave me. I'll never change," meaning, she teaches neighbours how to paint Easter eggs, enjoys serving *holubtsi* to Anglo-Canadian dinner guests, and, when she goes to church, goes to a Ukrainian one. The hyphenated consciousness allowed the ethnic to feel at home at a time when the Anglo-Saxon manor was double-locked from the inside and the Ukrainian cottage was fallen down, broken in the bush.

Making camp between two cultural solitudes was not, however, supposed to be a permanent condition. The ethnic compromise was a survival tactic employed while the environment was still hostile, suspicious, confused, and mercurial. Ethnicity was a culture of ambiguity, emphasizing now one, now the other identity on either side of the hyphen, depending on the prevailing political winds. When the Anglo-Canadian establishment was feeling vulnerable and defensive, the Ukrainian-Canadian community was careful to be more Canadian than Ukrainian. When the establishment was feeling secure and magnanimous, then the community reasserted its Ukrainianness. In the halcyon days between the War Measures Act and the formation of the Communist Party of Canada, Ukrainian-Canadians proudly manifested their ethnicity in very public ways; the *Sitch* marched in their uniforms in parades, church choirs entered competitions, dance groups joined festivals, all of it reflecting the "preservation of the good Ukrainian name." (Just a few years later, it would, of course, become a question of one's "good Canadian name.")

In the forties, with the "legitimization" of the Ukrainian-Canadian community through the suppression of the Communist party, the formation of the Ukrainian Canadian Committee and the post-war optimism about "national unity," closet ethnics came out into the light of day asking,

> What does it mean that we Ukrainian-Canadians are losing ownership of the lands which we first tilled . . . that we are veritably dissolving amidst the miscellany of Canadian life, and that in our endeavours to find a livelihood we have to foresake all that is great and holy for any other people? [435]

They went on to call upon the "identity," "unity," and "glory" of the Ukrainian people. Self-assertive language indeed, for a community so recently vilified and humbled. For the first time, too, academicians and social scientists were cited in support of the notion of biculturalism, particularly Watson Kirkconnell, whose statements on the "rich diversity of racial gifts on this earth" were reproduced a hundred times, almost as a mantra for those Ukrainian-Canadians still queasy in their "otherness."

> There is nothing so shallow and sterile as the man who denies his own ancestry. . . . We do not think less of the Scot in Canada because of his proud wistfulness towards the land of his origin. . . . As a Canadian, he is not poorer but richer because he realizes his place in a notable stream of human relationships down through the centuries. His sense of the family, the clan, and the race can scarcely fail to vitalize the quality of his citizenship. He grows greater than himself by virtue of his conscious pride in the past and his determination to be worthy of it.[436]

Imprecise and inflated, such language was nevertheless consoling in the face of the inevitability of assimilation and its concomitant, racial disparagement.

By the sixties, the ground had been prepared for a broad ideological assault on the prevailing assumptions about assimilation and the meaning of Canadianism. This was primarily the work of the Canadian-born generation, especially those members of it whose educational background and class expectations provided a lever with which to pry at the brick wall of the Anglo-Canadian establishment. Behind their rhetoric lay the fact that "people with funny last names make up less than one percent of the corporate elite, as defined by John Porter,"[437] that in spite of all their attempts to "pass" as successful citizens, the real power and influence in the country still resided with the Anglo-Saxon elite and that nobody in this elite had ever been fooled into thinking that Ukrainian-Canadians were anything but the second-class progeny of Galicians. These were people who had done all the right things – had accepted sacrifices to get an education, endured the apprenticeship of inferior working conditions and low pay at jobs in the ethnic ghetto, kept their political noses clean and subscribed to self-reliance, modesty, and patience. The understanding was that for "knowing their place" they would eventually be summoned forth from it to participate in the clubs of the Anglo-Canadians where the real rewards lay. But for a handful of cases, the pay-off had never come.

> Despite our smug conviction that our mosaic was a lot more genteel than the crass melting pot to the south, every ethnic knew in his heart that the only way to be taken seriously was to melt down to the Anglo-Saxon norm.[438]

Since it was impossible and in any case useless – the melted-down ethnic had only got as far as the tradesman's entrance to the clubhouse – another strategy altogether had to be employed.

Inklings of what it might be emerged in response to the political events of the sixties. The "quiet revolution" in Quebec challenged the exclusive status of Anglophone culture and political power in Canadian society and revived with impressive authority the argument that language retention and cultural survival were inseparable. Prime Minister Lester Pearson set up the Royal Commission on Bilingualism and Biculturalism and talk was not of one but "two founding races" and "two major distinct cultures" and "two societies." In the United States, radical blacks were propagandizing racial pride and the celebration of cultural difference. The Ukrainian-Canadians were not unmoved. If French-Canadians and American blacks could be taken seriously as unmelted cultural and political forces, then why not the "ethnics"? If Quebec was a legitimate "nation," then what about the third world of the non-Anglo-Saxon, non-Quebecois? The investigation into biculturalism was not going far enough.

> It ignored the ancestral backgrounds of 25 percent of Canada's population and in doing so made Canada a country in which over 50 percent of western Canada's population, in particular, appeared to be relegated to the status of second-class citizens.[439]

A conference of ethnic notables in Toronto, by way of retaliation, "overwhelmingly rejected biculturalism in favour of 'official recognition of the multicultural nature of Canada,'"[440] and in fact the terms of reference of the Bi-and Bi-Commission were expanded to include examination of the contribution of the "third force" to Canadian society. It was only judicious: by the end of the decade no single ethnic group, not even the Anglo-Saxons, represented a clear majority of the Canadian population.

Thus began the rhetoric and theoretical postulations. If nothing else, the Ukrainian-Canadians would argue themselves into acceptance. If they were never to "make it" as Anglo-Saxons, then, damn it, they would be summoned as ethnics. Writing at the time of Canada's centennial, Rev. Dr. S. Semczak of the Greek Catholic Church listed Ukrainian-Canadian contributions to Canadian society as "consolidation of Ukrainian element in Canada for common good and united purpose," "integration into Canadian life," meaning not assimilation and "annihilation as unity" but "the persistence to endure and to be what we are in the best sense of our culture, mental and social life," the "progress on all lines of Canadian endeavour" and, finally, "our ancient culture."[441] Paul Yuzyk, recently appointed to the Senate, speaking of the retention of "mother languages," argued that it stimulates cultural growth and grass-roots participation in culture, "provides for cross-fertilization and mutual enrichment . . . in the development of a common Canadian culture and national personality," makes Canada more effective in international relations and Canadians more "tolerant" toward the cultures of their fellow citizens.[442] He quoted the extended metaphors of a secretary of state, various prime ministers, and even Prince Philip as evidence of an historical predisposition on the part of the Anglo-Canadian elite towards multiculturalism, as in Sir Wilfrid Laurier's image of Canada as a gothic cathedral.

> For here, I want the marble to remain the marble; the granite to remain the granite; the oak to remain the oak; and out of all these elements I would build a nation great among the nations of the world.[443]

He resurrected John Buchan's 1939 exhortation to "remember your old Ukrainian traditions – your beautiful handicrafts, your folksong and dances, and your folk legends"[444] and reiterated the warnings of psychologists that "one's ancestry should be cheerfully accepted and used as a base to develop a fuller personality"[445] if one is to be a good citizen. Finally, he argued that all Canadians are united in purpose because of a "common experience of the land, the history, the democratic institutions and the economic prosperity" of Canada.[446] In perhaps one of the most mystical variations on all these idealistic themes of harmony, fellowship, pride, and purpose, M.H. Marunchak, in 1970, claimed that as a result of such "ideal inducements and high principles," the Ukrainian-Canadians have

> formed their own spiritual citizenship which imposes upon them unwritten laws. These laws are written in their hearts and are the natural reactions of noble minds, which command them to guard the cultural treasures of their people in relation to

themselves and to their motherland.[447]

Through the seventies, however, theoreticians of multiculturalism have evolved a decidedly less idealistic tone. As if encouraged by increased budgets from the federal government, the wide-spread popularization of folk cultures and the threatening rhetoric of more militant minorities, they have escalated their demands and toughened their analysis. Officially legitimized as a "third force" in Canada, these ethnics in the public eye have largely discarded the lyrical supplication of earlier decades. Stanley Frolick, for instance, at one time national president of the Ukrainian Canadian Professional and Businessmen's Federation, located "ethnic consciousness" in the "failure of the melting pot concept and the bankruptcy of the dominant WASP super culture and morality" and in the "yeast and ferment" of American blacks, chicanos, Jews, and feminists.[448] Dr. Manoly Lupul, professor in the University of Alberta's Department of Education, deplored the fact that "Ukrainians, despite appearances, common suppositions, or conventional wisdom at home or abroad, are less powerful than ever before and for all practical purposes will be a negligible political, social, and cultural force in another generation unless drastic changes are made inside and outside the Ukrainian-Canadian community."[449] He argued that "individual bilingualism on a regional basis" – for example, Ukrainian-English bilingualism in Alberta – "is the indispensable prerequisite to a meaningful multiculturalism." Ukrainian-Canadians are a community "whose language is under seige everywhere and who, therefore, along with the French Canadians, may rightfully claim that 'We too are not a people like the others' and need special consideration and aid,"[450] namely government-funded Ukrainian-language kindergartens, Ukrainian-language curricula, and Ukrainian studies.

The Fifteenth Congress of the Ukrainian Canadian Students' Union [SUSK in Ukrainian] in 1974 attacked the "discrimination" of the CBC in not providing Ukrainian-language programming:

The Canadian reality depicted in the media should be

multilingual, and only through use of it can Ukrainians in Canada effectively become a community.[451]

At the 1975 convention of the Ukrainian Self Reliance League, a resolution was passed calling on the federal government to create a ministry of multiculturalism. At the 1975 Canadian Showcase of Ukrainian Culture in Vegreville, Julian Koziak, Alberta's Minister of Education, evoked the "lesson" of Quebec: is it possible for the Ukrainian-Canadian culture to survive without the Ukrainian language? When, at this same festival John Munro, federal minister responsible for multiculturalism, announced that "a policy of multiculturalism is not reflected only in what can be called the purely 'cultural' events, but also applies to equality of access in the world of work as well," and, six months later, suggested that because of the emphasis of multiculturalism policy on folklore activities, "very real social problems are being ignored" and that henceforth some multicultural funds would be diverted from "small inward-looking groups" to help "groups that are only now beginning to fight their way into the mainstream of Canadian society," there was considerable objection from some Ukrainian-Canadians. Peter Savaryn of the UCC interpreted Munro's remarks to mean:

[a] horrible and uncalled-for change. . . . The most legitimate aspiration of the Ukrainians would be to preserve and develop Ukrainian culture and he [Munro] certainly doesn't go for that. He says there will be no support for teaching the Ukrainian language. In theory we have all the rights under the sun but that isn't what's being called for. If we aren't being provided with schools and teachers and textbooks, the right is empty. You might as well not have it.[452]

As contentious and alarmist as these statements may sound, they nevertheless bespeak the survival and revivification of the subculture of ethnicity and, in the seventies, are in many ways simply a more aggressive and self-confident expression of a point of view held throughout Ukrainian-Canadian history by numbers of noisy intellectuals and spokespersons who had consistently refused to take their medicine as second-class citizens. As lawyers, members of legislatures and parliament, school-teachers, newspapermen and women, and businessmen, they had all along urged their compatriots to insist on their rights as Ukrainian-Canadians and not as some soulless, assimilated facsimile of an Anglo-Saxon. They had pressured the establishment to open its ranks to the non-WASPs instead of keeping them huddled among the farmers and proletariat. Initially polite and suggestive in their demands, they were nevertheless sticking their necks out while most others were meekly blending into the Anglicized woodwork.

To the extent they did cause doors to middle-class success to open to more and more ethnics, they were the progressive leadership of a deprived minority. To the extent their aggressiveness and self-confidence spilled over into the routine consciousness of the whole community, they were an intellectual vanguard. Nowadays, the people of Two Hills are not apologetic about being Ukrainian-Canadians. They mention with pride how much the Anglo-Canadians "just run wild for Ukrainian stuff," buying *pysanky*, fishing for invitations to Ukrainian weddings, and driving out from Edmonton to get some "real" Ukrainian food. They are proud of their festivals and enjoy the admiration *of* outsiders when they "see the quality *of* our dancers and singers." They believe in the preservation of Ukrainian culture as a kind of local history, in the same way that old buildings and documents are preserved. They are proud of their Ukrainian-English bilingualism and are racially assertive.

> It took this long to get started because my parents' generation were so suppressed, so humble; they were followers, they didn't dare ask for things. But my generation is educated and not afraid to admit who they are. It's a quiet revolution.

To top it off, they are congratulated and encouraged by members of the Anglo-Canadian community whose own parents may have once calumniated and mocked them for the very Ukrainianness they now indulge. The Vegreville *Observer*, in its own day a bastion of Anglo-Canadian supremacy, thanked God in June 1974, that "affairs such as the Showcase of Ukrainian Culture can overstep politics and the foolishness of ethnic bigotry." An interesting phenomenon. When an Anglo-Canadian celebrates pyrohy and a Ukrainian-Canadian sings "O Canada" then the community has, by all the theories, arrived at the essential multicultural moment.

As to the ways and means of multiculturalism, these have been as diverse as the imagination and politics of the people and institutions undertaking them. A list of projects funded by the federal ministry responsible for multiculturalism in September and December 1975 reveals the interpretation made of the notion by community groups: dancing exhibitions; displays of traditional Ukrainian costumes; total immersion Ukrainian summer school; Ukrainian-Indian cultural exchange; recording of folk songs; a Ukrainian-Canadian University Students' Union symposium; Ukrainian Culture School; a Ukrainian festival; cataloguing of archival material. The groups and organizations initiating these projects – The Ukrainian National Federation, the Ukrainian Canadian Committee, Plast, the Ukrainian Women's Association, Ukrainian Educational Council Central Diocese, etc. – are uniformly moderate in tone and engaged for the most part in activities that fall within the narrow and innocuous parameters of "folk culture."

For obvious reasons, these are the groups who have the ear of governments, none more securely than the Ukrainian Canadian Committee, that brain-child of the federal government of the forties. It is to be understood that it is just as true of the seventies that official support of the Ukrainian-Canadian community extends only so far. As an executive member of the UCC explained,

> The UCC is an umbrella organization which includes the majority of the legitimate Ukrainian organizations in Canada. I mean non-Communist. There are some Communist-based groups which purport to be Ukrainian national organizations. The Communist organizations are simply operating under a

cover. It's international Communism under a cover of being a national organization appealing to the national feelings of the Ukrainians. The UCC has established a good rapport with the federal government and our experience is that we can carry on a dialogue with the federal government without any difficulty whatever.[453]

Thanks to the government's patronage, the UCC has sponsored regional festivals, the presentation of Shevchenko medals to archbishops of the Ukrainian Greek Orthodox Church, the request that the prime minister intercede on behalf of Soviet Ukrainian dissidents, the adaptation into the Ukrainian language of several National Film Board films, and a proclamation commemorating the twenty-fifth anniversary of the death of the commander-in-chief of the Ukrainian Insurgent Army. The Ukrainian Bilingual Association of Edmonton has obtained approval from the Edmonton Public School Board and Separate School Board and funds from the provincial government to set up a Ukrainian-English bilingual project at the kindergarten and elementary school levels. The University of Alberta is able to offer courses in Ukrainian Emigre Literature, Ethnic and Minority Group Relations, and the History of Twentieth Century Ukraine. A Ukrainian-born artist has undertaken to paint all of the Ukrainian churches in Alberta. The Continuing Education Division of Grant MacEwan College in Edmonton offered a course in Ukrainian church singing:

> Just as you don't have to be Ukrainian to enjoy cabbage rolls and pyrogies, neither do you have to be Ukrainian to participate in Ukrainian church singing.

The community of Two Hills has had a Ukrainian Dancing Club for eight years. And in Vegreville, they've put up a monstrous twenty-six-foot-long, five thousand pound, $50,000 aluminum Ukrainian Easter Egg, a project funded by the Vegreville and District Chamber of Commerce and the Alberta RCMP Century Celebrations Committee. Its dedication reads:

This Pysanka (Easter Egg) symbolizes the harmony, vitality and culture of the Community and is dedicated as a tribute to the One-Hundredth Anniversary of the RCMP who brought peace and security to the largest multicultural settlement in all of Canada.

How short their memories are! The "peace and security" of the community were paid for by the incarceration of native people on reservations and by many Ukrainian-Canadians themselves whose ULFTA halls were spied on, hunger marches busted, and grain strikes sabotaged by the RCMP. Upon all such endeavours, the governments have laid their blessings. Speaking to the Ukrainian Self Reliance League, John Munro's parliamentary secretary said,

At a time when multinational corporations, multinational trade unions, multilateral contracts and trade are proliferating, knowledge of the languages and cultures of the peoples of the world is a tremendous national asset. . . . Multiculturalism makes good economic sense.[454]

And Horst Schmid, Alberta minister responsible for culture, addressing the same group said

we – if we are to be worthy of the sacrifices of our fathers – will share also our cultural heritage in common. It is that simple.[455]

The implicit function of all such projects and pronouncements is the reaffirmation and benediction of a particular mythology of ethnic history and experience. Ukrainian-Canadians and Anglo-Canadians alike agree upon and publicize a version of Ukrainian-Canadian history that is fundamentally revisionist. From the relatively secure and comfortable perspective of their assimilated and respectable position in 1970s Canada, the ethnics review their past and serve it up in an attenuated and selective account which, coincidentally, the Anglo-Canadians find agreeable. And it is on the basis of this mutually gratifying account that the ideology and practice of multiculturalism, for one thing, are seen to be justified.

The official promulgation of multiculturalism, however, is only the formalization of a myth-making process which began with the first immigrant celebration of Canadian experience. As early as 1904, Michael Gowda wrote *To Canada* in which he rejoiced in the liberty and freedom from fear which settlement in Canada afforded, even though such settlement meant exile from the graves of ancestors, the "sacrifice and groan" of hard labour and exclusion from real citizenship. These penalties were endurable, however:

> But, Canada, in liberty we work till death
> Our children shall be free to call thee theirs.[456]

In another statement, an immigrant laments that

> It is sad to live in Canada
> In your youthful years

and that, much as he'd like to go back home, he cannot, so

> Work further in Canada
> You poor immigrant
> Canada is a free country
> And she is as good as a mother
> Believe in God, work diligently
> And you will have everything.[457]

Thus, from the accounts of the immigrants themselves, were derived the irreducible elements of the ethnic myth: life in Canada may be harsh but it's worth it because things will get better, the next generation will reap the rewards of the sacrifice, individual effort and unflagging persistence will sow the harvest of material security and increased social status and, besides, whatever one may think or feel, Canada is a free country where a person will be guaranteed dignity and justice. The immigrants, of course, had their reasons for indulging these optimistic scenarios. They had made the move to

Canada precisely on the basis of such promising alternatives to the wretched inevitability of a serf's life in the Ukraine. They required the psychological support of imaginary rewards as they lived out years of poverty, humiliation, and disappointment on their homesteads. They had perforce to make the best of things as there was no going back. They judiciously communicated their faith rather than their disillusionment about a country where, by a flip of the Immigration Act, they could be deported for subversive or immoral behaviour or even for being too poor. And many, because of their own increasingly good fortune or that of neighbours, sincerely believed in the propaganda that correlated hard work and dreams come true. For all these reasons, the intelligentsia among the immigrants, being in a position to do so, collected, made intelligible, and transmitted to the outside community the various elements of the immigrant mythology as a coherent mystique. In this choice to approve and celebrate the characteristics of a "good" ethnic rather than those of a dissatisfied, cynical, rebellious, and uncouth "bad" one, the mystique of the grateful and hopeful pioneer was confirmed. It had the singular facility of providing an agreeable explanation for a disagreeable truth: that, if immigrants and the children of immigrants had to sweat and heave against exploitation and injustice for every penny of their circumscribed prosperity, it was because they were such tenacious and self-denying people. The organized or spontaneous protests of the few malcontents were not to be taken seriously: they were disgraceful exceptions to the general mass of peaceable folk who gratifyingly, in effect, "put up and shut up." In part, then, the mystique was a survival tool, a political manoeuvre to deflect the repressive reflexes of the ruling classes against the grumbling horde of suffering immigrants. But it was also an opportune mechanism for those in the ethnic community who had most to gain from the Anglo-Canadian establishment's conviction that Ukrainian-Canadians were, after all, desirable.

In his novel, *Sons of the Soil*, the immigrant-writer Illia Kiriak vividly and poignantly described the cruelties and catastrophes of the pioneering era and ascribed the survival of the immigrants to "sheer fortitude and faith which from time immemorial had sustained their race."[458] A Ukrainian-Catholic priest, describing the bodies in pain and sleepless nights of immigrant field-workers, believed that "to endure this kind of work for few cents per day and sustain large families, Ukrainian farmers could do only on account of their unshakeable faith and spartan way of life."[459] The biographer of an immigrant family acknowledged the "ingenuity and perseverance" that were invested in securing the sheer necessities of life and that the "enduring, self-reliant, hard-working and thrifty" character, formed through centuries of oppression and exploitation, had served them "admirably to survive in the new land."[460] A member of the Basilian Order in Mundare, wondering "what was this mysterious driving force" that impelled the Ukrainian peasant to emigrate, concluded it was the "love of land and love of toil!"[461]

Inasmuch as all these explanations, attributions, and apostrophes were addressed within the community, they can be understood as forms of consolation and social stabilization: if members of the community were tired and despairing, let them be consoled by the mystery of their racial fortitude; if they were resentful and insolent, let them be reintegrated with the promise of imminent satisfaction. When the intelligentsia addressed the Anglo-Canadian community, however, their mystifications of the ethnic experience served additionally as mediations between an elite and the *lumpen*, with the Ukrainian-Canadian intelligentsia as trusted go-between. Thus a Mundare lawyer, George Szkwarok, speaking to the Edmonton Rotary Club in 1930, relieved his audience of responsibility and said the Ukrainian pioneers "did not care for their own comfort, small shacks of log or dugouts were their shelter." Assimilation was proceeding satisfactorily, the English language was in use and Anglo-Canadian culture was everywhere an object of admiration:

They will like your ways and customs, and they will assimilate them if they find them good. They will abandon their own if they are bad. They will learn of your ideals and will follow them.[462]

In a similar vein, Michael Luchkovich spoke in the House of Commons in 1928 as the UFA member for Vegreville constituency and argued, rather fancifully, that the most successful Ukrainian-Canadians were the ones who had arrived the poorest, the failures had arrived in luxury. The moral to be drawn was

that this is no country for mollycoddles; what we want is the hardy red-blooded pioneering type that . . . will roll up his sleeves and tackle without a murmur any obstacle that may confront him.

Blaming the economic problems of his constituents not on their vulnerability to the excesses of capitalism nor on the policies pursued by his fellow MPs, but on the ethnics' lack of character, he insisted that "true patriotism . . . also includes persistence and frugality even under trying circumstances."[463] And Peter Svarich, described in the Vegreville *Observer* as an "ardent lover of flowers" wrote in 1931 that, far from being subversive and unruly, the Ukrainian-Canadians' character is such that "they are not able to do any harm, menace, or disturbance to our government or its institutions." Why?

If they do fight, assault or murder anyone it would be their own countryman, as they have great respect for the English or any other people and will very seldom harm them.

Curiously, instead of deploring the low level of education of the mass of Ukrainian-Canadians, he pointed out that "had they more and better education, they would not . . . stick to the land as they did; and would not work for all their might. . . ." And he noted with approval that "school children learn and speak English not only at school but in private homes and in public places. They like it better than their own mother's tongue."[464]

As for Anglo-Canadian commentaries, they tended to repeat the substance of the mystique in their own observations, and there is a correspondence between their patronizing characterizations and the pacifying mythology of the Ukrainian-Canadians themselves. Arguing that the immigrant does, with their "reverence" for their new country and their "patriotism," revitalize the nonchalant and materialistic citizenship of the Canadian-born, J.S. Woodsworth believed that immigrants compel "us to make deeper and broader the foundations of our national life."[465] And Robert England, weary of the nonconformity and sombreness of some immigrant groups, praised the Slav's "deeply religious nature, his willingness to suffer hardship, his genius for self-expression," etc.[466]

Even if these mystifications were, illogically, true, they would be troublesome and disheartening. As half-truths, distortions, and outright lies, they are repugnant. I do not deny that the immigrants experienced hardships, that most survived one way or another, and that succeeding generations have had an easier time of it. I do not doubt that much of their endurance was grounded in a culturally-learned passivity, fatalism, and doggedness. I do not disagree that many believed in all sincerity that Canada was the promised land of freedom and justice. What I do deny and disagree with is the myth that it had to be so, that it was a good thing it was so, and that nobody minded it was so. On the contrary, as long as the myth has any viability or credibility, as it still does in the organizations and publications of the nationalist Ukrainian-Canadians, in the rhetoric of politicians and in the hearts and minds of second, third, and fourth generation Ukrainian-Canadians who don't know any better, it is a double-edged weapon. On the one hand, it has served to credit the "bohunk" with characteristics alleged to be admirable; it has kept ethnic memory alive in the face of Anglo-American cultural superiority and it has carved out a space for Ukrainian-Canadian autobiography within the collective Mother Goose rhymes of Canadian history.

On the other hand, it has traded in speciousness and

revisionism. It has implied as racial absolutes the features of a behaviour learned in another time and place. It has celebrated as respectable virtues docility, obsequiousness, and self-disgust – the psychological habits of the drudge – and romanticized the social habits of the poor: frugality, self-reliance, and stoicism. It has canonized as instincts what the ethnic had no choice in being – a pious, hard-working farmer – and passed on as certitudes what the ethnic merely hoped for: the democratic and humane regard of Canadian society. It denied or trivialized the reality of many Ukrainian-Canadian lives eked out of losses and failures, confusion and frustration, injustices and persecution. And it has dismissed as perverse and odious the struggles of those who resisted and fought back in the conviction they had nothing to lose but their chains. It idealized the Anglo-Saxon and often considered the culture of the Ukrainian-Canadian picturesque though dispensible; it patronized the farmer as a broad back and not very big mind that would tolerate and absorb any amount of abuse and exploitation. It popularized the self-congratulatory imagery of a replete and fulfilled generation building from nothing a spot of satisfaction, 160 acres thick with crop, a snug house, trim yard, and fragrant lilac hedge; a good supper in the belly, children playing in the weeds, the parents slumped in a big chair, their proprietors' eyes looking out over the miles of God's earth rolling around them, out to the horizon. The fact that this was a true picture of many Ukrainian-Canadian destinies does not justify the myth that it was the only one.

The son of immigrant Ukrainians confesses:

> In school, we were taught not to talk about our Ukrainian experiences and I knew that even though I was bitter about many things if someone had asked me I would have given a very romantic story.

Like him, the mythologists popularized an edited, sanitized and romanticized history which "cleaned up" the offending and provocative parts of a contradictory, unseemly account. They were in fact apologists for a history that was not all that the Anglo-

Canadian establishment might have wished it to be. Anxious to please and be rewarded, they repressed the bad news and exaggerated the good. Enjoying the privileges of their status within the Ukrainian-Canadian community, they invalidated the accounts of their opposition and circulated the conceits of their fraternity. Influential, they encouraged the powerless and meek to take pride in their oppression; it kept the peace.

Exploited people have had to find some saving grace about themselves, but I wouldn't call that pride. To call it pride that you make a good chambermaid? "If you're going to have to scrub toilet bowls, make sure you're the best toilet-scrubber there is." The minute you begin to analyse it, it sounds like, "I'm proud of my exploited self. I'm proud of the lowdown, mean dirty work I have to do."

There's nothing beautiful about exploitation, and if our people are screwed up and contradictory and craven it's because they have been exploited. The myth about the "grateful Ukrainian pioneer" came from the dominant English literature. Clifford Sifton and his ilk. Their conception of us. And Ukrainian-Canadians subscribed to it in the same way that a school-child faced with an exam will subscribe totally uncritically to anything the teacher says.

And so, a Ukrainian-Canadian raised within this self-conscious environment would acquire a Ukrainian identity based on a series of gratifying images not necessarily related to historical truths. A wall mural painted by a local artist of a "typical" Ukrainian village shows a charming scene of tidy thatched cottages, comely youths and maidens in colourful costume, a wise old *kobzar* plucking the strings of a *bandura* and a flock of fat geese at the edge of a scintillating pond – orderly and cheerful. Walls of church basements hold reproductions of famous paintings illustrating triumphant military heroes and manly, intrepid Cossack bands. Fables are recited about patient, long-suffering peasants, godly patriarchs and fair-haired, chivalrous noblemen. Dances choreograph the exploits of anti-Polish bandits and the *joie de vivre* of free-spirited mountain folk. Anthems, hymns, and eulogies celebrate the ancient and on-going thirst for national liberation and the sacrifices made for the cause. Women labour over cooking, sewing, and egg-painting to produce tokens of their esteem for the ancestors' genius. Laments are heard for the abandoned fruit orchards, the broken lovers' trysts, and the forgotten conviviality of the natal village. References are made to the Ukrainian Soul, Ukrainian Blood, and Ukrainian Destiny which theoretically unite all Ukrainians in a common purpose. Membership is mobilized around loyalist mottoes: "Native language in every parish!" "In every Ukrainian home also a Ukrainian press!" "A Ukrainian Patriarchate for the Ukrainian Church!"[467] Speaking for the Canadian-born, a speaker declares:

> The Ukraine is alive because we are alive and active. We, the descendants of the honest people of the Ukraine. We are demanding freedom and human rights for the Ukrainian people, even though we have never set our eyes on the land of our ancestors. Its geography is mapped in our hearts.[468]

That such idealistic images may bear little relation to Ukrainian social reality and even less to the here-and-now of Ukrainian-Canadian life is irrelevant to the person subscribing to them. It has always been easier to derive dignity and self-respect from an agreeable mythology passively received than to struggle actively for them through the discouraging muck of reality. Besides, demonstrably few others outside the community are concerned about the two-fold threat to Ukrainian identity from Russification in the old country and Americanization in the new; if it takes a sentimental, self-indulgent memory, and an inaccurate, distorted representation to preserve that identity and uphold the authority of the leadership, so, apparently, be it.

The question is, can the notion and practice of multiculturalism be anything but misconceived and misdirected when derived from such historical mystifications? For instance, since Ukrainian-Canadians are as much divided by class, politics, and religion as they are united by a shared ancestry, the effort to integrate them as a racially cohesive group into the Canadian middle-class mainstream is likely to be frustrated. If the cultural heritage that is celebrated and objectified has not been and is not in fact the culture of the people's everyday practice, then attempts to introduce it as an element of a common Canadian culture will be futile. If the "spiritual content" of Ukrainian-Canadians' lives has less to do with identification with the exploits of redoubtable Cossacks along the Dnipro some time ago than with the values and attitudes of North American contemporaries, then counting on the "honest conviction of the government circles that depriving the national entities of their language and cultural values only acts to the detriment of Canada"[469] is wishful thinking. If a Ukrainian-Canadian suspects or is aware that the history of the Ukraine has been characterized as much by ignominy as by glory, and that the society his or her parents or grandparents emigrated from was often humiliating as well as civilized, then the assumption that the honouring of and taking pride from a romanticized heritage will release the "creative energies" of Ukrainian-Canadians is tenuous.

Furthermore, a doctrine of multiculturalism which avoids confronting the nature and extent of assimilation is bound to be largely fanciful and irrelevant. The rhetoric may be reassuring and supportive of the idea of cultural retention but that doesn't make it conformable to reality. It is all very well for Prime Minister Pierre Trudeau to point out that "national unity, if it is to mean anything in a deeply personal sense, must be founded on confidence in one's own individual identity." And for John Munro, minister responsible for multiculturalism, to acknowledge that "much of the richness and vitality of our economic and social life is due to the energy of the many different cultural and racial groups that have made Canada their home." But the language is indefinite – unity, identity, richness, energy – and only begs questions. Unity around what? Identity as who? Confidence in what? Energy in what sense? In principle, the postulation is valid. In real life the question remains: is Ukrainian-Canadian an identity?

In a study published in 1971 of the "Ethnic Identification and Attitudes of University Students of Ukrainian Descent" at the University of Alberta, 93.8 percent of whom were Canadian-born, several findings relating to the question of Ukrainian cultural retention are noted. The majority of students were second-generation Canadian and nearly one quarter had one parent who was not exclusively of Ukrainian origin. Less than half the students were still members of a Ukrainian church. The majority were raised in homes where both Ukrainian and English were used, less than half had attended a Ukrainian evening or Sunday school, and, except for communication with relatives, English was their primary language. Over 90 percent subscribed to no Ukrainian periodical and had not read a single Ukrainian book during the previous year. While most of them could name Taras Shevchenko as a famous Ukrainian poet, less than 9 percent could name at least one of the major Ukrainian-Canadian organizations. Less than 20 percent claimed membership in any Ukrainian organization; 52.8 percent identified themselves as Canadians, 42.8 percent as Canadian-Ukrainian or Canadian of Ukrainian origin and 4 percent as Ukrainian. Of those married, 44 percent were married to non-Ukrainians; 71.5 percent felt that the status of Ukrainian-Canadians was at least "good" and 69.8 percent felt that assimilation is inevitable (although not necessarily desirable). Although assimilation into Anglo-Saxon norms was rejected, 92 percent felt that Ukrainian-Canadians should assimilate into a new Canadian identity. Conclusion:

> It is clear that, on the whole, assimilation into the dominant (British) linguistic-cultural group and the corresponding alienation from one's own minority group do increase with the number of generations born in Canada.[470]

There are further findings – 94.6 percent wished Ukrainian to be offered in school as a subject and 56.4 percent stated that they intend to teach their children Ukrainian – and another conclusion:

> The majority of students prefer neither an "ethnic ghetto" nor complete assimilation into the dominant Anglo-Saxon group, but an integration into a multicultural Canadian society.[471]

But these are statements of preferences, arising after the fact of perceptible, measurable, and definable assimilation patterns. The question remains: preferences aside, is there an identifiable Ukrainian-Canadian identity to incorporate into the ideal of a multicultural nation?

Let the surveyed students stand for my generation, the second Canadian-born one. English is our mother tongue. Our understanding of the Ukrainian language is imperfect and our speech even worse. (If we are successful writers, speakers, teachers, actors, and editors, it's because we have mastered the English language and excelled as members of an Anglophone community.) Not many of us bother going to church regularly, still less to a Ukrainian one and, when we do bother to observe an ethnic, religious festival, it's by means of a sentimental flurry at Christmas and Easter. We are ignorant of and indifferent to Ukrainian history. We don't feel prejudiced against as Ukrainians and have better things to do with our time than participate in an ethnic organization blathering on about "discrimination" and "rights." We feel as Canadian as, and sometimes even more Canadian than, the next guy and, even if we aren't in the ruling class, we don't feel very hard done by. We enjoy Ukrainian music, dance, crafts, and food but not much more than we enjoy Chinese food and classical ballet and much less than American movies and rock 'n' roll. The national origin of the person we marry is immaterial to our well being, and the ethnocentric value of running a "Ukrainian" home is inconsequential, compared to our, women's, need to be out in the real world of Canadian society. We identify our needs, ambitions, ethics, and biases as consonant with North American experience, not as semi-mystical vestiges of a genetic memory from a Galician village. Our political loyalties are to a Canadian future, and our various ideologies arise from an analysis of the time and place we actually inhabit. We do not deny we descend from Ukrainian nationals but that only describes us; it does not prescribe a Ukrainian way-of-being. Our foreparents came here to deflect their issue from a Ukrainian fate, to redirect us towards a Canadian one and so here we are: purposeful and at home in Canada.

How, then, is the "Ukrainian fact" to be discerned in the likes of us? Even if all multiculturalist dreams came true and we were to learn Ukrainian as a second or third language, to assemble a refuse of Ukrainianism in our apartments, to support the Ukrainian Canadian Committee as well as the United Fund, and to be appointed to the board of directors of the Bank of Montreal alongside McTavish and Plouffe, what would this prove? It would prove only, it seems to me, that we dabble in Ukrainian refinements as others dabble in Eastern philosophies, say; a way to live as more cultured and public people while committed to the deadly serious game of "making it" in the "Canadian fact." To "'think and act Canadian' is difficult to define," says Dr. Manoly Lupul,[472] deploring the non-involvement of most Ukrainian-Canadians in ethnic organizational work. But, compared to the difficulty of defining Ukrainian thoughts and acts, it is simplicity itself: when I listen to CBC, take a flight from Edmonton to Vancouver, join a union, order a pizza, or send Christmas cards, I am acting concretely, precisely, and confirmedly as a Canadian; when I wonder who to vote for, protest the economic hegemony of eastern Canada, daydream about a trip to Mexico, and devise schemes to save money, I am thinking typically, recognizably, and uniquely as a Canadian. Compared to this complex and vivid variety of Canadian experience (it certainly isn't just "British"), the remnants of my Ukrainian-derived behaviour and attitudes are scant and bloodless. Dr. Lupul goes on: "The North American climate of antipathy towards ethnicity is gradually choking us to death."[473] No one can dispute the self-evident fact of it, of course: global millions as well as Ukrainian-Canadians are being Coca-Cola-ized out of cultural singularity into the mass culture merchandized by American enterprise. The point is, I have yet to come across a convincing description from the multiculturalists of a Ukrainian-Canadian ethnicity that is anything more than a list of artifact-souvenirs and concert items and the ragtags of a language spoken hoarsely at the perimeters of the cities, as the towns and villages close up shop. This is not to disparage the souvenirs and ragtags. It is only to wonder: if this is all that my ethnicity has to offer against the irresistible and sensational content of the dominant culture then it hasn't got a chance. Then there isn't anything to "choke to death." The emotions and moods, the ethics and prejudices, the gestures and habits that bespoke a Ukrainian-Canadian and only a Ukrainian-Canadian expired quietly some time ago, when they laid down the hardtop on Highway 36 to Edmonton and the curtain closed on the very last production of *Oi Ne Khody Hrytsiu* in the Shepenitz Hall. They didn't even bother to take their dishes home.

It is with some skepticism, then, that one reacts to assertions that we ethnics, miraculously, live in times when we can still choose to resist what's already been done.

> When will [pro-assimilationists] learn that all people helped to open up the West, and their descendants to the nth generation will be proud of their ancestral roots and will not be shamed into an amorphous identity which ignores those roots.[474]

But simple pride of origin hasn't prevented most of us from reproducing ourselves as thoroughly typical Canadians, by all the measures that count: the way we make our living, the way we live as families, the way we live in social relationships to others, and the way we spend our money. If these ways are "amorphous," then the impalpable idealism of ethnic pride is in comparison a whistle in the wind.

> The ethnic identification . . . takes into consideration not only the bare symbolical interpretation but also its natural value. What the son considered to be an ideology, that was forced upon him by his father, the grandson regards highly as an information medium and a treasured history.[475]

If this is true – the principle of the third generation interest – it is because the grandchild, thoroughly at home in Canada and the beneficiary of the establishment's liberalism towards white middle-class arrivals at least, is free of the psychological equivocation between shame and defiance which so bedevilled the intervening generation and is free, then, to identify with information and a history that are finally unthreatening. The pursuit of ethnic information and the perusal of Ukrainian history are intellectual activities a Ukrainian-Canadian can now undertake without running the risk of confusing his or her identity with that of "bohunk" predecessors. It's not so portentous after all to be proud of one's ancestral Ukrainianness now that there is no organic Ukrainianness to haunt and scandalize the establishment.

Ukrainians are now a "legitimate" group because there are no more Ukrainians. Discrimination against us is gone because we are gone. We have accepted the premises of the majority group and once we were safely assimilated we were legitimized. So, Munro is just lying when he congratulates the Ukrainians on the preservation of their culture. We haven't preserved our culture! Here are a group of people who are a quarter generation away from expressing the Ukrainian culture in their daily lives; twenty-five years later they find themselves expressing it not at all in their daily lives, they go to an ethnic festival where the culture is "staged" and doesn't resemble anything like how they used to live and they are told by a lying politician that they are to be congratulated for preserving their culture. It's absurd! The political motive is to push the liberal myth that the system is once again operating for us, when all we're doing is living an idyllic memory of our past.

That said, it must also be said that there is, in my generation, a resurgence of ethnicity as identity which is not romantic or mystified and which rejects the easy notion that acculturation is the same thing as assimilation. The question also is, then: are we Ukrainian-Canadians allowed to assimilate? Whether or not to assimilate into the Canadian mainstream is not a simple decision of our will, it is also the decision of the elite which, according to the image it holds of the ethnics, will or will not allow us access to their structures. Thus, for me as for my parents, my security as a "Canadian," as middle-class, as a member of the intelligentsia, is directly dependent on the Anglo-Canadian establishment's indulgence of my social mobility; threatened or otherwise aroused, this establishment could withdraw, and has withdrawn, historically, my privileges by naming me, as my parents were named, "alien" and banished from the social contract it has struck within its own political territory. At that point, it would be irrelevant that I was socialized in much the same manner as the Anglo-Canadian bourgeoisie, that my values, attitudes, and postures were indistinguishable from theirs and my self-image profoundly associated with its aspirations and accomplishments, assumed by me as my own. In their eyes, I would be a "bohunk" and my situation suddenly determined by all the implications of the name.

It was the first Ukrainian-Canadian generation that made the point that, although they were manifestly not WASPs, neither were they "bohunks." That, although they were not allowed claim to Anglo-Canadian privileges, neither were they content to lie low in passive humility. While the compromise they struck may often seem to my generation to be nervous and overly-polite, it has provided us space in which to examine ourselves outside the glare of racism. Thus, we may luxuriate in our "ordinariness" as Canadians and yet still take account of the ways in which we are the "other," for that is also who we are as long as we are not among those classes which sit on the boards of directors of this country. For many of us, our Ukrainian-Canadian origins do describe our personality and life-style, however sentimentally or abstractly, and condition for us the nature of our family ties, some of our social activities, where some of our money is spent, and our reactions to the symbols of our ethnicity – an anthem, a prairie church, a flag. Like it or not, there does seem to be still an emotional significance in our continued attachment to the ethnic group.

Less abstractly, in these times of multiculturalism, it occurs to us that there is also political significance in the attachment: the ethnic group is now an interest group, a "lobby" as it were for those who cannot press their demands fully through class or regional or sex groupings. Ethnic consciousness is one of the ways in which we may understand our status, our legacy of wealth or poverty, our material and psychological security vis a vis other ethnic groups as well as the dominant group, our "place." Harold R. Isaacs, writing about the conditions which shape group identity, says the most "decisive" are the "political conditions in which the group identity is held, the measure of power or powerlessness that is attached to it."[476] And so, if I am really to understand my here-and-now, I have also to ask these questions (alongside the skeptical and revisionist ones) about my ethnicity: how much power and what kind do Ukrainian-Canadians have? How has this changed over the time of our being here? How do I see myself in relation to others? And, finally, where is home?

Home, as the saying goes, is the place where, when you go there, they've got to take you in. And so it is that no matter the alienation or mistrust or crossed purposes between generations, there is one thing that makes of the ethnic group a collective: we are all related. I may be denounced by the group, insulted, and ostracized, I may even leave it behind, but nobody can ever say I don't belong.

Not only is there a good deal of vagary around the idea of a viable ethnicity, there is also confusion between ethnic consciousness and political power. As long as the discussion is limited to the "spirit" of pride and unity and the "inspiration" or "dream" of free association and enriched diversity, etc., there is no problem. Such notions, inasmuch as they have more to say about the society we'd all like to live in rather than one we actually inhabit, do not have to pass the test of grubby reality. The problem begins with a statement like this:

> The Canadian type of unity rests on partnership in the enjoyment of freedom and fundamental equality and on power

> that stems from the solidarity of free men and groups
> appreciative of the political, legal and social guarantees which
> allow them to develop their potentialities freely, to worship and
> to create. . . .[477]

This is not political science, this is patter. Any basic text of sociology or economics will devastate the cosy assumption that Canadian society is organized around the "fundamental equality" of its vertically-positioned citizenry, the "solidarity" of its fractious classes, races, and sexes, and the "guarantees" that a northern Alberta Métis, for example, will develop potentialities as freely as Upper Canada College's class of '77. More to the point, the assumption is made that the freedom of a group to be its ethnic self is the same thing as "power" of that group. While it is true, as many Ukrainian-Canadians are quick to point out, that the cultural regimentation of an authoritarian state like the Soviet Union is anti-pathetical to individual self-determination, it does not follow that the reverse is *ipso facto* true. It's perfectly conceivable, indeed it's a fact of life these days, that a multicultural extravaganza may coexist with the familiar old inequities and swindles of the Canadian "system." An interviewee said,

> In theory, we were always free and welcome. But in practice,
> let's face it, the Anglo-Saxon has been supreme right across
> Canada and doesn't want to share power with the Francophone
> culture, let alone with the rest of us.

Budgeting for language training and showcases of Ukrainian culture is one, unbegrudged thing. A monopolistic and directorial power group voluntarily liquidating itself so the power can be spread around is another thing and not, God knows, what the minister of multiculturalism has in mind. "Multiculturalism," John Munro has said, "was seen as a way to build a more tolerant, compassionate Canadian community in which all cultures are respected. . . . The vertical mosaic will only be changed by changing the attitudes that keep it vertical." Anyone who believes that that is the way political change is effected, who believes that the Ukrainian-Canadian community en masse will get its fair share of political power through the simple exercise of winning affection for its *pysanky* and Ukrainian-language kindergartens, is in for a surprise.

The existing political structure can accommodate a wide variety of demands based on plugging menacing holes. It came up with unemployment insurance, Opportunities for Youth, the Bi- and Bi-Commission, the Royal Commission on the Status of Women, and, now, multiculturalism, which Charles Lynch interprets to mean that "the government didn't really mean to offend assorted European groupings with the assertion of the French fact, and is seeking to make amends."[478] A Ukrainian-Canadian would do well to review the history of the other "amendments" the government has made and discover to what extent Canada's youth, unorganized workers, women, citizens of Chicoutimi, and the family of Nelson Small Legs Jr. have experienced a meaningful change in their conditions of life. And then ask the proponents of multiculturalism if the icing on the cake that is "compassion" and "tolerance" will serve anybody who isn't securely installed somewhere in the snuggery of the middle-class.

> The contradiction between the ideal model of Canadian society as a mosaic, and the reality of major social inequalities . . . may lead us to ask whether the ideal of a mosaic is not a beneficial model for the two charter groups (Anglo-Saxons and Québècois) to espouse.[479]

And, for that matter, for ethnic leaders to espouse. Nobody for whom the "system" seems to be working well enough likes to look a contradiction in the eye.

The ultimate impotence of multiculturalism to change significantly the status and material condition of ethnics is implied, then, in the general reluctance to examine ethnics as members of socio-economic classes rather than of a self-contained culture. The 1971 survey of University of Alberta students, for instance, shows that for all intents and purposes they are already culturally assimilated and do not feel culturally oppressed or disadvantaged. But when one looks at the non-cultural descriptions of their status, it's another story. Almost half came from families with four or more children and 69.3 percent had parents earning less than $9000 annually. The majority came from farm and labour backgrounds (60.8 percent) and in an overwhelming number of cases their parents had never attended university. The Faculty of Education was the preferred choice of enrollment – half the female students were enrolled there – reflecting perhaps the Ukrainian-Canadian perception that teaching is still just about as far as they can go. (Considering that university students are the future elite of a community, one may well ask what the statistics will show about the income, occupation, and lifestyle of all those who didn't go to university.) The question is: would any of these statistics be changed by, say, the introduction of Ukrainian-language schooling or the students' education in Ukrainian history? Not likely. The oppression and exploitation that the majority of Ukrainian-Canadians experience is economic –"We are tired of being janitors in the corridors of power!" – and the agitation of the ethnic elite for more CBC programs and handicraft instruction is just so much prettification.

But there are those who are making their demands from a consciousness of their socio-economic powerlessness and of the potential political clout they have as an economic group united with others in the same position. Take, for instance, the 1975 provincial election in Ontario and the ridings of Downsview, Oakwood, Dovercourt, and Bellwoods. All had candidates of Italian origin representing various political parties. All elected those who had been active in community organizing, union organizing, and organizing injured workers as opposed to the more conventional cultural and ethnic organizations. Bellwoods riding was the most dramatic example of this switch where a wealthy businessman, Elio Madonia, came in a poor third behind the NDP winner, in spite of his heavy expenses and his support from other Italian businessmen. Take the native people who are resisting the label of "ethnic," and insisting instead that their fight for a better deal from white society is part and parcel of the wider struggle of all the poor and exploited against the "haves" of whatever race or culture. To go the way of other "ethnics" would mean

> they must see their culture as a minority culture reserved for ethnic activities which don't jeopardize the political and social status quo. . . . By becoming an ethnic culture and an ethnic people, the heritage of the native people is removed from having any fundamental impact on the daily order of our society. It is turned into a private observance brought out for the odd public display. Ethnicity turns a culture into a ghostly entertainment. . . . Nor can the immigrant farmer and labourer come to feel truly at home in the West, that this is his land, until he builds a new society dedicated to his dreams and not the dreams of those who brought him here. The immigrant farmer and labourer has yet to become a founding people. Up to now they have been pioneering workhorses in somebody else's house.[480]

Take the statements of some delegates to the Ukrainian-Canadian Students' Union Congress that "rather than working and building around government institutions we should start at the base of those institutions, i.e., the whole elite structure of our society" for "we are in a struggle for total existence, and all elements of our existence are political questions."[481] And the point of view of the Ukrainian-Canadian paper, Student:

> Multiculturalism as it stands presently does not seek to alter the structural foundations of the total social system but merely attempts to introduce reform within one particular dimension – treatment of its cultural minorities. It accepts the basic values engendered by a modern social system based on the capitalist mode of economic activity, i.e. the values of private enterprise, individualism and achievement. If cultural pluralism is sufficiently legitimized, each individual's opportunities for social

mobility would no longer be determined by ascribed characteristics, but by his abilities and achievements.[482]

Multiculturalism, then, is Business As Usual.

In the end, it is not surprising that the major, indeed, overwhelming emphasis of multiculturalists (ethnics and otherwise) has been on the cultural front of the power struggle. From the elite politicians' point of view nothing could be easier to negotiate. From the ethnic leaders' point of view, it's a gentlemanly way to get into the club. As Charles Lynch rather sarcastically points out, there's no harm done by institutionalizing ethnic tokenism:

> Hyphenated Canadians are as good as any other kind, and perhaps the Old Folks at Home will be gratified to know that their folkways, many of which they have cheerfully abandoned, are being perpetuated in the New World.[483]

Certainly the ruling class isn't likely to shake in its boots at the prospect of an ethnic aroused against the effrontery of being "deprived of the consolation of speaking and reading the language his mother taught him."[484] This should be the least of the ethnics' worries. The act of speaking Ukrainian four generations after immigration will not bring back the whole way of life and the whole communities subsumed within Anglo-American technological civilization and will not guarantee the collective dignity and security of people forced to live by the skin of their economic teeth.

> In convincing the Ukrainian-Canadian worker that his own social mobility is limited by cultural origins, his interest may be aroused. In providing services to him from the roots of his own community then there is a definite need created for him to return and develop his culture. But this as a strategy calls into question the structural foundations of the entire society; it threatens the hegemony of the ruling elite in the Canadian community.[485]

Revolution is not a tea party. The retrieval of a culture from the clutches of The Man is not like eating cake.

It's Ukrainian Day at the Vegreville Ukrainian Festival in June 1975. I wander among the booths set up in the recreation hall – it's a bazaar! – and realize that, these days, anybody can be a Ukrainian. (It's implied that someone will want to be.) Hot kobassa – the smell will always make me salivate – on a stick. Middle-aged women demonstrating how a *pysanka* is made. Teenagers flogging T-shirts: Drink Molson's Ukrainian! Kiss me, I'm Ukrainian! Just outside the open doors, the crowd passes through the midway; kids in Ukrainian-style, machine-embroidered shirts ride on the ferris wheel eating popcorn. I look for Slavic features in their faces, a flaring cheekbone or a dusky complexion underneath the wild hair and Maybelline mascara. At a booth of old photographs, "Taking Root in a New Land," I peer at the picture of a woman and child standing stoically in front of their "home," a few slender logs propped upright under a mass of grasses and branches, and try to find my own face in her inscrutable expression.

The program begins. The opening remarks are in Ukrainian, followed by a much-abbreviated English version. "Such days as today are very valuable for the patriotism of this country, etc." We stand for the national anthems. First the Ukrainian nationalist one, "The Ukraine Is Still Not Dead" (a rather negative way of putting it, I am thinking), and I am amazed yet again by the capacity of these people to be moved so artlessly and genuinely by the idea of the liberation of a country they have never seen.

> We will lay down our bodies, our souls,
> For our freedom.
> And we will show we are brothers
> Of Cossack blood.

Then we sing O *Canada* and their commitment to these words is no less sincere. For the first time in my life, I find this peculiar. I have been fifteen years gone from this community, fifteen years spent in uptown Canada learning my way around editorial offices and French restaurants, and I drop back in now like a tourist. Ah, yes, the hyphenated Canadian. I remember another time and another place. Vats of *holubtsi* in the hall kitchen, incense curling around my nose in the cathedral, the Jew's harp vibrating in the mouth of Baba. "*Oi dyvchena, shumy hai.*" We sit down. The Two Hills Dance Club dances a welcome for us, bearing bread and salt. I watch the old people watching them. Did the dancing ever look like this back in the *selo*? Young men dance the *arkan*, shouting and stamping in white shirts and tight, wide belts, sexy leg-kicks, and hip-twists. Very nice. I always did want to be a boy so I could dance like that, so I could dance too like the Indian chief in the rain dance. A young girl in the costume of Poltava comes forward and sings a mournful song, "*Ridna Maty Moya*" (Dear Mother of Mine). People wipe their eyes. More singing, more dancing, a couple of speeches. Applause. The end. We file out, "Freedom for Moroz!" leaflets under our feet. Before getting back on the highway, we eat hamburgers at Chico's Drive-In. "Chico" comes from Two Hills, originally.

It is the 1975 SUSK Congress. The discussion is all about language, the Ukrainian language, and how to learn it, or keep it, and why, and, well, why not? "I quit Ukrainian school. I never even learned the alphabet because the text was so boring." Confessions of a lapsed ethnic. Petitions of the reborn. "We are no longer just *pyrohy* eaters!" "Once we have our own language again, we can develop a Ukrainian psyche and Ukrainian impulses!" "We have to get out of a ghetto mentality." There is talk of Ukrainian private schools, an Institute of Ukrainian Studies (to embarrass Moscow!), teacher training institutes. There is a query about how to get the mass of Ukrainian-Canadians into at least one of the 103 Ukrainian ethno-cultural organizations in Alberta. There is conciliatory bravado: "You don't have to be Ukrainian to have a Ukrainian soul."

I go to the Taras Shevchenko concert sponsored by the Ukrainian Canadian Committee at the Jubilee Auditorium.

Everyone stands for the reading of Shevchenko's "Testament" – "When I die, O, bury me . . ." – as though this poem, too, were now a Ukrainian-Canadian anthem. A young man recites "My Thoughts" in a declamatory, rhetorical manner rather alarming in one so young. There follow songs, more poems, and a learned discourse on the "sources of Shevchenko's universality." The only English spoken is by the Honourable Bert Hohol, Minister of Higher Education – one suspects he doesn't speak Ukrainian very well, or not well enough for this sombre assembly – and the proceedings close with "The Ukraine Is Still Not Dead." I wait for O Canada but it doesn't come. In spite of the ethnic costumes, the harmonies of choirs, the portrait of Shevchenko festooned with beams of light, this has been a dour occasion. These Ukrainian-Canadians, it seems, do not take their folk heroes lightly.

I go to a folk concert at the hall of the Association of United Ukrainian Canadians. Straight-backed chairs, ordinary clothes, middle-aged and elderly audience. A plaque in the lobby indicates the hall is dedicated to the Canadian Communist, Mathew Shatulsky – "He Served the People" – and a big, bronze bust of him sits beside the stage inside. Otherwise, there are no pictures or decorations. The master of ceremonies introduces the program in Ukrainian, explaining that, after the last such concert, old people complained there had been too much English spoken which they didn't understand. O Canada, junior, intermediate, and senior dancers, women's choir, men's choir, mixed choir, duets and solos, children's orchestra of mandolins and accordians. So far, so Ukrainian-Canadian. Then a young girl sings "Whenever I Feel Afraid" from The King and I, and, for the final item, the men's choir sings an anarchist song from the Spanish Civil War.

A tourist I came, a tourist I leave. Like thousands and thousands of Ukrainian-Canadians of my generation and beyond, I only travel these ethnic sideroads when I need to find a breathing space awhile, away from the fumes of the cosmopolitan metropolis and all its works. But, metropolis is what I return to when it's time to go home.

It is, after all, where Baba meant to have me live, when she mortgaged her life so mine would be deflected as much from the CPR quarter as from the *kolkhoz*, near Tulova, in Galicia. When I look at the remnants of the cultural reality left from her history and finger them like curios in a Tijuana souvenir shop, it's not that I'm ungrateful or even unmoved. I can store them in a trunk, along with my high school yearbooks and my mother's wedding dress. But if I tried to use them, they would fall apart in my hands. I have other skills now and assignments to fulfill that Baba never dreamed of. Not that she wouldn't be pleased.

If there's any way at all that I carry on from where she left off, it won't be with her language, because I never knew it, nor with her habits, because they make no sense, nor with her faith, because I have lost it, nor with her satisfaction, because my needs have changed. It will be perhaps with the thing she had no choice in bequeathing: her otherness. As the alien, the bohunk, the second-class citizen, and the ethnic, she passed on to me the gift of consciousness of one who stands outside the hegemonistic centre, and sees where the real world ends and the phantasma of propaganda begins. As for the generation between us, my parents, her children, they gave me the possibility of action as one who is of this place and this time, free of the ghosts of diffidence. Seeing clearly and acting surely: the journey from Tulova ends here.

Notes

Chapter One

1. J. Skwarok, "The Ukrainian Settlers and Their Schools" (unpublished thesis, University of Alberta, 1962), p. 8.
2. Ibid.
3. Ukrainian Pioneers' Association of Alberta, *Ukrainians in Alberta* (Edmonton: Ukrainian News Publishers, 1975), p. 48.
4. Ivan Franko, *Poems and Stories*, trans. John Weir (Toronto: Ukrainska Knyha, 1956), p. 66.
5. Vladimir J. Kaye, *Early Ukrainian Settlements in Canada* (Toronto: University of Toronto Press, 1969), p. 322.
6. James G. MacGregor, *Vilni Zemli: The Ukrainian Settlement in Alberta* (Toronto: McClelland and Stewart, 1969), p. 78.
7. Ibid., p. 77.
8. Howard Palmer, ed., *Immigration and the Rise of Multiculturalism* (Toronto: Copp Clark, 1975), pp. 35, 38.
9. John A. Melnyk, "A Typology of Ukrainian-Canadian Folklore" (unpublished thesis, University of Alberta), p. 71.

Chapter Two

10. MacGregor, *Vilni Zemli*, p. 96.
11. Peter Krawchuk, *Shevchenko in Canada* (Calgary, Glenbow-Alberta Institute),p. 13.
12. Ukrainian Pioneers' Association, *Ukrainians in Alberta*, p. 49.
13. MacGregor, *Vilni Zemli*, p. 134.
14. Kaye, *Early Ukrainian Settlements in Canada*, pp. 324-5.
15. Ibid., pp. 330-1.
16. Ibid., pp. 338-9.
17. Rev. Nestor Dmytriew, "Canadian Ruthenia," *Ukrainian-Canadian Review* (1974), p. 35.
18. S. Woodsworth, *Strangers Within Our Gates* (Toronto: University of Toronto Press, 1972), p. 185.
19. Kaye, *Early Ukrainian Settlements in Canada*, p. 327.
20. Charles Young, *The Ukrainian-Canadians* (Toronto: Thomas Nelson & Sons, 1931), pp. 50-1.
21. MacGregor, *Vilni Zemli*, p. 88.
22. Young, *The Ukrainian-Canadians*, p. 53.

23. Ibid., p. 101.
24. Ibid.
25. Alexander Royick, "Lexical Borrowings in Alberta Ukrainian" (unpublished thesis, University of Alberta, 1965), p. 2.
26. Paul Yuzyk, *The Ukrainians in Manitoba* (Toronto: University of Toronto Press, . 1953), pp. 205-6.
27. Ukrainian Pioneers' Association, *Ukrainians in Alberta*, p. 48.
28. Melnyk, "A Typology of Ukrainian-Canadian Folklore," p. 210.

Chapter Three

29. MacGregor, *Vilni Zemli*, p. 105.
30. Palmer, *Immigration and the Rise of Multiculturalism*, p. 45.
31. Woodsworth, *Strangers Within Our Gates*, p. 239.
32. Palmer, *Immigration and the Rise of Multiculturalism*, p. 49.
33. Vegreville *Observer*, September 22, 1909.
34. Palmer, *Immigration and the Rise of Multiculturalism*, p. 56.
35. T.C. Byrne, "The Ukrainian Community in North Central Alberta" (unpublished thesis, University of Alberta, 1937), pp. 1-2.
36. Woodsworth, *Strangers Within Our Gates*, p. 112.
37. Kaye, *Early Ukrainian Settlements in Canada*, p. 343.
38. Young, *The Ukrainian-Canadians*, pp. 287-8.
39. Vegreville *Observer*, April 21, 1909.
40. Ibid., July 29, 1908.
41. Ibid., July 15, 1931.
42. Ibid., May 4, 1910.
43. Edmonton *Journal*, November 26, 1920.
44. Peter Bryce, *The Value to Canada of the Continental Immigrant* (Ottawa, 1928), p. 20.
45. Ibid., p. 23.
46. Remarks by Dr. W. Kushnir, *First Ukrainian Canadian Congress* (Winnipeg: The Ukrainian Canadian Committee, 1943).

Chapter Four

47. Yuzyk, *The Ukrainians in Manitoba*, p. 187.
48. *Friends in Need, The WBA Story: A Canadian Epic in Fraternalism* (Winnipeg: WBA of Canada, 1972), p. 63.
49. Edmonton *Bulletin*, October 29, 1914.
50. William Rodney, *Soldiers of the International: A History of the Communist Party of . Canada 1919-1929* (Toronto: University of Toronto Press, 1968), p. 12.
51. Helen Potrebenko, *Streets of Gold* (Vancouver: New Star Books).
52. Ukrainian Pioneers' Association, *Ukrainians in Alberta*, p. 43.
53. Yuzyk, *The Ukrainians in Manitoba*, p. 187.
54. Potrebenko, *Streets of Gold*.
55. Palmer, *Immigration and the Rise of Multiculturalism*, p. 189.
56. Edmonton *Bulletin*, November 28, 1914.
57. Vegreville *Observer*, January 3, 1917.

58. Ibid., January 23,1918.
59. Ibid., March 12, 1919.
60. *Family Herald*, June 21, 1916.
61. Yuzyk, *The Ukrainians in Manitoba*, p. 188.
62. Vegreville *Observer*, January 30, 1918.
63. Ibid., March 12, 1919.
64. Ukrainian Pioneers' Association, *Ukrainians in Alberta*, p. 214.
65. Rodney, *Soldiers of the International*, p. 15.
66. Ivan Avakumovic, *The Communist Party in Canada* (Toronto: McClelland and Stewart, 1975), p. 9.
67. *Friends in Need*, p. 64.
68. Rodney, *Soldiers of the International*, p. 17.
69. Martin Robin, *Radical Politics and Canadian Labour* (Calgary: Glenbow-Alberta Institute), p. 165.
70. Ibid.
71. Rodney, *Soldiers of the International*, p. 18.
72. Robin, *Radical Politics and Canadian Labour*, p. 165.
73. Vegreville *Observer*, June 27, 1917.
74. Avakumovic, *The Communist Party in Canada*, pp. 14-15.

Chapter Five
75. Young, *The Ukrainian-Canadians*, p. 98.
76. Ibid., p. 63
77. Ibid.
78. Ibid., p. 64.
79. Potrebenko, *Streets of Gold*.
80. Young, *The Ukrainian-Canadians*, p. 212.
81. Ibid., p. 219.
82. Ibid., p. 224.
83. Ibid., p. 231.
84. G.N. Emery, "Methodist Missions Among the Ukrainians," *Alberta Historical Review* (*Spring* 1971), p. 11.

Chapter Six
85. Young, *The Ukrainian-Canadians*, p. 179.
86. *Mundare Yesterday and Today*. Dedication souvenir of the Saints Peter and Paul Ukrainian Catholic Church, Mundare, Alberta, June 1969, p. 152.
87. Ukrainian Pioneers' Association, *Ukrainians in Alberta*, p. 54.
88. Young, *The Ukrainian-Canadians*, p. 191.
89. Ibid.
90. Ukrainian Pioneers' Association, *Ukrainians in Alberta*, p. 182.
91. Ibid., p. 185.
92. Skwarok, "The Ukrainian Settlers and Their Schools," p. 111.
93. Woodsworth, *Strangers Within Our Gates*, p. 244.
94. Ibid., p. 240.

436

95. MacGregor, *Vilni Zemli*, p. 214.
96. Skwarok, "The Ukrainian Settlers and Their Schools," p. 27.
97. Vegreville *Observer*, September 10, 1913.
98. Skwarok, "The Ukrainian Settlers and Their Schools," p. 108.
99. Ibid., p. 109.
100. MacGregor, *Vilni Zemli*, p. 231.
101. Ukrainian Pioneers' Association, *Ukrainians in Alberta*, p. 191.
102. Young, *The Ukrainian-Canadians*, p. 179.
103. Ukrainian Pioneers' Association, *Ukrainians in Alberta*, p. 193.
104. Ibid.
105. *Mundare Yesterday and Today*, p. 119.
106. Municipal District Records from Two Hills Area (71.3). Provincial Archives of Alberta.
107. Ibid.
108. Ibid.
109. Ibid.
110. Ibid.
111. Young, *The Ukrainian-Canadians*, p. 196.
112. Skwarok, *"The Ukrainian Settlers and Their Schools,"* p. 136.
113. John Charyk, *The Little White Schoolhouse* (Saskatoon: Western Producer, 1984).
114. Ukrainian Pioneers' Association, *Ukrainians in Alberta*, p. 187.
115. Municipal District Records from Two Hills Area (71.3). Provincial Archives of Alberta.
116. Ukrainian Pioneers' Association, *Ukrainians in Alberta*, p. 198.
117. William Darcovich, *Ukrainians in Canada: The Struggle to Retain Their Identity* (Ottawa: Ukrainian Self-Reliance League, 1967), p. 26.
118. Ukrainian Pioneers' Association, *Ukrainians in Alberta*, p. 85.
119. Ibid., pp. 88-9.

Chapter Seven
120. Skwarok, "The Ukrainian Settlers and Their Schools," p. 23.
121. Vegreville *Observer*, September 6, 1933.
122. Melnyk, "A Typology of Ukrainian-Canadian Folklore," p. 126.
123. Skwarok, "The Ukrainian Settlers and Their Schools," p. 24.
124. Ibid.
125. Woodsworth, *Strangers Within Our Gates*, p. 253.
126. Byrne, *"The Ukrainian Community in North Central Alberta,"* p. 47.
127. Ibid., p. 48.
128. Ibid., p. 56.
129. MacGregor, *Vilni Zemli*, pp. 164-5.
130. *Mundare Yesterday and Today*, p. 105.
131. Ibid., pp. 112-3.
132. Ibid., p. 114.
133. Ibid.,p. 115.
134. Paul Yuzyk, "The Ukrainian Greek Orthodox Church in Canada" (unpublished

    doctoral thesis, University of Alberta), p. 82.
135. *Mundare Yesterday and Today*, p. 112.
136. Yuzyk, *"The Ukrainian Greek Orthodox Church in Canada,"* p. 89.
137. Ibid., p. 90.
138. Ibid., p. 105.
139. Ibid., p. 109-10.
140. Ibid.,p. 109.
141. Ibid., p. 116.
142. Ibid., pp. 148-9.
143. Ibid., pp. 139-41.
144. Ibid., p. 149.
145. Young, *The Ukrainian-Canadians*, p. 144.
146. Vegreville *Observer*, July 31, 1935.

Chapter Eight

147. Records from the Townhall of Two Hills (74.68). Provincial Archives of Alberta.
148. Vegreville *Observer*, August 29, 1934.
149. Ibid., January 27, 1932.
150. Records from the Townhall of Two Hills (74.68). Provincial Archives of Alberta.
151. Ibid.
152. Ibid.
153. Young, *The Ukrainian-Canadians*, p. 71.
154. Ukrainian Pioneers' Association, *Ukrainians in Alberta*, pp. 310-1.
155. Records from the Townhall of Two Hills (74.68). Provincial Archives of Alberta.
156. Young, *The Ukrainian-Canadians*, p. 269.
157. Ibid., p. 276.
158. Byrne, *"The Ukrainian Community in North Central Alberta,"* p. 96.
159. Ibid.
160. Andrew Suknaski, *3c Pulp, Vol. III*, No. 7 (October 15, 1975).
161. Records from the Townhall of Two Hills (74.68). Provincial Archives of Alberta.
162. Ukrainian Pioneers' Association, *Ukrainians in Alberta*, p.151.
163. Ibid., p. 164.
164. Ibid., p. 165.
165. Ibid.
166. Ibid., p. 166.
167. Ibid.
168. Ibid., p. 168.
169. Ibid., p. 169.
170. Ibid., pp. 168-9.
171. Olha Woycenko, "The Ukrainians in Canada," *Canada Ethnica IV* (Ottawa: 1967), pp. 70-1.
172. Ibid., p. 69.
173. M.H. Marunchak, *The Ukrainian-Canadians: A History* (Winnipeg: Ukrainian Academy of Free Sciences, 1970), p. 430.
174. *Friends in Need*, pp. 115-6.

175. Ibid., p. 125.
176. Woycenko, "The Ukrainians in Canada," p. 67.
177. Kushnir, *First Ukrainian-Canadian Congress*, p. 7.
178. Young, *The Ukrainian-Canadians*, p. 89.
179. Ibid., p. 156.
180. Vegreville *Observer*, March 14, 1917.
181. Young, *The Ukrainian-Canadians*, p. 156.
182. *Mundare Yesterday and Today*, p. 190.
183. Kushnir, *First Ukrainian-Canadian Congress*, p. 164.
184. Ibid., p. 159.

Chapter Nine
185. Marunchak, *The Ukrainian-Canadians: A History*, p. 451.
186. Vera Lysenko, *Men in Sheepskin Coats* (Toronto: Ryerson Press, 1947), p. 217.
187. Ibid.
188. Ibid., pp. 222-3.
189. Vegreville *Observer*, June 3, 1914.
190. Quoted in Peter Krawchuk, *Shevchenko in Canada*.
191. Royick, "Lexical Borrowings in Alberta Ukrainian," p. 102.
192. Melnyk, "A Typology of Ukrainian-Canadian Folklore," p.160.
193. Vegreville *Observer*, February 21, 1934.
194. Municipal District Records from Two Hills Area (71.3). Provincial Museum of Alberta.
195. Royick, "Lexical Borrowings in Alberta Ukrainian," p. 59.

Chapter Ten
196. MacGregor, *Vilni Zemli*, p. 189.
197. Ukrainian Pioneers' Association, *Ukrainians in Alberta*, p. 369.
198. Robin, *Radical Politics and Canadian Labour*, p. 44.
199. Anne B. Woywitka, "Recollections of a Union Man," *Alberta History*, Vol. 23, No. 4 (Autumn 1975), pp. 6-20.
200. Stanley Frolick, "The Hillcrest Mine Disaster," *Canadian-Ukrainian Review* (1974), pp. 32-4.
201. *Friends in Need*, p. 49.
202. Ibid., p. 47.
203. Palmer, *Immigration and the Rise of Multiculturalism*, p. 88.
204. Darcovich, *Ukrainians in Canada*, p. 32.
205. Young, *The Ukrainian-Canadians*, p. 124.
206. MacGregor, *Vilni Zemli*, p. 135.
207. Woycenko, "The Ukrainians in Canada," p. 56.
208. Marunchak, *The Ukrainian-Canadians: A History*, p. 425.
209. Woycenko, "The Ukrainians in Canada," p. 464.

Chapter Eleven
210. Byrne, "The Ukrainian Community in North Central Alberta," p.35.

211. Vegreville *Observer*, May 31, 1933.
212. Municipal District Records from Two Hills and Area (71.3). Provincial Archives of Alberta.
213. Vegreville *Observer*, November 1, 1933.
214. Records from the Townhall of Two Hills (74.68). Provincial Archives of Alberta.
215. Ibid.
216. Ibid.
217. Ibid.
218. Ibid.
219. Ibid.
220. Woycenko, "The Ukrainians in Canada," p. 205.
221. Avakumovic, *The Communist Party in Canada*, p. 77.
222. Woywitka, "Recollections of a Union Man," p. 17.
223. Potrebenko, *Streets of Gold*.
224. Vegreville *Observer*, December 21, 1932.
225. Woywitka, "Recollections of a Union Man," p. 18.
226. Potrebenko, *Streets of Gold*.
227. Woywitka, "Recollections of a Union Man," p. 19.
228. Vegreville *Observer*, March 7, 1934.
229. Ibid., November 7, 1934.
230. Ibid., November 14, 1934.
231. Ibid., November 21, 1934.
232. Ibid.
233. Ibid., April 29, 1931.
234. Ibid., April 22, 1931.
235. Palmer, *Immigration and the Rise of Multiculturalism*, p. 106.
236. Vegreville *Observer*, December 12, 1934.
237. Ibid.
238. Ibid.
239. Ibid.
240. Ibid., June 12,1935.

Chapter Twelve
241. Ivan L. Rudnytsky, "The Role of the Ukraine in Modern History," *The Development of the U.S.S.R.*, Donald Treadgold, ed. (Seattle: University of Washington Press, 1964), p. 225.
242. Arthur E. Adams, "The Awakening of the Ukraine," Ibid., p. 231.
243. Young, *The Ukrainian-Canadians*, pp. 165-6.
244. Potrebenko, *Streets of Gold*.
245. Charles Lipton, *The Trade Union Movement in Canada* (Toronto: NC Press, 1973), p. 125.
246. Franko, *Poems and Stories*, p. 15.
247. Ibid., p. 53.
248. Percival Cundy and Clarence A. Manning, *Ivan Franko: Selected Poems* (New York: Philosophical Library, 1948), pp. 97-8.

249. Franko, *Poems and Stories*, p. 61.
250. Cundy and Manning, *Ivan Franko: Selected Poems*, p. 181.
251. Franko, *Poems and Stories*, p. 47.
252. Cundy and Manning, *Ivan Franko: Selected Poems*, p. 104.
253. Ibid., p. 84.
254. Franko, *Poems and Stories*, p. 39.
255. Ibid., p. 44.
256. Cundy and Manning, *Ivan Franko: Selected Poems*, p. xviii.
257. Ibid., p. xix.
258. Lysenko, *Men in Sheepskin Coats*, p. 223.
259. From *Rabochy Narod*, quoted in Krawchuk, *Shevchenko in Canada*, pp. 27-8.
260. C.H. Andrusyshen and Watson Kirkconnell, *The Poetical Works of Taras Shevchenko* (Toronto: University of Toronto Press, 1964), p. 330.
261. From the Greek Catholic Journal *Svitlo*, quoted in Krawchuk, *Shevchenko in Canada*, p. 69.
262. Andrusyshen and Kirkconnell, *The Poetical Works of Taras Shevchenko*, p. 150.
263. Krawchuk, *Shevchenko in Canada*, p. 68.
264. Andrusyshen and Kirkconnell, *The Poetical Works of Taras Shevchenko*, p. xvii.
265. Ibid., p. 272.
266. Orest T. Martynowych, "The Ukrainian Socialist and Working-Class Movement in Manitoba." Monograph.
267 Ibid., p. 19.
268. Avakumovic, *The Communist Party in Canada*, p. 36.
269. *Friends in Need*, p. 161.
270. Ibid., pp. 161-7.
271. Avakumovic, *The Communist Party in Canada*, p. 86.
272. Ibid., p. 120.
273. Young, *The Ukrainian-Canadians*, p. 146.
274. Yuzyk, *The Ukrainians in Manitoba*, p. 103.
275. Ibid.
276. Quoted in Rodney, *Soldiers of the International*, p. 34.
277. Ibid., p. 46.
278. *Winnipeg Free Press*, July 29, 1931.
279. Avakumovic, *The Communist Party in Canada*, p. 36.
280. *Vegreville Observer*, January 7, 1931.
281. Ibid., January 27, 1932.
282. Ibid., May 2, 1934.
283. Ibid., July 24, 1935.
284. Ibid., October 2, 1935.
285. Ibid., February 4, 1931.
286. Ibid.
287. Ibid., February 11, 1931.
288. Ibid., February 25, 1931.
289. Ibid.
290. Ibid., April 22, 1931.

291. Ibid., April 15, 1931.

292. Ibid., November 16, 1932.

293. Ibid., November 15, 1933.

294. Ibid., June 19, 1935.

295. Byrne, "The Ukrainian Community in North Central Alberta" p. 77.

296. Vegreville *Observer*, April 2, 1913.

297. Ibid., April 30, 1931.

298. Ibid., October 24, 1934.

299. Ibid., January 28, 1931.

300. Ibid., July 8, 1935.

301. Edmonton *Journal*, April 22, 1944.

302. Avakumovic, *The Communist Party in Canada*, p. 85.

303. Harry Piniuta, "Organizational Life of the Ukrainians in Canada" (unpublished thesis, University of Ottawa, 1952), p. 39.

304. Andrew Suknaski, *Suicide Notes Book II, Pulp Magazine*.

Chapter Thirteen

305. Avakumovic, *The Communist Party in Canada*, p. 199.

306. Ibid., p. 264.

307. Potrebenko, *Streets of Gold*.

308. *Friends in Need*, p. 198.

309. Yuzyk, *The Ukrainians in Manitoba*, p. 190.

310. Ibid., p. 199.

311. Ukrainian Pioneers' Association, *Ukrainians in Alberta*, p. 215.

312. Yuzyk, *The Ukrainians in Manitoba*, p. 6.

313. Ibid.,p.7.

314. Kirkconnell, *The Ukrainian-Canadians and the War*, p. 7.

315. Ibid.,p. 4.

316. Ibid., p. 5.

317. Ibid., p. 7.

318. Watson Kirkconnell, *Our Ukrainian Loyalists* (Calgary: Glenbow-Alberta Institute), p. 28.

319. Kushnir, *First Ukrainian-Canadian Congress*, p. 51.

320. Ibid., p. 50.

321. Yuzyk, *The Ukrainians in Manitoba*, p. 191.

322. Ibid., p. 190.

323. Kirkconnell, *Our Ukrainian Loyalists*, p. 7.

324. Ibid., p. 28.

325. Piniuta, "Organizational Life of the Ukrainians in Canada," p. 62.

326. Yuzyk, *The Ukrainians in Manitoba*, p. 192.

327. Edmonton *Bulletin*, February 9, 1942.

328. *Friends in Need*, p. 196.

329. Kirkconnell, *Our Ukrainian Loyalists*, p. 28.

330. *Star Weekly*, November 13, 1943.

331. Avakumovic, *The Communist Party in Canada*, p. 143.

332. Ibid., p. 140.
333. Ibid., p. 144.
334. *Canadian Tribune*, May 6, 1944.
335. *Friends in Need*, p. 209.
336. Piniuta, "Organizational Life of the Ukrainians in Canada," p. 41.
337. Ibid.,p. 38.

Chapter Fourteen

338. Yuzyk, *The Ukrainians in Manitoba*, p. 18.
339. Vegreville *Observer*, September 3, 1913.
340. Marunchak, *The Ukrainian-Canadians: A History*, p. 375.
341. Young, *The Ukrainian-Canadians*, p. 152.
342. MacGregor, *Vilni Zemli*, p. 219.
343. Kushnir, *First Ukrainian-Canadian Congress*, p. 6.
344. Marunchak, *The Ukrainian-Canadians: A History*, p. 475.
345. Edmonton *Journal*, July 11, 1928.
346. Marunchak, *The Ukrainian-Canadians: A History*, p. 396.
347. Ukrainian Pioneers' Association, *Ukrainians in Alberta*, p. 108.
348. Piniuta, "Organizational Life of the Ukrainians in Canada," p. 27.
349. Byrne, "The Ukrainian Community in North Central Alberta," p. 69.
350. Marunchak, *The Ukrainian-Canadians: A History*, p. 401.
351. Ibid., p. 402.
352. Ukrainian Pioneers' Association, *Ukrainians in Alberta*, p. 111.
353. *Mundare Yesterday and Today*, p. 144.
354. Woycenko, "The Ukrainians in Canada," p. 27.
355. Kirkconnell, *The Ukrainian-Canadians and the War*, p. 14.
356. Piniuta, "Organizational Life of the Ukrainians in Canada," p. 44.
357. Kirkconnell, *Our Ukrainian Loyalists*, p. 24.
358. Elizabeth Wangenheim, "The Ukrainians: A Case Study of the 'Third Force'" Peter
    Russell, ed., *Nationalism in Canada* (Toronto: McGraw-Hill, 1972), p. 82.
359. Kirkconnell, *Our Ukrainian Loyalists*, p. 22.
360. Potrebenko, *Streets of Gold*.
361. Kirkconnell, *Our Ukrainian Loyalists*, p. 26.
362. Kushnir, *First Ukrainian-Canadian Congress*, p. 4.
363. Ibid.
364. Ibid., p. 5.
365. Ibid.
366. Ibid., pp. 28-9.
367. Ibid., p. 28.
368. Ibid.,p. 11.
369. Ibid., p. 10.
370. Ibid., p. 29.
371. Ibid., p. 10.
372. Kirkconnell, *Our Ukrainian Loyalists*, p. 6.
373. Kirkconnell, *The Ukrainian-Canadians and the War*, pp. 15-6.

374. *Holos Spasytelya*, Ukrainian Catholic publication, private collection.
375. Piniuta, "Organizational Life of the Ukrainians in Canada," p. 59.
376. Potrebenko, *Streets of Gold*.
377. Paul Yuzyk, *Ukrainian-Canadians* (Toronto: Ukrainian-Canadian Business and Professional Federation, 1967), p. 47.
378. Kirkconnell, *Our Ukrainian Loyalists*, p. 25.
379. Ibid., p. 24.
380. Ibid.,p. 4.
381. Piniuta, "Organizational Life of the Ukrainians in Canada," p. 51.
382. Kirkconnell, *Our Ukrainian Loyalists*, p. 27.
383. Ibid.
384. Leon Trotsky, *For a Free, Independent and Soviet Ukraine*, in *Meta*, Vol. 2 (Toronto, 1975).
385. Marunchak, *The Ukrainian-Canadians: A History*, p. 407.
386. Piniuta, "Organizational Life of the Ukrainians in Canada," p. 104.
387. Kushnir, *First Ukrainian-Canadian Congress*, p. 6.
388. Martynowych, "The Ukrainian Socialist and Working-Class Movement in Manitoba," p. 22.
389. Byrne, "The Ukrainian Community in North Central Alberta," pp. 80-1.
390. Calgary *Albertan*, April 1945.
391. Ibid.
392. Calgary *Herald*, March 2, 1950.

Chapter Fifteen

393. Vegreville *Observer*, March 5, 1913
394. Ibid., August 2, 1918.
395. *Star Weekly*, November 13, 1943.
396. House of Commons *Debates*, March 26, 1945, p. 4. Speech by Anthony Hlynka, MP for Vegreville.
397. Kushnir, *First Ukrainian-Canadian Congress*, p. 90.
398. Byrne, "The Ukrainian Community in North Central Alberta," pp. 92-3.
399. Young, *The Ukrainian-Canadians*, p. 169.
400. Skwarok, "The Ukrainian Settlers and Their Schools," p. 114.
401. Marunchak, *The Ukrainian-Canadians: A History*, p. 717.
402. Darcovich, *Ukrainians in Canada*, p. 20.
403. *Mundare Yesterday and Today*, p. 135.
404. Byrne, "The Ukrainian Community in North Central Alberta," p. 61.
405. Young, *The Ukrainian-Canadians*, p. 76.
406. Edmonton *Journal*, November 26, 1920.
407. Byrne, "The Ukrainian Community in North Central Alberta," p. 93.
408. Woycenko, "The Ukrainians in Canada," p. 66.
409. Byrne, "The Ukrainian Community in North Central Alberta," p. 86.
410. Ibid., p. 86.
411. Young, *The Ukrainian-Canadians*, p. 159.
412. Lysenko, *Men in Sheepskin Coats*, pp. 240-2.

444

413. Ibid., p. 239.
414. Yuzyk, *The Ukrainians in Manitoba*, p. 208.
415. Kirkconnell, *The Ukrainian-Canadians and the War*, p. 9.
416. Young, *The Ukrainian-Canadians*, p. 281.
417. Byrne, "The Ukrainian Community in North Central Alberta," p. 97.
418. Piniuta, "Organizational Life of the Ukrainians in Canada," pp. 104-5.
419. Yuzyk, *The Ukrainians in Manitoba*, p. 208.
420. Palmer, *Immigration and the Rise of Multiculturalism*, p. 123.
421. Marunchak, *The Ukrainian-Canadians: A History*, p. 716.
422. Ibid.
423. Ibid.
424. Melnyk, "A Typology of Ukrainian-Canadian Folklore," p. 209.
425. Ibid.
426. Robert Klymasz, "Ukrainian Folklore in Canada: An Immigrant Complex in Transition" (unpublished thesis, University of Alberta), p. 127.
427. Ibid., p. 128.
428. Lysenko, *Men in Sheepskin Coats*, p. 243.
429. Kushnir, *First Ukrainian-Canadian Congress*, pp. 166-7.
430. Ibid., p. 91.
431. Ibid., p. 89.
432. Charles W. Hobart, "Adjustment of Ukrainians in Alberta: Alienation and Integration," C.J. Jaenen, *Slavs in Canada* (Edmonton: Ukrainian Free Academy, 1971), p. 70.
433. Ibid., p. 71.
434. Ibid., p. 82.

Chapter Sixteen

435. Kushnir, *First Ukrainian-Canadian Congress*, p. 6.
436. Yuzyk, *The Ukrainians in Manitoba*, p. 210.
437. Sandra Gwyn, "Multiculturalism: A Threat and a Promise," *Saturday Night* (February 1974), p. 15.
438. Ibid.
439. *Ukrainian-Canadian Review*, No. 3 (1972-3), p. 5.
440. Gwyn, "Multiculturalism: A Threat and a Promise," p. 16.
441. Rev. Dr. S. Semczuk, "The Ukrainian Catholic Church" (Winnipeg, 1967, Special Collections, University of Alberta), p. 6.
442. Yuzyk, *The Ukrainian-Canadians*, p. 83.
443. Ibid., p. 74.
444. Ibid., p. 85.
445. Ibid., p. 87.
446. Ibid., p.77.
447. Marunchak, *The Ukrainian-Canadians: A History*, p. 725.
448. *Ukrainian-Canadian Review*, No. 3. (1972-3), p. 33.
449. Ibid., p. 3.
450. Ibid., p. 8.

451. Notes from the 15th SUSK Congress, Winnipeg, Manitoba, August 1974.

452. Radio interview, CKUA, Edmonton, Alberta, 1976.

453. Ibid.

454. Edmonton *Journal*, July 6, 1975.

455. Ibid.

456. Yuzyk, *The Ukrainian-Canadians*, p. 82.

457. Melnyk, "A Typology of Ukrainian-Canadian Folklore," p. 253.

458. Illia Kiriak, *Sons of the Soil* (Toronto: Ryerson Press, 1959), p. 121.

459. Semczuk, "The Ukrainian Catholic Church," p. 2.

460. Ukrainian Pioneers' Association, *Ukrainians in Alberta*, p. 45.

461. *Mundare Yesterday and Today*, p. 102.

462. Edmonton *Journal*, April 18, 1930.

463. Municipal District Records from Two Hills Area (71.3). Provincial Archives of Alberta.

464. Vegreville *Observer*, March 18, 1931.

465. Palmer, *Immigration and the Rise of Multiculturalism*, p. 124.

466. Robert England, *The Colonization of Western Canada*, (University of Alberta collection), p. 224.

467. Marunchak, *The Ukrainian-Canadians: A History*, p. 270.

468. Dr. Roman Olynyk-Rakhmanny, address to the annual banquet of the Ukrainian Canadian Committee, Montreal, Quebec, February 15, 1975.

469. Marunchak, *The Ukrainian-Canadians: A History*, p. 721.

470. Bohdan K. Bociurkiw, "Ethnic Identification and Attitudes of University Students of Ukrainian Descent," University of Alberta case study, *Slavs in Canada* (Ottawa: Inter-University Committee on Canadian Slavs, 1971), p. 35.

471. Ibid., p. 37.

472. *Ukrainian-Canadian Review*, No. 3 (1972-3), p. 9.

473. Ibid., p. 10.

474. *The Ukrainian-Canadian Review* (November 1973), p. 67.

475. Marunchak, *The Ukrainian-Canadians: A History*, p. 721.

476. Harold R. Isaacs, "Basic Group Identity: The Idols of the Tribe," Nathan Glazer and Daniel P. Moynihan, eds., *Ethnicity: Theory and Experience* (Cambridge: Harvard University Press, 1975), p. 32.

477. Yuzyk, *The Ukrainian-Canadians*, p. 77.

478. Charles Lynch, "Ethnic Tokenism Unleashed," Southam Press, May 18,1973.

479. Baker, p. 13.

480. George Melnyk, "What's This About 'Ethnic' Native People?" Edmonton *Journal*, May 17, 1975.

481. Notes from the 15th SUSK Congress, Winnipeg, Manitoba, August 1974.

482. *Student*, Vol. 8, No. 31 (1975).

483. Lynch, "Ethnic Tokenism Unleashed."

484. Quoted in Yuzyk, *The Ukrainian-Canadians*, p. 80.

485. *Student*, Vol. 8, No. 31 (1975).

Myrna Kostash

Myrna Kostash was born in Edmonton. The publication of her first book, *All of Baba's Children*, had a profound effect on her life because it placed her squarely in the context of her ethnic community and give her intellectual work its main focus. She has also written *Long Way from Home* (1980, Lorimer), the story of the sixties generation in Canada, and *No Kidding* (1987, McClelland and Stewart), a wide-ranging report from inside the world of teenage women. She continues to write for magazine and radio and has had two stage plays produced. Myrna has been a member of the executive of the Writers Guild of Alberta and the Writer's Union of Canada and is active in PEN. A forthcoming book is based on her travels to Slavic Europe throughout the 1980s and again in the turbulent fall of 1991.